THE TRIBES TRIUMPHANT

By the same author

Tribes with Flags
Money for Old Rope
The Northern Front

CHARLES GLASS

The Tribes Triumphant

RETURN JOURNEY TO THE MIDDLE EAST

'When the government is unable to provide for their safety, they will band themselves into tribes.'

SIR JOHN BAGOT GLUBB,
Britain and the Arabs: A Study of Fifty Years, 1908–1950

HarperPress
An Imprint of HarperCollins*Publishers*

Harper Press
An imprint of HarperCollins*Publishers*
77–85 Fulham Palace Road,
Hammersmith, London W6 8JB
www.harpercollins.co.uk

Published by Harper Press in 2006

Copyright © Charles Glass 2006

1

Charles Glass asserts the moral right to
be identified as the author of this work

A catalogue record for this book
is available from the British Library

ISBN-13 978 0 00 713162 4
ISBN-10 0 00 713162 3

Map by Leslie Robinson

Set in PostScript Linotype Sabon by
Rowland Phototypesetting Ltd, Bury St Edmunds, Suffolk

Printed and bound in Great Britain by
Clays Ltd, St Ives plc

The author dedicates this book
to his friend Noam Chomsky
and to the memory of another friend,
Edward Saïd.

'Between the Arabian Desert and the eastern coast of the Levant there stretches – along almost the full extent of the latter, or for nearly 400 miles – a tract of fertile land varying from 70 to 100 miles in breadth. This is so broken up by mountain range and valley that it has never all been brought under one native government; yet its well-defined boundaries – the sea on the west, Mount Taurus on the north, and the desert to east and south – give it unity, and separate it from the rest of the world. It has rightly, therefore, been covered by one name, Syria.'

REVEREND GEORGE ADAM SMITH
The Historical Geography of the Holy Land (1894)

CONTENTS

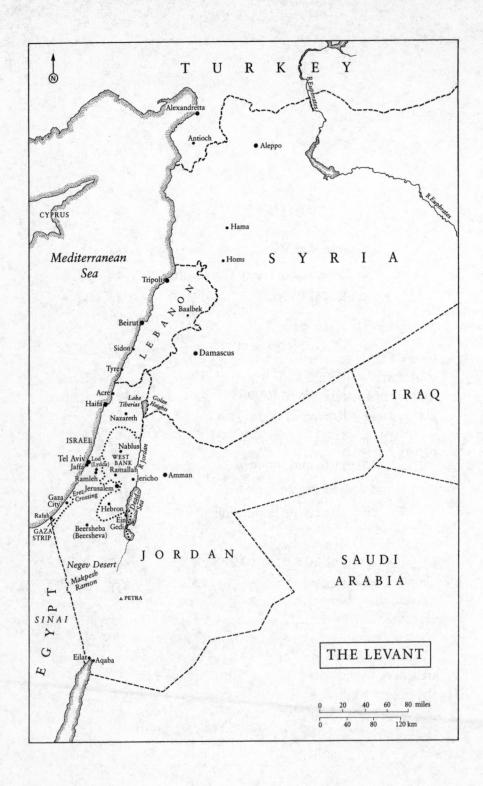

ONE

Imperial Wars

'It is the atmosphere in which seers, martyrs, and
fanatics are bred.'
REVEREND GEORGE ADAM SMITH
The Historical Geography of the Holy Land (1894)

11 September 2001

IT WAS NOT ENOUGH to sail or drive to Aqaba. I had to take
it by force, galloping with Arab tribal warriors to the gates of
its ancient fortress, storming the citadel and raising the colours
above the battlements. The Ottoman Red Sea garrison would
surrender, as it had to Captain T. E. Lawrence in the summer
of 1917, or my sword would taste the defender's flesh. All Syria
– its sandy plains and snowy summits, oases and castles, nomad
camps and ancient cities, fractious and competing believers in
the One God – would lie open to my advance.

Years later, of course, I might regret it. Lawrence of Arabia
certainly did. Was Johnny Turk any worse to the Levant than
his successors – Britain, France, America and the advocates of
Zionist colonization? A region that had remained united for
four centuries within the Ottoman Empire – and for many more
Hellenized centuries before that – was divided, abused and
rendered impotent. Lawrence himself acknowledged his betrayal of the Arabs, as America's Lawrences later confessed their
treachery to the brave Afghan tribesmen who had beaten back
the Soviet empire. Foreign adventurers promising freedom to
the earth's wretched – among them the Arabs of 1917 and the
Afghans of the 1980s – knew in their souls that what they

1

offered the native warrior was so much dust. Empires employed the *indigenes* to destroy rival empires: the British vanquished the Ottomans, as America did the Soviets, with local trackers, guides and killers.

I was halfway from London to Aqaba, by train and ship, when massacres of my countrymen in the United States altered the nature of a journey I had been contemplating for fourteen years. My intention was to complete a Levantine adventure. In 1987, while on my way from Alexandretta in southern Turkey to Aqaba in Jordan, politics stopped me dead. In Beirut, a Shiite Muslim militia, the Hizballah, cast me into chains. After my escape, I returned home to my family in London rather than resume the journey south. The Hizballah had kidnapped many other foreigners for political ends; and it had nurtured the suicide bomber, that mysterious and sometimes anonymous figure who expelled the US Marine Corps and the Israeli occupation forces from Lebanon. The tactic of the human delivery mechanism reached its horrible fruition in the wilful murder of thousands of innocent human beings in New York, Washington and western Pennsylvania on 11 September 2001. I was in Florence when it happened.

After watching the World Trade Center's towers collapse on Italian television, I called friends in New York's downtown. The telephone lines were down. It did not occur to me that the mass murders in the United States would affect my plans, until Julia, my sixteen-year-old daughter, called from England. Seeing the destruction of a solid structure from which we had enjoyed the Manhattan vista the previous summer shocked her. Making a connection that I had not, she feared that the events we had witnessed via our televisions would have an impact in the Middle East. American administrations had bombed Muslim countries for less, and Julia worried that people in the Arab world would attack American citizens in revenge for American vengeance. I promised her that, if I anticipated any threat to myself, I would come home.

I had already reserved a wagon-lit that night to Brindisi on

Italy's east coast and berths on ships from Brindisi to Greece and Greece to Port Said. That would leave time to cancel if an outraged Arab world reacted by killing or kidnapping the Americans in its midst. Julia's entreaties had the effect of making real to me the horrors that I had yet to absorb in the preceding hours. Her life had perhaps made her more sensitive to political danger than most children in the complacent West. Political-religious revolutionaries in Lebanon had abducted her father when she was two. The father of two of her close friends, British military attaché Colonel Stephen Saunders, had been assassinated in Athens by the notorious November 17th group two years earlier. As she worried for me, I thought of my older son, George, in Turkey. Although no harm was likely to reach him there, I called him, as Julia had me. I asked him to return to Rhodes, where my ship was stopping. We could sail on together from there. Thus, under threat, we seek refuge among our own tribes – in this instance, among fellow Christians in Greece – lest we offer targets to the other side. Rhodes, itself a haven to Knights Hospitaller driven from the Holy Land in 1309, lay close to the Turkish shore on the frontiers where Islam brushed against Christendom. No harm came to any Westerners in Turkey.

On that September day, I was in the Florentine house of friends, Adam and Chloe Alvarez, set within the walls of a garden so vast that it is best described as a wilderness. Weighing on me were Julia's fears, New York in chaos, the impossibility of telephoning friends there, the reports of more and more deaths and the brutality of the attacks. In the Alvarezes' sitting room, Britons and Italians alike worried for New York friends while watching, again and again, the collapse of the Twin Towers. Unable to endure another replay, I walked out to a cypress grove at one end of the garden. In the Mediterranean, cypresses grow in graveyards to point the soul's way to heaven. People in my native land were dying and in agony and in fear. It would not be long before American anger would manifest itself in the deaths of Muslims. I must have been about to weep, when someone called from the house to say the television had more news. That was before we knew how many had died, who had done it and why.

An Italian woman I had loved years before called me at the Alvarezes'. The deaths in New York, where she had once lived, left her too distraught to see me off, as planned, at Santa Maria Novella Station. We had said enough sad goodbyes when we were in love. I left without a farewell, boarding the train alone like a spy skulking into the night and not as a soldier dispatched to the front with farewell kisses. Later, snug in my bunk reading about nineteenth-century Palestine, I answered my cellphone. My younger son, Edward, was calling from England. What were my plans? Would I be safe? He was seven when Hizballah captured me.

The next day, on an empty beach near Brindisi, I wrote, 'What am I to do? I'm commissioned to write a book in the Middle East, and I have to go. But I don't want to cause hurt to my children, as I had in 1987. I'll see when I get to Rhodes.' In 1987, I embarked on a journey through all of geographic Syria to write *Tribes with Flags*. Beginning in Alexandretta, the Syrian Mediterranean port that the French ceded to Turkey in 1938, in the spring, I had intended to reach Aqaba on the Red Sea – after exploring Syria, Lebanon, Israel and Jordan – in time for the seventieth anniversary of Lawrence's victory in July. But, by July, I had already been a captive of the Shiite Muslim Hizballah movement for a month in Beirut. After my escape on 19 August, I did not complete the journey. Finishing something that I started fourteen years before was no excuse for making my family suffer again. I would go, but I would avoid risk

Boarding the *Maria G.* of Valletta that evening in Brindisi harbour brought me back to the Levant. An old woman, who looked as if she had not left the farm once during her sixty-odd years, stepped ahead of me. In a rough cotton dress, the tops of her dark stockings rolled at the knees and a scarf knotted around her white hair, she could have been a peasant from any Mediterranean village. Faced with a moving escalator, she stared as if at a ravenous sea monster. A Greek crewman took her arm. She fell, and the sailor righted her with a quick shove. She trembled while the metal stairs carried her towards the landing. At the top, she refused to budge. I stepped back to avoid crashing into her, but to no avail. The woman stepped on my big toe, from which a chiropodist had only recently removed an in-growing toenail. Passengers bashed into me from behind, and we were all tumbling over one another. The crewman pulled the woman out of our way. She waited, petrified, unwilling to risk the second ascent to A deck. The sailor forced her up to the top, where several other sailors shifted her like luggage. On A deck, she stepped on my toe again. How could this Italian matron have lived for more than sixty years without confronting an escalator?

That evening, while the sun descended on Brindisi harbour, I sat on the aft deck with a book and a drink. The old woman, restored to safety, stopped at the rail with her husband. They were speaking Italian. 'These Greeks,' she said in disgust of her fellow passengers, 'are *primitivi*.'

The sun went down, and Brindisi's lights went up. An aeroplane took off in the north. It ascended slowly and seemed to hold still in the sky. Who on that day, seeing an aircraft on the wing, did not imagine for an instant what he would do to save himself if it flew straight for him? The *Maria G.* of Valletta, its flag flying the Maltese Cross that once terrorized the infidels of the East, sailed six minutes early at 7.54 in the evening. On the eight o'clock news of the BBC World Service – a small transistor radio has accompanied me for thirty years – a newsreader predicted, 'Life for Americans will never be the same.' I did not want to believe him.

Slow Boat to the Levant

As the ship approached Patras the next morning, the BBC World Service reported that Israel's prime minister, General Ariel Sharon, had sent Israeli forces to attack Jericho, a Palestinian city in the Jordan Valley. Sharon, a lifelong Arab fighter, appeared to be making use of the American declaration of war on terrorism. No longer would General Sharon be attacking Arabs to kill them, to prolong Israeli occupation of the West Bank, to plant more settlers to displace more Arabs and to eliminate resistance to illegal military occupation. From then on, he would be fighting terror arm in arm with America.

At nine in the morning, winches lowered guide ropes to tie the *Maria G.* to the quay in Patras harbour. The bar in which I'd had a cold espresso was emptying, as passengers lost themselves in the exit queues. Only the canned jazz remained. This was Patras, Greek Patras, my first Levantine port. The town of squat apartment blocks and storage sheds was uglier and more functional than the colourful, tourist-friendly seaports to the west, St Tropez, Portofino, Porto Ercole. The East had abandoned beauty for high returns – minimum investment for maximum return. The new world of the East was more hideous than it had been on my 1987 tour, but it was more convenient: mobile telephones, cash dispensers, the end of exchange controls and more relaxed customs regimes. Ashore in Patras, I withdrew drachmas from a cash machine, took a taxi to the central bus station and boarded the bus to Athens.

If the Levant began at Patras, the Third World opened its doors at Piraeus, Athens' ancient port. Perhaps because Greece was then building a new airport for the Olympics, it had left its harbour to rot. Signs indicating separate windows for EU and non-EU citizens meant nothing. I waited behind a Jordanian, a Dane and an Israeli in the EU queue. Most of us took more than an hour to clear passport control, then wandered the dock without anyone telling us how to find the ship. Some of us went right, others left. It took time and ingenuity to find the *Nissos Kypros*. My father with his years at sea would have called her a rust bucket. Praying she would not sink, I boarded and made for the bar. There, an Egyptian barman told me that the millions of drachmas I'd withdrawn at the bank machine in Patras were useless on the *Nissos Kypros*. The ship, he explained, accepted only Cypriot pounds.

I drank beer on deck. The BBC World Service reported that the US was preparing to attack Afghanistan. Friends called from the United States and Tuscany to question the wisdom of my journey. My only agony so far was caused by the bad muzak (is there such a thing as good muzak?) of the *Nissos Kypros* bar. A couple whom I had met in the passport queue joined me. Anne Marie Sorensen, and Juwal, pronounced Yuval, Levy were, I guessed, in their late twenties. A Dane, she had a degree in Arabic and Hebrew. Juwal was born in Switzerland to Israeli parents and had completed high school and military service in Israel. He was hoping to go to university, probably in Denmark. They were motorcycling from Denmark, where they lived, to his family in Israel's Negev Desert. After visiting his family, they would fly to New Zealand and Australia. He planned to return alone to Israel to ride the motorcycle back to Denmark and join his wife there.

They were among those lucky – or blessed – married couples who go well together, relaxed, listening to each other, interested in what the other said. We talked about – what should we have called them, bombs? – the hijacked aeroplanes and mass murders in America. Every few hours the radio raised the death count. By then, it was thought to be about three thousand. We talked about Israel. The people whom Juwal seemed to detest were not the Arabs so much as fanatically religious Jews. They did not recognize his marriage to his Danish wife and accused him of, in his words, polluting the blood. Anne Marie and Juwal had Bedouin friends who sounded more sophisticated – with university degrees – than more traditional nomads I had known in the deserts of Jordan and Syria. Some were academics who had, like Juwal, married Danish women.

In the morning, the radio raised the body count in America, speculated about possible culprits and predicted global economic calamity. The *Nissos Kypros* docked at the island of Patmos, where I had a breakfast of cheese, olives and what the Greeks call 'Greek' coffee. From there, we cruised beside the Turkish shore towards Rhodes. When we arrived, I went looking for my son George.

He was waiting, as promised, in an old hotel beside a forlorn, disused mosque in the centre of the Crusaders' fortress. Twenty-three, healthy and sunburned from a week's sailing, he took me to dinner in a tiny place he knew. The restaurant, with no name posted anywhere, lay hidden in a tight passage amid crumbling houses. Its plump and maternal proprietress had already adopted him. She was about my age and had lived in England. My son, she said, did not eat enough. She put us at a large table that more or less blocked the alley and covered it with cold beer, lots of mezze and a bountiful platter of mixed grilled meats. George was on his summer break from studying Middle East history at London's School of Oriental and African Studies (SOAS). Like me, he speculated on the impact of the attacks in America. Like his sister Julia, he had misgivings about my proposed trip. We would stop in Cyprus for a few days. If the hangings of Westerners started in the Middle East, I'd fly with him back to London and postpone my trip to Aqaba a second time.

After lunch, we toured Rhodes' old town, where Ralph Bunche, America's United Nations mediator, negotiated the 1949 truce that interrupted the war between Israel and Egypt and led to Israel's subsequent truces with Jordan, Syria and Lebanon. The accords he signed at the Hôtel des Roses left 700,000 Palestinian Arabs, three-quarters of Palestine's Arab majority, permanent refugees. Under Bunche's agreements, the UN recognized the Israeli army's conquests of 1948 and 1949. UN Security Council Resolution 181 of 1947 had partitioned Palestine into an Arab and a Jewish state with Jerusalem as an international city. The proposed Jewish state was 55 per cent of Palestine, but Israeli victories awarded the Jewish state 78 per cent. The Rhodes and subsequent agreements left the West Bank in the hands of King Abdallah of Jordan and allowed Egypt's King Farouk to keep the strip around Gaza City next to Sinai. The Palestinian Arabs got nothing. With the West Bank and Gaza, Jordan and Egypt inherited hundreds of thousands of refugees cleansed from what had become the Jewish state.

The Palestinian Arabs, then as subsequently, were not consulted. Israel, the Arab states, the United Nations and the United States were content to leave most of them as wards of the UN. The UN established two temporary agencies – the UN Troop Supervisory Organization that monitored the disengagement lines and the UN Relief and Works Agency that fed, housed and educated Palestinian Arab refugees. Both have been in the Middle East ever since. The UN's pro forma Resolution 194 of 1948, renewed annually, required that Palestinian Arab 'refugees wishing to return to their homes and live at peace with their neighbours should be permitted to do so at the earliest practicable date'. No one enforced it, and the 700,000 refugees became, with their descendants and those expelled in the 1967 war, more than three million. Ralph Bunche, setting a precedent, accepted a Nobel Peace Prize for negotiations that produced – not peace – but more punishing wars.

Back on the deck of the *Nissos Kypros*, where the muzak blended with the engine's rumbling, Juwal, Anne Marie, George and I discussed the Middle East to which we were sailing. Juwal told us a story about his father, Udi Levy. Udi Levy had demanded that the word 'Jew' be removed from his national identity card. In Israel, nationality did not mean citizenship. It meant racial origin. Udi Levy was proud to be a Jew, but he did not accept being defined as one by the state, especially when the state gave its Jewish citizens privileges it denied to Arabs. He fought through the courts and won. Juwal had inherited some of his father's dissidence, refusing to serve in the army of occupation in the West Bank and Gaza. As with many other refuseniks, the military found a way to avoid prosecuting him. They let him serve in the navy. The sea was not occupied.

Where Juwal came from, kids made tougher decisions than ours had to. Some joined the army. Some ran away to other countries. Some went to prison rather than shoot Palestinian children, demolish houses and enforce a military occupation in which they did not believe. On the Palestinian side, youngsters threw rocks at tanks, ambushed settlers or committed suicide

9

in order to kill other kids they believed were their enemies. Some Palestinian boys worked for the Israelis, as labourers in settlements or as police collaborators; others languished in Israeli interrogation rooms or prison cells.

Dreams on Maps

When the *Nissos Kypros* reached Cyprus, my friend Colin Smith met us at Limassol port. Colin lived in Nicosia. When we met first in Jerusalem, he was the *Observer*'s roving correspondent and I was working for ABC News in Lebanon. A few months later, we covered the independence war in Eritrea together with the photographer Don McCullin and Phil Caputo of the *Chicago Tribune*. A couple of weeks of hell in the desert with guerrillas who got us lost, denied us water and nearly left us for dead started our long friendship. Caputo went on to write novels, and Colin had collaborated with the journalist John Bierman on books about Orde Wingate, the British officer who more or less created the Israeli army, and on the battle of El Alamein.

That night, Colin, his wife Sylvia and their grown-up daughter Helena took us on foot to a Greek restaurant in an old house near the Green Line between Turkish and Greek Nicosia. The Aegean's owner was a Greek Cypriot political fanatic named Vasso. Vasso, with a beard as long and black as an Orthodox archbishop's, could have given lessons in political intransigence to Israeli settlers and Palestinian suicide bombers. His cause was Enosis, the union of Cyprus with Greece. The décor of his courtyard hostelry gave his politics away. Pride of place went to a huge wall map that showed Cyprus as part of Greece – not just politically, but physically, a few hundred miles closer than it is on the earth. The eastern Mediterranean was the region of creative map making. Syrian maps included Turkish Alexandretta in Syria and left a blank for Israel, a void that Syrian politicians called 'the Zionist entity'. Many Israeli maps included Judaea, Samaria and Gaza in 'Greater Israel'. Some Arab nationalists' maps, based on those of the eighth century, showed an Arab state from Morocco to Iraq. A Kurdish map delineated Greater Kurdistan from the Mediterranean to Armenia and Iran.

When Colin introduced me as his American friend, Vasso said, 'I am strongly anti-American . . . policy.' The delayed 'policy' seemed to come out of consideration for the thousands who had died a few days before. It was clear he did not normally add it. He confessed that, despite his politics, he sympathized with Americans over the massacres. Perhaps the struggle between Christendom and Islam took precedence over his hatred of Henry Kissinger, who, as secretary of state in 1974, had supported Turkey's invasion of the Cypriot Republic. Turkey was reacting to a coup attempt by the Greek Cypriot National Guard, whose leader, Nikos Sampson, had championed Vasso's dream of Enosis. Since then the island had been sliced into Turkish and Greek halves. Vasso ran a good restaurant in a stone house whose style anyone but Vasso would have called Ottoman. The wine was rough, the food deliciously grilled. We stayed late, arguing politics with a band of Greek actors at another table and, as usual with Colin for almost thirty years, drinking too much. We walked home along the Green Line. Colin nearly led us into a Turkish checkpoint. That detour would be harmless in the morning, but at night a Turkish conscript might shoot.

During our week in Cyprus, while the US assembled its forces around Afghanistan, George played tennis in the mornings with Colin and I made calls to Israel, Jordan and Lebanon. The US was not bombing any Arab countries, and no harm had come to Americans in the Arab world. I could leave Cyprus for Aqaba, having kept my promise to my daughter. George flew back to London and his final year of history at SOAS. I read some Somerset Maugham short stories and came across the dictum 'The wise traveller travels only in imagination'. I should have heeded him on my first journey through Greater Syria in 1987.

If not for Britain's invasion and division of the Ottomans' Arab provinces, I might not have made this journey or the one that was curtailed in 1987. T. E. Lawrence and his masters had created the conditions for the wars that I had come again and again as a journalist to report: not only the many between Israel's Jewish colonists and the Arab natives, but between Arabs and Kurds, Christians and Muslims, Iranians and Iraqis. The empires brought border wars, where there had been no borders; tribal wars, where tribes had always lived; anti-colonial wars, where empires had always ruled over colonies.

I was a dual citizen: of the vibrant American empire and of its British predecessor, now a mere kingdom of northern Europe. Two passports and many allegiances. My ancestors had originated from subject peoples in Ireland long before its independence and from Mount Lebanon under the Ottoman Sultan in Istanbul. Both families were Catholic, one of their many legacies to me and another claim on my loyalty. Part native, part double imperialist, I would enter Aqaba from the Red Sea. Lawrence's route had been, like the man himself, more circumspect. He had led a detachment of Arab irregulars from the Hejaz north through the desert to Wadi Roum, the rosy-rocked Greeks' Valley in what became Jordan. Disabling Turkish batteries along the way, they struck south to surprise the Ottomans from the rear.

I could have gone that way, but that was not where the real war was fought, not where decisions were made. Lawrence's five-hundred-mile march and the capture of Aqaba were episodes in the Arab myth of self-liberation. Reality was the British army, preparing to assault Gaza from Egypt. Reality was the Royal Navy, cutting Turkey's communications between Aqaba and the Ottoman troops concentrated in the holy city of Medina. The naval guns of Great Britain had reduced the seaward walls of Aqaba's Mamluke fortress, where a few hundred Turkish imperial troops sheltered for safety. Lawrence wrote of Aqaba in 1917: 'Through the swirling dust we perceived that Aqaba was all a ruin. Repeated bombardments by French and

12

British warships had degraded the place to its original rubbish. The poor houses stood about in a litter, dirty and contemptible, lacking entirely that dignity which the durability of their time-challenging bones conferred on ancient remains.' By the time Lawrence reached Aqaba, it was as a walkover.

The capture of Aqaba transformed Britain's eastern war. Captain Basil Liddell Hart wrote, in his biography *Colonel Lawrence: The Man Behind the Legend*, 'Strategically, the capture of Aqaba removed all danger of a Turkish raid through Sinai against the Suez Canal or the communications of the British army in Palestine.' In Hart's words, it also inserted an 'Arab ulcer' in the Turkish flank.

Aqaba perched at the crux of two thighs – African Sinai in the west and Asian Arabia to the east. The penetration of Aqaba from above by Lawrence and below by the Royal Navy created the breach that would subordinate the Arab world to Great Britain and its French ally. The Ottoman loss of Aqaba presaged the novel division of Turkey's Syrian Arab provinces into what became Syria, Lebanon, Jordan and, until 1948, Palestine, thereafter Israel. Another British campaign against Turkey in Mesopotamia would forge Arabs and Kurds against their will into a new country the British would call Iraq. The region has had no peace since.

I chose the way of the warships – the gods of the story, the powers that granted Lawrence and the Arab tribes the illusion of independent action. By the time of my journey, the United States Navy had succeeded Britain's fleet in the Red Sea and just about every other wet region of the globe. America's warplanes would soon send thunder and lightning from the heavens over Afghanistan to give heart to Afghan warriors assaulting their tribal enemies. Alliances with some of the natives had the same rationale in Arabia as in Afghanistan: to reduce the dangers to imperial forces. If giving guns to the Arabs saved British lives in 1917 and 1918, using Afghan against Afghan would achieve the same for Americans nearly a century later. It was the cheapest way to fight an imperial war.

13

TWO

Aqaba, Fourteen Years Late

'From time immemorial it has served as both the ingress
and egress between sea and land, between Arabia and
the highlands of Sinai and Palestine, "The Gateway
of Arabia".'

REVEREND GEORGE ADAM SMITH
The Historical Geography of the Holy Land (1894)

Port of Entry

THE AFTERNOON SHIP from Sinai carried four tourists: an
old Australian woman, her grown son, a Japanese man with a
red backpack and me. The rest of the passengers were Egyptian
workers, a few with wives and children, bound for Jordan, Iraq
or Saudi Arabia. They were the Arab world's gleaners, who
collected the leavings of oil potentates, gun sellers and concrete
spreaders. They washed Saudi dishes, painted monuments to
dictators and provided the muscle to erect alien forms on Oriental landscapes. After a few years, or a lifetime, working in the
Arabian sun, they returned home to Egypt with enough Iraqi
dinars or Saudi riyals to open a shop selling Coca-Cola beside
the Nile. They smelled of happiness, these moneyless but smiling
young men. They waited hours without complaint for the ship
to embark. Before that, they had stood in long queues at embassies for work permits and visas. In the dingy embarkation hall,
a warehouse with a coffee stall and some broken benches, Egyptian policemen made them wait before taking their passports,
stamping them and, at the quay, returning them in confusion.
Aboard a bus that carried us from the departure building to the

14

dock, the workers jumped up to offer their seats to the Australian matron.

Neither the heat nor the prospect of near-slavery in the desert suppressed their laughter. The Egyptian fellaheen, the peasants, had laughed at Pharaoh. They built his pyramids to quell his terror of death, and they got the joke that he did not. Two things mocked Pharaoh's dogma of eternal life: real, undeniable death without end, without immortal soul, without reincarnation; and the fellaheen's laughter. When Pharaoh's mummified corpse lay dormant within gilded chambers, they robbed his grave and laughed. They laughed at Egypt's conquerors – Alexander the Great, the Vandals, the Caliphs and the British – and still they laughed at its modern dictator, Hosni Mubarak. They called him, for his resemblance to a processed cheese logo, '*la vache qui rit*'. They laughed even more at fat Saudi princes whose vanity required them to waste their countries' fortunes on drugs, alcohol, prostitutes, palaces and physicians to deny their mortality. If the fellaheen had known why I sailed with them to Aqaba, they would have laughed at me too.

Our ship cruised out of Egypt's Nuweiba harbour past vacant beach chairs, umbrellas and thatched bars. This would be another year without tourists. North of the luxury beaches that Israel had occupied in 1967 and tried to keep until 1988 lay the apartment blocks, many-storeyed and unlike anything an Egyptian had ever conceived or wanted. The six- and seven-storey boxes might have blended into an American federal housing project in a cold urban ghetto, but they defaced the Egyptian shore. Architects misunderstood Egypt and its soil, its most eminent contemporary architect Hassan Fathy wrote fifty years before. They needed to design in the vernacular with bricks made of Egypt's mud-rich earth. Egypt's architects, however, mostly studied in the West or worked for Western firms. Contractors made money with cement and nothing from mud-brick. The last structures I saw in Egypt were cement monuments to American immortality.

The ship moved north-north-east, Africa to Asia. Arabia's

ochre hills sliced into the water to form half of an invisible chasm that emerged in the north as the Jordan and Bekaa Valleys and in the south as the Great Rift. The sun was casting Africa's half of the valley into shadow, while the desolate, treeless slopes of the Arabian side shone against the coming darkness. A cartoon in white rock on the Saudi slope pointed our way. It was an open book perched atop a scimitar as large as England's prehistoric chalk horses and overendowed men. In the Kingdom of Saudi Arabia, it could have been only one book, *the* book, the Koran. The sword of religion, Saef ed-Din, protected, as in the past it had delivered, the Word of God. From the middle of the Gulf of Aqaba in the northern Red Sea, I could almost touch four countries – Egypt, Israel, Jordan and Saudi Arabia. To my left were Taba in Egypt and Eilat in Israel. To my right, only a stroll away, was the Saudi desert. And ahead, in the middle, was the town with the fortress that had been my destination when I set out from Turkey fourteen years before.

When Captain T. E. Lawrence invaded in 1917, there were no Eilat, no Taba, no Saudi Kingdom. Apart from the invisible demarcation between British-occupied Egypt and the Ottoman Empire that the Bedouin ignored, borders were unknown. 'For months,' Lawrence wrote in *The Seven Pillars of Wisdom*, 'Aqaba had been the horizon of our minds, the goal: we had had no thought, we had refused thought, of anything beside.' Modern Aqaba lacked any characteristic to make it anyone's horizon. It was, like Eilat next door, a minor beach resort with large, empty hotels and palm trees dropped in for decoration. Yet it had obsessed Lawrence, and it had eluded me in 1987. I had attempted and failed to reach it that July for the seventieth anniversary of Lawrence's triumph. Halfway between Alexandretta in southern Turkey and Aqaba, my Beirut oubliette was as much a legacy of Lawrence's military campaign as the mini states born of the myth of his Arab Revolt. Out of the 1917 fall of Aqaba came flag-swinging little Syria, Lebanon, Israel and Jordan, whose squabbling and land grabs had led to the wars and mayhem and kidnappings that blocked my way in

1987 – an inconvenience compared to the tragedies imposed upon the natives.

The last words I read before disembarking at Aqaba, painted in black on the wheelhouse of the cargo ship *Al Houda*, were 'Safety First'. A Jordanian officer – Jordan's police and soldiers are the best dressed in the Middle East with their starched tunics and regimental headgear – took our passports and instructed us to board an old bus. On the quayside, Jordanian flags dropped from dark masts, the red–green–white–black motif replicated like an Andy Warhol portrait series, the shade of each depending on the way it caught the sun, how weathered it was or how it dangled from its lanyard. In Jordan, as in Egypt, flags were outnumbered by only one other artefact: pictures of the leader. When we set sail from Sinai, I was relieved that a giant effigy in Nuweiba port of President Hosni Mubarak, the air force officer whose luck had made him Egypt's vice president when soldiers assassinated his predecessor in 1981, would be the last for a while. In Jordan, young King Abdallah's visage proved as ubiquitous. It greeted me at the dock, welcomed me on the bus, invited me into the immigration hall, watched with unaffected lack of interest while an official stamped my passport, looked up at me from the ten-dinar banknote that I used to buy a Jordanian visa with his family coat of arms upon it and smiled as I walked through several interior checkpoints where soldiers of different units examined my documents. Outside, the young king hovered over our long taxi queue.

An old Toyota taxi took me half a mile to the next portrait of the king at what turned out to be the real taxi stand for cars going to Aqaba town. Here, we admired more images of the monarch in costumes that signified his many roles: father, soldier, tribal chief, descendant of the Prophet, bridge builder, peacemaker, Bedouin warrior, businessman, friend of the people. Like Mubarak and every other Arab leader, Abdallah was Ram ad-Dar, head of the house. In all traditional Arab houses and shops, the head's picture – usually retouched in black and white, of an old man framed under glass on a wall above door height

– dominated the most important room. President Mubarak, King Abdallah, Saddam Hussein in Iraq, Bashar al-Assad in Syria and King Fahd in Saudi Arabia translated to the public sphere the senior male's leadership of the family. I would see them in Israel, the modern society that created itself to cast off the old ways of the ghetto and of subservience at foreign courts: the same patriarchal portraits in the same positions, alone, high on a wall, old, wise and revered, a father, a grandfather or a rabbi – the Lubavitcher rebbe, a long-dead Talmudic scholar or, in some settlements in occupied territory, the American killer rabbis Moshe Levinger and Meier Kahane. Photographs of prime ministers, who came and went, sometimes in disgrace to return later, were to be seen only in government offices. No one blamed the father, the king, the president for mistreatment by his minions. If the leader knew what was done under his portraits, he would bring to justice all sergeants, bureaucrats or ministers of state who abused the leader's trust.

My First Evening

I turned on the television in my luxury hotel suite. The state channel played Jordanian music videos in homage to King Abdallah. Montages of a young man wailing in Arabic dissolved into the object of his worship, '*Ya Malik, ya Malik*' – O King, O King. Ten minutes later, while I unpacked and washed for dinner, the news began. The lead story was neither war in Afghanistan nor murder in the West Bank. It was King Abdallah's courtesy call on a school. This blockbuster, hard to surpass for news value, led on to further exclusives: King Abdallah at a cabinet session, King Abdallah pouring cement on something and, the *coup de grâce*, the king and his queen, a beautiful Palestinian named Rania, touring another school. I liked the way the producers began and ended their broadcast on the same theme and wondered what other risks they took to keep the populace informed.

I went outside to the new Aqaba. It was a dull, quiet place at Easter 1973, when I'd hitchhiked down from Beirut and slept on the beach. Aqaba had since matured into a mini Miami of gaudy hotels and private beaches. But it was still dull and quiet. The seafront Corniche looped east and south from the Israeli border and boasted scores of modern hotels, restaurants, pharmacies and cafés where young men watched television at outdoor tables. In 1973, Aqaba and I were poorer, making do with simple fare: grilled chicken at open-air rotisseries under dried palm branches on wooden frames. There were only two big hotels. A long stretch of sand separated Aqaba and the border fence, then closed, with Eilat. On this, my first visit in twenty-nine years, the border fence had opened to turn Eilat and Aqaba into one city. Once, Aqaba had been distinctly Arab with overgrown parks, neglected beaches, wedding-cake minarets and a few camels; Eilat was defiantly Euro-Israeli, concrete slabs, grey socialist-realist architecture, bars and women in bikinis. Now, they looked the same – the same hotels, shopping centres and other investments in concrete. Despite the open fence, Aq-elat, or Eil-aba, was as segregated by race, religion and language as most other cities. The transnational corporations, which gambled on prosperity in Jordan after its 1994 treaty with Israel, were losing. The Palestinians rose against Israeli military occupation in September 2000, and the result in Aqaba was that the Radisson, the Movenpick and the rest had fewer customers than staff. I walked along the Corniche to the Movenpick, Aqaba's largest hotel, for dinner.

The Movenpick was said to be *the* new hotel in a town where hotels were under construction on every spare plot. Its vast edifice straddled, via a bridge, both sides of the Corniche. It occupied acres of seafront and its own man-made hill. Its vaguely Greco-Roman columns and mosaics were ornamented with modern versions of *mushrabieh*, lattices and lathed woodwork that protected windows, as in old Jeddah and Yemen, from the sun and strangers' eyes. Despite the traditional balconies clinging like spiders to flat marble walls, the Movenpick looked more MGM-Las Vegas, sans casino, than *Arabian Nights*.

I was the only diner. The waiter, though cordial, spent most of his time in the kitchen. Like most solitary travellers, I had for companions a book, my thoughts and whatever I happened to see. I watched the lobby. A Filipina nanny came in with a flock of fat children in American clothes. She tried to persuade them to get into a lift. The children – loud, spoiled, rich – ignored her and ran through the restaurant. They rushed past my table, upset chairs and headed towards the swimming pool. When the empty lift closed behind the nanny, I thought she would cry. The children were learning young what their parents discovered after they earned money: they could abuse servants, at least servants whose families were too far away to take revenge. New money had taken them far from their Arab traditions, which required them to treat their household, including those paid to care for children, as family.

The walk back along the Corniche put me in melancholy mood. Only in the gaps between the new and half-completed hotels could I see the water. In patches that the developers had yet to fill, old Arab men played backgammon and smoked their glass-bowled water pipes. The brighter neon of Eilat, no longer hostile and no longer out of reach, was the model for Aqaba's honorary entry to the modern, Western world. A few young Jordanians smoked narghiles – water pipes – like old men. The narghile was becoming fashionable again in the Arab world. The boys sucking plastic- and wood-tipped tubes were wearing, not the keffiyehs of proud desert warriors, but baseball caps. And they drank Coca-Cola.

A Ramble with Staff Sergeant Amrin

In 1973, I had spent the best part of a day searching for the fortress that Lawrence had conquered in 1917. Everyone I asked then had an original notion of its whereabouts – in the hills, on the King's Highway, somewhere near the Saudi frontier. When I found it on the beach near the old town, I slashed through a jungle that had grown in and over it. Forcing a path along the ramparts, I was rewarded with the Turkish commander's perspective of the Red Sea when the pillars of his empire were falling. Below the ramparts were storerooms and the yard where deserters and rebels had been hanged. Later, I asked to meet old people who might have remembered Lawrence from fifty-six years earlier. Some helpful Jordanians took me to a café to meet a man who could not have been more than forty. Much discussion ensued, until I asked how a man as young as he could have known Lawrence. He sorted through papers in a beefy leather wallet and produced a photograph of himself in black desert robes with Peter O'Toole as Lawrence in David Lean's film. Indicating the fair-skinned actor, he asked, 'What do you want to know about him?'

Early on my first morning back in Aqaba, Ahmed Amrin came to my hotel. At five foot six, he was taller than the man he most admired, the late King Hussein. His get-up was pure California, as if he'd shown up for work as assistant director on a Hollywood set: big Wild Foot boots, Nike baseball cap, grey Levis and a V-necked sweater over a grey T-shirt. His dark goatee was trimmed like a sail, and his left hand sported a wedding ring and a Timex watch. He spoke English as a British soldier would, and he knew his job. He was a guide.

Mr Amrin had taken his degree in English at the University of Amman. His favourite playwrights were Shakespeare and Marlowe, fellow partisans of royalty. He enlisted in the Jordanian army, serving three years in England at Catterick Barracks, near Darlington, North Yorkshire, studying electronics. When he returned to Kerak, his home town between Amman and Aqaba, he married. Jordan and Israel signed a treaty of peace in 1994, and former Staff Sergeant Amrin moved to Aqaba to claim the promised riches of peacetime tourism. He studied his country's archaeology, history, even its geology, flora and fauna. He became a first-class tour guide in a land without tourists.

'In the tenth century BC,' he informed me, marching over a seaside dig next to the Movenpick, 'this was a Solomonic port. It served the Nabataeans and the "Ptolemites"'. Mr Amrin was a rare figure for the Middle East, an honest interpreter of history. Some Arab guides omitted the connection between the land and the ancient Israelites, as most Israeli archaeologists and tour companies avoided references to the Arab, his culture and his history. To Mr Amrin, who was once Staff Sergeant Amrin of the Royal Jordanian army's engineering corps, the story was incomplete without Jews, Arabs, Greeks, Romans, Nabataeans, Turks and the British. The 'Ptolemites', descendants of Alexander the Great's General Ptolemy, had ruled Egypt from Alexander's death until the Roman conquest.

Mr Amrin explained how the other side of the Gulf came to be called Eilat: 'In the Muslim era, this was called Ela or Wela, which means "palm tree".' The ruins were so far beneath our feet that all I could see were brick-lined trenches. The archaeologists had a way to go, but they had forced the government to preserve the ancient Nabataean–Ptolemaic remains from burial under a hotel. It may have been an economic calculation: Aqaba had plenty of hotels but not much history. Walls two millennia old gave it an edge over Eilat, whose oldest structure dated to 1949. The earthworks that Mr Amrin showed me were a small portion of the Roman achievement, a link in the empire's land–sea communications between the fertile hills of Felix Arabia, now Yemen, and garrisons in Egypt and Palestine. The rest of it was under either the Movenpick Hotel, where no one would see it, or the Red Sea, where anyone with goggles and flippers could have a look.

Aqaba as it came to exist was the creation of Islam's third Caliph, successor to the Prophet Mohammed, Othman. Mr Amrin's tale jumped from the pious Othman, one of the four 'rightly-guided' Caliphs, to modern Jordan. He said the Emirate of Transjordan was born of the Meccan Sherif Hussein bin Ali's struggle during the First World War. Without prompting from me, he said, 'Don't forget the English and the French, of course.'

On our way to the Turkish fortress, our shoes collected the dust of Roman and early Muslim digs. We passed beaches where Jordanians above the age of twelve wore enough clothing for an English winter and children were stripped down to bathing suits. Mr Amrin said this was the 'free beach', one of the last that had not been sold to developers to serve the foreign tourists who no longer flew to Jordan or anywhere else in the Levant. Beside the shore, tiny plots of garden, bordered by squares of raised earth, sprouted green vegetables and spiky herbs.

Mr Amrin was, like most other native Jordanians, a monarchist. It was not the system he admired so much as the man, or the men. He talked about the dynasty that had given its name to the Hashemite Kingdom of Jordan. His story began with the patriarch, Hussein bin Ali, already an old man when the British encouraged him to lead a tribal – in Lawrence's fantasy, national – revolt against the Ottoman Empire. His sons, Abdallah, Feisal, Ali and Zeid, harassed the Turks in the east, while Britain advanced from the west. Hussein, meanwhile, practised politics, conspiracy and diplomacy in Mecca. The Arabs were more successful at fighting than Hussein was at politics. The old man subsequently lost Mecca itself to another of Britain's Arab supplicants, the Al-Sauds from the inland desert of Nejd. Britain's favourite among the Hashemite sons, Feisal, became King of Syria. His throne in Damascus lasted almost a year, until France took its share of the Ottoman Arab spoils and expelled him. In compensation and for its own purposes, Britain awarded him a richer prize, Iraq with its fecund earth and its oil. The British killed at least ten thousand Iraqis to impose Feisal upon them; and his dynasty lasted until a year after the British left and a mob got its hands on his grandson, Feisal II, in 1958. Another of old Hussein's sons, Abdallah, founded Jordan – 'Don't forget the English and the French, of course' – in the desert between Iraq and Palestine. Jordan was the booby prize. Until Abdallah, it was nothing more than the desert waste that kept Iraq and Palestine apart, the Crusaders' *Outre-Jourdain*. But it was the only one of the four Hashemite crowns – Jordan, Syria, Iraq and the Hejaz – that survived. Abdallah's successors were his son Talal, Talal's son Hussein and Hussein's son Abdallah, whose picture gazed upon the ruins.

'I can say the late king was the creator of modern Jordan,' Mr Amrin informed me, referring to Hussein. 'He was humble. He listened to the radio to hear the people's complaints. He created a sense of love among the people.'

And the son?

'I believe the same is happening with Abdallah.'

The land around the citadel had been cleared since my 1973 visit, and there was no longer any need to scratch my way through the brush. We stopped outside the walls, as Lawrence did before the Turks surrendered. Above the vast, open Mamluke gate were two metal flags, painted by hand. 'People think that is the Palestinian flag,' Mr Amrin was pointing at one. 'It isn't. It's the flag of the Great Arab Revolt.' A British officer had designed the red–white–green–black standard of Sherif Hussein bin Ali's Arab army in 1917, and most Arab flags were variants of it. The Lebanese with its green cedar between red stripes was the exception. The Palestinians – the last standard-bearers of Arab nationalism – adopted the Sherifian flag without alteration. With that flag came lies: that the Arabs were an independent nation, albeit temporarily separated into states with their own flags; that the Arabs would liberate Palestine; that Arab warriors had somehow defeated the Turkish, French and British empires; and that, one day, they would expel the American empire's pampered child, Israel, from their midst.

An old gatekeeper asked us to pay a fee. When Mr Amrin explained my purpose, the man invited us in as his guests and sat down again in the shade of the massive iron gates. Mr Amrin pointed to some writing, carved into the wall, in beautiful Kufic Arabic script, a lavish calligraphic style that originated in Kufa, Iraq: 'This inscription honours Kalsum al-Ghuri, one of the leaders who fought the Portuguese from 1505 to 1520.' Portuguese raiders in the sixteenth century were discovering and claiming the more vulnerable parts of Arabia, India, Africa and the Americas. Kalsum al-Ghuri appeared to have saved Aqaba, and thus Syria, from the massacres of Muslims, Jews and heterodox Christians that accompanied Portugal's Renaissance conquests further east.

Mr Amrin showed me, between the testament to the Mamluke chief al-Ghuri and a carved verse, or *sura*, from the Koran, 'a secret passage to leave the place in wartime'. I looked deep inside the walls, where a tight corridor disappeared into darkness. We didn't go in. Next came the courtyard, a stone parade ground protected by four high walls. 'It's very different, if you were here in '73,' he said. The difference was that I could see it. Then, weeds hid the well, the storerooms and the stairs below the ramparts. Now, it seemed like the Alamo, a barren shrine to a mythic struggle. On the stones where Ottoman levies had once borne aloft their Sultan-Caliph's flag and guarded the southern approach of empire, Turkish officers chose surrender over siege and annihilation in 1917. If they had fought to the death, and if the Turkish governors to the north had not antagonized the Arabs of the cities by hanging their leaders, might their deaths have inspired their comrades to rally and repulse the British? Would the cry 'Remember Aqaba!' have saved the Ottoman Empire from destruction? Turkey still held the holy cities of Medina and Jerusalem in 1917, and many thousands of Turks would die before their armies retreated for ever from Arabia and Syria into Anatolia. If the Turks, like the British, had bribed and made false promises to the Arabs, they might have made the conquest of Syria too costly for the British to carry on. Like the American empire of the twenty-first century, Turkey took Arab acquiescence as a constant in all their calculations. It was a mistake.

We marched across the quad, up and down the circling staircases, and along the ramparts. We saw where the Turkish soldiers had slept, where they ate and the vast chambers in which they received their imperial commands from the Prophet's successor on earth, the Sultan-Caliph, in Istanbul. The dates of the inscriptions accorded to the Muslim lunar calendar. 'We are in the year 1422,' Mr Amrin informed me. 'That is 5762 or 63 in the Jewish calendar.' The Muslim Year One was AD 622, the time of Hejira, Mohammed's flight from Mecca to Medina.

What fascinated me was Mr Amrin's interpretation of history. No two people, no two books, related the fables in the same way. The teller might be an Arab, an Armenian, a Turk or an Israeli. Each saw the world from the vantage of his religion, his sect, his school of philosophy and of law, his village, his tribe, his family. Mr Amrin was born in Kerak, known in Jordan for a beautiful Crusader castle and its Bedouin hospitality. 'The first place the Muslims got to,' he said, referring to Islam's earliest forays outside the Arabian peninsula, 'was Kerak. It was called Mu'ata, and it had a famous university. There, they had their first clash with the Christians.' They lost. Two thousand Muslim horsemen needed more than belief to vanquish a force of 200,000 Byzantine regulars. 'The Muslims had to withdraw,' Mr Amrin said. 'Three of their leaders were killed in that battle, and they elected Khalid bin Walid in the field.' That was in AD 690. Seven years later, Khalid bin Walid led the Muslims to victory against Byzantium's forces at Yarmouk. As the British and Arabs would dispatch a weakened Ottoman Empire north to its Anatolian heartland in 1917 and 1918, the Muslims of Arabia drove the Greeks from Syria to their defences beyond the Beilan Pass in Asia Minor. If the Byzantines had held at Yarmouk, if the Turks had stopped Lawrence at Aqaba, if . . .

Empires always get it wrong, something my country was learning, and denying, in the Middle East and the Asian subcontinent. The Ottomans, however nostalgic I may have been for the splendour of their court and the tolerance of their pre-First World War governors, also failed. 'You know Kerak?' Mr Amrin asked. I did. The Bedouin there had invited me to a huge *mensef* – a feast of boiled mutton and rice served on a communal platter that we ate without knives, forks or bread – twenty years before. Its Crusader castle had fascinated me. Its markets overflowed, its women were the most beautiful, its lambs the tastiest . . .

I rhapsodized like an Arab court poet. Mr Amrin was not interested in my memories of Kerak. He had his own: 'In 1910, Kerak had a famous revolt. The Ottomans sent people to the top of the tower and threw them down. Sixty-five people. They had refused to work in the army. This created anger against the Turks. After that, it was easy for Sherif Hussein bin Ali. The people were ready.'

An ingenious system of rain gutters and cisterns had kept the Turkish garrison in Aqaba supplied with water for men, animals and crops. A giant granite millstone had ground the wheat for their bread. Indicating the rust-red hills above Aqaba, Mr Amrin said the granite for the millstone and to construct the walls had come, like Lawrence's surprise invasion, from there. When he said the rocks were from the pre-Cambrian period, I nodded as if I knew when that was.

'This castle,' Mr Amrin added, bringing the story forward several millennia, 'was used as a khan for pilgrims from Egypt.' The land route to Mecca passed through Aqaba, until Israel occupied the Negev and Eilat in 1949. Pilgrims, at least those who did not take the sea route from Suez to Jeddah, would have found within Aqaba's caravanserai the water, the camel forage and the imperial protection they needed to continue south through the desert to Mecca and Medina. Those with more time or fervour added Jerusalem, where their father Abraham had attempted to sacrifice his son Isaac on an altar of stone that had, since the seventh century, been sheltered within a golden-domed mosque.

This citadel belonged in Aqaba, while the town's steel and cement hotels and offices might have been in Marbella or Atlanta. New high-rise projects for Aqaba's poor used gas heating in winter and electric air conditioners in summer, wasteful and unreliable. The Mamluke architect Khair Bey al Ala'ai knew what he was doing in the sixteenth century. He erected a fortress of clay roofs, arched and open to the breezes, with ramparts of stone mixed with clay. And it held until the twentieth century. 'This is perfect for the climate,' Mr Amrin said.

'It's cool in the sun, then warm in winter. It's not like it is if you live in cement.' Mr Amrin, since he had moved with his family from Kerak, lived in cement.

We ascended the staircase, following a Russian couple and their young daughter, to walk the ramparts. From the walls, Mr Amrin showed me his adopted city. 'You see the buses?' An array of camel-beige coaches glided through the town. 'Aqaba is not just a tourist centre. It does business. Those buses are taking people to jobs.' In the south-east, ships were waiting to dock. Mr Amrin said four ports made Aqaba a commercial hub: one harbour each for cement, phosphates, cargo and passengers. The caravan-like stream of buses carried workers back and forth to ports that worked around the clock. The sea trade meant that Aqaba could survive without tourists. Not all that well, if the squalor of its old city indicated anything, but well enough. There seemed to be two losers amidst the mirage of Aqaba's prosperity: big hotel owners and Iraqi refugees. The hotel's shareholders – who lived in America, Japan and Europe – could sell or wait or close down. The Iraqis starved.

'You see those women in black?' Mr Amrin asked me. This was later in the afternoon, when I was hotter and thirsty. We had left the fortress and were walking in the town's commercial heart. All I wanted was a cup of coffee, but Mr Amrin, leading me with casual indifference past beckoning cafés and the fragrance of coffee boiling with cardamom, had a favourite place that seemed to lie miles away. 'You see those ladies?' he repeated. I saw them, squatting on the pavement, their backs against concrete walls, veils shading their foreheads. They were handsome-looking women, who, despite opening their palms to receive coins from strangers, retained more dignity than many who had grown up as beggars. 'They are from Iraq. They were very rich people.'

I had seen women like them in Baghdad, once the most prosperous and modern city in the Arab world. In the first years after the war over Kuwait and under an international boycott, they sold their jewellery. Next came the silverware, the old books and the Irish linen that foreigners like myself could buy from outdoor stalls downtown in what Baghdadis called the 'thieves' market'. I was never sure whether the thieves were the sellers or the buyers. In time, the paintings went, then the extra furniture, the kitchen appliances, the better clothes. Finally, some of the women – and these had been among Iraq's proudest and best-educated – sold themselves. A British television cameraman in Baghdad had told me he had sex with an upper-class Iraqi woman while her husband waited alone in a bare living room for them to finish. The cameraman then had coffee with them both, as if he had been an invited guest, before leaving a discreet gift of one hundred dollars. The American embargo starved and bled Iraq for twelve years, until the American invasion of 2003 made life there even more precarious.

The two Iraqi women in black had, nestling in the folds of their cotton cloaks, about three Jordanian dinars between them. With that, they could have bought a sandwich each at any of the cafés I longed to stop at. At the Movenpick, which was the sort of place they had once been accustomed to, they might have shared one cup of tea.

An Oriental Garden

After a long walk and many stories of Moses, of Moabites, of Edomites and of Nabataeans, and then bumping into Mrs Amrin with their young son Qais, we had our coffee in a shaded park. Tall, thorny and mangled trees that the Arabs called *sidr* provided shade. Young men provided the coffee, tea and sandwiches in a green Pepsi-logo'd hut. Mr Amrin knew the owner, Bassam Abu Samhadana. Both were from Kerak. Mr Abu Samhadana would sit with us every few minutes between spells of overseeing his waiters. Most of the white plastic tables hosted large families. The mothers, fathers, grandparents and uncles talked. Children ran amok among the *sidr* trees. In a corner of the garden – itself a triangle of open land surrounded by city streets, restaurants and business buildings – was a lone table where three women smoked narghiles, sucking hard on the long tubes to make the water bubble and the smoke fly. Their laughter, their girth, their hair piled high in colours that might have come from tubs of ice cream, their skirts cut miles above plump knees, their jewels casting sunbeams through the *sidrs'* shadows, their shoes tight and black, everything about them, said: we are not from here. They might have hung 'For Rent' signs around their necks. '*Sharameet,*' Mr Amrin explained. Prostitutes. The picture cried out for Delacroix and the caption, 'Hookers with hookahs' or 'Oodles of odalisques'. Mr Amrin admitted they were Jordanian, but they were not from Aqaba. They were most assuredly not, he said when I asked, from Kerak.

Was Mr Amrin a Bedouin? He was, but a few generations back. 'You can say 99.99 per cent of the original Jordanians,' by which he meant the half of Jordan's population who were not refugees from Palestine, 'are Bedouin.' Most had settled in cities, towns and villages. 'Bedouin are peaceful people. They are very straight. If they like you, they say they like you. If not . . .'

Was it, I wondered, a good idea for him to have left Kerak for tourism in Aqaba? In Kerak, he had been an army-trained electrical engineer. His wife had had a job there. She came from a prominent Jordanian family, the Mejallis, who had given the country politicians, lawyers and a prime minister. In Kerak, Mr Amrin had a house and a father, mother and siblings.

In Aqaba, he said, he had seen the president of the United States. It was in 1994. Israel's prime minister, Yitzak Rabin, King Hussein and Bill Clinton were opening the border between Israel and Jordan. 'They were crying,' he said. 'The newspapers said it was because of the treaty' – the Israel–Jordan peace – 'but it wasn't. It was the dust.' The royal family kept a palace in Aqaba, and he had often seen the young princes. He had met many foreigners. Aqaba showed him more than Kerak. On 11 September 2001, he was driving American tourists in Wadi Roum, the desert through which Lawrence had marched to Aqaba in 1917. 'One guy's mobile rang in the back seat. He woke up and jumped. "What? The World Trade Center is destroyed?" He was very upset. His brother was on the eighty-second floor, but he was worried about another man in the building who owed him money.'

Maybe it was just as well the Americans no longer visited Aqaba. Mr Amrin did not understand them. He said he was not a businessman. I could see that when he refused payment for my day's tour of Aqaba, its ancient citadel, its souks and Bassam Abu Samhadana's coffee garden.

Bassam Abu Samhadana poked in and out of our conversation, administered affairs in the café and gave us lunch he'd made himself at home. We feasted on a large pan of kafta, minced and spiced lamb in yoghurt, that we ate communally. Each of us grabbed bites from the flattened circle of meat with our silver spoons or pieces of Arabic bread and took billows of white rice from a bowl. While we ate and drank tea, Bassam Abu Samhadana told us Aqaba's gossip in a manner so relaxed he might have been stretched on a divan smoking a narghile and musing on visions rising from its smoke. He motioned to me to eat more kafta, then said that England's Prince Edward had once visited Kerak. Bassam, as royalist as his Kerak compatriot, had tracked down the youngest son of England's queen to present him with a Persian carpet. Did Edward like it? Mr Abu Samhadana was not sure. He smiled to make me follow his eyes to the far table, where the three professional women were receiving a Saudi gentleman. A young Jordanian in a black leather jacket hovered behind.

Ahmed and Bassam, as they instructed me to address them, blamed the Saudis for attracting prostitutes to Aqaba. Saudi millionaires brought their money and sexual frustration a few miles over their border to a conservative Arab town that, compared to any city in their kingdom, was Gomorrah-on-Sea. Ahmed and Bassam did not rate the three Jordanian prostitutes. 'The prettier ones are the gypsies,' Bassam said. 'And the high-class women come from Iraq.' The Saudi gentleman, however corpulent he was under his dark cotton gown and whatever price he was then negotiating with the leather-jacketed procurer, gave the impression of a man on a budget. He and the jacket reached an agreement. The Saudi paid for the women's narghiles and colourful cocktails and accompanied them across the street to a Lebanese restaurant, the Ali Baba. How, I wondered, would he manage three such well-proportioned women after a large lunch?

In the evening, I walked alone along the beach, read the newspapers, ate a Lebanese dinner at the Ali Baba and returned to Bassam's outdoor café. The day's heat had settled, leaving Bassam's garden cool and silent. Long necklaces of fairy lights, every other one out like a blind eye, dangled among the branches. My first day in Aqaba: was it a success? A few hours earlier, I had watched children swim at Aqaba's last free beach – a dirt shore where women coddled babies and let the sea brush the hems of their long dresses. Boys, no more than eight or nine years old, charged by on lithe and small Arab mares, plumes and spangled bridles ablaze in the sunset. Blankets and rugs hugged dry earth nearest the water, where men and women, not one of them immodest enough to strip down to a swimming costume, wrapped the remains of picnics and called their young in from the waves. Away from the shore, boys in jeans or shorts kicked footballs, while others bought ice cream and popcorn from a two-wheeled stall. Wet children wrapped themselves in large towels, crouched with their backs to the wind and shivered. The wind rose, from the north-west, like Lawrence's Arabs, hurling desert sand and pebbles at the dying day.

When someone travels to write about a place, he looks for what makes it different from other places. That evening in Aqaba, I could have been anywhere. The beach, apart from the modesty of the adults, resembled the quiet sea at Brindisi or the Santa Monica sands in California where I had grown up. Aqaba's particularity lay hidden in its history, those rare occasions when some emperor or general captured it and left mud-brick remains like the Nabataean–Ptolemaic harbour or the Mamluke citadel that the Turks surrendered to a young

British officer and his few hundred Arab irregulars. If not for its past, Aqaba might not have been worth the visit.

Out of the darkness of the garden café, between my chair and the kiosk, where the staff prepared coffee and food, Bassam approached wearing a red-check keffiyeh around his neck. He unwound the fluffy headscarf and handed it to me. 'My mother made this,' he said. 'It's wool.' Stretched out, it was a yard of white cotton into which his mother had sewn dyed wool in elaborate patterns. People used to tell me that red-check keffi-yehs like that were for the Bedouin. Peasants, the fellaheen, wore black and white. Bassam told a waiter to bring me tea and a narghile.

The waiter dropped the water pipe and a box of hot coals to keep us warm beside the table. 'You want more coal?' Bassam asked. I was warm enough. The waiter ran back to the hut for a smaller coal carrier with chips of charred wood, *fahm* in Arabic, for the pipe. He placed the embers on a mound of wet tobacco at the summit of the silver stem above a glass vase of water. The ceremony proceeded: he tested the tobacco, blew on the coals and inserted a plastic mouthpiece into the wood tip of an accordion cord. The sweet smoke, filtered through clear water, let me dream like a Turkish pasha.

Bassam, rubbing his hands close to the fire, asked if I liked the tobacco. Pleased, he said, 'It's apple.' He flavoured his tobacco with other fruits, but apple was his favourite. He told me the story of his business. He had come to Aqaba as an inland tourist a year after Jordan ended its official state of war with Israel. He saw a disused plot of trees and shrubs and weeds between a traffic roundabout and some restaurants and asked the town's government for a permit to sell coffee on it. It was agreed that, if he cleaned the site and the public liked his coffee, he could stay. 'I opened with a half kilo of coffee, two kilos of sugar, two kilos of bananas, and two kilos of oranges.' He spent what little money he had in the bank on clearing the weeds and rubbish and building the kiosk. With his profits from sales of tea, coffee and fresh juice, he bought more coffee, more sugar, more fruit. 'I cannot drink juice here any more,' he said. 'I see it too much. But if I go to Syria, I drink orange juice every day.' The business prospered. Pepsi put a canopy on his kiosk and provided a cooler for its bottles. Bassam was joining the world economy.

Israelis came to his café, usually on day trips from Eilat, and Bassam welcomed them. An Israeli guide named Menachem brought group tours to rest and drink tea under the *sidr* trees. I assumed Bassam had to pay him something in return. There were problems with the Israelis. What? Stealing, he said. What did they steal? Glasses. Glasses? 'We cleared the tables,' Bassam recalled. 'Twenty glasses were missing. I asked Menachem to get them back. Menachem said they were taking them to drink later. I told him we had plastic cups for that.'

Despite the thefts, Bassam served the Israeli day-trippers and counted glasses before they left. When the Palestinian uprising against military occupation began at the end of September 2000, the Israelis stayed in Eilat. Western tourists, apart from a few hearty pilgrims, avoided the entire region. The source of Bassam's suffering was neither the Israelis who stole glasses nor the foreigners who feared visiting Jordan, but the Jordanian bureaucracy. One conscientious bureaucrat almost cost him his business, his investment and his livelihood. This officer of local government took it upon himself to enforce the law with an efficiency that many Western financial consultants believe the Arab world needs if it is to assume its place in the scheme of transnational, universal, utopian capitalism. This functionary was new to Aqaba, a man who knew the regulations, a man to help forge a land of laws and not of men, an arbiter of right and wrong, the kind of man whose rightful home might have been in the FBI, an 'I'm-all-right-Jack' British trade union of the 1950s, or middle management at an American corporation. He did not belong in Aqaba.

Having been posted to the town from Jordan's more austere north, the official visited Bassam's café. He tasted the coffee and must have observed that Bassam's clean kitchen conformed to the rules of health and safety. He noted that previous local officials had issued Bassam the papers necessary to maintain the green kiosk, its cooker, its juice squeezers and its refrigerators. The kiosk-café had a valid permit. The plastic tables and chairs, scattered among trees for the relaxation of families and occasional tourists, did not. And the observant bureaucrat saw tables where the law did not allow tables. He saw people sitting in chairs that the law did not sanction. He must have seen glasses of tea and cups of coffee on those permitless tables. Perhaps he heard a bit of laughter in the shade and observed children running round the prohibited tables on the earthen paths that Bassam had cleaned and swept amid grass that he had cut. The bureaucrat, this northerner, did his job. He had come to Aqaba to enforce the law, and he enforced it by sending men to seize every table and every chair and lock them in a government warehouse.

Patrons who had come to enjoy Bassam's garden and to muse over Persian tobacco smoke and Turkish coffee went elsewhere. Aqaba's citizens were not Italians to stand at a counter for a quick espresso before rushing to an office or shop. They had time for the rituals of the day, to wait for coffee to brew with cardamom seeds in a brass pot, to watch a young man light the coals and pack the tobacco into a hookah, to observe from a chair the universe revolving around them. Bassam lost them to other cafés, none so congenial as his had been, but where they might feel a chair beneath them and bang a table when the argument suited. His business declined, and the little garden resumed its empty, forlorn state. Bassam stopped sending money to his two sisters at university. Helping his father in Kerak, a filial duty, became difficult.

Bassam Abu Samhadana did what any good Jordanian whose prosperity was threatened by bureaucracy would have done: he wrote to the king. A new monarch had ascended the throne, a young man who had not been tested. The old king, as Bassam and many others among his subjects abjured, would have dealt with the legal threat to Bassam's survival swiftly and justly.

Young Abdallah, however, was a modern man. His mother was English, and his education came from the Western world where law and by-laws and regulations and rules were said to prevail. Such a modern king might leave the enforcers of law to do their work without royal interference. Abdallah's training – his English was more fluent than his Arabic – should have inclined him to let Bassam's remaining clients drink on their feet or drink elsewhere. Writing to such a king – unlike to his father, who had behaved like the true father of all his subjects – held perils. What if King Abdallah read the letter and rebuked Bassam for going over the head of a government official, accused him of demanding favours, prosecuted him for asking the king himself to violate the law? Bassam was a man of Kerak, and the men of Kerak were not afraid. He sent the letter, and he waited. A week is a long wait when your business is dying and your sisters and father depend on you. Bassam waited many weeks, then many months. He survived in part courtesy of loyal customers like Ahmed Amrin, who were willing to stand rather than seek another café.

King Abdallah's letter arrived, and Bassam rejoiced. The king had read the petition, weighed the facts of the case and concluded that the Governorate of Aqaba must restore to Bassam's café all its chairs and tables. Bassam took the letter to the government office building and showed it to the bureaucrat who had seized his property. Despite what amounted to a royal proclamation, the bureaucrat did not relent. While conceding that the king had written the letter, the man said it had no legal force. Instructions to release confiscated property had to be processed through channels. There were not only regulations – and the official had demonstrated his devotion to those – there were also procedures. And to the procedures, he was just as loyal. To enforce his decision in the case, the king would have to instruct a minister, who would pass the order down to the regional governor, who would send it from one office to another, where it would be signed and stamped by the appropriate officials, until it reached the desk of the bureaucrat in Aqaba. The chairs and the tables remained locked in the warehouse.

Bassam had an acquaintance, also from Kerak, who knew the king. The Kerak man was a soldier, who had trained the then Prince Abdallah years before in some aspect or another of military practice. Bassam contacted the soldier – by telephone or letter, I was not sure which – and asked him to tell the king what happened to royal decisions in Aqaba. The king had to be informed that, despite his ruling to the contrary, the tables and chairs remained locked away and Aqaba's finest garden café was empty. The soldier promised to bring the matter to King Abdallah's attention. Further days, then weeks, passed without action from the palace or a call from the soldier. With business suffering, Bassam called Amman, the capital and home of the officer who had been a mentor to the young prince before he became the king, to impress upon his Kerak compatriot the urgency of the case. If his tables and chairs were not restored soon, the café would close and Bassam would return to Kerak a failed man. His disgrace would not fail to dishonour King Abdallah, whose writ would be seen not to run as far as Aqaba, as well as the officer from Kerak.

While I listened to Bassam's tale, told in a tranquil voice without rancour, and puffed my narghile, I imagined the dilemma of the officer in Amman. As at all royal courts, the man would have to await the right moment – perhaps when the monarch and his courtiers were talking about Aqaba or the people of Kerak or coffee or even tables and chairs. Such moments do not present themselves every day, yet his fellow son of Kerak was calling every day from Aqaba to demand justice. A man had to be careful when making requests of a king, but the same man had to protect his reputation among the people of Kerak. Months later, when Bassam had to consider bankruptcy and admitting to all in Kerak that his king and his Kerak intercessor had both failed him, King Abdallah was made aware of the insubordination of the assiduous bureaucrat in Aqaba. The fresh decision and its implementation were immediate, and, in

Bassam's view, just: the bureaucrat was transferred to a desolate corner of the northern desert and eight tables and thirty-two chairs were delivered from the state warehouse to Bassam's garden. He was back in business.

The tobacco was burning down and the coals had turned to ash. Several empty coffee cups and tea glasses had collected on the table. Bassam told the waiter to bring a last tea before he went home. I tried to pay him for the coffee, the tea and the narghile, but he would not accept anything. All he allowed me to do, when the table was cleared and the kiosk locked, was tip the waiter. It was after midnight when I walked along the shore to the hotel. The Red Sea, as still as the open eye of a corpse, caught the lights of four countries within a compass of forty miles. The map lines made no impression on the night. Aqaba was the reason for the lines, the frontiers, the divisions. Aqaba had been the goal of a revolt against an empire on behalf, not of the rebels themselves, but of more distant empires. The fall of Aqaba was a romantic, cynical saga, that had bequeathed a century of separation, of exodus, of bloodshed. The Turks could not hold Aqaba and, with it, the rest of what had been Greater Syria. Those who conquered it, occupied and divided it, had yet to destroy and remake it wholly in their image. Bassam did not take my money for the coffee and tobacco, and he sent what he had to his father in Kerak. This was no way to run a Starbuck's.

When the Arabs realized that France, Britain and Zionism were claiming sovereignty over them after 1918, they resisted, longer perhaps than any other colonized population. And they were still holding out. In small ways, their lives could not conform to the standards set for them by the empires – first Britain's and France's, then America's – because they ate with their hands from a shared bowl, because they took time to brew coffee and prepare their tobacco, because desert traditions of hospitality and vengeance survived in their city houses, because they believed in angels. The Western world had destroyed the mass forms of their protest – their nationalism, their socialism – and was even then bombing its latest manifestation: fundamentalist, violent Islam. Standing on ruins the Greeks had left more than two millennia before, I looked at the shores of Egypt and what are now called Israel, Jordan and Saudi Arabia. This land was indigestible. Its history was too long, its cultures too strong, its faiths too pervasive. The cost of their stubbornness has been high, but they go on paying. They have absorbed the good and the bad of civilizations that have passed here, but they have not been absorbed. They are the world's spoilers. Imperial histories chronicle expedition after expedition – by Pharaoh, by Titus, by the Shahs of Persia, by the legions of Byzantium, by Sultans in Cairo and Istanbul, by the British army and the American armed forces – to suppress their rebellions, contain their passions and possess their wealth. Perhaps that was why I had returned, not out of pity, but in admiration.

THREE

Royal Cities

'Here is a land blessed more than most with health and
fertility, but its health has been paralysed by its danger,
its fertility checked and blasted by the floods and
barbarism to which it lies exposed.'

REVEREND GEORGE ADAM SMITH
The Historical Geography of the Holy Land (1894)

Seeking the Nabataeans

LAWRENCE'S FORCES rode north from Aqaba to disrupt Turkey's railway communications and to guard Allenby's right as his Egyptian Expeditionary Force advanced from Gaza. Eighty-four years later, I followed the Arabs' route in an old Toyota taxi through canyon and desert. In the gorges above Aqaba, not a plant grew in the granite. Fertility lay miles north, where Lawrence feared the peasants would resist his Arab national army as they would a Bedouin raiding party. Centuries of Bedouin raids – sheep theft was as common as on the Scottish–English borders – had made the fellaheen wary. Some attacked their liberators. A half-hour out of Aqaba, a customs officer stopped us at an anti-smuggling roadblock. When the driver told him I was a foreigner, he let us pass the Jordanians whose cars were searched.

One by one, sprigs of life exposed themselves beside the road: sage, an acacia, a donkey. The first work of man was a stone monument, left for centuries in the wind to revert to bare stone. Then, evidence of civilization: a cemetery within walls of grey rock housed a regiment of marble markers. Next to it, a village

40

of newly painted old mud and new cement breeze-block houses, all but a few single-storey, sheltered a population half that of the graveyard.

On the right, parallel to the road, a railway line accompanied us north. The track had, until Lawrence, carried pilgrims, soldiers and supplies from Istanbul all the way to Mecca. Perhaps the peasants had been right to oppose Lawrence's desert Arabs. Thanks to Lawrence, the Hejaz railway never ran again. In Damascus, there remained a beautiful Ottoman Hejaz Railway Station and a modern Hejaz Railway Commission whose members – Turkey, Syria, Jordan and Saudi Arabia – distrusted one another so much that not one mile of the track blown by Lawrence's sappers had been repaired. Like Arab unity, rebuilding the railway was relegated to the realm of millinerian expectation.

The modern era's power pylons, telephone poles and water pipes defaced the landscape. At noon, we reached a sign that read 'Amman, 275 Kilometres'. Another sign advertised 'The Farm for Sale'. The car stopped, and I looked from a ridge across the sands for the farm. Nothing grew for a hundred miles. I understood why the farmer wanted to sell, but where would he find a buyer? The drought that parched his land could not be blamed on global warming. It began at the end of the Ice Age.

We turned off the main Aqaba road at the King's Highway to Wadi Musa and Petra. In the shade of a ridge, a lonely pool of snow resisted the change of season. Beyond were villages with abundant cypress, pine and olive trees on the slopes. A two-lane asphalt road floated along the hilltops into Rajif, a large village of flat-roofed houses, a white schoolhouse, a playground and as many vegetable shops as houses. We had to wait for old men in red keffiyehs to squeeze past us in the tightening streets. More open road took us into Taibit, splashed across the slopes of many jagged hills. There were two Taibits, the new town that had grown closer and closer to the windy summits, and Old Taibit – Taibit Zamen – near the base of a wadi. The old town's earthen hovels with lovely arched entryways had occasional mounds on their level roofs and tiny gardens in open central courtyards. Old Taibit, nearer the water that coursed down the hills, stored rainfall in cisterns that fed their trees and crops. It was a place of stone, clay and mud. Above it loomed the new cement town, itself dwarfed by a new mosque. In the streets, old men paraded everywhere in cotton robes and keffiyehs or trousers and shirts. When I asked the driver why there were no children, he rubbed his thumb against his index finger and said, 'No money.'

To reach Petra, the ancient Nabataean capital that the Swiss explorer Johann Ludwig Burkhardt rediscovered in 1812, we had to pass through New Petra. Here were the Movenpick, Petra Panorama, Marriott, Nabataean Castle and Grand View hotels, freshly built and doomed to bankruptcy. In 1973, this town with its shops, restaurants and amusement centres did not exist. Nor did the Visitors' Centre, bookshop, souvenir kiosk and ticket office. Then, I had slept outside in a place called Nazal's Camp, where I saw in the night sky every star that man had ever counted. And, counting them, I had fallen asleep.

If I fell in love with Petra as a graduate student on an Easter excursion, love went cold now. It was like revisiting an old mistress, her beauty diminished by cosmetic surgery rather than age. Petra then, six years after the June 1967 war and barely three years after the Black September civil war between Palestinian commandos and the Jordanian army, was an enchanted city of empty tombs and palaces, discovered but not desecrated. It was like no other city of antiquity – no fortifications, no encircling walls, no natural water source and no cramped streets. It was larger than other ancient cities, about 65,000 acres spread over rocky ravines, desert plain and mountains. The Nabataeans had lived in elaborate caves and freestanding palaces. They funnelled rainwater from the hills – a great natural flow collected at Petra's base – and cut channels to carry water from Ain Musa, the Spring of Moses, to their commercial metropole. They relied on the narrow valleys, the towers of natural sandstone and their own mobile defences to protect them from marauders and invaders.

In 1973, Bedouin lived in a few of Petra's higher caves. I met some of them and, like any other tourist, took pictures. They gave me coffee and talked politics. The only visitors disturbing their tranquillity, apart from me, were Jordanian schoolchildren on a day trip. The only people who demanded money were the young men who hired horses. They had told me – what did I know aged twenty-two? – that I was required to enter Petra on horseback. So it was that I had my first glimpse of Al-Khazaneh – the so-called Pharaoh's Treasury – at the end of a long gorge called the Siq, on horseback. Burkhardt entered on a noble Bedouin steed, but mine was a nag who looked so hungry I should have carried her.

Jordan had used the interval of nearly thirty years between my two visits to effect 'improvements'. At the Visitors' Centre near the Bab Al Siq a ticket seller charged ten Jordanian dinars for entry. At a tollgate, I showed my ticket, as if in a cinema, and walked in. The horse hirers were still there, but government officials watched to guarantee they did not cheat the few foreign visitors. This time, I walked. The route was the same but the path had been paved and provided with little waste-baskets bearing the logo 'Edico'. Workers in Edico uniforms swept the path, and signs in English explained everything. 'Al Siq,' the first read, 'is 1207 metres long and 3 to 16 metres wide. It is a natural gorge of spectacular geological formation, which the Nabataeans widened in parts by carving out the rock . . .' No one needed a sign to tell him the gorge was spectacular. It was like reading in the Louvre 'Beautiful painting of a woman with an enigmatic smile by the Italian Leonardo da Vinci'.

I overtook a family that I assumed were Americans from the Midwest. The father carried a baby on his chest and wore a 'J + B Scotch' T-shirt, Nike trainers and a baseball cap. His wife and daughter licked ice creams and wore blue jeans. But they were speaking Arabic. In 1973, Jordanian men did not wear baseball caps or carry babies. Jordanian women – when in

Jordan – wore long dresses. Petra and its indigenous visitors were adapting or assimilating to the new global empire as the Nabataeans had to Greece and Rome. I rushed ahead of them lest anything come between me and my first sight through the narrow cleft at the end of Al Siq.

The gorge opened and up shot a magnificent tomb, mountain-high, that said, 'Stranger, beat this.' Invaders coming to Petra by this route would have entered single file, there to be cut down one at a time by Nabataean archers on the plaza of their king's mausoleum. It was a good place to die, overwhelming in its beauty and surprise. I did not die but the new Coca-Cola kiosk and souvenir stands were killing me. Tour guides were explaining, perhaps for the thousandth time, that the treasury, Al-Khazaneh, was never a storehouse of gold and jewels but the burial place of a king. They did not explain why Jordan had permitted the desecration of this once-solitary shrine.

I sat on a bench, listening to guides and tourists, and looked at the tomb. A headless eagle – defaced, no doubt, by iconoclasts of one monotheism or another – sat poised to soar from the perch on which Nabataean sculptors had placed him a century before the Crucifixion. Then I wandered among Petra's palaces and tombs and theatres. In 1973, when I had slept out at Nazal's Camp, Bedouin lived all over Petra. Like Nazal's Camp, the Bedouin had been removed. No longer in their caves along the ridges, they lived miles away and sent their children into the ruins to beg from tourists. Some of them sold coloured rocks. 'No, thank you,' an American woman with legs larger than her trousers said to a little Bedouin girl. 'I think the rocks should stay in this place.' She also thought her money should stay in her handbag.

The children approached me. When I gave a dinar to one of the boys, his sister said I had to give another one to her. Six or seven years old, they were determined entrepreneurs. Another child, who said her name was Rima and looked about ten, gave me a stone of the same rosy stripes as the Treasury. In English, she asked if I preferred to see the Monastery or the Bedouin camp where her family lived. We came to a tea shop, whose proprietor tried to sell me silver jewellery. When I declined, he said, 'For your wife.' No wife. 'For your secretary?' He chased Rima away, perhaps resenting the competition, and gave me a glass of tea.

An American family on camels trotted behind a camel herder. Some Russians – father, mother, daughter – asked the tea vendor for directions to the Monastery. I walked on to an amphitheatre. A goat grazed near the stage on which the Nabataeans had thrilled to the tragedies of Greece. Other tourists, people like me, shooed the goat aside and took pictures of themselves. Rima and the other children tried to make them buy stones. I should not have come back. The driver, asleep in his car near the Bab Al Siq, woke and drove me to an indifferent lunch at a restaurant near the Turkish bath. He asked if I had enjoyed Petra. I didn't answer.

The best book in English on the Nabataeans – the book that made me appreciate their achievement – was *The Lost Civilisation of Petra* by an Israeli who had fought in court to erase the classification 'Jew' from his identity card. He was the father of Juwal Levy, the young man my son and I had met aboard the *Nissos Kypros*. Udi Levy was, although he did not know it, waiting at home in the Negev to show me the rest of the Nabataean empire.

Ancient Philadelphia

Amman was dark by the time we reached its outskirts. Thrown like a Bedouin blanket over a batch of hilltops, the city had outgrown the Circassian village where Prince Abdallah of the Hejaz pitched camp in March 1921. Abdallah had embarked on a quixotic mission to restore his brother Feisal's throne in Damascus after France had massacred Feisal's Arab army at the Maysaloun Pass and robbed the Arabs of their independent state. Abdallah's adventure, if allowed to proceed, threatened war between Britain and France. Winston Churchill, by then colonial secretary, persuaded Abdallah to accept a principality to be called Transjordan with its capital in Amman. This involved compromises for Abdallah, who must have known the French would annihilate his Bedouin troops; for the Arabs of Greater Syria, a vast majority of whom had told the American King–Crane Commission of their desire for independence and unity; and for the Zionists, whose territorial ambitions included both banks of the Jordan. Until then, Britain and its Zionist protégés had called the country Eastern Palestine. Britain revised its League of Nations Mandate in 1922 to exclude the East Bank from the Balfour Declaration's proposed 'Jewish home'. It assumed responsibility for Prince Abdallah's foreign policy and, under the able direction of General John Bagot Glubb, organized his army into the Arab Legion. Zionists who rejected the revision of the Mandate and insisted the future Israel comprise both banks of the River Jordan came to be called the Revisionists. Its leaders would be Vladimir Jabotinsky, Menachem Begin, Yitzak Stern, Yitzak Shamir and, later, Ariel Sharon.

Jordan, removed from the Palestine Mandate, did not escape the Palestine problem. Half of the lighted hilltops of night-time Amman belonged to Palestinians, whose refugee camps were as much a part of the city, albeit poorer, as the East Bankers' neighbourhoods. Jordan had fought three wars over Palestine. In 1948, Abdallah – who became king of independent Jordan in 1946 – captured East Jerusalem and the West Bank. In 1967, his grandson, King Hussein, lost Abdallah's 1948 conquests. In both wars, Jordan absorbed refugees whom the Israeli army had expelled. Then came the third war. The refugees, led by Yasser Arafat, and the native Jordanians under King Hussein waged ferocious battles in 1970 and 1971. The Palestinians lost, and the Hashemite throne survived.

The city we entered had grown to include a million people on the hills where Abdallah had found about three thousand Circassian settlers and a few hundred Arabs. At one of Amman's many traffic roundabouts, twenty young men were dancing in a large plaza. Clasping one another's shoulders, they formed a line and kicked their legs out to the beat of the tambour, the Arab drum, and the clapping and singing of boys and girls. They were having great fun. Dance festivals had evolved over millennia: pagan feasts absorbed by Christian holidays, Christianity giving way to Islam, sacred holidays secularized by the nation. And in all of Syria, there was the *dabke*, a communal dance like a Scottish reel. There were the *chababi*, a pipe, and the tambour, and clapping, and the mixing of sexes, ages, classes. I used to see this dancing at the great *mahrajans* in Mount Lebanon, at regional festivals in Jebel Alawi in northern Syria, among the Druze and in the towns of the West Bank. They might celebrate a birth, a wedding, a harvest, a saint's day. These boys, girls, men and women danced in the forecourt of Amman's telecommunications centre, under blazing floodlights. Above them loomed a quadruple-life-size, Hollywood-style portrait of King Abdallah holding a cellphone to his ear. Amman had a new mobile telephone network! An ancient ritual that had been paganized, Christianized, Islamized and Arabized was now commercialized. How else to herald the new era?

Welcome to Amman

Penury and loyalty dictated my choice of hotel, the Shepherd's in Jebel Amman. The old place was far less costly than the modern chains, the InterContinental, Marriott, Hilton, Radisson et al. I was not on expenses, as I had been as a journalist. My publishers' advance was so meagre that I could not have survived on it all year if I'd slept in a tent. The Shepherd's belonged to the Shalhoub family, whose daughter Norma had been at the American University of Beirut when I was studying philosophy there. I was twenty-one then, and she was a year or two younger. We had not gone out together, despite my repeated attempts to woo her. On my student travels, I had stayed at her family's hotel. Then, it was managed by her father, a gregarious and well-known Amman character named George Shalhoub. For a time, he had – persuaded by his son Nader that it would be good for business – opened a British pub on the roof. George Shalhoub had died, and Nader was in charge. The pub had closed, but Shepherd's retained the fading charm of George Shalhoub's times.

There were only one or two other guests, like a seafront hotel in winter, and the service was nothing if not personal. I received a call as soon as I reached my room. Norma Shalhoub was inviting me to lunch the next day. How did she know I was there? Amman was a village, and Shepherd's was a village hotel. This was the wrong place for me to bring a Jordanian maiden for the night, not that I knew any.

'The West Bank is killing Jordan,' Norma Shalhoub said at lunch. She was not discussing attacks by Palestinians or the arrival of West Bankers in search of work. She was talking about perception. 'I've been to trade fairs in Japan three times.' The Shalhoubs had opened a travel agency to complement their hotel business. 'The first time, the Japanese asked if we could hear the bombs in the Iran–Iraq war. The second time, could we hear the bombs in Lebanon? And the last time, did we hear the explosions from the West Bank? They think it's all the same.' Amman had been tranquil since 1970.

We were at her mother's house. Norma lived next door on one side, her brother and his family on the other. Norma's mother gave us rice, vegetable stew and chicken grilled in the Lebanese way with lemon and garlic. Although they were patriotic Jordanians, the Shalhoubs' ancestors had migrated to Amman from Lebanon – from the same Christian mountain village that my great-grandmother had left for France and Massachusetts in the late nineteenth century. Her food was like my grandmother's. As a gesture to me, Norma had gone out to buy cans of beer. Like most other people in Jordan, where alcohol was legal, the Shalhoubs did not drink.

When the Israeli border opened in 1994, they built the Palace

Hotel in Petra. Mrs Shalhoub remembered Udi, an Israeli tour operator, coming to the house for lunch. He was pleasant and polite, and they looked forward to working with him. But he warned them: 'This is just the beginning, but wait. I promise you that after a year of doing business with Israelis, you'll be anti-Semitic.'

The anticipated profits from the Palace Hotel in Petra did not materialize. Most Americans toured the Middle East on Israeli package holidays. Only the more adventurous – and such people are few – came to Jordan on their own. 'The day tourists,' Norma said, 'would bring their own food – even their own water – from Israel.' Israeli tour operators bussed the tourists to Petra for a few hours, stopped by the Palace or some other hotel to buy postcards and bussed them back over the border. It was to make them pay something, Mrs Shalhoub told me, that the government introduced the ten-dinar entry fee. Again there were stories of Israeli tourists stealing glasses. But Udi the tour operator failed as a prophet. The Shalhoubs were spared anti-Semitism by the kindness of Jewish families in America. When Mrs Shalhoub's younger daughter, Lena, moved with her American husband to Pittsburgh, she stayed home all day with two small children in a foreign country while he worked. In Jordan, her mother, sister, aunts and cousins would have been with her. In Pittsburgh, she became isolated and unwell. Mrs Shalhoub said, 'The only people who offered to help were Jewish.'

Norma drove me on a tour of Amman's newer quarter, Abdoan, and its shopping centre – a mall I thought I had seen under another name in the San Fernando Valley. The logos of American suburbia beckoned: Baskin-Robbins Ice Cream, Planet Hollywood, Dunkin' Donuts, McDonald's. An American atmosphere pervaded Abdoan, kids in fresh-washed cars, boys and girls eyeing one another through the black lenses of reflecting sunglasses, families at outdoor tables eating hamburgers and drinking Coca-Cola. Did I want to see the new American Embassy?

The previous embassy had been a modest stone office building whose front door opened onto the street opposite the main journalist hotel, the InterContinental. It dated from the days when anyone could walk into a US Embassy without being searched, scanned and security checked. It took a few bullets during the Black September 1970 battles but it was otherwise unharmed. The new embassy, not far from the mall, was a citadel of the American world order. It lay within a perimeter of walls that an Olympic pole vaulter could not scale. Jordanian army tanks surrounded the compound, guns pointed outwards. The embassy itself was a gargantuan block of stone, trimmed in satellite dishes, television and radio aerials and, higher than them all, a flagpole. Norma told me the embassy was self-sufficient. Its PX sold cornflakes and peanut butter so the staff would not have to buy Arab food outside. It could have been a French Foreign Legion fort in old Africa, awaiting the inevitable and futile assault by the natives.

At dinner that night, in an Italian restaurant called Romano's, I ate alone with a book of conversations with Middle East historians – *Approaches to the History of the Middle East* by Nancy Elizabeth Gallagher. The author's first interview was with Albert Hourani, whose *History of the Arabs* remained the standard fifteen years after its original publication. 'Between the powerful and the powerless,' Albert said, 'there cannot be an easy relationship of friendship. Having power is quite different from being under someone else's power, which is a far deeper experience, just as victory is a much less profound experience than defeat.' Albert was one of two historians – the great Mediterranean and Crusades' scholar Sir Steven Runciman was the other – who had advised me on *Tribes with Flags*. Both had since died, and I missed their counsel. Reading Albert's reflections was like having lunch with him, as we used to in London at the Oxford and Cambridge Club. In the most diplomatic manner, he would tell me that I had misinterpreted the histories of Islam, the Crusades or the Ottoman Empire. Sitting in Amman with my book, I saw couples – well-dressed men and women – at other candle-lit tables. I thought about Albert Hourani and

Steven Runciman, two of Britain's grandest old men of letters. Ageing was sadder for the loss of your mentors. Solitary travel too was becoming a trial, when you ate alone and all the pretty women in the restaurant were with other men.

Notables in Exile

'We're not very numerous,' Usama Khalidy said of his family. 'We're probably not more than three or four hundred.' The Khalidys had for five centuries contributed generation after generation of scholars to the Muslim world. Their longevity as nobles of Jerusalem had prompted Usama's younger brother, the historian Tareef Khalidy, to respond to the accusation that the Khalidys were decadent with: 'Decadent? Three hundred years ago, we were decadent.'

Usama was the middle of three accomplished brothers. The oldest was Walid, another academic who lived in Cambridge, Massachusetts. Tareef, the baby, taught history at Cambridge, the one in England. Before Cambridge, he taught at the American University of Beirut. Throughout Lebanon's long war, he resisted the deadening effect of military occupations by Syria and Israel, massacres and the anti-intellectual bias of Lebanon's Muslim and Christian sectarian barbarians.

The three Khalidy brothers – Walid, Usama and Tareef – grew up in Jerusalem during the British Mandate. Their family owned beautiful houses and a library of rare and ancient Islamic manuscripts within the stone walls of Jerusalem's old city. Like many other Arabs and Jews, they had built villas away from the squalor of the old city – whose rain-fed cisterns sometimes bred unhealthy bacteria – on the open hills to the west. In 1948, when the Arab inhabitants were expelled or fled the violence, West Jerusalem became Jewish Jerusalem.

Usama's father, a teacher and scholar like most of his family, had written some of the first textbooks in Arabic. 'He did an experiment with me,' Usama said. 'I did not go to school until

I was nine. I knew every cave in the area. I knew where to catch scorpions. I knew every plant. I knew every shepherd. I did not know how to read and write.' Illiteracy did not impede his progress through academe. A tutor taught him enough one summer for him to pass his exams for the third-form elementary. He was nine. By the time he celebrated his nineteenth birthday, he had a degree in biochemistry. By then, he lived in Beirut. By then, there were no Khalidys in West Jerusalem.

'I am one of the few who has had the honour of being occupied by the Israelis three times,' Usama said, proud of his record. He spoke without anger. The way he sat, almost as if his body had fallen into a restful sleep, said he would be at home wherever he escaped. Usama Khalidy's apparent indifference to his treatment by Israel's armed forces was inexplicable in a man who, again and again, had been on the losing side. His first Israeli occupation took place in April 1948, when he was sixteen. The Khalidys – mother, father, three boys and two girls – remained at home south-west of Jerusalem's old city. 'I was coming back from school by the Jaffa Gate,' Usama said. It was his last term at the Rashidieh School. 'I saw the people who had been captured in Deir Yassin and been left in the sun for three days,' he said of the most famous massacre of Palestinian Arabs, about three hundred of whom were killed by Menachem Begin's Irgun with assistance from the Haganah over the night of 9/10 April 1948. 'They were dropped at the Jaffa Gate. It created panic.'

Before dropping them at the Jaffa Gate, the Irgunists had put Deir Yassin's survivors in cages and paraded them through Jerusalem's Jewish neighbourhoods. 'No less disgusting [than the massacre],' the Labour Zionist historian Jon Kimche wrote in his 1950 book, *Seven Fallen Pillars*, 'was the subsequent publicity parade by the Irgun of a number of poor Arab prisoners through the streets of Jerusalem.'

Was it, I asked, when they had been displayed in cages?

'It was after they had been in the cages,' he answered. 'There were twenty or forty, I don't know. They were mainly women.'

I told him that Deir Yassin, now a part of Israeli Jerusalem called Givat Shaul, had become the site of a mental hospital.

'Very appropriate,' he said. 'I remember an argument between my father and my uncle. My father was in the Arab Higher Council. My uncle wanted to tell the story completely. My father said they should play it down, because it would cause a panic. My uncle won.' The Palestinian Arabs lost. Arab leaders advertised the massacre to show the Western world that they, not the Zionists, were the victims. The world did not care. Zionist leaders, especially Menachem Begin of the Irgun underground movement, used the events at Deir Yassin to inspire other Arabs to leave their homes. Begin wrote in his memoir, *The Revolt*, 'Out of evil, however, good came ... This Arab propaganda spread a legend of terror amongst Arabs and Arab troops, who were seized with panic at the mention of Irgun soldiers. The legend was worth half a dozen battalions to the forces of Israel.' He said that Deir Yassin helped in 'the conquest of Haifa': 'all the Jewish forces proceeded to advance through Haifa like a knife through butter. The Arabs began fleeing in panic, shouting: "Deir Yassin!"'

I asked Usama whether the massacre at Deir Yassin had inspired him to fight.

'There weren't enough weapons to give even to adults,' he answered, smiling to dismiss any notion of him as a warrior. Shooting between the two sides often kept him awake, but no one in his neighbourhood fired at the neighbouring agricultural school run by 'Madame Ben Zvi'. Mr Ben Zvi, a colleague of David Ben-Gurion, became Israel's second president. The Khalidys were evicted, not by the Israelis, but by the Red Cross. 'The Red Cross asked us to leave so they could make the house a refuge for displaced persons from both sides,' he said. Israeli forces occupied the area and announced that no Arabs, even those who had complied with a humanitarian request from the Red Cross, were allowed to return.

Usama went to Beirut, where he earned his bachelors and masters degrees in biochemistry, and then to Michigan for his doctorate. He returned to the American University of Beirut's hospital to teach for twenty-five years. In 1967, on a year's sabbatical, he taught in the children's department of Jerusalem's Augusta Victoria Hospital. The Augusta Victoria, a late German Gothic stone edifice, dominated the eastern half of Jerusalem from a hilltop that Glubb Pasha's Arab Legion had held in 1948. In 1967, Israel and the Arab states fought another war. 'When the war started, Dr Najib Abu Haidar' – Abu Haidar was a highly regarded physician I had known in Lebanon, a contemporary of Usama's – 'and I went up to the hospital. I was put in charge of the blood bank. We never got any blood.' The bloodless blood bank fitted the Arab logistical profile in 1967: Jordanian troops defending East Jerusalem did not receive ammunition or other supplies. Israeli artillery next to a Jewish hospital, Hadassah, shelled the Augusta Victoria. 'They fired mortar shells and napalm shells. The top of the hospital caught fire. We stayed for three days in the basement with our patients. It was very frightening, especially with the roof on fire. I kept working there, until the Israelis came to occupy the hospital. They held us for three or four days, then let us go.'

When Usama emerged from the hospital, he saw the bodies. They lay, like abandoned cars, unburied and unmourned, on either side of the road. They were all Arabs, like him, Palestinian civilians and Jordanian soldiers. They would not be buried until the Israeli army granted permission. Usama did not speak of the war as an act of injustice. He did not, as many Palestinians did, list the villages the Israeli army demolished in 1967. Nor did he bemoan the destruction of the Moroccan Quarter in the old city to clear the ground for a Disneyesque viewing platform beside the Jewish Western, or Wailing, Wall. A scientist, Usama told me what he saw – no more, perhaps much less. As with 1948 – the year the Palestinians refer to as their national *nakhba*, catastrophe – he left it to me to supply words like tragedy, pity, injustice. His languid posture, his monotone, his frequent and paced drags on his cigarette spoke of resignation. Events were like chemical reactions observed under a microscope. If a mix of substances exploded, that too was an event. He would not explode with them.

What did he do after he walked down the hill from the Augusta Victoria?

He went to his family's old house near the Bab az-Zahir and waited. 'We were going to leave anyway at that time,' he said. His sabbatical from the American University Hospital was over. 'I went over the bridge and never went back.'

Jerusalem had been 'reunited', according to the joyful Israelis who danced on the new plaza where Arab houses had stood the day before. It had been 'conquered' and 'occupied', in the words of United Nations resolutions and of the Palestinians who remained in Jerusalem after June 1967. The Khalidys had lived there for a thousand years, an offshoot of the tribe of Beni Khalid – sons of Khalid – who had migrated with the seasons between Syria and the Persian Gulf. For five hundred years at least they had been Jerusalem's judges, teachers, diplomats. They had earned respect by remaining aloof from the tribal battles that blooded Jerusalem's older feudal Arab families, the Nashashibis and the Husseinis. The Khalidys had collected manuscripts, written books and kept records of the Arab presence – Christian and Muslim – in Palestine. It was no accident that one of the best volumes of documents on the Palestinian conflict, *From Haven to Conquest*, had been edited by a Khalidy, Usama's brother Walid.

For a man like Usama to say 'I went over the bridge and never went back' was to conceal thoughts and emotions that could not have died. He did not elaborate, although I asked him to. Five centuries of scholarship? The beautiful stone houses, the fountains in verdant courtyards, the libraries? The cousins and aunts and uncles left behind?

He lit another cigarette, offered me more Turkish coffee and related the third act in his saga of Israeli occupation. He had resumed teaching at the American University Hospital in Beirut, experimenting with a method of instruction through problem solving that had been developed at McMaster University in

Hamilton, Canada. By the early 1970s, when I was living in Lebanon, the Palestinians had come to dominate West Beirut, culturally, politically, militarily. Young Palestinians were fighting for their independence – from Israel, from the Arab states, from Western domination. Usama, perhaps in accord with familial tradition, did not join any of the movements with their abundance of alphabetical acronyms, PFLP, PDFLP, PFLP-GC, PLF et al. Commandos who launched raids across the border from Lebanon were usually killed. They often attacked civilians on beaches or in buses. When captured, they were tortured. Many of their sympathizers in the West Bank and the Gaza Strip were also taken to the interrogation centres and the prisons. Others – in Lebanon, Syria and Jordan – also went to the cells and the torture chambers. The disparate, tribal, sometimes juvenile, brave and desperate Palestinian organizations inspired a defeated people – not only Palestinians, but many other Arabs. They did not end Israel's occupation, impede its confiscation of land or prevent the construction of all-Jewish colonies that were displacing Palestinians from the territories that Israel conquered in 1967. But the Palestinian commandos would not let the world – especially the Arab world – forget the injustice done to them. They made trouble, in Israel, in Jordan and, then, in Lebanon. In 1982, Israel invaded Lebanon.

At the time, Usama and his wife were living in an apartment building that also housed the Palestine Research Centre. Just above Rue Hamra, with its Café de Paris, cinemas and dress shops, the Research Centre was far from the Palestinians' military structure in and near the refugee camps of Sabra, Shatila and Borj al-Barajneh. It should have been left alone, but it wasn't. Between 1979 and 1983 it was bombed five times, by a Syrian-run commando faction called As-Saiqa, by Christian Lebanese and by Israel. In 1982, after a three-month Israeli siege, the Palestinian commandos evacuated Beirut by sea. Under the terms of an agreement guaranteed by the United States, Israel was to remain outside the western half of the city. It violated the agreement, sending tanks and infantry across the Green Line from the Christian, eastern side. Israeli defence minister Ariel Sharon invited Christian militiamen to eliminate 'terrorists' in the Sabra and Shatila refugee camps. Although all armed Palestinians had gone, the Christians butchered hundreds of women, children and old men while Israeli troops guarded the camps' entrances. When Israeli soldiers reached the Palestine Research Centre, they loaded all of its archives, its books, precious documents, computers and its internal files onto trucks that took them to Israel. (Scholars who wished to consult its documents on Palestinian history could do so, with security clearance, at the Hebrew University in Jerusalem.)

'We were at home until the Israelis got close,' Usama said. 'Then a car bomb destroyed most of our house.' The Israelis later admitted they had used car bombs in Beirut to assassinate Palestinian leaders. Sharon said later that his only regret about Lebanon was that he had not 'liquidated' the PLO leader, Yasser Arafat, when he had the opportunity.

After the car bomb, Usama moved into a friend's apartment. While the Israeli army looted the Research Centre on the first floor, soldiers broke into all of the flats above. 'They walked into our house,' Usama said. 'They shat on things. One had to appreciate their ability to shit on top of a refrigerator. They tore a lot of books. It was more vandalism than theft.'

Usama's outrage was nowhere evident in the telling. His conclusion: 'I don't think it was fun, to put it mildly.' He had left West Jerusalem in 1967. In 1982, he stayed in Beirut. Eventually, after the Lebanese suicide bombings, the Israelis were the ones to leave. Usama restored his flat, replaced his books and continued to teach. In 1983, the largest car bomb of all demolished his building. Twenty-two people died, including the wife of the Research Centre's director, Sabry Jiryis. Jiryis had grown up in Israel, spoke and wrote Hebrew and had been in Israeli prisons for non-violent political activity. A fine writer and scholar, he was among the few Palestinians to urge his people to understand the Israelis, to compromise, to reconcile. After his wife's funeral, he left Lebanon for another exile.

The bombing wounded Usama and his wife. Six months later,
when they recovered, they moved to Jordan. Their flat on the
ground floor of a new stone building could have been in Jerusalem, so much had its walls and floors and shelves been covered
in Khalidy memorabilia. 'This was the grandfather of my grandfather's father,' Usama indicated a reproduction of an old painting of an old man attired in the style of his Sultan – a dark robe,
a turban, a beard. 'Mohammed Ali [Khalidy] was the deputy
judge of Jerusalem. The chief justice was a Turk, who never
came to Jerusalem. So, Mohammed Ali was in effect the chief
judge. He died in 1862.' To be a jurist in the Ottoman Empire
was to be a scholar, and a Muslim judge adhered to one or
another of the schools of legal philosophy that defined the
nature of one's belief in Sunni Islam. The law had been as
significant in the consciousness of an Ottoman Sunni Muslim,
whether Turk, Kurd or Arab, as it remained for strict Orthodox
Jewish rabbis. The law and the devout study of law – law giving,
law making, legal interpretation, the source and legitimacy of
legal precepts – involved not only jurisprudence, but philosophy, history and theology. The law made the Khalidys into
scholars, and the tradition persisted among the latest generations – academics, but not a lawyer among them.

Usama Khalidy did not subscribe to the Islamic school that
proscribed and condemned visual representation of the human
form. He lived surrounded by family portraits of long-dead
Khalidys in Ottoman robes of office and of his two modern and
wildly beautiful daughters. I asked about a black and white
drawing propped against the books behind him. I'd been looking at it for some time: six men on their feet, four seated in
front, all eyes fixed on the artist. 'This is one of the oldest
pictures in the Middle East of my ancestors,' Usama said.

The ten, who looked like a difficult jury to impress, divided
into two phases of Ottoman history. The elders, frail in white
turbans atop snow-white beards, had grown up in the last years
of a Sultanate that had not absorbed the cultural lessons of its
military defeats by the once-insignificant Christian kingdoms of

Europe: in Greece, in the northern Balkans, in much of North Africa. The younger men, all fresh and trendy in sporty tarboush and twirling moustaches, were coming of age when the Sultan understood that weakness required concessions to the foreigner and new arrangements with the more dissatisfied natives. In the mid-nineteenth century, those Khalidys in the fezzes were the new men of reform, of progress, of enlightenment. The Sultan would govern under the new men, reorganize the empire, invite the hated Europeans to train his army and buy the new steel cannon of Krupp and the Maxim gun. Soon, the Sultan's subjects would be wearing trousers and conspiring to depose him.

'This is our ancestor, Yusuf Dia Khalidy,' Usama spoke with a certain pride of this man, one of the oldest in the picture. 'Yusuf Dia was sent as a judge to Kurdistan. He wrote the first dictionary of the Kurdish language.' The dictionary was in Kurdish and Arabic, languages that flourished under the Ottomans, but which had been banned – except for prayers in Arabic – in the modern Turkey that Moustafa Kemal Atatürk created after the First World War. Usama said I should buy a copy of the dictionary, still in print from the Librairie du Liban, when I reached Beirut.

Usama's two daughters, Mouna and Ramla, lived in Beirut with their husbands and children. Ramla, Usama said, was an old Arab name, so rare that I'd not heard it except as the name of an Arab town in Palestine. More Christians than Muslims, he said, gave their children the ancient names. The Christians were more tribal, following the traditional pattern of marriage within their *Jund*. *Jund*, classical Arabic for army, was also a division of land: great west–east stretches between the Mediterranean and the desert, self-sufficient and parallel regions of fish and commerce beside the sea, fruit and timber in the coastal mountain range, wheat and vegetables in the fertile plain, and, at the desert's edges, the Bedouins' meat, milk, yoghurt and cheese. *Jund Dimashk* went from Beirut over Mount Lebanon to Damascus and the Syrian Desert. To its south were *Jund al-Urdun* and *Jund al-Falastin*. There would be more family ties hundreds of miles across the *Jund*, from Hebron over the Jordan to Kerak or from Jerusalem to Salt in Jordan, than between towns a few miles north and south of one another in different *Junds*. The Christians, few as they were, preserved tradition. Usama said that they were the last in Jordan to perform a ritual operation on their babies to remove the uvula from inside their mouths. 'They say it improves their speech,' Usama explained. 'I was told there is a Yemeni tribe who do that as well. It's similar to circumcision.'

Usama had retired, but for him retirement was a mission. 'Traditionally, when people became my age, sixty-nine, they had the job of deciding who married whom,' he said, implying that it was not a role for him. 'Of course, they hardly ever became my age.' Rather than play patriarch, he studied the flora and fauna of the desert. The Jordanian government had set aside 12,000 square kilometres for the Badia Research Project to document aspects of desert life. 'I'm interested a bit in plants,' he said, 'for example, to find out how to grow black iris out of seed. I've developed a method for extracting the smell of some desert plants. Wait a minute.' He left the room. I examined his books. Most were science, biology or chemistry, but there were also Arabic–English dictionaries, a book on Ottoman architecture, Tony Clifton's *God Cried*, about Israel's 1982 invasion of Lebanon, Jonathan Randal's *Going All the Way* on Lebanon's civil war, and a book of old photographs of Palestine, *Before their Diaspora*, edited by Usama's brother Walid. I was looking at the last when Usama returned with a vial of black liquid that looked like molasses.

'Put your finger in,' he ordered, delighted to be teaching. 'This is the essence of a desert plant, from near the Iraq–Syria border.' In Arabic its name was *shih*. Usama leafed through a botanical index. 'Here it is in English, it's artemisia. *Herba alba*. It's a kind of wormwood.' My hand would smell of wormwood for a week.

Usama had become a calligrapher, not in the traditional Arabic fashion of ink on parchment, but in three dimensions.

He took me to his workshop, a small room off the corridor. Here I saw the tools – arrayed in neat rows on the wall – with which he chiselled, scraped and sculpted Arabic letters into vibrant shapes in wood, iron and brass. A simple word like *hua*, he, looked like the statue of a man, its contours unconfined to the flat page. The most beautiful, as in traditional Arabic calligraphy, was *Allah*, God, whose image can never be painted or carved by a good Muslim, any more than a devout Jew can speak his name.

'At about the age of forty,' Usama said, 'I decided that Arabs don't know how to retire.' Arab presidents and kings fitted the general pattern. 'I went to Iraq al-Amir, where there is an old, eighth-century palace or fort. The Jordanians have crafts industries there. I went down to teach them how to make paper.' He gave me some dark paper, thin but sturdy and as absorbent as an egg box.

I felt the paper and looked at Arabic words come to life. Why was Usama Khalidy content to leave the medical school to the next generation of instructors and to allow his daughters to choose their husbands and not to tyrannize his family or those exiled Jerusalem Muslims who might look to a Khalidy for leadership? What made tribal chiefs, family patriarchs, kings, policemen and dictators cling to power until death? What drove out or suppressed the most interesting, the most creative and the most original within the Arab family? Why did the Arab world fight against its best self?

Did Usama, who felt these questions in a more profound way than a visitor like myself, despair? He thought for a few seconds and said, 'No.' Why not? 'We're passing through a funny phase. At the same time, one has to remark that the Arabs are probably the world's oldest living tradition. A child can read something written in Arabic fifteen hundred years ago and enjoy it. You cannot do that in English, for example. A child today cannot understand Chaucer and would have problems with Shakespeare. Our tradition is there. It has survived. It will survive. It's getting much poorer, of course.'

Usama, amid his bottles of desert scent, his bold script statues, his library, his relics of old Jerusalem and his ancestral pictures, did not mention the West. He did not blame Britain and France for drawing lines all over the map that erased the harmony of the *Jund* and brought European Jews to displace him and put compliant dictators in charge of the oil that could, perhaps should, have propelled Arab civilization into the vanguard of intellectual and artistic discovery. The dictators kept the Arabs in servitude and, for the most part, misery. For this failure of leadership and of society, his gaze turned – not in anger at the United Nations or Great Britain or the United States – but in regret at the tribes.

'Our main problem is education.' He said that Arab education prepared the young only for examinations, the *tawjihi*. Pass the *tawjihi*, and you continue to university. Fail, and you stay in the village or the slum. The *tawjihi* system produced students who memorized set answers to set questions, not those who thought or questioned or looked at things in an original way. 'Reforming the education system will help, but it needs a revolution. We take the best students. They have to study medicine or engineering. The worst go on to schools of education. Worse than that, they go to schools of theology. The worst are in charge of our brains, the best in charge of our muscles.'

In the 1930s and 1940s the Palestinians were led by the obstinate and self-destructive Haj Amin Husseini. Then came Yasser Arafat. Neither was known for intellect or wisdom. Had the leaders improved in half a century? 'Not very much. The Palestinians deserve better leadership. The whole Arab world deserves better.'

Before I left him to the study of plants and the manufacture of words, I asked him about identity. Was he an Arab, a Palestinian, a Jordanian, a Muslim? The concoction of tribalism, faith and nationalism bedevilled Israelis and Palestinians alike. Who is a Jew? What is an Arab? Juwal Levy's father had gone to court to take the word Jew off his identity card. Some Arabs believed in the Arab nation, divided into states that could never be nations. Some were Lebanese or Egyptians first, Arabs second or not at all.

'Arabs don't know the word *huwiya*,' he said. *Huwiya* meant identity, and it was also the identity card that policemen in Israel and the Arab world demanded from Arabs. 'It's a very new word. We don't think of identity. We think of loyalties. Unlike identity, which is exclusive, loyalties are multiple. You can be loyal to your family, your religion, your state and so on. It depends on the situation. If my child is sick, that is my first loyalty.'

When loyalties conflict, does identity dissolve?

'You noticed after 1948, as the Arabs lost faith in Arabism, they ended up going to religion – either the religion of communism or real religion. It happened after '48. It's happening now.' With communism dead, Islam remained.

Allegiance, loyalty, identity. Race, sect, tribe. The Zionists came to the right address. Every question the Zionists asked had its equivalent among the natives. Who is a Jew, a question debated in Israel's civil and religious courts, translated as, who is an Arab? Was it blood or language or geography? There was no Platonic ideal of Arab or Jew, and everyone refined his identity: Ashkenazi or Sephardi Jew, Arab of the Mashrak, the East, or the Maghreb, the West in North Africa. There were Arabs in Syria who had no Arab blood of the tribes from the Arabian peninsula. In Russia, millions of Jews traced their ancestry to the Gentile Khazar people and not to any of ancient Israel's Twelve Tribes. No one had found the Arab or the Jewish gene. Usama Khalidy believed only a racist would try.

A History Lesson

Kamal Salibi, whom I knew when he taught history at the American University of Beirut, had moved to Amman. Like most other Eastern Christians whose forebears had become

Protestant, Salibi was de-tribalized. Protestant Arabs were the first to read the Bible in Arabic and take degrees from Beirut's Syrian Protestant College. The most famous, and brilliant, of the Protestants' offspring was Edward Said, who taught at Columbia in New York and wrote, among other books, *Orientalism*. The College became the American University, where I first met both Salibi and Said. During the Lebanese civil war, Salibi used to tell me the Palestinians were making the fatal error of becoming another Lebanese tribe.

He stayed to teach throughout the civil war, the Israeli invasion and the years of anarchy under West Beirut's Muslim militias. Fanatic Shiite fundamentalists threatened him, and Christian friends were kidnapped. Already author of a history of Jordan, he had a friend in King Hussein's brother, Prince Hassan. In 1997, when Lebanon was again at peace, then-Crown Prince Hassan invited him to head Jordan's Inter-Faith Institute. Salibi had lived in Amman since then, although a few years later he would return to Beirut.

His new house was, he said, 'near the Fifth Circle'. The city's neighbourhoods were often named for the number of the nearest roundabout. Shepherd's Hotel was near the First. Salibi's modern flat did its best to recreate the Ottoman charm of his old Beirut apartment with Persian carpets and mother-of-pearl furniture. As in Beirut, he smoked cigarillos. Also as in Beirut, he offered me whisky. If Usama Khalidy's house was Palestine, Salibi's was old Beirut. If Usama had his doubts about Palestinian politicians, Salibi was ashamed of Lebanon's. He condemned Lebanon for its mistreatment of the Palestinian refugees. From the time the PLO retreated in 1982, Palestinians had been massacred by Christian militias with Israeli support and by the Shiite Muslim Amal militia with Syrian connivance. The Lebanese government excluded them from most employment and denied them state-funded medical care. Lebanon's establishment, Christian and Muslim, blamed the Palestinians, rather than themselves, for a war that lasted from 1975 to 1991. Salibi was angry that the Lebanese contrived more ways to punish the Palestinians, twenty years after they lost all power in Lebanon. 'They are now making laws that any Palestinian refugee who owns a house or land in Lebanon cannot pass it on when he dies,' Salibi said. 'The bloody Lebanese parliament passed it almost unanimously.'

What should Lebanon do?

'I think that, in Lebanon, the Palestinians ought to be acknowledged as Lebanese citizens with all social and political rights. Once they become Lebanese, they will do what all Lebanese do and emigrate.' Lebanon had always refused to make the refugees, who had lived there since 1948, citizens. The only state that had granted citizenship to the refugees was Jordan. With almost 400,000 refugees registered with the United Nations, the Palestinians made up 10 per cent of Lebanon's population. In Lebanon, Christians feared turning so many Muslims into citizens, and the Shiites resisted being outnumbered by the Sunnis. There were no Palestinian Shiites and not many Palestinian Christians in Lebanon.

'The idea of Zionism is tribal,' Salibi said. 'The idea that something binds you together around the world, that it is more important than any other allegiance and you have to be all together in one place, this is tribal.'

Tribal or not, Israel was a fact. If most Arabs did not accept Israel's moral right to displace most Palestinian Arabs and put others under military occupation, they recognized its strength. Salibi was one of the few people I knew in the Arab world who did not disparage the Palestinian leadership.

'What surprises me,' he said, 'is the maturity of the Palestinian leadership. There is no more of that "throw the Jews into the sea" nonsense. They are asking to live only on what they have.' They had the West Bank and Gaza Strip, barely 22 per cent of Mandate Palestine, and they were losing much of that to Israeli settlers. 'Palestine since my infancy has been socially divided between effendis and peasants. The effendis always despised the peasants and still do. If they hate Arafat, it's because he's not from their class. I tell them Palestine is no longer yours. It belongs to those who fought or who tilled the soil. I'm not sure it's a bad thing.'

The 1993 Oslo accords between Israel and the Palestine Liberation Organization had allowed the Palestinian leaders to return home and govern under the Israelis. Since then, Israel had doubled the number of settlers in the West Bank and Gaza. Salibi was one of the few who did not see the Oslo accords as a disaster.

'What's wrong with the Oslo agreement?' he asked. 'For the first time, it gave the Palestinians something.' Having been to the West Bank and Gaza many times since the accord, I disagreed. Oslo had given the Israelis something: a Palestinian administration that policed the occupied territories while the settlers took more Palestinian land. Salibi believed Oslo was less the problem than Israeli refusal to implement all its provisions on schedule. 'The Israelis are behaving like savages. They are going to be the losers in the end. They are going to have to accept a settlement, even if it means a Palestinian state on a few metres. It will puncture the Zionist balloon. Zionism is a package deal. It's Eretz Israel, the Bible land, heritage. They want to get all the Jews from all the world and cram them there. The whole thing is a package deal conceived in a seminar room. The least puncture and the speed with which it will deflate will amaze you.'

He thought the Israelis were 'damned if they do, damned if they don't' over making peace with the Palestinians. The wiser course was to make peace. 'The more generous they are, the better it is for them,' Salibi concluded, even if it meant punching a hole in – or setting a limit to – Zionism's dream.

Did he imagine that the Arabs would accept Israel? Not as a tactic, but as a long-term proposition?

'Yes,' he said. 'The minute there is a settlement, you cannot imagine what will happen. The Arabs are very forgiving. Think of Lebanon. Twenty years of fighting and the minute the fighting stopped, East Beirut and Jounieh filled with Muslims. The Christians flocked to West Beirut. There were Eid al-Fitr tents in Jounieh.' East Beirut and the seaside resort of Jounieh were Christian ghettoes, and Eid al-Fitr was the Muslim feast to celebrate the end of the Ramadan fast. 'Arab society is very forgiving. Grudges are not borne for long – except by one family against another. The hatred does not last.' Salibi was from Bhamdoun, a Christian village in the Shouf hills of Mount Lebanon. In 1983, when Israel withdrew its army from the Shouf, the Druze massacred Christians and sent most of them north in an act that Yugoslavia's wars would later give the term 'ethnic cleansing'. 'I don't bear a grudge against the Druze,' Salibi said. 'People are going back.' He thought that Europeans took longer to forget. 'I was in England in the 1950s. The Dutch students refused to listen to German music.' During the bloodiest days of Lebanon's war, Christians swooned to the voice of a Muslim diva, Oum Kalsoum, and Muslims never lost their love of the Christian singer Feyrouz. But the end of the war did not end the Lebanese animosity to the Palestinians. What was Israel to make of that?

Salibi went on, 'Jordan made peace with Israel. Not one Israeli visitor was hurt. Palestinian refugees over the age of fifty who had shops refused to sell to them, but everywhere else they were accepted. They object to their stealing – not to their being Israelis.' The only people who objected in principle to Israel, he believed, were the Islamists. But in Jordan, unlike in Egypt, they did nothing to harm Israelis.

'Listen,' he urged me. 'The Jordanian army is on cordial terms with the Israeli Defence Forces. The Palestinian Authority was the same. If there is an agreement, then the whole hatred of the West in the Arab world will vanish. Abracadabra!'

Abracadabra?

'It's originally an Aramaic word that means, "vanish like a word". The wind will be out of the sails of the Islamic movement in the Arab world.'

I reminded him that, in Lebanon many years before, he had told me Syria would never make peace with Israel. Its existence and strength depended upon keeping Israel isolated from the rest of the region. He had told me to think of the map. With Israel excluded from the region, all east–west Arab trade had to pass through Syria. There was no other land route between the Mediterranean and the Persian Gulf. If Israel were accepted, trucks could collect goods at Haifa port and drive them to Iraq and Saudi Arabia through Israel and Jordan. Pipelines and railways would leave Syria out. Acceptance of Israel would deny Syria its leverage and render it insignificant. Having an Israeli enemy also justified Syria's military dictatorship and police repression, he had said then. Now he believed peace between the Palestinians and Israelis would change that. 'Syria will lose her blackmail position. It will sign a deal only after the Palestine question closes and only then.'

Problems lingered, I said. I had imagined that, once Israel withdrew from Lebanon in 2000, Hizballah would end its war against Israeli occupation. Yet Hizballah fought on – for a small area called the Shaba Farms that Israel did not leave. Hizballah said it was Lebanese territory and Syria agreed. Years before, however, Damascus claimed Shaba was part of Syria.

'Shaba is a small mountain town,' he explained. 'It's Sunni Muslim. In 1967, Israel occupied that area when it took the Golan Heights.' Until 2000, Syria had claimed Shaba for itself. 'Israel pulled out of Lebanon to the last bit, because Syria and Iran told them to.'

The real battle was not at Shaba, a containable sideshow. The struggle for Israel, for Palestine, was under way in the West Bank and Gaza. 'Things have changed since 1948,' Salibi said. 'If there were a few shots then, many people fled. This time, the Israelis destroy whole cities and only a few people leave. They've been hardened. Israel is turning the Palestinians into lions. The Israelis don't know what they are doing. They don't know what they have done. They have, how many Sharons? Three or four? How many Palestinians will be suicide bombers?'

Kamal Salibi was born in 1928, when France was occupying Lebanon and Syria and the British held Iraq, Jordan and Palestine. His parents, his teachers and all the elders of Bhamdoun had been Ottoman subjects. The era of independence had done more to disrupt their lives by moving large numbers of people – Tolstoy's definition of history – than had the Ottoman centuries. History was being made in the West Bank and Gaza, where Israeli settlers were moving in to force Palestinian Arabs out.

Salibi gave me some books to read, as he used to in Beirut. His houseboy went out to find me a taxi. That evening, he was having dinner at Usama Khalidy's house. For them, Amman was a little like Beirut. In my taxi, between Salibi's house and Shepherd's, I looked at the vast hotels, Kentucky Fried Chicken shops and elegant stone houses. Amman was an unexciting city, but it had not surrendered to the vulgar brutality of Beirut and other Arab capitals. Houses had to be built of native stone, as in Jerusalem over the river. Streets were swept and washed. The cars were mostly new.

I dropped the books at the hotel and went for a walk. In the all-male cafés, men played cards and backgammon. There was no real souq, no central bazaar as in Istanbul or the other old Ottoman cities. Beirut's souq had been a proud centre, until the civil war and the property developers reduced it to powder. Damascus, Aleppo, Jerusalem and Nicosia had kept their ancient marketplaces. Amman had never had a real souq, not having been a city since the days when the Romans called it Philadelphia. It had retained the culture and appearance of a large Arab–Circassian village in the Cotswolds, all quaint stone and ordered life. It was a town for driving in rather than walking. 'In Jordan,' Salibi had said, perhaps explaining his choice of Amman over Beirut, 'they did not repudiate what the British taught them. If they build a road, it's a good road. Look at the Pan-Arab Highway. The Jordanian part is beautiful. The bumps start in Syria.' That much was true. But, as good as Jordan's highways were, they were neither as vast nor as smooth as those next door in Iraq and in Israel.

Amman's surrender to British and then to American culture made a kind of sense. Amman did not have much to cling to. Most of its people came from elsewhere. Its rulers were Hejazis from the Holy City of Mecca in what became Saudi Arabia. Their subjects had come there from other parts of Jordan, attracted by the royal court, administrative jobs, the army and business. Other Arabs had moved there from Lebanon, Syria and Iraq to marry or to enjoy its relative political stability. Half the city had escaped there from Palestine in the cataclysms of 1948 and 1967, unwillingly driven from towns and villages to which they believed they – or their children or their children's children – would return. It had no claim on their loyalty.

The Grand Vizier

Everyone told me to see Zayd Rifai, former prime minister, former ambassador and now chief of the Senate. 'He's a great raconteur,' the Syrian-born artist Ali Jabari said. A young woman at the Foreign Ministry told me, 'He's brilliant. He's well read. When I met him, I just listened.' (The young woman, Raya Qadi, was so beautiful that when we met I just listened.) Prince Talal bin Mohammed, a first cousin of King Abdallah, said that Rifai was a champion story-teller whose stories were sometimes true. True or not, they were good.

The first thing I noticed about Rifai was not the dark suit, possibly from a tailor in Savile Row, or the cigar, from Havana, but the blue eyes. Everything else in his Senate office spoke of Arabia. We were served Bedouin coffee – boiled cardamom – from a brass pot by a man in immaculate robes and keffiyeh. There were Persian carpets and tribal décor, a ceremonial sword and photographs of Jordan's four kings. Rifai had the tanned skin of the desert and looked like a shrewd Arab politician. But the eyes spoke of the Ottoman Empire, whose Turks, Circassians, Bosnians, Kurds and Chechens mingled with the tribes of Arabia and Syria. Rifai, it seemed, numbered Circassians and Turks among his ancestors.

'The family is originally from the Hejaz,' he said. 'One of our grandfathers went to Iraq, where he created the Rifai school of thought in Iraq in the eleventh century.' The Rifai school was a sect of Sufis, Muslim mystics. 'A lot of followers of the sect took on the name. There are now about twenty million Rifais in Lebanon, Jordan, Syria and Iraq. The family were civil servants in the Ottoman administration. They moved from one city to another. My grandfather was born in a village of southern Syria, in the Hauran. He met my grandmother in Marjayoun and married her. My father was born there.' Marjayoun, a large town in south Lebanon, was mostly Greek Orthodox. The Israelis had made it their military headquarters and base for their mercenary South Lebanon army from 1978 to 2000.

'My uncles were born in Tyre and Sidon,' Rifai said. 'My grandfather retired to Safad.' Safad, a mixed Arab–Jewish city in the Galilee, was just south of Lebanon's Marjayoun. 'My father grew up in Safad, and he worked for the British Mandate administration in Palestine. He was seconded in 1921 to Trans-jordan to establish the new administration. I was born here in 1936.'

Rifai said his father, who had served as prime minister to Jordan's first three kings, advised him to avoid politics. 'He said I should choose engineering or medicine. He really wanted me to be a doctor.' He became a diplomat instead. His education at the Bishop's School in Amman and Victoria College in Egypt, where Edward Said would also study, was pure British colonial. Then he made the transition, as the Arab world would, from the British to the American system. He went to Harvard. Did he study medicine? 'Political science,' he said. 'I graduated in 1956. Then I did international law and relations at Columbia. I still go back and give lectures.'

In 1956, King Hussein had dismissed the British general John Bagot Glubb – Glubb Pasha – as commander of the Arab Legion. Reacting to anti-colonial criticism from Nasser's Egyptian press, the young king had to prove his Arab nationalist credentials by putting his armed forces under an Arab. I wondered whether Rifai had known Glubb Pasha.

'He was a wonderful man,' Rifai recalled. 'He became more

Jordanian Arab than British. A lot of injustice was done to him. My father had to tell Glubb to leave.' His father found the duty distasteful. Glubb had given his professional life to Jordan within the context of his loyalty to the British Empire. I had known Glubb's son, Fares, in Beirut in the early 1970s. Short and thin like his father, he looked like photographs of Glubb Pasha as a young man. Fares spoke flawless Bedouin Arabic, had converted to Islam and was close to the Marxists of the Popular Front for the Liberation of Palestine who in 1970 had attempted to destroy the Hashemite crown that his father had sworn to defend for thirty-five years.

'I went as ambassador to London for a few months,' Rifai remembered. 'Glubb Pasha used to call on me. He always referred to King Hussein as His Majesty, or our lord – *sayedna*. He had contributed enormously to the establishment of the army, to administration and order in this society.' The discipline, the starched uniforms and the army band's bagpipes owed something to Glubb Pasha.

Back in Amman with his Harvard and Columbia degrees, Rifai went on to represent Jordan in Cairo, Beirut and London, as well as at the United Nations. In 1971, he started work in the royal palace. 'I thought I'd have a change after all we had been through.' What Jordan had been through included the June 1967 war, when Israel captured Arab Jerusalem and the West Bank from what had been Glubb Pasha's army; the Arab–Israeli War of Attrition that followed; and the 1970 Black September war between Palestinian commandos and Jordan's army.

'The most dangerous time was the period after the '67 war,' Rifai said. 'For Jordan, it wasn't a six-day war. It was a four-year war. There was the battle of Karameh in 1968. There were daily bombardments and air raids by the Israelis. There was anarchy with the presence of Palestinian commandos. We had fifty-two commando organizations, including the Red Brigades, Baader–Meinhof and Carlos the Jackal. We had no idea they were all here until September 1970.' He described a time of chaos, when Palestinian commandos briefly held the Western press corps hostage in the InterContinental Hotel.

'The borders were open. We had Iraqi troops in the country. We had no idea the Palestinians were so well dug in. They planted land mines and had rocket-propelled grenades. They took control of this city. Our army was on the front lines with Israel. The Palestinian commandos put up checkpoints. They stole cars. They took donations to the cause by force. They kidnapped. They had their own newspapers. Remember their slogan, that they would liberate Jerusalem by liberating Amman. The army almost revolted. When soldiers came to spend weekends with their families in Amman, the commandos would kidnap, kill and mutilate them. Battalions in the Jordan Valley would hear what happened to fellow soldiers. The units would come up here on their own. I would go with His Majesty and Zayd Bin Shaker' – Bin Shaker, King Hussein's uncle, was the army commander – 'to stop them. There was a decision by His Majesty. We waited and waited.'

On 15 September 1970, King Hussein appointed a military government to force the commandos out of Amman. The Jordanian parliament sent a delegation to ask Yasser Arafat to evacuate without a fight. Rifai's version of Arafat's reaction was, 'He told them, "The situation has run out of my hands. The best I can do for you is to give King Hussein twenty-four hours to leave the country."'

Hussein stayed. After two weeks of intensive fighting, during which Jordan's Bedouin troops massacred Palestinians and bombarded their camps, it was Arafat who left. Negotiations between King Hussein and Yasser Arafat in Cairo may have caused the heart attack that killed Gamal Abdel Nasser the night after the two Arab chiefs left. With Nasser's death, Arab nationalism retreated and left the field to the steady advance of political Islam.

Did Arafat, who made several attempts on Hussein's life, reconcile with the king? 'Oh, yes,' Rifai said. 'They made up. Arafat often came here. He was received as a head of state.

With politics in the Middle East, you can't afford to have a long memory. You won't be able to talk to anyone.'

After the war, Arafat's commandos assassinated Jordanian prime minister Wasfi Tel outside the Hilton Hotel in Cairo. Someone also tried to kill Rifai, when he was ambassador in London. 'We were in a narrow road coming from Regent's Park,' he said. 'The driver was making a right turn. They were standing on a little traffic island and started shooting point-blank. I was reading the paper. The car was a big Daimler. It was *The Times*, I remember. I was crouching like this.' Rifai bent forward. 'The first bullets hit my hand and ear. I reacted quickly. I threw myself to the floor. They found forty bullets, and the fire was concentrated on the back seat. A Scotland Yard inspector said he didn't believe a canary would survive.' Rifai blamed the clandestine arm of Yasser Arafat's Al Fateh, Black September, for the attack.

The Jordanians responded in kind, assassinating PLO officials in their post-Amman headquarters, Beirut.

That evening, an old friend of Rifai's met me for a drink. I told him the story about the attempt on his life. 'Black September?' the friend asked. 'Maybe. We always thought they were London gangsters trying to collect gambling debts.'

Farewell to Amman

I saw old friends in Amman, among them Riad and Zein Khoury, Prince Talal and his beautiful Lebanese wife, Princess Ghida, and the children of both couples. All of them worried, not about Jordan, but about the neighbours. They hated the Israeli occupation of the West Bank and Gaza and what it was doing to the Palestinians. They hated the economic embargo of Iraq on their eastern border and the cost in lives of Iraqi children. It was a rare Jordanian who had no relations or friends west of the River Jordan or east of the great desert in Iraq. They did not love Yasser Arafat, who they said was a useless leader, or Saddam Hussein, a vicious tyrant. The United States sustained the wretchedness of Palestinians and Iraqis. America paid for Israel's illegal settlements on illegally occupied land, and America enforced the boycott that deprived Iraq's children of medicines and treated water. It would soon invade Iraq, making life there even worse. Yet none of my Jordanian friends dared to suggest a public gesture – boycotting American goods, severing diplomatic relations or closing an American hotel – to affect Washington's policies.

The bullet holes I saw on my first visit here in 1973 had been erased. Monster buildings had transformed the terrain of battle between the brave fedayeen and the hardy Bedouin into a zone of combat for market share, for the greater triumph of AT&T and Sheraton and for the acquisition of newer cars and cellphones. Amman sustained the dullness from which its Hashemite monarchs, the British and several wars had not redeemed it. Its sleepy hills, in which a few thousand Circassians had lived in their huts of rock, did not welcome disturbance. It was not a land of flooding rivers or icy precipices or earthquakes. Amman perched on gentle hills, and its inhabitants closed their doors on excitement. It had been the wrong stage for the Palestinians to enact their revolutionary drama. I did not linger in Amman.

The car journey from Amman to Jerusalem should take an hour and a half. But it does not take an hour and a half. It takes many hours. If you are a Palestinian, it can take for ever. For me, it was five hours in several taxis and one bus, most of that time absorbed, not on the highway observing the wildlife, but waiting at the border.

If I curse Britain and France, despite having lived in and loved them both, it is for these borders. Travelling from Beirut to Damascus, or Damascus to Amman, or Amman to Jerusalem – all simple trips along good roads with no insuperable natural obstacles – constituted an ordeal for all travellers. So mutually suspicious were the mini-states of Greater Syria that they mistreated all who entered or left. All showed Europeans and Americans less discourtesy, and the Jordanians were more polite to Israelis. The Syrians and Lebanese would not admit Israelis or anyone with an Israeli visa in his passport. Every border policeman – Israeli, Jordanian, Syrian or Lebanese – made a point of humiliating any Arab who came his way.

On the way to the River Jordan, the road sticks to the earth's contours, flowing like water through the easiest downward passages. The Jordan Valley was the hot land, where the wool cloaks of mountain shepherds yielded to the peasant's light cotton robe. Here were sandy wastes, lush meadows, small farms and greenhouses dressed in plastic sheets. In December 1917, when the British captured Jerusalem, Allenby's forces fought to link their army near here with the Hashemites who were advancing north on a parallel march. But the linking was not to be. The British were repulsed by Turkish forces north of the town of Salt, and Lawrence was unable to take Ma'an in the east. In the event, each army made its separate way up to Damascus. By then, each understood that its interests and objectives diverged from the other's. The Arabs, Lawrence knew, were fighting for independence in all of Greater Syria. The British planned to divide the land into European colonies with one corner, western Palestine, set aside as a reserve for Europe's Jews. Palestine's Arabs would be sacrificed to pay for European anti-Semitism. The Arabs reached Damascus, but Britain prevailed.

Signs indicated the Dead Sea to the south and, later, the King Hussein Bridge straight ahead. A little stand at the side of the road sold boxes of oranges, as on the pre-freeway California highways of my childhood. You could buy the oranges by the box or the kilo, or a man in a straw hat would slice them in two and squeeze them into a pint glass. Nearby, other farmers stacked celery stalks and lettuces on barrel tops to sell to the few passing drivers. We came to a village where I'd have romanticized the unchanging life of donkey carts, camels and its graceful mosque but for the neon and paint logos of the Arab Bank, Sharp, Coca-Cola, the Internet Café and the Green Saloon. At the largest and dustiest roundabout, a cement frame larger than a movie screen surrounded a portrait of the late King Hussein in Prince of Mecca garb: white robes and white keffiyeh, the keffiyeh held by a black *egal* tied around his head, the robes offset by a belt with a curved dagger in a golden sheath. It was not a poster. Someone had painted the fresco onto wet cement. King Hussein had not been dead long. A complicated man, he had saved his throne from overthrow by socialists, nationalists, communists, Palestinians and Muslim fundamentalists. Like a true Bedouin chief, he had never severed contact with his enemies – whether Nasserite, Israeli or Palestinian – and was wary of his friends – the other Arab monarchs and the Americans. He had outlived the dictators of Syria and Egypt, who had once sworn to replace all the Arab kingdoms with republics like their own. The republican dictators instead adopted regal succession, appointing their sons to replace them when they died. Could it have been otherwise? The Ram ad-Dar, the head of the household, did not leave the fate of the tribe to the masses, as if they could choose a leader with wisdom and strength to lead them. That decision was his, and the only one he could train to confront the world's cunning and evil ways was his son.

Monarchy went against my beliefs. I knew about Jordan's prisons. The best that could be said of them was that they were probably not as bad as those in Syria, Iraq, Egypt or Saudi Arabia. People were repressed, but less so than elsewhere in the region. Palestinians in Jordan had a difficult time, but no one stole their homes and threatened to expel them en masse as in Israel and the territories it occupied. No state official prevented them from taking jobs, as in Lebanon. They were not denied passports, as in Syria and Lebanon. The crown that Hussein had passed to his son left Jordan more peaceful than its neighbours.

Beyond the valley's villages were the Bedouin tents, rows of them in white, beside white sheep and a tethered white donkey. About five miles short of the river was Jordan's lazy border post. Within its walls, a triangular yard was bounded by an arrival hall, a departure hall and a café. A rusting bus waited in the middle to deliver the day's last shipment of travellers to the other side. I made the mistake of walking into the departure building, whose offices were locked and whose windows for three different categories of traveller – Arab, Jordanian, non-Arab – were shut. A policeman in starched khaki guided me to the arrivals building. Since the *intifadah* began in September 2000, one room served both purposes. I filled in forms and a polite official stamped my passport. I paid the five Jordanian dinar departure tax and boarded the unlit bus with a driver and three other passengers: an old man in a white keffiyeh; his wife in a white scarf and a beautiful olive dress embroidered in scarlet eagles' wings and pink rosebuds; and a younger man in a lightweight business suit. He called the old man 'Haj', a title of respect for someone who had made the pilgrimage to Mecca. Christians who had gone to Jerusalem were also called 'Haj'.

At five o'clock, the driver pulled the door shut. After a few warm-ups, the engine started. As the bus turned to leave the post, we saw the last royal portrait, of the two kings, father and son, Hussein and Abdallah. A gold crown hovered in a fair blue sky above them, a trinity whose spirit might pass from head to head but was eternal in its protection of the people, of the family, of the tribe.

I was thinking of something Prince Talal had said to me the night before. Talal, like his uncle, the late king, and his first cousin, King Abdallah, had received his formal education abroad. His school was Harrow, and his undergraduate and graduate degrees were from Georgetown. He rode motorcycles and liked Western music. He was a crack shot and a good horseman. He said that Western politicians who met people like himself thought of them as 'good Arabs'. I paraphrase what he said, because I did not write it down. It went something like this: 'I dress like them. So they think I am not really an Arab. It's like being an honorary white. But I am as much an Arab as any Bedouin who has never left the desert. And, if I have to choose, I choose to be an Arab.'

He had just told me that Jordan had arrested some of the Islamic fundamentalists of Osama bin Laden, who had tried to blow up a Jordanian phosphate plant. The Jordanians were passing information about threats to Americans in the US and the Middle East to Washington. They wanted to help, especially when the fanatics were as opposed to the Hashemite throne as to the American government. But they could not go all the way, as President George Bush demanded with his 'You're either with us or against us' speech. Nor could Jordan support General Sharon's self-proclaimed 'war on terror' that was a war on Palestinians under military occupation. Jordan could not, however much it disapproved of Saddam Hussein's atrocities, favour the sanctions that deprived Iraq's people of medicine and of equipment for the restoration of sewage treatment and other basic services. To Talal, there were no good and no bad Arabs, measured on a scale of Americanization. There were good and bad people based on their humanity.

The sky in the king's fresco was a clearer blue than the one towards which our bus rumbled across the deserted plain. We came to sets of metal gates and a long runway, as if we would fly into the darkening horizon over the River Jordan and into Canaan in our sweet chariot. This was no-man's-land, the nether-world that separated each state of Greater Syria from the other. No one lived here. No one governed the tribal buffer. No farmers farmed, no livestock grazed and no trees cast shadows to obstruct the view from either side of the other. Concrete pillars – dragon's teeth, in American military parlance – stood sentry at intervals of ten yards on both sides of the highway. I don't know if the land was mined against infiltrators, but nothing grew out of that cement-powder soil. Two miles of protected desolation brought the bus at last to the 'Police Security Directorship – Bridge Security'. Metal screamed on metal, as the ancient brakes of our border shuttle stopped us crashing into the gates. A Jordanian policeman boarded and collected vouchers that confirmed we had paid the departure tax. The driver slammed the doors, fired up the engine again and released the brake. We rolled past a sign, the last I would see in Jordan. It wished us all 'Bon Voyage'.

The first Israeli fence was a little further. We stopped. We waited. We waited a long time. The old man sitting in front of me, who had been patient for a quarter of an hour, was the first to speak. 'Why are we waiting?' 'Who knows?' the driver answered. His daily route between the two border stations had accustomed him to waiting. This was his last trip of the day, and he would return empty. The old Haj repeated his question: 'Why do they make us wait so long?' The other passenger, the man in the suit, told him, 'Be patient, Haj.' The Haj looked at his wife, who smiled at him, and shrugged. The driver got out and opened all the luggage compartments for inspection by two Israeli soldiers. He drove on to a second gate, where a sign said, 'Welcome to the Allenby Bridge Crossing Point'. We were still on the East Bank, waiting to cross a tiny suspension bridge that the Israelis, following the British, named for General Allenby and the Jordanians called the King Hussein Bridge.

Impatient, the driver took the bus up to the gate and said to a woman soldier inside the guard post, 'This is the last bus.' She told him to reverse to where he had been. He backed up to our original position twenty yards away, with the perilous grinding of old gears and brakes. The moment he stopped, the woman soldier waved to him to come forward again. At last, we were going through.

FOUR

Over Jordan

'Palestine, formed and surrounded as it is, is a land of
tribes. That it can ever belong to one nation, even
though this were the Jews, is contrary to Nature
and Scripture.'

REVEREND GEORGE ADAM SMITH
The Historical Geography of the Holy Land (1894)

On the West Bank

INSIDE THE ISRAELI BORDER SHED the old Haj asked me
to fill in his forms. At this crossing between an Arab country
and occupied Arab land, there were no Arabic entry cards. All
were in Hebrew and English. The old man gave me his and
his wife's Jordanian passports and I wrote their names and
addresses on the questionnaire. He was born in 1932. City of
birth: Bethlehem. I hesitated at country, wanting not to com-
plicate his entry, before writing what it said in the passport:
Palestine. The purpose of their visit was to see their daughter.
They thanked me and went ahead to the passport booth, where
a young policewoman was polite to them both. The man
laughed at something she said and then, taking his wife's hand
and wheeling his smart new suitcase, walked outside to a taxi.

Next at the passport counter came the man in the suit. After
presenting his American passport, he answered the policewoman's questions in an amiable but apprehensive way. Born
in the West Bank in 1960, he now worked as a businessman in
Jordan. The purpose of his visit was to see business associates
in Jerusalem. Unfortunately, his passport had stamps from many

81

trips to Europe. The Israelis took him apart, first the suitcases, then his dignity. Israeli police did not treat American citizens of Arab origin as they did other Americans. They looked on them as security risks. This man would have a hard time. I had done a story the year before about another Arab American, a young man named Anwar Mohammed, from Florida. The police had arrested him as he was leaving via this same border. They took him to the Moscobieh, the security headquarters in Jerusalem known in English as the Russian Compound. He was chained to a chair, interrogated, abused, held for two months and released without charge. He was lucky, saved perhaps by the cockiness that came from his youth, his karate black belt, his belief in his American passport and, just as important, the fact that there was no evidence against him. If he had been a Palestinian with no passport, only a refugee identity card, he might have stayed for years. The American Embassy lodged no protests on his behalf. An American diplomat pointed to a warning on the State Department website that Israel did not necessarily respect the American citizenship of Arabs born in Arab countries, Israel or the occupied territories. The State Department permitted the Israeli police to determine who was and who was not an American citizen.

Outside, in the dark car park, I found an Israeli taxi driver and asked him to take me to Jerusalem. The road from the Allenby–Hussein Bridge cut through the occupied–disputed Jordan Valley, knocking aside all obstacles in its straight path. Jericho, whose walls came tumbling down, sparkled on the dark horizon. 'That her walls fell at the sound of Joshua's trumpet,' the Reverend George Adam Smith wrote in 1894, 'is a summary of her history.' No one had ever defended Jericho. Her low-lying position on the frontier between eastern desert and western mountain was indefensible and prey to raiders from both directions. Under the Oslo accords of 1993, Jericho was the first town that Israel allowed the new Palestinian administration to govern for itself, within limits.

As the road had created its way through the plain, it

resculpted the hills beyond. On the Jordanian side, it had rambled with the land like the rolling English road's drunken path of no resistance. Israel's was an American highway for which mountains and villages and forests made way, a proud, broad road that would have me in Jerusalem for dinner. 'There is no water,' Reverend Smith wrote, 'from Jericho till you reach the roots of the Mount of Olives.' There was no traffic either. Israeli settlers were afraid to drive at night, and the Israeli army kept the Palestinians confined to their towns.

Daughter of the Final Solution

Lily Galili had asked me to meet her in front of the American Consulate in West Jerusalem at 7.15 in the evening. An Arab taxi took me from the American Colony Hotel across the 'seam', as Israelis called the old Green Line between east and west, to the consulate. The car stopped opposite the late-nineteenth-century consular building, and security guards raced out of their post towards the car. I asked the driver to go another hundred yards uphill to avoid an hour's questioning. I got out and walked towards the consulate. An Israeli security guard asked me what I wanted. I was meeting a friend. What was the friend's name? What was my name? I ignored him, standing as I was on a public pavement, and walked further down the hill in search of Lily. Another security guard, a young woman, followed and said, 'Lily said she would wait for you at the corner.'

Lily's corner was dark, out of range of the consulate's spot-lights, near a passage between two stone houses that led to her friend's flat. She apologized for choosing the consulate as our rendezvous. She had forgotten about America's security worries. We talked a bit in the dark, catching up before we went to the dinner. Her voice was like a precocious child's, whose judgements, criticisms, observations and stories were astute and unexpected. She was leaving soon for Krakow, the city of her birth where she said her spirit was most at home, to celebrate her fifty-fifth birthday. Lily looked a good ten years younger than I did, and I was fifty. She was a journalist at *Ha'aretz*, a Tel Aviv daily that employed more talent – among them Danny Rubinstein, Gideon Levy, Amira Hass and Daniel Ben Simon – than the top ten Western newspapers combined. Lily and I had met in Cambridge, Massachusetts, when she was a Nieman fellow at Harvard. My friends Bernard Avishai and Sidra Ezrahi had taken me to a dinner that Lily cooked at her place, and we became friends. She once called me from London on my British cellphone, when I happened to be in a kosher restaurant in Krakow's old ghetto. Klezmer music played behind me, and she told me about her love affair with Poland's most beautiful Renaissance city. After the war, her family had returned to Krakow. Her mother brought her to Israel in 1956. She was ten.

Lily was clutching a bottle of wine for our American hostess, who she said had 'made *aliya*'. In the protected garden of an Arab house that looked as if it had been built around the same time as the American Consulate, were a group of English-speaking immigrants. They had all 'made *aliya*', that is, immigrated or 'risen up' like a wave to live in Israel. There were two South Africans, Benji and Anne Pogrund; a British couple, the Goldmans; and a woman who appeared to be Canadian and did not say much. During the introductions, Anne Pogrund told me that her black eye, which I could not make out in the dark, was not what I thought it was. I didn't think anything. She said she had really walked into a door. Her husband, a rotund ex-journalist with a bearded, friendly face, did not look like he would hit anyone, especially his wife. Benji Pogrund had been a journalist on the *Rand Daily Mail*, a brave and honourable opponent of South African apartheid. He and Anne, a painter, had fled Johannesburg for London and then for Israel. Bob Goldman was a videotape editor in the ABC News Jerusalem bureau. Our hostess worked for an Israeli millionaire named Stef Wertheimer.

After a drink in the garden, we went into the flat. It was a redesigned Arab house set on different levels, with a dining table next to the open kitchen. We'd finished our hostess's first and only bottle of red wine in the garden, and someone opened the one Lily had brought. Our hostess drank white, and there wasn't much of that. Dinner was *à l'américaine*, no first course, spaghetti on the boil in the kitchen going limp while she stirred a tomato and onion sauce, green salad with more vinegar than oil. That was all. She put two bowls on the table, and we served ourselves pasta and salad. We sipped Lily's red wine. We talked. About newspapers. About television. About Israel. About the Middle East. About the massacres in New York and Washington. About Osama bin Laden. Polite. Civilized. The Goldmans' children had disappointed their parents by leaving Israel. The Pogrund children had done the opposite. They went religious and would never leave. Their mother and father did not dwell on similarities between the race-based society they opposed in South Africa and the one in which they subsequently raised their children. They sounded like people who would have preferred their children to resist military service in the occupied territories or live in the West.

Someone said that an internet website was criticizing the ABC News anchorman, Peter Jennings, for being too favourable to the Arabs. 'He had an Arab wife,' Benji Pogrund said, confirming the internet verdict. Jennings had married a beautiful Lebanese woman, Annie Malouf, in 1973. They divorced, and his next two wives were Jewish, including the one he had now. 'So,' Benji said, 'Jewish wives. That's why he likes Arabs.' Peter Jennings, whose journalistic integrity made him scrupulously fair, was said to be anti-Israeli by people accustomed to the anti-Arab bias of American television. Later, other journalists told me Benji Pogrund was a 'good guy', who invited speakers with divergent points of view to address Israel's Anglo-Jewish community.

My argument that night was not with Benji, but with his wife, Anne. She was a painter and an interesting woman. She had made paintings from old studio photographs of South African

blacks, formal portraits for family occasions; and she was looking for similar family photographs of Arabs in Gaza. When she
discussed the September 2001 attacks in the United States, she
lost me. We spoke in a polite, civilized way, but we were arguing. Her case was a psychologist's rationale, that the killers
acted out of envy. They wanted what they admired but could
not have. America's democracy and its high standard of living
had made it their target. Perhaps, I said, there was another
explanation. Holland, Norway and Canada had democracies
and high living standards, but no one hated them. Why did they
hate the United States? Not because it was richer – per capita
there were wealthier lands – or more democratic. Could it be, I
asked her, that the Norwegians and Canadians did not install
and maintain regimes that robbed their people, did not break
open the doors to their markets and did not bomb or invade
them? This went on and on, towards no conclusion. There was
a widespread belief in the United States that Americans were
attacked because of their goodness; as many Israelis were convinced that Arabs attacked them – not because Israel occupied
their territory and confiscated their land – but because they were
Jewish. If anti-Semitism motivated the Arabs, would they have
given their lands and their homes gladly to any other people
who came from outside to displace them? Is it likely that they
would have moved to make way for Albanians, Basques,
gypsies, South Africans or any other group of Gentiles? The
discussion went on and on and, like the political conflicts themselves, got no further than the arguments of fifty years before.

I left dinner early to meet Andrew and Emma Gilmour in the
Ottoman courtyard of the American Colony Hotel. There, I
drank the red wine I'd been deprived of at dinner. We talked
about politics, the *intifadah* and, Andrew's special interest,
negotiations to end the fighting. Andrew worked for United
Nations negotiator Terje Roed Larsen, and Emma was a physician. Andrew's older brothers – David, Oliver and Christopher
– were probably my closest friends in Britain. Emma was
expecting their fourth child in December. They invited me to

stay in their house at Abu Tor, an Arab neighbourhood above the old city. Even with the discount that Pierre Berclaz, the Colony's Swiss manager, had kindly allowed me on a good room, my advance would run out soon.

Upstairs in the Pasha Room, dance music played. An American was marrying a Ramallah girl. One of the hotel guests complained about the noise, as I did once in 1987 during a wedding reception at the New Omayyad Hotel in Damascus. Then, it annoyed me so much that I left. Now, I loved the noise of a wedding. Perhaps I had improved. The music stopped at one-thirty, when I fell asleep. In Damascus, it had gone on all night.

Daughter of the Revolution

I had my first lunch in Jerusalem with Nadia Sartawi. Her father, Dr Issam Sartawi, was one of the heroes of the Palestinian cause. He acted on behalf of what he believed were his people's interests – not in line with the cant and slogans of the revolution. Any journalist who reduced him to the status of 'Yasser Arafat's special envoy', as a few did, enraged him. He insisted with pride that he was no diplomat. Along with Sabry Jiryis and Sayed Hammami, Issam pioneered the Palestinian dialogue with the Israelis. In 1982, during the Israeli invasion of Lebanon, I invited Issam and Israeli general Mattityahu Peled to lunch at a Lebanese restaurant, Fakhreddin, opposite Green Park in London. When I asked Peled if he were a Sabra, meaning someone born in Israel, he nodded and said, 'Issam's a Sabra too.' They were already friends, both born in northern Palestine, each a patriot to his own people, both working to spare the next generation of Israelis and Palestinians more warfare. Issam saw early the futility of the armed struggle for a people as militarily weak – but with a strong moral case – as the Palestinians. He had once headed a small commando organization and knew the effect of raids into Israel: unarmed Israelis killed, world outrage against Palestinian terrorism, more hostility and retaliation by Israel. Arafat never understood. Nor did he understand that no leader could abandon certain principles, like self-determination, and maintain his enemy's respect.

When I asked Issam why the Palestinians had not produced leaders more capable than Haj Amin Husseini and Yasser Arafat, he said, 'We had a good leader once, but we crucified him.' He accused Syria of doing more harm to the Palestinians than Israel. He called for the United Nations to declare the Syrian regime a threat to world peace and dispatch a force to overthrow it. A few months later, in the spring of 1983, the hired assassins of the Palestinian radical Sabry al-Banna, known as Abu Nidal, shot Issam dead in the lobby of a hotel in Portugal during a conference of Europe's Socialist International. The Syrians, Abu Nidal's benefactors at the time, may have put him up to it. Abu Nidal had already assassinated the director of the PLO's London office, Sayed Hammami, in 1977, for the same supposed crime of meeting with Israelis. Issam Sartawi's criticisms outraged Yasser Arafat, whose security service was secretly cooperating with the CIA and thus indirectly with Israel's Mossad. In 1982, Arafat evacuated Beirut, claiming victory over the Israeli army. Issam made a public declaration: one more Palestinian victory like Beirut, and the Palestine National Council would hold its next meeting in Fiji. No one said that Arafat had killed Issam, but many Palestinians believed he had 'withdrawn his protection', exposing him to Abu Nidal and to Syria. Abu Nidal would himself be murdered by another benefactor, Saddam Hussein, before America invaded Iraq in 2003.

Issam was a gentle, well-dressed man, who had trained as a physician and married another Palestinian doctor. I remember him at our house in London, playing with our children when they were small. Having lunch with his daughter at an Arab restaurant near the American Colony, I listened to a woman young enough to have missed most of her childhood playing with her father. She had grown up in Paris and spoke perfect French. Her English had a French rather than Arabic accent, like many Lebanese women in Beirut. Ahmed Querei, a member of Yasser Arafat's cabinet and one of the Palestinian negotiators at Oslo, had hired her as special assistant. I asked what her father would make of her working for Abu Ala, the name by which Qurei was known. She ignored the question. Would she introduce me to Nurit Peled, the daughter of Issam's friend Matti Peled? I knew that, after Issam's assassination, the two families had become close. A few years after Issam's assassination, Matti died without having seen the Israeli–Palestinian dialogue that he and Issam pioneered lead anywhere. In 1997, a Palestinian suicide bomber took the life of Nurit's young daughter, Matti's granddaughter, in West Jerusalem. Smedar was thirteen. Phil Jacobson, the former *Times* correspondent, had written a heart-breaking account of the suicide bombing that had killed Smedar and its effect on Nurit and her husband, Rami Elhannan. Nadia said that when the prime minister of the time, Benyamin Netanyahu, offered to pay his respects to the Peled family, Nurit told him not to bother. She blamed him for policies that had led to her daughter's murder.

In my view, one not shared by everyone, Dr Issam Sartawi would have condemned the agreement that his daughter's employer had negotiated at Oslo in 1993. Issam had recognized Israel's 'right' to exist, although the 'right to exist' is not a concept in international law, years before any other PLO leader. Recognition and dialogue did not mean surrender, and even surrender did not require self-annihilation, the price exacted at Oslo. What the Israelis and the Palestinians got instead of democratic neighbours was the submission of one, weak tribal leadership to the power of the other. It left Israel a permanent military oppressor, with all that implied for Israeli society, and the Palestinians as helots to acquiesce when settlers wanted their land, when settlers needed their water or when the Israeli army confined them to their villages. Nothing in the agreement prevented Israel from expanding old settlements, constructing new ones or building roads between them – activities that required the seizure of what little land the Palestinians had. While

Palestinian Authority police protected the demographic shift caused by a doubling of settlers in the West Bank, no one protected Palestinian farmers and householders from having their land taken. Was this intended to establish peace or to extend the occupation? Was it consistent or inconsistent with the old Zionist aim of seizing Palestine 'goat by goat, dunum by dunum'? Oslo's terms compelled the weaker tribe to wait until it was strong enough to redress the imbalance or so close to suffocation that they exploded. At the end of September 2000, that explosion came.

It was a year into the explosion when Nadia and I met for lunch. The last time I had seen her was the year before, when the uprising began. Then, she went to her office and hoped the Israelis would propose some compromise that would allow the Palestinians to end the *intifadah* and resume discussions. In the meantime, the Israeli electorate chose General Ariel Sharon as their prime minister. Now, Nadia said, Israeli checkpoints prevented most of the Palestinian Authority from reaching their offices. She was living – more of the confusion of this area – in an old Arab part of the Jewish, western half of Jerusalem. She was renting an Arab house, whose original residents had either fled or been expelled in 1948, from an Israeli landlord. She was an Arab, but she carried a French passport. The passport allowed her not only to live in a Jewish-owned Arab house, it permitted her to clear the Israeli checkpoints to reach the Palestinian Authority offices in Ramallah. Other PA staff in Jerusalem could not reach Ramallah, as those in Ramallah could not go to Jerusalem. The only Palestinians moving freely within the occupied territories were those who – through marriage or some other accident – had foreign, non-Arab passports. As natives, they could not go anywhere. Only new visitors to this lunatic asylum noticed that the set-up, both on paper and in reality, was untenable.

Nadia was one of many Western-born or Western-raised Palestinians to return to the homeland after Oslo in 1993, when they imagined they would build a state. You would meet them in the offices of the Palestinian Authority, private companies and charities, all speaking perfect English with British, American or Canadian accents. Many were studying Arabic for the first time. The country had not seen such idealism, hope and talent since young, educated European Jews answered Zionism's appeal to build the kibbutzim, irrigate the desert and learn Hebrew. Working for Abu Ala, one of the most egregious proto-types of the unpopular Palestinian politician with big body-guards and bigger cigars, had made Nadia more cynical than I remembered from the year before. Her belief in working within the PA towards statehood was becoming harder to maintain. Israel was dismantling its institutions and the PA's leaders were stealing from it. My criticisms of the PA annoyed her, and she talked about what help she might offer me. Like a Lebanese aunt, she told me which was the best hotel in Gaza, where to rent a cellphone and how to lease a car for a few months. She also made me write down a dozen useful telephone numbers. Abu Ala must have found her indispensable.

Palestinian Neighbours

Emma Gilmour, pregnant and every inch a natural beauty, was driving me through West Jerusalem with her three children in the back seat. The car was a big Land Rover, white with United Nations number plates. We stopped at a red light near Yemin Moshe, the pretty collection of old stone cottages that Jerusalem's mayor lent to visiting artists and writers. The driver of a car beside us motioned to me to roll down my window. His knitted kippa covered most of his clipped hair above a short, patchy beard. He pressed a printed sign against his window for us to read: 'UN UNwelcome No Bodies, Go Home!' This spontaneous act of bravery seemed to please him. The light changed, and we went our separate ways. Later, I told a friend at another United Nations agency about it. She said the settlers did that all the time: 'They hate us.'

At six in the evening, the Gilmour children were having tea in the kitchen of their house in Abu Tor. The lights went off. Caitriona, one of the prettiest and most fey three-year-olds I knew, cried. She was not noisy. She was afraid. Emma lit candles so that the children could see their food. Outside, all the streets and houses of Silwan and Abu Tor were in darkness. In the distance, the Jewish quarters of west Jerusalem were in full light. Their power was never off. Ours came on again an hour later, while the children were in a candlelit bath.

From time to time at the Gilmours', Palestinians neighbours would drop by. One was a young woman, who, like Emma, was about to have a baby. You meet people and don't think much about them, until someone tells you that this pregnant woman with a bridal veil of dark hair had spent two years in prison. And you look at the young mother, playing with her children, and you ask yourself, as you would in a country where people were free, what she could have done to merit a two-year sentence. Later, Emma told me her story.

After the Israeli security forces shot dead fourteen unarmed young men for throwing stones in the Al Aqsa mosque grounds, Intisar took a knife from her kitchen and went down to Jerusalem to take revenge. Several other Palestinian women – not in concert or with any plan – did the same. They went, each on her own, to the Jewish Quarter of the old city to stab an Israeli settler. Did Intisar stab anyone? No. The soldiers searched her, found the knife, put her under arrest and sent her to the court that passed judgement. Two years later, she went home.

Another woman came to the Gilmour house one evening to babysit the children, so that Emma, Andrew and I could go to Fink's Bar for dinner. She did not say much. Her dress was black, and her long hair had almost as many white strands as brown. In the car on the way into the city, Andrew and Emma told me that the Israelis had shot and killed her husband at the end of the June 1967 war. She raised five children on her own. Her husband's family offered her no help, unusual in Arab society in which children are the responsibility of the paternal

family. She refused payment for babysitting the Gilmour children. To look after the younger son, Xan, I'd have demanded a
year's salary. In return for the favour of watching her neighbours' children, the widow expected reciprocal favours: a ride
into Jerusalem, help with her shopping, advice. It was an
exchange between equals.

Defending the Doomed

At nearly ninety, Mrs Valentine Vester was the *grande dame* of
old Jerusalem. Proprietress of the American Colony Hotel, she
was the niece of Gertrude Bell, the English Oriental traveller
and linguist who helped to create modern Iraq when Britain
occupied the country during the First World War. I had met Val
and her husband, Horatio Vester, in 1972. The Colony belonged
to his family, descendants of nineteenth-century American
religious pilgrims. They also had an ophthalmic hospital in the
old city. Horatio, whose urbane demeanour reminded me of
Noël Coward, ran the place in those days. Raconteur and *bon
vivant*, Horatio was loved, especially in the bar, by the hotel's
guests and staff. When he died, Val employed a Swiss company
to manage what was beyond doubt Jerusalem's finest hotel. She
went on living there and kept an eye on the place, as she always
had. With her snowy hair and benevolent smile, she oversaw
the Israeli gardeners and the Palestinian receptionists. She had
known them for generations.

Perhaps I should not have repeated to Val the joke that
Andrew Gilmour told me about her hotel restaurant's fame for
slow service. She had returned the day before from a visit to her
son in London. Her hearing was beginning to fail, and I had to
shout without letting the head waiter, Ahmed, and the rest of
her long-time and loyal employees hear. 'Do you know how
the Jordanian army lost Jerusalem in 1967?' The Jordanian
general staff were having lunch here at the American Colony.
When they heard that the Israelis were invading, they asked

for their bill. By the time it arrived, the Israelis were in Jericho.

Val laughed. Ahmed watched us from his corner of the garden, and I knew I would wait longer than usual for my club sandwich. Ahmed was just as slow to bring Mrs Vester her rabbit risotto. She didn't mind the wait, she said. She's had thirty-eight years to get used to it.

My favourite place to meet people was the courtyard where we had lunch. It may have been the stone walls and the parapets or the oriental arches or the gushing fountain and the scented blossoms. It may also have been the mix of Palestinians, Israelis and sojourners in a setting that predated the British occupation, Zionism, nationalism and uprisings. It was the most tranquil corner of Jerusalem, and there were days when I hated to leave it for the chaos outside.

Jonathan Kuttab, a Palestinian-American lawyer whose practice was in Jerusalem, came to the courtyard for coffee. I had met him first in the spring of 2000, a few months before the failed negotiations that Bill Clinton had staged between Yasser Arafet and Israeli prime minister Ehud Barak at Camp David. I had come to Israel to do a story on torture for American television. The Israeli High Court had just banned certain forms of torture. The court's decision meant that, in the absence of laws authorizing the mistreatment of detainees, anyone who committed torture could be held to account in the civil courts. The decision had two consequences: it reduced torture, and it prompted Likud Knesset members to introduce legislation to protect torturers from lawsuits.

Jonathan Kuttab, a University of Virginia graduate, had represented hundreds of security detainees during the first *intifadah*. After the Palestinian Authority was established, it detained Jonathan's brother, a respected West Bank journalist named Daoud Kuttab, for criticizing Yasser Arafat. Amid Valentine Vester's flowers, the fountain, and the bougainvillea, Jonathan and I ordered Turkish coffee.

I asked if the High Court ban on torture had expired with the new *intifadah*.

94

'Totally,' he said.

Jonathan was more than a lawyer. Like all other Palestinians, he was a political analyst. He augmented the basic knowledge that circumstances gave every Palestinian with lessons from the political prisoners he represented, from the Israeli military and civil courts in which he worked and from his American formal education. The last time we had met, before the Camp David failure and the uprising, he told me that disaster was inevitable.

'The Israeli grand design to have and to expand settlements and contract out security to the Palestinian Authority could not work,' he said, one year into the new *intifadah*. 'In fact, if this *intifadah* had not been against Israel, it would have been against the PA.'

The question that confronted Palestinians about Yasser Arafat was: is he governing for us or for the Israelis? If for the Palestinians, he should have been moving politically to dismantle the Israeli settlements and give the land back to their owners. If for the Palestinians, he should have made his executive accountable and open to them. If for the Palestinians, he would have made it impossible for his ministers to steal and to help the Israelis construct settlements. But, if he governed for Israel, he would arrest Palestinians who attacked settlements, allow his advisers to grow rich selling cement to the settlements, cooperate with the intelligence agencies of Israel and America to suppress resistance to occupation and demonstrate his contempt for those who criticized him in the Palestinian legislature, media and civil society.

'Arafat,' Jonathan said, 'I think, sensed it wasn't going to work. It wasn't so much Jerusalem or the refugees, but Barak's insistence at Camp David that this was it, the end of the road. There was no possibility you could improve the terms. He couldn't do it. His people would not have gone along with it. From that day to this, Tenet, Mitchell' – meaning the missions of the two Georges, the CIA director and the former senator – 'everything has been an attempt to revive security cooperation. If Arafat hits Hamas, the Israelis will stop hitting him. Nothing else. It's simply not going to work.'

What will work?

'A two-state solution.'

To many Israelis that was an unacceptable, maximalist demand. It was, however, the result of an evolution in Palestinian thought born of eighty years of defeat and a compromise of their previous ideal of a 'secular, democratic state' in all of Palestine. It had taken generations for them to realize they did not have the strength to win back the part of Palestine – 78 per cent – they lost to Israel in 1948. By the first *intifadah* in 1987, they were ready for independence in Gaza and the West Bank. The settlers and Israel's then prime minister Ehud Barak told Palestinians they were unreasonable to demand *all* of the West Bank and Gaza, *all* of Israel's 1967 conquest, all of the 22 per cent. At Camp David, where Bill Clinton caused a conflagration with his quixotic pursuit of a Nobel Peace Prize to redeem his tarnished presidency, Barak had excluded the largest settlement blocs from discussion and was prepared to consider adjustments only to the rest of the occupied territories. Under Barak's vague proposals, Israel would have kept about 30 per cent or more of the land, 80 per cent of the water and all of the sky above for its right to fly and use the airwaves. Even a leader as craven as Arafat could not say yes to a mere 15 per cent of all Palestine on which to build his Arab Bantu-stine.

'Israel holds all the cards,' Jonathan said, 'and they know it. They are furious with the Palestinians for failing to recognize that. This is more on the left than on the right.' Jonathan had discussed this with the foreign minister, Shimon Peres. 'Peres told me, we are not negotiating with the Palestinians. We are negotiating with ourselves.' The Israeli leadership regarded its decision on what to 'give' the Palestinians as an internal matter rather than as a subject for negotiation with the occupied people.

'When subcontracting control to the PA failed,' Jonathan concluded, 'the left had nothing else.' Israel turned to Sharon 'with his policy of hit them and hit them harder'. Sharon had his critics, but Jonathan said they were even further to the right, demanding that the old Arab killer 'get tougher, expel'. The Palestinians were making the settlers feel insecure on their roads in the West Bank and Gaza. 'Palestinians now have guns and are willing to use them,' Jonathan said. 'The Gaza settlers are no longer safe. Period. Palestinians can exact a daily price, which means Israelis don't hold all the cards.'

In response, he admitted, 'The Israelis made life absolutely miserable.' Sharon was, he said 'absolutely furious. And he's trying to keep it going. More incursions, more killings.'

In his pink Ralph Lauren shirt with preppy button-down collar, Jonathan Kuttab was as much American as Palestinian. But he misjudged the United States, as parts of the world did when the attack on Afghanistan was beginning. 'America needs the Arab world,' he said. 'It cannot invade Afghanistan without neutralizing this place. Pakistan, Egypt, Iran and the rest will not go along with this crusade unless the Americans do something about the Palestinians.' He was wrong. The United States let Sharon deal with the Palestinian problem as if its only dimension were security, as if Israel provided the model for the US to deal with Osama bin Laden and the tribes of Afghanistan. It did not seek or obtain Arab support. 'The only basis for optimists,' Jonathan said, 'is that you cannot ignore one billion Muslims for ever.' Jonathan, a Christian, may have been wrong about that as well.

We went back to the local conflict that was emblematic of the larger dispute between an all-powerful America and a helpless, supine Arab world. And we were back where we began more than a year before: that total weakness of the man in the torture chamber. 'It's not pure sadism,' Jonathan said. 'In the first *intifadah*, the problem was that ordinary soldiers were doing the interrogation. That's sadism. They beat them up. But it was not effective. They have to force them to give information and to sign confessions. And they need professionals to do that. When you physically weaken someone, humiliate him, you can force him to do what you want. They use sleep deprivation and violent shaking. They are more effective. They study this. They are scientific and methodical. There are time limits, when people are vulnerable. If they have not broken down by the fiftieth day, they let them go.' Did he know anyone who had taken it longer than fifty days? 'I had a client who did. They released him on the fifty-fifth day. He had a few teeth broken. He was tired, weak, but in very good shape.'

The ones who survived the best were those who neither confessed nor implicated their comrades. Franz Fanon, the psychiatrist who wrote *The Wretched of the Earth*, based on his experience of French repression in Algeria, had observed the same phenomenon. Those who cracked, who named names, left prison ashamed and broken. Those who held out – despite being tortured longer – recovered. One of Fanon's other observations was that those most in need of psychiatric treatment were the torturers. He told of a French policeman who came to Fanon begging for help. He wanted to stop beating his wife and children but to continue torturing Arabs. A journalist at *Ha'aretz* told me of an Israeli psychiatrist who specialized in torturers, some of whom found their only remedy was to quit.

What had the Palestinians achieved with their suffering? In my lifetime, the Vietnamese had driven out the French and the Americans. The Algerians had expelled the French. The Belgians, the British, the French and the Portuguese had left Africa, the Dutch abandoned the East Indies. The whites of South Africa had surrendered power to the majority. Yet the Palestinians were left behind, ignored by the great powers, betrayed and used by the Arab states, beaten down by the Israelis. Young Palestinians emerged from the Russian Compound to repair their damaged spirit and flesh, then grew old to watch their sons relive the experience.

'Let me tell you something,' Jonathan said. His elbows were on the table. His black hair and moustache made him look like a sombre Charlie Chaplin. I leaned forward to listen. 'I never defended anyone accused of possessing, manufacturing or buying communications equipment. Give me a break. I've defended thousands of security defendants. How come no one is trying to listen to the Israelis? This is so embarrassing. In terms of armed struggle, we Palestinians are not serious.' It wasn't the coffee or Valentine Vester's young blossoms that filled the morning air of the courtyard just then. It was despair. Jonathan, who for most of his professional life had attempted to defend Palestinians in the military courts, said that he had switched to business law.

Hidden Treasure

Papa Andrea's restaurant was empty. I liked the place, not for the food, but for its open roof in the Christian Quarter. Most of the old city's landmarks were nearby, all Jerusalem's domes and spires and rain troughs and polished stone roofs. Just below were the souvenir shops, whose owners had set tables and chairs to play cards with one another outside. The largest shop, Yasser Barakat's, was shuttered and padlocked. Two years earlier, in preparation for Pope John Paul II's visit, the shopkeepers had no time for cards. The streets were crammed with pilgrims and tourists along the Via Dolorosa to the Church of the Holy Sepulchre. Today, the large fountain where five streets met was dry. Flies swarmed over discarded cans of Coke and Pepsi where clear water should have collected. At street level, the cobbled walkways, the deserted businesses and the broken fountain made the old city a forlorn setting. Between the street and the roofs were the windows of the settlers' flats. Each window sprouted a flag and blue metal mesh shutter. Tiny T-shirts and large underwear dripped in the sunlight. In one window, children pressed against the grille to watch the Arabs at their card tables. Their parents had settled there with the express purpose of forcing the Arabs out, as they had forced other Arabs out of Jaffa, Lydda, Ramleh and, more recently, much of the West Bank.

Would those young faces one day rebel against their parents' radical hatred and learn Arabic and play cards in the street with their neighbours? Or would they, like their mothers and fathers, find some subterfuge to seize another flat and evict its Arab residents?

A middle-aged settler – her hair bundled under a scarf and her legs hidden inside a long skirt, like so many modest Muslim women – limped past the card players. Dragging her groceries in a bag from the Jewish Quarter, she did not look at the men. They did not glance up from their cards. Neither existed for the other, the Arabs living in their pre-Israelite past, the settler in some Arab-free future.

The Armenians dwelled, like ghosts, between the two. 'There are two thousand Armenians in the old city now,' George Hultunian, community historian, said. 'Their children have no future.' Armenia was the first kingdom in history to embrace Christ, and its priests were among the earliest to establish hostels for pilgrims visiting the scene of their Saviour's execution and resurrection. Most of the two thousand lived within the walls and gates of St James's Convent. The Armenian Quarter had no shops apart from a few groceries, Vic Lepejian's ceramics factory, the Armenian Tavern and a photo shop.

Benjamin Disraeli, who came to Jerusalem in 1830 and 1831, later compared its Jews and Armenians in his novel *Tancred*. Eva 'the Jewess' noted the similarities between her people and the Armenians:

> Go to Armenia and you will not find an Armenian. They too are an expropriated nation, like the Hebrews. The Persians conquered their land, and drove out the people. The Armenian has a proverb: 'In every city of the East I find a home.' They are everywhere; the rivals of my people, for they are one of the great races and little degenerated; with all our industry, and much of our energy; I would say with all our human virtues, though it cannot be expected that they should possess our divine qualities; they have not produced Gods and prophets and are proud that they can trace up their faith to one of the obscurest of the Hebrew apostles [St Gregory the Illuminator] and who never knew his great master.

The resemblance turned to tragedy in the twentieth century when both peoples were subjected to genocide.

The Armenians of Jerusalem were cut into factions and sects and categories as if they had been a million. By faith, they were Gregorian (Orthodox), Catholic and Protestant. By Armenian politics, they were Hanshak or Tashnak, dating from the pro- and anti-communist fights of the Russian Revolution and its Soviet conquest of non-Turkish Armenia. They were also, like the Arabs of the West Bank and Gaza, either local families or descendants of refugees from massacres. Many were Palestinian nationalists while others just wanted to get by, no matter who governed Jerusalem. George was from a native Jerusalem family, a Gregorian and a Palestinian nationalist. His friend Albert Agazarian, he said, was a refugee from northern Syria, a Catholic and also a Palestinian nationalist. Neither he nor Albert had strong views on Armenian politics, having made their stand as Palestinians. Eight Armenians languished in Israeli prisons for resisting occupation, and one Armenian, Artin Gouzelian, had given his life for Palestine.

George said that an organization to which he belonged had sent 350 Bibles in Arabic to Christian political prisoners in Israeli custody. Christians, including the Armenians, were leaving the country. Muslims, particularly since the new *intifadah* began, were leaving as well. Christians went to the West, whose countries gave them visas. Muslims, more than 100,000 in the previous year, went over the bridge searching for work in Jordan. Natalie Zarour, one of the managers at the American Colony Hotel, was emigrating with her family to Canada in a few weeks. Christians from Bethlehem, the Zarours were tired of the violence, the restrictions, the settlers who treated Arabs as sub-humans. I had known Natalie for years and would miss her beautiful face behind the Colony's reception desk.

George took me upstairs to the refectory of the Armenian Convent. Among long tables of stone and marble, under vaulted ceilings, I imagined the monks eating in silence and awaiting an unwelcome visit from the city's Turkish governors. A bridge, under which I had often walked and driven, formed part of the refectory. George indicated a hidden door. 'If the Turks came,' he explained, 'the monks would disappear through here.' It was an Armenian Bridge of Sighs, along which the monks would, like Casanova, escape. It was built in AD 1370. Until 1830, he said, the Ottomans did not collect fixed taxes. Instead, they demanded money when they needed it. 'The Turks raided the monasteries. They were a good source of income, because of the pilgrims.' The monks would clamber through the priest's hole, across the covered bridge and onto a roof. After that, they hid or dispersed in the gardens on the other side of the city wall.

As we stepped onto the convent roof, guarded by a sixth-century gable, George explained the economics of Jerusalem life before the British occupied the city in 1917. 'Three or four hundred people lived in the convent,' he said. 'It had about eight hundred rooms. They filled with pilgrims at Easter. In fact, at the times of pilgrimage, the whole city's population grew about ten times. This convent could take in eight to ten thousand people.' After the Armenian genocide by Turkey, the convent filled with refugee families. Some of them, like Albert Agazarian's, were still there.

'In 1917,' George said, 'three days before they left Jerusalem, the Turks demanded the Treasury.' The convent's treasure of gold, silver and jewels lay hidden behind another secret door within the church. George opened it, but swore me to keep the secret of its location until I died. 'The Armenian patriarch filled wagons with the treasure in sealed boxes. He covered the boxes in coal.' Horses pulled the Armenian community's wealth to safety outside the city until the Turks withdrew. It seemed strange that no Turkish sentry would question a load of coal *leaving* the city in winter. George referred me to Sir Ronald Storrs' *Orientations*, where the tale is recounted as he told it.

The Cathedral of St James, beyond a small plaza near the iron-door entrance to the monastery, was more beautiful to my eye that any other church in Jerusalem. 'In sharp contrast to the sombre weariness of the Holy Sepulchre,' Fr Jerome Murphy-

O'Connor wrote in *The Holy Land*, 'this church mirrors the life and vigour of a colourful and unified people.' I was not sure about the unity, but the ceilings and walls let loose tributes of colour and vigour. In terms of icons per square foot, St James's could hold its own with any Greek church. It also contained one of the holiest relics, the head of St James the Less. Herod the Great's feeble son, Herod Antipas, had done with the apostle's head what his father had to John the Baptist's, in AD 44. George, with great patience for a man who must have shown the church to hundreds of ignorant visitors, told me the story of every panel, every painting, every door.

Three hundred and fifty candle-bearing lamps, all lit and suspended from ropes, could be lowered and raised via small pulleys. Each bore the inscription of its Armenian donor community. Much of the church's beauty was the gift, George said, of an eighteenth-century patriarch called Gregory the Chain-bearer. In Gregory's time, Armenians elsewhere were neglecting their church in Jerusalem. He went to Constantinople to shame them. 'He put a chain around his neck and sat in front of the churches to raise money,' George said. Gregory's takings paid for the grand plaza, or porch, at the church door and for much of the restoration within. The cathedral was a warren of hidden doors and secret passages. Some led to chapels, others to refuges from tax collectors – the world's first tax shelters.

George and I wandered through the convent grounds. They comprised about a sixth of the old city and almost the entire Armenian Quarter. At the Convent of the Olive Tree, there was indeed one olive tree. 'This is, of course, a very young tree,' George said, 'but they say it is Ananias's tree.' By very young, George meant a few hundred years. Ananias had been a high priest two thousand years ago, when, legend claimed, Christ had been tied to the tree and whipped. Interestingly, both a non-Armenian church and a mosque stood within the grounds of the Armenian Quarter. St Mark's, believed to have been the house of St Mark's mother, Mary, was a Syrian Orthodox church. And the tiny Yaqubieh, or Jacob, Mosque had once been the chapel of the martyr St James of Persia. He was known as St James the Cut-Up, because the martyr's singular form of execution was to be chopped to pieces.

The entire Armenian Quarter was clad in the smoothest stone I had ever seen, as slick as a seal's back. The roofs, the court-yards and the plazas all had surfaces you could run your hands over or run barefoot across without taking a scratch. The roof-tops and walkways formed an intricate system of water collec-tion. Every massive stone was set to point the water towards a channel, and every channel made its way to a reservoir. 'Under every church,' George said, 'there is a cistern. Before the rainy season, people spend weeks cleaning the roofs.' Like the Naba-taeans of the desert, the people of Jerusalem saved every drop the sky gave them. To waste water was a sin. To run dry was death.

The Armenians, like the Arab Christians of Palestine, were running out of people. We walked by the yard of the Armenian school, where a few boys played basketball. 'The children have no future,' lamented George, himself unmarried and childless. 'Our generation didn't care about the future. Albert and I, for example, have no possessions. We are a proud generation. We lived under Arab sovereignty and dignity. We were treated as normal citizens.' He looked at the children, all born long after Israel conquered the old city in 1967. 'They have known only occupation. They have had only humiliation. They challenge it in the *intifadah*, but that is superficial.'

The Armenians had survived genocide by Turkey. They would survive the Israelis, I said. Jerusalem, he reminded me, was a long way from the massacres in Anatolia, northern Syria and Mesopotamia. Jerusalem, in the last years of the Ottomans' chaotic empire, was a refuge. 'The Turks,' he said of those who ruled the old city, 'wanted money. These people want the land.' The monks hid their money or begged for more. Land cannot be concealed or replaced.

George, a bespectacled and subdued man in a grey cardigan, hated the Israeli occupation of East Jerusalem and the indignity meted out to both Arabs and Armenians. He told me that the only way he had found to endure was, like the monks of old, to seek a refuge. His refuge, he said, was the nineteenth century.

The View from the Convent

Jerusalem had always been a real estate scam, Albert Agazarian told me. George had left me at Albert's house inside the convent. Albert lived there with his wife, son and two daughters. At home in his Syrian stone house, where every room opened on the courtyard as in old Damascus and Seville, Albert was a pasha. Madeleine, whom he had married when they were still in their twenties, brought coffee, tea, tobacco and sweets without his asking whenever anyone dropped by. He often had a guest – a journalist, a diplomat or an instructor from Bir Zeit University where he worked and his children studied. He usually received them in his library, a cluttered, domed room, with overstuffed sofas, shoe-sized ashtrays and books in no discernible order that he pulled down to quote some passage or other. There was no point in making an appointment to see Albert. He and Madeleine rarely bothered to answer their telephone.

God, could Albert talk. 'You went to the leather tannery?' he asked me. The 'leather tannery' was Dabbagha Square, just below Papa Andrea's rooftop restaurant. 'Up until 1860, that place stank like hell. After the Crimean War, the Russian pilgrims started coming. There was a wedding here between Russian piety and generosity on the one hand and Byzantine cunning on the other. It was Eftimos, the Orthodox treasurer, who got rid of the tannery and the smell from those dead cows and rotting hides.' He said it as if the aroma had just cleared his nostrils. 'Eftimos built the first well and the first hotel in the old city. It was not a khan.' A khan, or caravanserai, was common in the Levant of the nineteenth century. Travellers stopped for shelter, but brought their own blankets and food. A hotel that provided beds, linen and meals was an innovation.

'This hotel was the Hospice of St John, the first modern hotel in Jerusalem. This is where the settlers have been since April 1990.' Those were the blue-grilled windows with Israeli flags that I had seen at lunch.

Madeleine, supporting a tray of coffee and cakes, pushed through the door and cleared space among the papers on the coffee table. Albert got up, opened a drawer and searched for something. Whatever it was, he did not find it. Madeleine poured the coffee and started for the door. I asked why she did not stay. Friends were waiting for her in the kitchen, and their conversation was more interesting.

'The hotel was successful,' Albert continued. 'Its success instigated the Greek Orthodox to open the Grand Hotel and Grand New Hotel.' The two hotels, built of Jerusalem stone in the high splendour of late Victorian and Habsburg design, dominated the western portal of the old city at the Jaffa Gate. 'The Grand changed its name to the Imperial when Kaiser Wilhelm visited in 1898.'

The period from the Egyptian invasion of 1830 to Kaiser Wilhelm's pilgrimage in 1898 made modern Jerusalem. The Christian powers – Russia, England, Austria-Hungary, Germany, France and Italy – erected churches and hospices in the Christian Quarter, on sites they bought in the Muslim Quarter and on hills outside the walls. German Christians erected the Augusta Victoria Hospital on a summit where the Kaiser was said to have had his first view of the Holy City. Prior to that, Imperial Russia staked its claim to Jerusalem with the construction of the Ascension Church, all onion domes and multicoloured like St Basil's in Moscow, in 1870. Most of the modern Christian Quarter was built with foreign Christian donations in the late nineteenth century. England and Prussia opened the first Protestant church in the Holy Land, Christ Church, near the Jaffa Gate in 1849. It was a time when ideas born in Europe invaded the near Orient, Jerusalem in particular: imperialism, *la mission civilitrice*, the romantic Christian Zionism of Lords Shaftesbury and Palmerston (who suggested in

1840 that Europe's Jews should be removed to Palestine and originated the phrase 'land without a people for a people without a land'), nationalism, the forced opening of Ottoman markets to European trade with all its dislocating effects, the political Zionism of Leo Pinsker and Theodor Herzl and the first purchases with Rothschild money of Arab land for Zionist settlement. The Kaiser's well-publicized procession through the Holy Land attracted Herzl from Vienna. Herzl paid homage to Kaiser Wilhelm and requested German sponsorship for the colonization of Palestine. At the Herzl Museum in West Jerusalem a photomontage in badly focused sepia depicted the elegantly dressed, bearded Father of Zionism on foot and doffing a white pith helmet to the mounted Kaiser. The Kaiser did not sponsor the Zionist project, whose architects wisely turned to Britain.

'Before 1831,' Albert said, 'the population of Jerusalem was never more than 10,000. There were 4000 Muslims, 3000 Christians and 2000 Jews. The gates of the city were locked at night.' From 1840, with the European Christian building programme and the missionary attempts, mostly failed, to convert Muslims and Jews to Christ, the modern age began. Britain in 1917 accepted the *status quo* in the old city, freezing the Jewish, Christian, Armenian and Muslim land holdings where they were. Israel, after 1967, was more flexible. This took Albert back to Jerusalem's first hotel, the St John Hospice, where I had watched settler children staring through wire mesh at the Arab world below them. 'The settlers got in through the protected tenant,' he said, 'who unfortunately was an Armenian.'

He dropped his pipe in an ashtray and jumped up to find a book. Then another. He handed them to me. One was Robert Friedman's *Zealots for Zion* and the other Dilip Hiro's *Sharing the Promised Land*. 'Look on page ninety-nine,' he said, pointing at the Friedman book. There it said that an Armenian named Martyros Matossian had received $3.5 million to assign his family's protected tenancy in the hospice to a group of Israeli settlers. The Hiro book, on page twenty-two, made the same allegation, but said Matossian, who then fled the country, received $5 million.

Albert explained that most of the property in the Christian Quarter belonged to the churches – with the Greek Orthodox owning most. 'For example,' he said, 'my mother has leased her house from the Greek Orthodox Patriarchate since 1932. The leases are with local tenants, and tens of people in a family could have shares in the same house. The settlers find the one who needs money. They ask him to sell his room in the house. Then they elbow their way in.' Albert knew families who had settlers in one cramped bedroom of their house. 'If there is an explosion,' he said, meaning a Palestinian bomb targeting Israelis anywhere, 'the settlers will get angry and beat everyone in the house. They go on the rooftop and pee in the water tank.'

The old city settlers were, for the most part, extremely religious. 'Traditionally, the Jewish religious establishment opposed Zionism,' Albert said. 'Ben-Gurion told them, we have a state and it must be based on the rule of law. We have conscription. We have state education. We have public transport on Saturday. The money we receive is for all the Jewish people. You must reach an accord with us. And they did. It was the new *status quo*.' The religious establishment, who believed Jewish nationalism contradicted the centrality of Jewish faith, arrived at a mode of co-existing with the state. The religious were exempt from military service. They sent their children to religious, rather than secular state, schools. Public transport did not trespass in their neighbourhoods on the Sabbath. They took a share of government expenditure to disburse among their own as they saw fit.

'From 1948 to 1967,' Albert recalled, 'the father of Avraham Burg, the speaker of the Knesset . . . his father, Yossef Burg, was the longest-serving Knesset member. As head of the National Religious Party, he served in all of Israel's governments. He did not get involved in Israeli politics. Instead, he represented religious interests. It created a strange relationship. He used your money to attack you, the government. After 1967, a completely new relationship emerged.' The religious colleges, the Yeshivas, developed a new theology and, with it, a new politics. 'Their interpretation was original. For the first time, they said, we now have Hebron. We have Jerusalem. This means we are living in Messianic times. Our mission is to redeem the land. This line of reasoning surfaced in 1972 in Hebron when the Gush Emunim grabbed its first settlement.'

Gush Emunim, Bloc of the Faithful, settled in a Hebron hotel. To persuade them to leave the centre of the Arab city, the Labour government allowed them to establish Kiryat Arba on a hill it confiscated above Hebron. 'After Kiryat Arba, the religious settlements began to proliferate, like amoebae, under different names: Ne'vot David at St John's, El Ad and the rest. These are now the people who are holding the government by the balls.' The settlers had also returned to Hebron, where they regularly abused and attacked the Arab inhabitants. One of them, Baruch Goldstein, had shot and killed twenty-nine men in the Grand Mosque.

Albert showed me one of the settlers' slogans, in English, on that most American of political advertising media, the bumper sticker: 'G*d is a religious Zionist.' He laid some of their literature, booklets and pamphlets on the table. There were biblical passages from Genesis, Exodus, Deuteronomy and Joshua on ridding the land of Canaanites and Philistines. 'I predict,' Albert said, as if sermonizing from a pulpit, 'that within ten years, the religious will take over the army.' The army, in Albert's view, was already leading the country. Sharon remained more soldier than politician. His tanks and helicopters swarmed all over the West Bank and Gaza, but he did not know how to pass a budget. 'This is a government that serves the army,' he said. 'How far can this go?'

From time to time during my stay in Jerusalem I would stop by Madeleine's kitchen. It was no accident that my visits often coincided with lunch. She cooked well, and her food was the closest to Lebanese in Jerusalem. Neither the Palestinians nor the Israelis were great cooks, but the Lebanese and Armenians were. Among the Armenians, Madeleine Agazarian was one of the best. I understood why Albert and the children lunched at home almost every day. It was rare that I was the only guest. Sometimes, George Hultunian was there in a tattered cardigan. Often, women of the Armenian Quarter or further afield appeared. There were occasional academics and journalists, but I never saw a priest.

During one lunch, the women were talking about 'the settler'. There were so many settlers in old Jerusalem that I did not know why they singled out this particular man. Madeleine and one of her friends had seen wives of the Arab labourers who had worked for him restoring his old house. They were standing outside his door, begging for their husbands' unpaid wages. One of them had a small baby. '*Haram*,' one of the Armenian women said. Pity. I asked what was going on, and Albert said it was not important. I pressed the women, and they told me the story.

'The settler' was an American, who had taken a house on Ararat Street next to St Mark's Syrian Orthodox Church. It was at the edge of the Armenian Quarter, not far from Habad Street in the Jewish Quarter. The house he took needed work, and he hired Arabs to do it. When the time came to pay them, he replaced them with other workers. The labourers demanded their wages, and he ignored them. They were afraid to tell the police. Arabs from the occupied territories could not approach the authorities without being arrested themselves for working without permits. Their wives went to the settler's house to shame him. But, the women said, he refused to give them any money. It was the scandal of the Armenian Quarter, and no one had the power to make the settler pay.

In the evening, I walked from Armenian Patriarchate Road into St James's Road, a footpath too narrow for cars. At the Ararat Grocery, I asked the way to St Mark's. 'That's my church,' the young man behind the counter said, not without pride. There were a few hundred Syrian Orthodox in Jerusalem, and he was one. He took me outside, and under the feeble lamps of the ancient city carefully pointed the way. Passing under the arches, the vaults and sky, I found the Church, no larger than a small chapel, of St Mark. Behind it, extending in a graceful curve over the lane, was the house of the American settler. I recognized it by the new, unfinished cement steps built by the unpaid workers. A ramp, with two-by-fours nailed to it, led to the front door. This was where the neighbours said the workmen's wives had stood crying and begging for the money their husbands had earned. I went to the door, but no one was home. What was I going to say? Would I tell him, American to American, to pay the men? Or would I ask him for his side of the story? Taking a man's labour without paying him was slavery, and we had fought a civil war over that.

The Room Down

Next door in St Mark's Church I met the remarkable Sister Yostina al-Banna. An orthodox nun from Nineveh, which she called 'the great city of Jonah', she had three brothers who were priests. One of the three, George Yusuf al-Banna, taught geology at a university in Portland, Oregon. The second lived in Jordan, and the third was still in Nineveh. Sister Yostina had left Iraq, homeland of most Syrian Orthodox, little more than a year before.

'This is the first church in Christianity,' she said, making it one of the many first churches I have seen. The early Christians had no churches. They gathered in synagogues and, when uncircumcised Gentiles were admitted to their communities, in one another's houses. They gave themselves the name Christian at Antioch, where I visited a cave in 1987 that also claimed the distinction of first church. The Turks had turned it into a museum. St Mark's was still a church.

Sister Yostina said St Mark's, built in AD 37, had been destroyed three times. 'The first time was in 71, when the King Titus come to this city and destroy Jerusalem. Everything high, he cut it. The twelfth century was the last time.' The nun, like the church itself, was old and small. But, also like the church, warm and welcoming. She showed me an Aramaic inscription that she said had been discovered in 1940. Aramaic, or Syriac, was the language of Palestine, spoken by Jews as well as Gentiles, at the time of Christ. The Syrian Orthodox still used it for their liturgy, as Lebanon's Catholic Maronites did until Vatican II instructed them to use the vernacular. She said of the inscription, 'It's old, fifteen hundred years old. It is written in Aramaic, the language of Jesus, from right to left.' Then she translated it: 'This is the house of St Mark's mother, who was chosen of Christ from the Apostles.'

St Mark's mother, Mary, lived in the house below the church. That was the legend. If true, it was where St Peter took refuge when the angel helped him out of prison. The church was a museum of Christian legends. 'In the upper room of the house down [down meant the levels below the church itself], Jesus made the Last Supper,' she told me, adding another astonishing detail, 'and, also, the washing of the feet.' The Virgin Mary, she believed, was baptized here; although the New Testament did not mention her baptism. There were more stories, not all of which I understood.

Sister Yostina said, 'Jesus sent St Peter and St John. He told them, "You shall enter the city Jerusalem, and you shall see a man carrying a jar." In those days, only women carry jar. This was the miracle from God. St Mark went and stand and carry a jar. And they follow Him until He reach the house of his mother. So, they prepare for Him the upper room of the house down.' That was not all. 'After the cross, the Apostles with the Virgin Mary were afraid. They don't know where they can go. They are strange in this city, so they turn back to the house of St Mark's mother. They remain three days, until Jesus appear to them, after He be in this life, after three days.'

Sister Yostina knew the story well. In fact, she knew all the stories. 'Before Jesus rise to heaven, He asked the Apostles to remain here, not to leave this city until He sent for the Holy

112

Spirit to be strong. After ten days only after Jesus rise, the Apostles with the Virgin Mary, with Mark's mother, with those around them, they recognize the Holy Spirit in the upper room of the house down. Because of that, they choose to be the first church in Christianity.'

When I walked into the tiny square chapel, through its arched door, I had not suspected that it was anything more than another of the city's many churches for another of its un-countable sects. If it harboured evidence for half of what Sister Yostina believed, the site was at least as important as the larger and grander Church of the Holy Sepulchre hundreds of yards to the north. The wonders the aged Syriac nun revealed to me were, however, only beginning. 'We have the first baptism for a baby in Christianity down,' she said. 'Only four years after Jesus rise, they complete the building of this church. Because the house down belong to St Mark's mother, they call this church a second name, St Mark's Church. But, as a first name, the Virgin Mary Church. Today, we say the Church of the Virgin Mary in the Monastery of St James.' She led me through the church to a cloth on the wall behind the baptismal font. 'What is important now,' she said, 'is you shall see the real face of Jesus and the real face of the Virgin Mary, as St Luke painted in the first century on a skin of deer. St Luke was one of those who wrote the New Bible, one of those Apostles who remained with Jesus three years. So, he saw Him as a young man. St Luke was a painter.'

She raised the cloth. The painting, so far as I could see it in the church's penumbra, was a stylized, Byzantine prototype for all Madonna and infant portraits. Raphael had rendered his own beautiful version of St Luke painting Mary and the baby Jesus, based upon the legend that Sister Yostina believed. 'When he tried to paint Jesus as a child with his mother,' Sister Yostina explained, 'he painted His face as a young man, because he saw Him as a young man.' It was true. The face was not an infant's, but a mature, suffering man's face on the child's body. It was unnatural, allowing for the already anti-naturalist context of icon-like two dimensions. No child sat for this portrait, as in Raphael's presentation.

'What is important,' Sister Yostina said, 'is God allowed many miracles to happen here with the Virgin Mary. The last miracle happened here in November 2000.' She told me the story of an Anglican priest, who visited the church. He was suffering, she said, from prostate cancer. He sat for three hours contemplating St Luke's portrait. She swore that he left the church cured. To prove her point, she showed me a letter from the Reverend John R. P. Ashby of Eastbourne in East Sussex, in which he attested to the miraculous preservation of his life.

Fr Jerome Murphy-O'Connor's scholarship in *The Holy Land* questioned the authenticity of this ancient Christian relic. 'The painting is in fact very old,' Fr Jerry wrote, 'but does not antedate the Byzantine period.' That period began with the Emperor Constantine's establishment of his capital in Byzantium, or Constantinople, in AD 300 and the legalization of the Christian religion in AD 313. St Luke would have been dead for at least two hundred years when *The Virgin Mary from Life* was painted. Fr Jerry, however, did not dismiss the 'extraordinary number of traditions' associated with the church, which gave 'a sense of identity and pride to one of the smallest Christian communities in Jerusalem'.

Sister Yostina was nothing other than proud when she announced, 'We shall go down to the upper room.' I was uncertain, as if I were following Vincent Price into the pit to see the pendulum. The hidden stone stairway twisted down towards, not a dungeon of horror, but an ancient storeroom of wonders. In a descent of twenty feet, we shed twenty centuries to see where Christ may have eaten the Passover supper from which the Eucharist was born. If not the Cenacle itself, it was at least a contemporary whose now-subterranean windows may have witnessed some event of the Saviour's last days on earth. The final step brought us to the firm floor of the upper room. Luckily, Disney had not discovered the site and placed a faux Last Supper table with animated wax figurines of the Apostles breaking bread. The room was empty, apart from a chair and a small altar. 'The first Bishop of Jerusalem sat on this chair,' Sister Yostina said, 'after Jesus rise. It was James, Jesus's brother.' The altar, she said, contained many holy relics. There was not much to do or see in the tiny room where so many miracles may have taken place, so she took me down another level.

There was, if anything, less to see further down than above: a stone bowl 'for the first baptism for a baby in Christianity', a large clay jug, a wooden crutch and an icon of St Catherine. 'St Catherine,' Sister Yostina said, 'lived in the fourth century. She wrote a book in Aramaic about the house of St Marco's mother and about the Last Supper.' I was not sure why St Mark became St Marco downstairs, but I listened without asking. 'This big jar,' she said, tapping the ancient clay. 'We don't know this jar from which century, but St Mark carried a jar and the Apostles know him.' She told me about the crutch. 'Before seven months, a lady came from France. She told me she want to marry, but no one want to marry her because of her bad leg. She sat in front of the icon for three hours. She said the icon became the Virgin Mary. Then, no more problem in her leg. She threw that crutch.' There it lay, where the lady from France had left it.

Many Roman Catholics, even some Muslim women, sought help from the Virgin at St Mark's. I hoped that the wives of the workers next door would try the same thing. Raising the dead, however, was nothing compared to making an American racist pay the wages he owed.

Hitch-hikers and Taxis

An Israeli taxi driver who was taking me to the American Colony Hotel in East Jerusalem said that the man in his back seat, wearing a black fedora above a face full of hair, was one of about 15,000 Orthodox Jews returning from Ukraine. They had gone to the tomb of Rebbe Nachmun. 'It's the Jewish New

Year,' the driver explained. The man in the back seat did not speak English and paid us no attention. 'God writes the names of those who are for life and those who are for death. These people,' the driver was referring to the black hats like the man in the back, 'pray to the Rebbe to ask God not to put them for death.' The way the year was shaping up, I wished I'd asked Rebbe Nachmun for his intercession. We talked about the military action in Afghanistan. The driver was all for attacks and invasion: 'America has to show the world who is the boss.'

I wasn't showing anyone who was boss. I'd agreed to give a lift to the Hasid in the back seat; and I assented again when the driver, as secular a man as any I'd seen in Israel, asked whether we might drop this other passenger first. There turned out to be one difficulty: the man did not know where he lived. He had an address of a small flat in a side street near Agudat Israel Road in a religious quarter of Jerusalem. The driver made a strenuous effort to find it. The man in the back was no help, holding a piece of paper with the address in Hebrew to the driver's face each time he asked for more details. The driver stopped another Hasid, who'd been taking an evening stroll, and asked if he knew the address. It seemed he did, because he jumped into the back seat next to his fellow believer and barked directions in a high, excited voice. We were in the depths of the religious quarter. The newcomer told the driver to stop. He and the first Hasid exchanged a few words that indicated we had reached the place. They got out. The first one took his suitcase and paid the driver, while the second, with a farewell, ran into an alley.

'These people,' the driver said, 'they never go out, so how can they know how to find their way home?'

I said that there were many men out walking.

'At night. But all day, they stay inside studying the Torah.'

Another Jerusalem taxi driver told me, 'I was in the paratroops. For thirty-three years. I was in the '67 war, the '73 war, the '82 war. I was at Karameh in '68. I was in Lebanon in '78. I believe this war will never end. Never. Not for three thousand years. And what are you Americans doing in Afghanistan?

Afghanistan is not enough. America must bomb Iraq and Iran.' The respected president of the Hebrew University, Rabbi Judah Magnes, had said in 1947, 'If I do not want a Jewish state, it is because I do not want perpetual war with the Arabs.'

An Interrupted Lunch

A cafeteria defiantly calling itself Quick Lunch in Zahara Street was known for its home-cooked Arab food. Quick it was not. It lay just outside the old city walls in the midst of Arab Jerusalem's commercial area. The owner, a smiling old woman whom everyone called Khaltie – My Aunt – told us, as my Lebanese great-aunts did – what to eat. Four of us crowded into a booth to eat vine leaves stuffed with rice, pine nuts and morsels of lamb; boiled rice with a stew of okra; and pans of *kibbeh be-saniah* – a purée of minced lamb, cracked wheat, onion and spices roasted in the oven. The customers were working people. The food came at disconnected intervals, and conversation around us was high-decibel. The Arabic news, from a radio on a shelf near the kitchen, announced that three men had just fired automatic rifles at the Khadera bus station in Jerusalem. The restaurant went silent. The radio said two people died before the three gunmen were killed. Khaltie turned up the volume, so everyone could hear. Her cooks stopped work.

'Why,' Khaltie asked, 'do they have to choose civilians?'

The radio had news of another killing: a drive-by shooting of an Israeli on the way to his kibbutz. The news came from Voice of Israel's Arabic service. It did not mention, as the BBC did later, that Israeli forces were conducting military operations in the West Bank to find and punish the assassins of tourism minister Rehavam Ze'evi. Palestinians killed five Israelis that day. That was news. Israel's killing of more Palestinians in the occupied territories was not. At Quick Lunch, where all the staff and customers were Palestinian, the murder of Israeli civilians prompted no rejoicing. The men and women ate their food

without a word. What had been a noisy working-class restaurant went as silent as a church. There was little connection
between the people and the armed struggle. In fact, many Palestinians said, the leaders had launched an armed struggle when
the people themselves were taking power into their own hands
during the first *intifadah* of 1987 with civil disobedience, mass
demonstrations and stone throwing. Yasser Arafat, and even
Hamas, knew that some of those stones were meant for them.
On both sides, it was a dirty war.

The militant Islamic Jihad group claimed that its fighters had
shot up the bus stop at Khadera. If the murderers had brought
the Palestinians a day closer to independence or led the Israeli
government to any action other than military retaliation that
took Palestinian lives, an excuse might have been contrived. But
there was no excuse. There was no strategy. There was no
leadership. There was no hope.

FIVE

O, No, Jerusalem!

'They have disfigured the neighbourhood of Jerusalem,
and threatened the rest of the land, with rival sanctuaries,
planted side by side as even at Gethsemane.'
REVEREND GEORGE ADAM SMITH
The Historical Geography of the Holy Land (1894)

Peace for Sale

JERUSALEM THE ANGEL'S HORN called from the summit of
Judaea's hills to mystics, seers, lunatics, killers, weapons dealers,
scholars and, most dangerous of all, those selling visions of
peace for the Promised Land. Daniel Lubitzky was one of the
last. Lubitzky described himself as a self-made multimillionaire.
A Mexican Jew, he ran a company in New York called Peace
Works. At dinner in Al Pasha, an outdoor Arab restaurant near
the American Colony, he outlined to Andrew and Emma
Gilmour and me his scheme to negotiate a statement of principles between Palestinian Arabs and Israeli Jews via email, the
internet and the newspapers. He would invite as many Israelis
and Palestinians as possible to compose and refine a letter of
agreed principles so that the maximum number could sign.
Armed with the letter, each side would pressure its leaders to
resolve the dispute along its lines. Virtual peacemaking. Lubit-
sky, who spoke Spanish, Hebrew and English, did not seem as
moronic as his plan.

Lubitzky was trying to persuade Lily Habash, an intelligent
young woman from Ramallah whose family had been forced
out of Lydda in 1948, to work for him. Lily had already assisted

119

in the establishment of the NSU, Negotiation Support Unit. The NSU's young, Western-raised Palestinian lawyers and techno-crats provided expertise to match Israel's. During the 1993 Oslo talks, only the Israeli negotiators brought maps and lawyers. The Palestinians had been sent by Yasser Arafat without either. The NSU attempted to redress the balance in post-Oslo talks on implementation.

No one listened to them. One NSU volunteer, a Yale-educated lawyer, told me he had once passed a note to Ahmed Querei, Nadia Sartawi's boss, during a meeting with the Israelis. The note contained pertinent data to support the Palestinian argu-ment. Querei, also called Abu Ala, refused to read it. Later, he warned the young lawyer, 'Never do that again.' To Abu Ala, taking advice from a younger man meant loss of face. To the lawyer, a negotiating team was just that – a group that mar-shalled its members' knowledge to win the best agreement. Abu Ala would no more admit in front of his adversaries that there was something he did not know than Yasser Arafat would have sought advice from Abu Ala. That ubiquitous picture of the father, the chief of the tribe, stared not only from the walls but from within. The young lawyer quit the NSC.

'It's hard,' Lily Habash said, while Lubitzky pitched his peace plan to the UN through a somewhat sceptical Andrew Gilmour. 'It's hard to keep good people, when the best are hired away for more money by foreign NGOs and foreign companies. They leave, not only for the money, but because the PA ignores them.' PA ministers treated them like expensive pets. They would brag that they had Harvard MBAs, Yale law grads and scientists from MIT working for them. But they did not listen to them. The idealistic Canadian and American Arabs arrived from exile with an innocent faith in their country and left disgusted with its leaders.

Lily Habash's pay was so low that she listened politely to Lubitzky's offer. He would more than triple her salary. This was her first night out of Ramallah in a month. Curfews and endless delays at the Israeli checkpoints had, until this evening, kept her at home. After dinner, she would wait for more than an hour for a taxi willing to drive her to the last Israeli checkpoint. From there, she, like all other Palestinians, would be searched before walking to the other side. Then, she would have to find another taxi to take her home or she would walk. A few days later, she told me, she turned Lubitzky down.

The BBC World Service's morning news reported that Pakistan's President, aka General, Pervez Musharraf, promised Afghans 'a broad-based multi-ethnic government representing the contours of Afghanistan freely chosen by the Afghans without outside interference'. No outside interference, apart from the American armed forces. At the same time, Israeli prime minister Ariel Sharon told an audience at Kiryat Motzkim what kind of Palestinian state he could accept. The man who, as an army officer and later as minister of defence in Menachem Begin's government, had proposed turning Jordan into the Palestinian state, was now willing to let the Palestinians govern themselves, albeit on his terms, in parts of Palestine. Sharon's Palestinian state would be 'demilitarized, Israel will control its border passages and it won't be allowed to enter into treaties with states hostile to Israel'. Although the Sharon concept of a Palestinian state was no state at all, his minister of tourism, Rehavam Ze'evi, and the development minister, the Russian Avigdor Liebermann, resigned from the governing coalition to protest against giving the Palestinians anything. Denouncing their resignations in the Knesset, Sharon accused Ze'evi and Liebermann of treason. Ze'evi, another former general but with an undistinguished war record, had said of the Palestinians, 'Let them go to Mecca.' He had also called them 'cockroaches'. The day after Sharon condemned his treason, Ze'evi was assassinated.

Two young Palestinians found Ze'evi in his room at the Hyatt Hotel, part of which lay in territory occupied in 1967, and shot him dead. They fled in a rented car. The security forces sealed the hotel and interrogated its employees. Many of the staff happened to be Arab. That was in the early morning. Within a few hours, Israel knew who had killed Ze'evi and why. It was not so much police work as the fact that the Popular Front for the Liberation of Palestine in Damascus claimed that it assassinated Ze'evi in response to Israel's assassination of its leader, Abu Ali Mustafa. At four in the afternoon, Sharon blamed Yasser Arafat for Ze'evi's death. (While Sharon was still accusing Ze'evi of treason in the Knesset, Arafat had been travelling from London to The Hague to ask Europe to redress America's unconditional and lavish generosity to Israel.) The Israeli Defence Forces closed all roads, except those between the settlements, in the West Bank. The search for the PFLP assassins, despite the blame Sharon heaped on their rival Arafat, was on.

Ze'evi, who consistently urged his government to expel all Arabs from the land of Israel, was known to his army comrades as Gandhi.

Do-gooders

The Knight's Palace, in the Christian Quarter on Latin Patriarchate Road, was a pilgrim hostel with clean rooms and kind staff. Swedish Protestants were sponsoring a meeting on 'The Current Situation – An Assessment' in a basement reception room. The featured speaker was none other than Albert Agazarian.

Albert looked dapper in a grey suit with pressed white shirt and solid tie. His hair and goatee had been trimmed the day before at Abu Majed's barber shop in the Christian Quarter, where I too had my hair cut. His lecture, from notes, began, 'Okay, I accept that you were in a burning building and had to jump.' Many Israelis used the burning building as a symbol for the Nazi Holocaust. They had not meant to hurt the Palestinians upon whom they landed. 'Okay. You jumped and, when you fell on top of me, you broke my neck. Okay, I can accept that. But why do you have to go on breaking my ribs, my legs, my arms? For every bone after the neck, you are responsible.'

He said Israel's leaders declined to recognize that the Palestinians too had a history. Israel dictated the framework of dialogue between the two sides, and it was not a discussion between equals. The only rights Palestinians had were those that Israel granted. 'If there are masters and servants,' Albert said, 'at least the servants have quarters where they can eat.' The masters had taken, and were still reducing, the servants' space. Since the Olso accords, the settler population had doubled to more than 200,000 in the West Bank plus another 170,000 in Arab East Jerusalem that Israel had annexed in 1967. The Israeli budget for the year 2000 had set aside twenty-seven million shekels for settler by-pass roads in the occupied territories and up to two hundred and sixteen million shekels for land confiscation. 'This leads to apartheid and control. Apartheid was much better than this. In South Africa, you could drive for two days without seeing a roadblock. It is impossible here to drive more than five miles in any direction without hitting an Israeli roadblock. In South Africa, there was no collective punishment.'

For the seven years of the Oslo order, the Palestinian leadership cooperated with the Israeli police and army on security. 'Maybe it was necessary for confidence building,' Albert said. 'The question is, at what price? Just to give certain individuals' – he meant Arafat's senior officials – 'rights of passage? The Palestinian Authority has been treated as a junior, reserve branch of the Border Police. When Sharon went to the mosque, people said, "No. This is not the deal." If there is no reference to internationally accepted rules, we have a problem, and what a problem we have.'

A woman named Nora Cort, whom I had interviewed ten years earlier for a BBC television documentary based on Said Aburish's *The Forgotten Faithful*, stood up to speak. A friend of hers had died a few days before in Ramallah. The Israelis would not allow her to drive from Jerusalem on the direct road through the Kalandia refugee camp to pay condolences to the family. She tried another route, driving down to the desert via Jericho and up again through the Judaean hills to approach

Ramallah from the other side. Despite an extra two hours' drive, she was again not admitted to Ramallah. She changed the subject: 'I remember when [the assassinated tourism minister] Rehavam Ze'evi said on television, "You Palestinians are like cockroaches".'

A Swedish woman of a certain age rambled through vague notions of love and peacemaking without asking a question. She ended, 'I've worked among Jews and Arabs. You need to be sensitive. Israeli kids have been blown up. Israeli leaders have been assassinated.' She sat down. 'We Palestinians,' Albert answered, 'should never underestimate what the Jewish people have gone through in the Holocaust. The Israelis must recognize the havoc they have caused in the lives of the Palestinians. I do not underestimate what the Israelis have gone through, with buses blown up and people killed. But this is the effect. What is the cause?'

Later, by the fountain in the American Colony courtyard, an American told me what he had seen the day before outside the village of Beit Rima. A former journalist, he was working for the United Nations. A convoy of ambulances had taken him there to evacuate Arabs wounded by Israeli gunfire. 'I begged the Israeli soldiers to let us in, but they wouldn't.'

Why not?

'They're like the American army. They don't give reasons. Their commanding officer came over, and it was chilling. He said we didn't need to go in because there weren't any wounded.' My friend, a former colleague who had once filed reports on similar scenes, said that the officer was telling him that, one way or another, all the wounded Palestinians in Beit Rima were dead. The Israeli soldiers left the village. 'They marched their guys out instead of putting them in troop carriers.' Better pictures, he guessed. The cameras and the journalists, like the ambulances, were not allowed inside to see what had happened in Beit Rima. Rehavam Ze'evi was avenged.

The Producer

Abu Dis was a suburb of Jerusalem, an unfinished Palestinian new town that had been elevated to a potential capital – a pseudo-Jerusalem – of the potential state of Palestine. Past an Israeli checkpoint, beyond blocks of semi-constructed breeze-block shops and houses, in the centre of Abu Dis, the village's largest uncompleted structure loomed over all the others. Its twelve or so storeys of unclad concrete made it tall enough to attract attention, but not impressive enough to hold the eye for long. Rumour had it that it would be Palestine's new parliament. The Palestinian Authority, in characteristic form, would not say what it was or when it would be finished. When I drove past it in my rusty car rented from the Palestinian Dalla Company, no one was working on the site. Bags of cement, blocks of wood and stacks of iron rods hinted that builders might return. I had been instructed to drive to a smaller office building to meet Nadia Sartawi's employer, Ahmed Querei. Querei was born in Abu Dis in 1936, the year the Palestinians launched their first *intifadah* against British rule and unlimited European Jewish immigration. As speaker of the Palestinian Legislative Council, he had opened an office in his home town when Israeli closures made travel impossible between Abu Dis and the PA offices in Ramallah. Although I had known or interviewed most of the Palestinian leaders from the time I moved to Beirut in 1972 until they left ten years later, I had not heard of Querei. Abu Ala, Querei's *nom de bataille*, won his fame as Arafat's representative at the secret conference in Oslo in 1993. He was not a lawyer, not a diplomat, not a freedom fighter and, from any reading of the Oslo accords, not much of a negotiator. He was, before he joined Yasser Arafat's Al Fatah in Jordan in 1968, a banker.

His was a banker's office, name on the door, new carpet on the floor. There were two types of Palestinian politicians' offices: those that were slick, modern and well-furnished with computers and well-dressed secretaries, where the civilized ambience reassured American diplomats; and the others, like the old PLO offices in Beirut, at the top of dark, dirty concrete stairs, with posters of Che Guevara or Palestinian martyrs, broken wooden desks, telephones that sometimes functioned, masses of mimeographed position papers, records of Israeli war crimes, ashtrays that were sometimes empty but never clean and lots of chairs for refugees, widows and other supplicants.

An assistant guided me from an anteroom to Abu Ala's inner sanctum. Querei stood behind his desk to shake hands and offered me a chair. Would I like coffee or tea? I felt as if I had come to ask for an overdraft. The first thing I asked was about his mortgage on Palestinian lives and livelihoods, the Oslo accords. 'I don't think the reason things went wrong is the Oslo agreement,' the Oslo negotiator said. 'The problem is the implementation of the agreement.'

At the time of the agreement and of its White House photo opportunity, Edward Said had warned that Oslo could not benefit the Palestinians or lead to their independence, as the word is normally understood, in the West Bank and Gaza Strip. Said blamed Arafat for betraying the people he claimed to lead and dismissed Abu Ala as a nonentity. As Said and others had predicted, Oslo allowed Israeli settlements to absorb more Palestinian land. Was the problem implementation or the agreement itself?

Abu Ala would not utter a *mea culpa*. 'Each Israeli prime minister,' he said, 'had his own interpretation. Rabin implemented the agreements.' This was how the PLO cut itself loose from the consequences of Oslo: all went well until an Israeli extremist named Yigal Amir assassinated Yitzak Rabin in 1995. The excuse did not stand up. 'Rabin delayed withdrawing troops from parts of the West Bank,' I said, 'and he expanded the settlements.' Rabin's Labour government had seized thousands of Palestinian acres for settlements, settler roads and army bases to protect both.

Abu Ala shrugged and tapped a cigarillo on the lip of an

ashtray. 'Then we had Shimon Peres, Benyamin Netanyahu, then Barak, now Sharon. Put these five prime ministers there, and see the contradictions. I believe Rabin and Peres were honest. Likud voted against Oslo, and Netanyahu said he would renegotiate it. Barak put in only the parts of Oslo that he wanted. Sharon doesn't want any of it.' He accused Rabin's successors of bad faith and of violating the Oslo agreements. He said they had brushed aside Oslo's timetable for withdrawing Israeli troops from parts of the West Bank and Gaza. Worse, he said, was 'the second, very dangerous violation of Israel's expansion of settlements and by-pass roads and new settlements'. While correct about the scheduled withdrawals, he was wrong on settlements. Having read the accords when they were published, I told him that they did not prohibit Israel from building new settlements and increasing the size of old ones. Doubling the number of settlers between 1994 and 2001 may have been illegal under international law, but it did not breach Oslo. He disagreed. If I had been requesting an overdraft, it would not have been forthcoming. I asked to see the agreement. My copy, all two kilograms of it, was in London. He called an assistant into the office and told him to find the Oslo accords.

'The third violation,' he said, 'was that in the third year of the interim period' – that would have been in 1997, when Benyamin Netanyahu had succeeded Shimon Peres – 'we were to discuss the future of the settlements, Jerusalem and other outstanding issues, whether the settlements were to remain, be dismantled or whatever.'

Abu Ala's assistant opened the door and said they had no copies of the accords. There might be some, he speculated, in the Ramallah office. Abu Ala promised to send me one at the American Colony Hotel. (It would be six weeks and twenty reminders before a box arrived at the Colony containing the 'historic' agreement that Abu Ala and his colleagues had negotiated in Norway.) We talked more about the settlements. 'Look here at Ma'ale Adumim,' he said of the massive urban complex that I had passed on my way to Abu Dis. 'It is tripled from

127

1994. This is a violation of the agreement.' I repeated that it was not a violation, but we would have to see the document itself. He complained of the 'by-pass' roads between the settlements. These modern highways that Palestinians were not permitted to use had eaten up acre after acre of Palestinian orchards and farms. Again, he said the roads were prohibited under Oslo. I insisted that Oslo specifically permitted the roads to secure the safe passage of settlers through areas from which the Israeli army was meant to withdraw.

'The last serious violation,' he added, 'is the continued mentality of the occupier: closures, the resort to military power, assassinations.' I did not doubt that the mentality of occupation had remained constant post-Oslo, but, again, it did not violate any section of the agreements. Was Abu Ala really surprised? 'No doubt, I was not expecting it to go on this way. I thought that their need for security and our need for peace would work together, but this is not the case.' Perhaps he should have read Menachem Begin's memoir, *The Revolt*, that said it was a strategic error to assume your enemy will behave humanely.

The process of which Abu Ala had been an integral part had failed. This was what the United States called 'the' peace process, thus – as Noam Chomsky wrote at the time – excluding all other initiatives, whether by the United Nations, the European Union or anyone else. By equating peace with Oslo, to the exclusion of all else, its failure meant there could be no peace. For seven years Abu Ala and his Israeli 'peace partners' had pretended the problems were solved and the conflict had ended. The Palestinian Authority did its part, albeit inefficiently, in arresting – and sometimes torturing and executing – Palestinian opponents of the Oslo version of peace. The Palestine Liberation Organization became the Palestinian Authority, a pseudo-government under Israeli suzerainty that had nominal governance of patches of the West Bank and Gaza called by the Oslo accords A Area enclaves. B Areas were under Israeli military and Palestine Authority civil rule, while the C Areas were run directly by the Israelis. It was a mess, more unstable than the

Bantustan arrangement that South Africa's apartheid rulers attempted to impose on the black majority. The phoney peace collapsed at the end of September 2000. Abu Ala's Israeli 'partners' – how absurd this terminology sounded even then – said that Yasser Arafat and the rest of the Palestinians rejected peace and embraced war when they turned down prime minister Ehud Barak's 'generous' offer. Barak's defenders alleged that during President Clinton's Camp David conference in August 2000, Barak offered Arafat 95 per cent of the West Bank and all of the Gaza Strip. Why did he say no to the best offer Israel had ever made and was ever likely to make?

'First of all,' Abu Ala said, 'why 95 per cent? Why not 100 per cent? Why not UN Resolution 242, which rejects occupation by force? Why, if you want to implement the Resolution, do you offer only 95 per cent?' Abu Ala was leaning forward, elbows on desk and cigarillo at full smoke. In the year since Camp David, he must have heard my question a hundred times and stayed up nights thinking about it. Had the great negotiator really said no to ending the occupation of 95 per cent of the West Bank?

'Barak offered 91 per cent,' he said. 'And he was going to swap another 1 per cent near Gaza, giving 92 per cent. That's what he said. But, at Camp David, Latrun and the areas around the Dead Sea and Jerusalem were not included. The real offer was less than 83 per cent.'

While we spoke, Israel had 100 per cent. Its forces were besieging Ramallah, Qalqilya, Tulkarm, Nablus and Bethlehem. They had Hebron under curfew. Soon, they would invade most of the West Bank cities, pulling in and out of them as Ariel Sharon directed. The IDF controlled all movement to and from, as well as within, the Gaza Strip. Fear of Israeli bombardment, claustrophobia, malnutrition and hunger were depriving Palestine of its most precious asset: people. Many were going to Jordan or, if they could afford it, even further afield. Those who found spouses and work there would not return. Some time later, Israel's former air force commander Eitan ben Eliah

129

would tell Israel Radio's Channel Two that 'we have to step up [Jewish] immigration immediately and in some way also thin out the number of Arabs here'. The thinning out was under way.

I asked whether Abu Ala, who was on good terms with much of the Israeli Labour Party, had met Sharon. 'Four or five times,' he said. What were his impressions? 'He's deep. It's not easy to see what he wants. Because he is a soldier, he believes that what he thinks will be imposed. The problem with Sharon is that he came without a political programme.'

What did he make of Sharon's son, Omri, who had been acting as his father's emissary to the Palestinians?

'I met him once,' he said, 'in a long meeting. He's polite, but he needs more experience.' People said the opposite of the father. Why had Sharon sent his son rather than his foreign minister, Shimon Peres, or an official from his Likud Party? 'I think he has no other choice. I think Omri has influence with his father, more than anyone else.' It may have been that tribal chiefs preferred family contacts to institutions. If so, Sharon and Arafat had something in common.

Abu Ala missed his Labour Party friends, although they had made what he called the less-than-83 per cent offer at Camp David, expanded settlements, allowed Sharon to promenade in the Haram ash-Sharif and sparked the *intifadah*. He still spoke to them on the telephone. 'They are sad,' he said. 'This is not the situation they expected. I mean Yossi Beilin, Shlomo Ben Ami and Avraham Burg. Avraham Burg and I went together to the European Parliament. He's a good man. He has a vision. He believed security cannot be made without peace with the Palestinians.'

Behind Abu Ala on the otherwise bare wall was a mounted colour poster, like an old movie billboard, of Jerusalem's Haram ash-Sharif complex with the golden Dome of the Rock twinkling in the morning sky. Abu Ala reminded me of a Hollywood producer, surrounded by well-groomed assistants and telephones and cigars, who just couldn't get a film made any more. After the flops at Oslo and Camp David, he was no longer bankable. He went through the daily routine of putting scripts into development and calling actors' agents about the next project, but the stars themselves and the big money boys did not return his calls.

'Yesterday,' he told me, 'I had a big interview in the *Ma'ariv*.' *Ma'ariv* was a Hebrew daily, to the right of *Ha'aretz* and less populist than *Yediot Ahranot*. 'Many Israelis called me and said it's very good.'

Outside, in a new, dusty street of Abu Dis, I bumped into an acquaintance from the PLO. We were both looking at the massive, empty parliament that was not a parliament. What was it, really?

He said, 'The Israelis say it's a parliament, and they don't want it within Greater Jerusalem. The Japanese gave $600,000 to furnish government ministries, and Abu Ala used the money to build this.' A tower that high would cost millions. 'The $600,000 was to start it. It cost more.' But I asked, is it a parliament? 'No one knows what it is yet. There's a conference hall inside for five hundred people, but we have only eighty-eight members of parliament.'

It didn't look like much work was going on, I said.

'No. They ran out of money.'

The Hill of Evil Counsel

Government House, the British High Commission of Mandate days and since 1949 the United Nations Troop Supervisory Organization Headquarters, wrapped itself around the summit of the Hill of Evil Counsel above Jerusalem. Where the British once played the irreconcilable roles of protectors of Zionist settlement and of non-partisan judge between settler and native, the United Nations went through the motions of preserving peace along the two remaining hostile borders, with Lebanon and Syria, and of mediating peace between the settlers, who had built a state with an impressive armed force, and the natives, who had not. A rolling metal gate protected the entrance from attack, but as I drove up in my shabby Palestinian rented car, the gate slid open. I stopped anyway, and a guard inside his concrete hut asked, 'Are you here for Father Jerry's talk?' Indeed, I was. I was so accustomed to the Israeli checkpoints, where soldiers demanded passports and asked questions, that I waited for the UN guard to search the car. He didn't.

Inside Government House, Fr Jerome Murphy-O'Connor, OP, was beginning his annual lecture series on the history and archaeology of Jerusalem. I sat on a folding chair near Emma Gilmour and Mrs Vester, herself part of the history of Jerusalem. Most of the audience were wives of diplomats, UN officials and foreign journalists. Fr Jerry, who stood a good six foot four, was a popular figure in the expatriate community, many of whose marriages and baptisms he had performed. He had told me that, despite having lived in Jerusalem for thirty years, he had no Palestinian or Israeli friends. He refused to take sides, and, sooner or later, they all expected him to. His friendships with expatriates, who left after a few years, were short-lived or maintained at a distance. Such was the priestly life of an Irish Dominican archaeologist in Jerusalem.

He was a captivating speaker. He began at, well, the beginning. People had inhabited Jerusalem since at least the fourteenth century before Christ. Its ancient name, *Yara Shalin*, meant Foundation of the God of Twilight. 'The name,' he said, in one of many caustic asides he left out of his book *The Holy Land*, 'may have a certain value today.'

A series of slides accompanied the lecture, an old-fashioned presentation that suited the subject. Colour photographs and diagrams of the city's shape and position as it altered over the ages popped up behind him, magically illustrating his themes. The earliest Jerusalem, that of the Jebusites, was outside the walls of the city that took much of its present form under Herod the Great in the first century BC. 'The greatest mystery,' he said, 'is how did it ever become an important city? It had very little water and no natural resources. It was not on any trade route.'

A slide snapped onto the screen showing ancient commercial passages from Gaza north up the coastal plain and east towards the Jordan Valley and Petra, bypassing Jerusalem altogether. 'In the great trade routes,' he said, 'Damascus was always a crossing point. The coastal route was called the King's Highway. The mountain route, across the ridges, was always avoided.'

A map showed the topography on which the Jebusites and, later, King David had constructed the city. There were two hills, the eastern hill and the Mount of Olives, and three valleys. David's genius was to site his capital outside the territory of Israel's Twelve Tribes, on neutral wasteland. His predecessor, Saul, had placed his within the area of his own tribe and suffered the predictable jealousy of the rest. Jerusalem lay at the edge of Benjamin's tribal frontier, where Horites, Hittites and Jebusites lived. No Israelite tribe claimed the Gentiles' Hills. 'David made it the capital of a federation,' Fr Jerry said, 'not within any member state, like Canberra or Washington. David put the Ark of the Covenant in Jerusalem. Politics and religion were mixed from the very beginning. Jerusalem worked as a political capital because of a religious symbol.' He might have added that it was also good for business. Pilgrimages by Jewish believers, followed later by Christians and Muslims, brought money to compensate for lack of resources and trade.

Next came a series of outlines of the city walls, growing, contracting and moving like amoebae: Solomon's city climbing north up the hill, the Maccabean city completing its rectangle shape, Herod's walls nearly doubling Jerusalem's size and Titus reducing it to a small corner he called Aelia Capitolina. Israel's history was written in those changes: expansion, contraction, destruction. In 586 BC came the first of many annihilations, when the Babylonians took the Children of Israel across the desert to their empire near the fertile plains and foothills that Abraham had left. Fifty years later, the Persians conquered the country and permitted the Jews to return. Ten of the Twelve Tribes elected to remain in the Fertile Crescent, and the two which went back to Jerusalem were not allowed to rebuild its walls. They made do with a settlement smaller than the one established by Solomon five centuries before.

The lecture, the first in a year-long series, would be supplemented by Fr Jerry's walking tours of the old city, Masada, Galilee and other archaeological sites. He invited his audience to visit, among other places, the museums. Israeli museums, he said, charged admission in cash but never had change. 'If any of ya comes without change to get into the museums,' he said, more Irish boxer than priest, 'I'll kill ya.'

The summer before, Fr Jerry had undergone heart surgery in Ireland. Jeff Price, an old friend of ours who had been the *Baltimore Sun*'s Jerusalem correspondent and then foreign editor, called me the next day and asked how Fr Jerry was recovering. I was able to tell him the old priest was feistier than ever.

That morning, long before Jeff's call, helicopters woke me. They were headed towards Beit Jalla, the small Christian village near Bethlehem that had endured a bad year of Israeli bombardment, tank fire, shooting and confinement. I listened to the BBC World Service, which reported an IDF announcement that its forces were withdrawing from some of the six A Area towns it occupied. The process would take a few days. In Afghanistan, the US continued its attacks but could not prevent the capture of Abdul Haq, a pro-American Afghan commander, by the Taliban.

Lovely Lily

'I cannot ever forget the day we arrived in Israel,' Lily Galili said. We were having drinks in the bar of the King David Hotel, the west side's larger and grander version of the American Colony. I had known her for about five years, but was aware only of basic facts: that she grew up in Poland, that she married and divorced a man named Galili who left her the sweet rhyming name that suited her, that she was a first-rate journalist, that she was an Israeli patriot whose soul contained no anti-Arab hatred and that she was the mother of two grown-up sons. She had recently published a series of long articles in *Ha'aretz* on Israel's mixed cities of Arabs and Jews. Elegant, cool, sophisticated, she sat with her legs crossed. Her dainty fingers held a cigarette from which she took languorous drags. All she needed were long white gloves to be a 1950s fashion model.

The King David's art deco bar seemed also to date from the 1950s. It was of the 1950s, when Lily came to Israel, that she spoke. 'It was 29 October 1956, when I came with my mother from Poland,' she said. 'We landed at Lod. We went straight to an air raid shelter, because there was a siren. That was the beginning of the Sinai War.' It was an appropriate, if terrible, welcome to their new country. 'My mother was terrified. She was a Holocaust survivor. She had taken me to a land she still called Palestine. I was nine at the time and didn't want to leave Poland. And then we ended up in a shelter. She looked at me in despair and said, "Why did I bring you?" I said, "Don't worry. You'll be okay, as long as you're with me." '

Lily was not the only child of a survivor I knew who became a parent to her parent. Nor was her mother the only woman to emerge from those factories of murder with a morbid fear of harm befalling her child. Lily was not, however, telling me about her arrival to make a point about survivor syndrome. 'Later, I learned that, at the same time we were in the shelter, there was a massacre at Kfar Kassem.' Kfar Kassem was a village in Israel inhabited by Palestinian Arabs, most of whom were peasant farmers. 'The Arabs, who did not know about the curfew, were killed when they were walking home from their fields.'

It was a black day in Israeli history. The Israeli army would never have shot Jewish farmers unaware of the curfew order. On that day, Israel launched a war of conquest in collusion with Britain and France to allow the region's former imperial powers to occupy the Suez Canal that Egypt had nationalized earlier in the year. The idea was for Israel to provoke a war with Egypt by occupying the Gaza Strip and Sinai Peninsula. An Anglo-French force would, and did, land in the Canal Zone under the pretext of separating forces. Israel's reward was to be control of Sinai and Gaza. Britain and France would keep the Canal. And Egypt's Arab nationalist president, Gamal Abdel Nasser, would be discredited or deposed. It almost worked, but for one miscalculation Israel would not repeat: they forgot to ask the United States. President Dwight Eisenhower ordered all three countries to withdraw, and they did.

'Forty-five years later,' Lily said, 'it's the same thing. I'm feeling pretty miserable and thoughtful. It's as if the whole burden of Israel is on my narrow shoulders.' This was the first time I had seen her in a melancholy state, and I wondered why. She had survived bad times in her forty-five years as an Israeli: the wars of 1956, 1967, 1973 and 1982, the *intifadah* of 1987 to 1993 and a year of the second *intifadah*. What was the difference?

'I was born on 6 October,' she said. 'This was the first year in twenty years that no Palestinian friends called on my birthday. Usually five or six called. They didn't call this year.'

In the year that Lily was born in Poland, 6 October was Yom Kippur, the Day of Atonement. Her birthday fell on Yom Kippur again in 1973, when Egypt and Syria launched a war to regain the lands they lost to Israel in 1967. It was now Wednesday 29 October, the anniversary of the day her mother brought her to Palestine and they hid in a shelter while Israeli troops shot and killed Arab farmers.

'The twenty-ninth of October makes me feel awful,' she said, 'like I'm back to square one. I'm old, and things are exactly the same.'

She ordered another drink, lit another cigarette and curled into the upholstered chair as if to make herself smaller, as if to disappear. She talked about her mother, who discovered in 1993 that she had a brain tumour. 'I stayed at her bedside for five months,' she recalled. 'My mother had a sense of drama. It was 13 September 1993, the moment Rabin and Arafat signed for peace. My cellphone rang at the American Colony.' Israelis and

Arabs who believed in the agreement were celebrating at the American Colony. Journalists, politicians, writers, lawyers, businessmen and diplomats watched the broadcast from Washington and thought it was finally over – the fifty and more years of hatred, massacres, petty abuse, torture, terror and dispossession. The tyranny of death would be succeeded by Israeli picnics in the hills above Nablus and Palestinian family dinners in the Jewish restaurants of Tel Aviv. No one had at that point read the agreement. Until her cellphone rang, amid the noise of celebration, Lily Galili did not know her mother was dead.

Lily went straight to the hospital. 'I stayed with her body a long time,' she said. 'Then I went home. The first call, by coincidence, was from a friend in Dhaisheh refugee camp.' Dhaisheh camp was in Bethlehem. The caller was a Palestinian woman friend named Amina, whom Lily had met at a conference in Italy. Lily said the conference's Italian organizer knew nothing about Israel or Palestine. 'Maria Luisa said to us, "I love you both. I want to come and see the two of you." Amina asked her, "Where are you going to stay in Dhaisheh?" And she said, "There must be a Hilton I can stay in." Amina and I looked at each other.' Lily and Amina belonged to the same place and to each other. And it was Amina, her refugee friend, who called her on the day her mother died. 'Amina turned out to be the first person I told that my mother died.' They wept together.

Refugees, the victims of 1948, had not been her concern. 'I'm of the left, who look back to 1967, to undo 1967,' she explained. 'I didn't think much about 1948. Working on this series' – her *Ha'aretz* articles on the Arab–Jewish towns in Israel – 'I was faced with 1948. It was staring at me. Every time I saw the results and the people of '48, I had a mental image constantly of them and my mother. Wherever I was facing these moral questions, I chose my mother. Where could she go, the only survivor in her family?'

Lily nonetheless felt alone. 'I'm not part of any tribe,' she said. When she chose her mother – her flesh and her traditions

– over the victims of 1948, she was clinging to her tribe. The first person in whom she confided the loss of her mother was a victim of '48. And, now, on her most recent birthday, her friend the refugee had not called. Dhaisheh was surrounded by Israeli tanks, and some of its children had died. It would have been hard for the Palestinian woman to call Lily, who was from the tribe of the enemy. All they could share were tears for the dead, for the cruelty of their lives, for the impossibility of their friendship.

The next day, Israeli forces killed six Palestinians in Tulkarm and Hebron on the West Bank. The slick, Americanized former prime minister Benyamin Netanyahu told CNN that Yasser Arafat ran 'a classic terrorist state' and that Israel needed the 'moral clarity to win against terrorism'. The ambassador to Pakistan of the dying Taliban regime claimed the American bombardment of Afghanistan had so far killed 1500 civilians. In New York, a sixty-one-year-old Vietnamese immigrant named Kathy Nguyen died of anthrax poisoning. And, for the first time in eight years, American domestic production shrank. It was down 4 per cent in the third quarter.

Death in the Family

A diplomat told me that the Israeli government, in violation of recent promises and Shimon Peres's assurances, was constructing a new settlement near Ma'ale Adumim. I drove out to see it, but the traffic along the 'seam' – the highway along what had been the Green Line between Arab and Jewish Jerusalem from 1949 to 1967 – stopped dead at French Hill. In Jerusalem, driving was usually slow, but not that bad. I turned off at French Hill, a settlement built on occupied Arab territory so long ago that most people, including many who lived there, did not know it was a settlement. I drove back to the American Colony. A few minutes after I arrived, ambulances blared from French Hill. Someone said a bomb had exploded there. Another report said that a gunman had shot up a bus. An off-duty soldier then shot the gunman. The first report on the radio said three people on the bus had been wounded. This was updated to two dead.

I went up to the Church of Notre Dame that dominates the hill facing the old city's New Gate and Christian Quarter. Part of the massive Gothic building was a hospice that had closed a year earlier for lack of custom. Upstairs was a chapel. I was planning to attend the six o'clock Roman Catholic Mass, but the Mass was at six-thirty. In the lobby, sterile as a school, other Catholics seemed to have made the same mistake. Six Filipinas, all dressed properly for Sunday service, sat speaking Tagalog. An African priest in a grey tunic was pacing the floor. After a few minutes, he approached me. He had lived at Notre Dame as a diocesan priest for twenty years. The morning Mass had been his to say, and this evening's would be by a French Carmelite. 'It's in English, though,' he added, lest I seize the excuse to escape.

In a circle of chairs near the Filipinas, I resumed reading. The priest left, went into a doorway and, a few minutes later, returned. 'Since you're early,' he announced, 'you can read the First Lesson.' I wanted to tell him the truth: I'm a back-row Catholic, ineligible to receive Communion. However, I don't know anyone raised within the bosom of Holy Mother Church – who studied at Catholic schools and made his confirmation – who knew how to say no to a priest or nun. I had been in jails for refusing to obey policemen, and I have ignored armed men who were blocking my way to places I needed to reach. I have jeopardized domestic tranquillity by ignoring sound advice from women. Yet, let one old priest or tiny nun make the most pointless, ridiculous or unwelcome request, and I perform like a circus dog. How could I blame Israeli Jews for heeding their rabbis, or Palestinian Christians their priests, or Palestinian Muslims their mullahs? Gamely, I mounted the pulpit and stumbled through an Epistle from St Paul to the Gentiles. I was never early for Mass again.

It was shortly after my debut at Mass that the mother of my

139

former wife died in England. I had to find a cheap ticket to attend the funeral. Call David, a friend advised, and he'll get you a ticket for half the price. I called David, who proposed a combination of return fares to London that were indeed half the going rate. Instead of the scheduled all-night flight from London back to Lod on British Airways, David's return charter left London at noon. The catch was that I had to pay cash and meet David at the Jaffa Gate.

From the gate, I called him on his mobile. A few minutes later, we found each other on the steps of the Petra Hostel. The Petra in 1900 was the grand Mediterranean Hotel, rival to the Imperial fifty yards away. Now, it was a flop house for illegal workers, travelling students and drunks. David invited me to come up to his office. That meant following him past the money changer on the ground floor and up a flight of decrepit stairs to a lobby, where a Western woman in her late twenties lounged on a torn chair, one Levi'd leg over its arm, watching an old television. A cashier stood behind the counter staring, so far as I could see, at nothing. A fragrance of Middle Eastern dormitory hung over the vast and ill-kept lobby, not the spices and brewing coffee of the souq, but the unwashed bodies and rancid garments of those who had given up.

David seemed out of place in the Petra, his energy and enthusiasm reproaching old, unwatered plants in plastic pots and comatose humanity awaiting miracles. He was young and moved like an athlete up the stairs and through the lobby. He was losing his hair, but the baldness was premature – as if, like its bearer, his hair were in a hurry to get to the point. David raced ahead of me up stone steps to the roof, where we negotiated washing lines and television aerials to reach the parapet. He pointed at the old city, its domes popping up like breasts on their flat, rain-catching roofs. 'This is a two-million-dollar view,' he said. David was a businessman, not a poet. The sight of Caliph Omar's golden dome, of the churches and synagogues and ancient houses and hospices, of the Mount of Olives beyond, made pilgrims swoon, knights commit holy massacres and artists abandon hope of capturing it. It had been measured in beauty, in love, in spiritual rapture, in music and in poetry. For some, the real measure was real estate – for Christian churches of the nineteenth century, Zionist land agents in the twentieth and David the travel agent in the twenty-first.

He led me to a little roof-top room. The tiny space with unmade bed, brass menorah and miniature desk was his office. It was like a low-rent brothel. David kept ticket prices low by keeping overheads down. The modern flat where he lived was on the west side near the Knesset, far from the two-million-dollar view. A computer screen displayed flights and fares. 'I call them and negotiate a lower price,' he said. The prices on-screen seemed low enough, but David was determined to better them. He would have a ticket at a lower rate for me in twenty-four hours. He asked me to collect it from him in Ramat Gat. 'It's twenty minutes from here.' I asked him to leave it at the American Colony.

'Do you trust me with your money until I get the ticket?' he asked. I did.

'Lots of people say that. A guy gave me money the other day for a dozen tickets – I do a lot of work with the Christian pilgrims – and he said I have an honest face.' He did.

David called the 'consolidators' on the telephone and negoti-ated in Hebrew until they came down to his price. His Hebrew sounded fluent, and I asked him if he spoke Arabic as well. 'I'm learning,' he said. He was from Argentina, 'part Polish, part Spanish and part Italian'. And all business.

I had breakfast the next morning in the Colony's courtyard with Caroline Hawley, a young BBC reporter who had a degree in Arabic from Oxford and lived in Amman. We went to the bookshop, whose proprietor, Munther Fahmy, complained more than usual that people were not buying enough books. A taxi driver sent to me by David the travel agent arrived, put my bags in the back of the van and drove me towards Ben-Gurion International Airport in Lod – once the Arab town of Lydda. An Israeli army checkpoint at the airport's entrance stopped cars long enough for the soldiers to have a good look at the drivers before waving them past. David's Arab driver predicted the soldiers would pull us over.

He was right, which explained why most travellers used Jewish drivers for the airport. We waited for a policeman to return our passports, while fifty or more cars sped past. Finally, a policeman told us we could leave. There was no brutality, just routine checking of an Arab driver, his van and documents that added twenty minutes to the journey. Two hours later, I was in the air.

In Sussex, at a rain-drenched graveside service, my children buried their grandmother in a simple coffin next to her husband, their grandfather. We went back to the house where my wife had been staying with her mother in 1987 on the morning she had received the news that I had escaped my cell in Beirut. My captivity and her suffering ended, as did our marriage, when I returned that summer from Lebanon. I consoled my children, especially the youngest, Julia, as well as I knew how. And, more than anything, I regretted that I was no longer the man to soothe my former wife during this loss as I had when her father died. That was her new husband's task.

During my week away from the Promised Land, the war in Afghanistan gathered momentum. Mazar-e-Sharif fell to the Americans and their anti-Taliban Afghans. Next, on 13 November, came Kabul. From then on, it would be a matter of chasing Al Qaeda and Taliban die-hards out of their last redoubts and into their mountain caves, of counting the dead and of imposing a new regime, as the Soviet Union had once done, on Afghanistan. The war would end, and resistance to foreign occupation, as with the Soviets, would begin.

O, No, Jerusalem!

Return to the Asylum

The young Israeli taxi driver who picked me up at Ben-Gurion Airport looked like a soldier. His hair was clipped to stubble, his face freshly shaved. He was strong and in good health, an embodiment of the post-ghetto, free, warrior Jewish man that Zionism's pioneers sought to create. I wanted him to take me to Andrew and Emma Gilmour's house in Abu Tor. He had not heard of it and asked if it were in East Jerusalem. Another driver told him Abu Tor was near the old Jerusalem Railway Station, on the edge of the west and closed for many years. I offered him the option, if he felt unsafe, of leaving me at a hotel where I could change to an Arab taxi. My proposal offended his pride. Off we went to Jerusalem in the evening, passing Kastel and the other landmarks of Israel's heroic 1948 battles that opened the road to West Jerusalem, the empty spaces where the Arabs had once lived and, finally, the vice of settlements squeezing the city.

Once in the new city we passed the King David Hotel and the Montefiore Windmill. On the Bethlehem Road near the Palestine Railway Station, I asked him to turn right into the Hebron Road. It had taken me some time, on previous visits, to realize that the Hebron Road went to Bethlehem and the Bethlehem Road went nowhere. That was the way with Israeli or Palestinian roads. Taxi drivers had explained in vain, for example, why there was both an old–new and a new–old road between Tel Aviv and Jerusalem. In the wide Hebron Road, we passed one of my favourite Israeli cafés and the grocery where I picked up my morning newspapers. I was happy to be back amid the Hebrew shop signs and the inane horn-honking traffic.

At the first traffic light I asked the driver to turn left into something called the Forest of Peace. It was a small pine grove below the Hill of Evil Counsel. From the turning, the Gilmours' house was less than a mile. Entering the mixed neighbourhood of Israelis and Palestinians, the driver changed mood. I had been thinking how similar his cab was to an Arab's: the same evil-eye talisman dangling from the rear-view mirror, pictures like holy cards on the dashboard. Where a Palestinian driver in Ramallah might place a photograph of his family or Yasser Arafat, his was of Rebbe Nachmun of Ukraine. Unlike an Arab driver approaching rows of Arab stone houses and a field of pines, he was afraid. He was a courteous and intelligent man who did not want me to see his fear. I assured him that the road, on which half a dozen huge monuments donated by Canadian and other Diaspora Jews faced the old city, was safe. It was badly lit, and the asphalt had potholes. A road as neglected as this meant only one thing: Arabs lived here. He did not believe the way ahead was secure.

'I am Israeli,' he said. He refused, however, to turn back. He drove slowly through the forest to the first house. He stopped, looked at me and drove on. Then, he slowed down even more. We saw two trucks that I knew belonged to one of the Gilmours' Palestinian neighbours. Someone was filling them with diesel. The driver's caution turned to panic. He stopped the car. He looked at a Palestinian in a long galabieh and remained transfixed. A minute went by.

I said I would walk the rest of the way. He did not speak. I assured him 'I know these people. They're okay.' He waited again, slipped into first gear and inched forward. We passed the men beside the trucks, and I greeted them in Arabic as I always did when going to the Gilmours'. They returned my greeting. The driver's fear mixed with something new – suspicion. Was this a trap? Was I luring him to his death? He stopped and refused to go further.

I paid him, and he tried to turn the car around. A skilled driver, he jerked the car right and left, slipping gears and nearly going off the road. It took him several attempts to point the car in the opposite direction. I waited with my suitcases and thanked him again for coming that far: he did not return my goodbye and had an awkward moment trying to pass the trucks. I walked towards him to show I would help if he had any problem. He cleared the track and sped away.

He had nothing to fear, but he was no coward. This was a neighbourhood of families whom I knew, a friendly place whose people helped one another with baby-sitting and shopping. To him, it was enemy territory. Palestinians had murdered Israelis in dark places far from their homes. Palestinians had the same fear, whenever they went into an all-Jewish town or settlement. I knew whites in my home town, Los Angeles, who were too terrified to stray into African-American neighbourhoods like Watts or Crenshaw. I had met young black men and Mexican-American boys in Los Angeles, who would not go to Beverly Hills where the police would question them and the store-owners accuse them of shoplifting. Terror was not confined to Israelis and Palestinians. It was the human condition in segregated societies.

The Palestinian men around the trucks offered to carry my suitcases. Up the hill on the way to Andrew and Emma's, most of the neighbourhood was gathered around an open fire. Every-one was smiling, and a few were singing. I saw soft drinks and food and children. Everyone – even the men at the back of the truck – looked happy. Why the fire? Why all the smiles? What were the people in this corner of Abu Tor celebrating?

When I reached the house, Emma told me, 'Intisar had her baby today.' Intisar lived next door, and this was her third child. Everyone in the neighbourhood was happy for this young mother who had survived two years in an Israeli prison.

Emma Gilmour, I was convinced, could do anything. She had three children and was carrying a fourth. Having me as her guest must have been like having a fifth. She was a physician, tall and striking and the mainstay of her household during Andrew's many trips to Gaza, the West Bank and UN headquarters in New York. She was also something of a political activist. UN officials, diplomats and foreign journalists stayed out of the conflict between occupier and occupied. Their spouses, how-ever, attended anti-occupation demonstrations. I had often seen Emma alongside the wives of the *Daily Telegraph* correspondent and European diplomats at checkpoints to protest against the siege of Palestinian towns. Emma, as doctor and mother, had a particular disdain for Israeli soldiers who prevented pregnant women from reaching hospitals to deliver their children. Many babies, and several mothers, had died as a result. A few women gave birth in cars at the checkpoints.

Some mornings and evenings when I was staying with the Gilmours, Emma and I would sit in her kitchen to talk. If we had been in England, our conversations would have been about her husband Andrew's older brothers, all old friends of mine. Or we would have discussed her girlfriends who had had the misfortune to go out with me. Here, in Abu Tor, we discussed the occupation. Many of the British women she knew belonged to something called Checkpoint Watch. Matrons were more effective than men at embarrassing Israeli soldiers into behaving correctly. At the entrances to Palestinian cities, their vigilant scowls occasionally lessened the mistreatment. No one wanted nanny to watch him bullying Palestinian kids. Imagine a dozen Margaret Thatchers staring out at you.

The women worked only during the morning and evening rush hours. If they had been able to stay all night, she said, they might have saved some of the babies whose mothers were not allowed to reach Bethlehem's Holy Family Maternity Hospital. That was where Emma had decided, having visited all the maternity wards around Jerusalem, her baby should be born. If the soldiers did not allow her into Bethlehem, there would be trouble.

Until I could pick up another wreck from my friends at Dalla Car Rental in Beit Hanina, I was on foot. When the sun shone, walking to the city from the Gilmours' was an easy downhill stride with stops along the way for newspapers and coffee. One morning, I was about halfway to the American Colony, at the base of the Kidron Valley, when I gave up and hailed a taxi. The car came to a stop below Suleiman the Magnificent's walls, and I was about to get in when I noticed two people in the back seat. I told the driver I'd wait for an empty taxi. The man and his daughter in the back had no objection, so I got in the front.

Was I, the man behind me asked, a tourist? 'Worse than that,' I said, 'a journalist.' He talked about the BBC, whose World Service had kept his father informed during the British Mandate. He did not think it was as good as it used to be. Who did? The car was taking him and his daughter to his shop on the west side in Ben Yehuda Street. They were Armenians, who, like Albert Agazarian, lived in the St James Convent. His shop was in a large building that, like the convent, belonged to the Armenian Church. I said he was lucky the Church had not sold it. When he said the Armenian Church did not sell land, the driver interrupted, 'What about the Imperial Hotel?'

The Armenian ignored the question. It was better, he said, to keep the buildings and collect rent to support the Church and its clergy. I asked him if there were many Armenian priests, and he said there were fifteen. In the West, I said, not many young men wanted to become priests any more. 'We have the same problem,' he said. When he and his daughter got out, he invited me to his shop anytime for coffee.

The driver talked the rest of the way. He was a Catholic and his name was Charlie. He said that the Catholic Church, unlike the Armenian and Greek Orthodox, never sold its property. He had often worked with journalists and accompanied some the previous Christmas to the Catholic Church in Bethlehem. How was it? 'Bad.' And this year? 'It will be worse.'

The State Department announced that Secretary of State Colin Powell would deliver a major speech on Monday at the University of Louisville. This would be his first statement since 11 September on America's foreign policy goals and was expected to concentrate on the Middle East. Perhaps – and this was the most Palestinians hoped – he would explain what President Bush meant when he referred to a Palestinian state. Whenever Ariel Sharon put the words state and Palestinian together, he meant a Bantustan of tiny, discontinuous ghettoes. Was it, as most Palestinians suspected, the same for Bush and Powell?

The next day, 14 November, the *Jerusalem Post* reported

one of those inexplicable incidents that reminded people that nothing in the Levant was simple. 'Atallah Abu Aida,' Israel's English-language, right-wing daily wrote, 'the Negev man arrested over a week ago on suspicion of dealing weapons to Palestinians, is a Likud central committee member, Channel 2 reported last night. Nine months ago, Abu Aida was a guest at Prime Minister Ariel Sharon's home in the Negev. Sharon's son and advisor, Omri, said he has a friendly relationship with Abu Aida.'

The facts seemed simple. Atallah Abu Aida was an Arab in the hierarchy of an anti-Arab party whose leader, Ariel Sharon, stood accused of massacring Palestinian Arabs on many occasions between 1953 and 2001. The Arab had been a guest at Sharon's ranch. The police arrested him for selling arms to other Arabs. In a land with no immune system to repel conspiracy theories, rumours bred like bacteria: Abu Aida was sending arms to Palestinians opposed to Arafat. Sharon was asking him to funnel weapons to Palestinian irregulars, who would fire on Israelis and provide Sharon with a pretext to reoccupy Palestinian towns and destroy the apparatus of the PA's proto-state. Abu Aida, who had already betrayed his own people with his membership of the Likud, was now betraying Israel to make money as an arms dealer. The one version no one put forward was that police had made a mistake.

Living Within the Walls

I made Jerusalem home base, returning from sorties to the Negev, Galilee, Gaza and Ramallah, to catch up, read my notes and see more people. For some time, I stayed in the old city at the Knight's Palace Hotel. Its management and staff worked hard and made me as welcome as if I were at the American Colony. It was clean. The rooms, except those that faced a schoolyard, were quiet. It had a location that Conrad Hilton would envy, within the walls but on a road that cars could reach. It was yards away from my barber, Abu Munir, who shaved me every morning. It was also near the Al-Ma'mal Gallery, whose young proprietor, Jack Persekian, provided the only exhibition space in the old city for modern artists. The Knight's Palace had one other attraction that eclipsed the rest: it was very cheap.

The Knight's Palace, in the pilgrim hostel tradition, locked its front door at midnight. After that, I had to ring a bell that woke the nightwatchman. He was good about it, unless a woman were with me. While not disapproving, he would tell me not to let the hotel's owner see her in the morning. Staying there meant returning to the city gates every night and walking within its protective walls each morning, like every pilgrim or traveller before the twentieth century. It allowed me to learn the cobbled paths among its four quarters – Muslim, Christian, Armenian and Jewish – and make sense of what had, in previous years, been a baffling labyrinth.

The closer you are to a place and the longer you remain, the less romantic, the less exotic, it becomes. Its life, once strange, is ordinary. That is when you come to know it, as you would a new language or a lover. My favourite cities have always been those designed to be walked, and the old city of Jerusalem made the car, the van and the truck uncomfortable. Some of its prime routes were so tight that people on foot could barely negotiate them side by side. In walking cities, there are more places to rest – cafés, restaurants, bars, shops and friends' houses. Cafés and shops offered hospitality. And I had a home at the Agazarians' house, walls within the walls of a fortress convent within the walls of a fortified city.

Albert Agazarian and I regularly talked politics and local history. I came to know him better, one of the luxuries of staying so long. He had graduated in history from the American University of Beirut in the summer before I started there in the graduate school of philosophy. He had taken part in the legendary student strike of 1971, when police had beaten and arrested students occupying the administration building. We had many common friends in Lebanon. We were the same age in years, but life's experiences had made him my senior. He had endured Israeli occupation. He had taught at a university whose students and teachers were often detained, interrogated and tortured. He attended the funerals of undergraduates shot during demonstrations against the occupation. Raising children in that charged environment, he somehow sustained a dialogue with Israelis in the belief they would one day metamorphose from occupiers into neighbours. I had seen more of the world, but had positioned myself on the periphery to watch and comment on it. Albert had the wisdom of the man in the centre. His hair was greyer, wilder and longer than mine. A dark goatee enhanced his gravitas. He was flamboyant and loved to tell stories. I preferred to listen.

One day, Albert and I were drinking coffee at the big table in Madeleine's kitchen while she prepared stuffed vine leaves. She wrapped them around morsels of lamb and rice and then dropped them into a big tin pot. Albert said he was the youngest of three brothers. When he left the university in Beirut, he returned to Jerusalem and took a safe job at Barclay's Bank in Salah ed-Din Street. But he would not settle down. The number of his girlfriends and the speed with which he left one for another scandalized Jerusalem's conservative Armenian society. 'My mother said, "You are going to kill me one day,"' Albert confessed, beginning the story of how it all changed. It was an instructive tale of playboy become respected gentleman. 'I was taking a taxi to work in Salah ed-Din Street from the Jaffa Gate. The driver almost crashed into a woman who was crossing the road. She shouted at him, "May God make you blind!" And behind her was Madeleine. Afterwards, I went to the bank. I worked and went on my lunch hour. When I was walking, I saw her a second time. I went back to the bank and finished working. Then I was with a friend near Herod's Gate, and I saw her again. Three times in one day.'

Madeleine went on laying out vine leaves and wrapping them into cigar-sized parcels of meat and rice. She did not say anything, but she listened. 'That day at the bank, a customer wanted to change a large sum of money. I made a deal, and the bank earned a quick buck. That evening, I celebrated and came home a bit tipsy. My mother said that this behaviour was unacceptable. And I said, "I've found her." My mother understood. She asked, "Is she Armenian?"'

I could hear an Israeli mother asking, 'Is she Jewish?' or my grandmother, 'Is she Catholic?'

'I said, "I think so." It was possible she was a girl I had seen, before I went to AUB, when she was thirteen. She had a uniform of the Armenian school. My mother and sister went on querying me. "Who is she?" I didn't know, but I said I think she lives in the Christian Quarter. They found out who she was, the way women do. My mother came back and said, "Nora Cort said she was a charity child." Then she said to me in Turkish, "You take us to the wilderness on a horse and then on a donkey and then let us walk."'

Turkish proverbs eluded me, but I gathered, from the way Albert spoke, that his mother thought Madeleine's family were cut from the wrong social cloth.

'I didn't like it, and I told her, "The Armenians came here with nothing, and now you dare look down on people."' Albert seemed so exasperated with his mother, more than twenty years later, that he stopped talking.

Madeleine popped another rolled vine leaf into the pot. 'His mother and sister came to my mother's shop,' she said. 'They said Albert is interested in the woman. Before he makes a step, he wants to check her out.' There was more toing and froing between the two families. Investigations were conducted, approvals granted. They got married. Four days later, they went to Washington for him to do a masters at Georgetown University.

'You forgot,' Madeleine said. 'Your family wanted to see this girl. But Albert said, "I just want to hear her voice." It's the traditional way.'

'For the next twenty-five years,' Albert said, 'she has kept my inner front intact.' Madeleine said, 'Here is this extremely flirtatious man and a womanizer who ends up with a very conservative woman.' At the time of the wedding, Albert was twenty-seven and Madeleine twenty-three.

Madeleine put some snacks on the table, and Albert poured two glasses of arak, added cold water and dropped in some ice.

'I carry the spirit of Omar Khayyam,' Albert said, appreciating his loaf of bread, jug of wine and Madeleine beside him. 'He loved good food and good wine. He loved science and knowledge. He hated the dirty politics of his time, and so do I. I have happiness, *humdul'ilah*' – thank God. He put his arm around his wife and said, 'You are the backbone, *habibati*' – my dearest. He toasted her with his arak.

> Come, fill the Cup, and in the fire of Spring
> Your Winter-garment of Repentance fling:
> The Bird of Time has but a little way
> To flutter – and the Bird is on the Wing.

The telephone rang. Israeli soldiers at the checkpoint near Bir Zeit University had beaten and detained some students. It was Albert's job to act as liaison, as soother, between the occupying army and the university. He called the Israeli army commander at Beit El near Ramallah to plead for the students. 'I've been working hard not to hate,' he said. 'Once you hate, it's weakness.'

An Incident After Dark

On the evening before the month of daylight fasting, Ramadan in the Muslim lunar calendar, a young Palestinian woman was walking along the Paratroopers' Road towards the New Gate of the old city. She told me later that a boy, who seemed to be about sixteen, bumped her from behind and walked past. Alerted, she watched him until he turned a corner. A few minutes later, she saw him coming towards her. As they crossed, he grabbed her indecently from behind. To him, she may have looked European. She lived in Britain, and she wore chic Western dresses. He could not have anticipated her reaction.

She swore at him in Arabic. Some young men in a car parked nearby heard her and chased the boy. They caught him and dragged him back to her. Holding him tight, they asked her what she wanted done to him. She did not answer. Instead, she slapped the boy ferociously across the face. Her rescuers then released the boy.

I asked who the men from the car were. She answered, 'They were either Palestinians, who had nothing better to do, or Israeli plainclothes police, who spoke fluent Arabic. I couldn't tell.'

Before dawn peered over the Mount of Olives to light the gold of Omar's dome, the muezzin was urging the faithful from their beds. 'Prayer is better than sleep,' the call went, as it did every morning. On this day, the sixteenth day of the Christians' November and the first of Islam's Ramadan, something else was better than sleep: food. Old men trudged the passages of the Muslim Quarter, beating drums. 'Wake, wake,' they cried. 'Wake and eat.' Sleepy Jerusalem had an hour before the day-light fast began, and the old city was breathing the aroma of baking bread, fresh thyme and flowery tea.

I had been up all night and was walking through the old city's deserted streets, enjoying their stillness and waiting for a café to open. In the dark, as the drummers passed, I heard families scuttling indoors to their kitchens. They were forced by the power of their belief, before the first sparkle of sunlight found the city, to gather around their tables and eat enough to sustain them until their next meal, their *fitr*, or break-fast, after the sun disappeared into the Mediterranean. This was the first day of a month's daytime starvation. During the hours of darkness, Ramadan could be the happiest time of the year.

In her book *Approaches to the History of the Middle East*, Nancy Elizabeth Gallagher quoted an Arab historian at the University of Damascus, Professor Abdul Karim Rafaq. He had studied the craft guilds and property deals of Arab cities, like

153

Damascus and Jerusalem, in the Ottoman Empire. He said, 'No community lived in a ghetto-like situation. In fact, during the three centuries that preceded the impact of Industrial Europe and the domination of the world capitalist economy in the nineteenth century, which caused socio-economic and communal riots, no such riots occurred at all.'

At ten o'clock each night, a watchman closed and locked the iron door to the Armenian Convent of St James. From that hour until early morning, no one came in. No one went out. Madeleine Azagarian said it made her feel safe.

Refuseniks

Most people in Jerusalem lived outside the walls and rarely felt safe. Israelis feared Palestinian gunmen and bombers. Palestinians were afraid of arrest, interrogation, humiliation, torture and, in some cases, assassination. The new city – that is, the vast metropolis that choked the medieval town – was, like Gaul, divided into three parts: the Arab east, the Jewish west and the illegal Israeli settlements on Arab land. Israel had built fortress-like, all-Jewish enclaves east of the city and incorporated them into Greater Jerusalem. When Ehud Barak discussed ceding some of the territory Israel conquered in 1967 to Palestine, he had excluded the Jewish 'neighbourhoods' from the discussion.

One outpost of Israeli control in East Jerusalem would not form part of any negotiations, because it had not fallen to Glubb Pasha's Arab Legion in 1948. This was the Hebrew University on Mount Scopus, which remained an inviolable island inside Arab territory from 1949 to 1967. One of the finer institutions of higher learning in the world, it had been founded in 1925 and had become an island again – of Israeli liberalism in Jerusalem's rising sea of religious fundamentalism and settler orthodoxy. Its History Department did not offer chairs to post-Zionist historians like Ilan Pappe, Avi Shlaim or Tom Segev, but it had been home to such humanistic scholars as Rabbi

Judah Magnes, Rabbi Yeshayahu Leibowitz and Israel Shahak. Arab students felt out of place there. One, an undergraduate student in Middle East history between 1977 and 1981, had told me, 'Literally and metaphorically, I could not breathe at the Hebrew University.' Yet it tolerated radicalism and made space for that most dangerous type of Israeli, the one who refused to serve as a soldier in the occupied territories.

'I am a soldier, and I will be a soldier,' Menuchin Ishai, a political scientist at the university and an army reservist, said. We met in the university's cafeteria. 'But I am not going to do anything against humanity.' To occupy another people, to bulldoze their houses, to expropriate their land, to implant citizens of the occupying power, to kill the occupied people and to enforce laws on those who had no voice in their legislation, Israel needed a strong and obedient military force. Menuchin Ishai wanted to deprive the state of the use of its citizen army for all purposes but the defence of the Israel that came into being during the war of 1948. That was the line that he and several hundred other Israeli soldiers had drawn. Their movement, founded during Ariel Sharon's 1982 invasion of Lebanon, was called Yesh Gvul. In Hebrew, 'Yesh Gvul' means 'There is a limit'. Ishai said, 'It also means, "There is a border". Basically, enough is enough.'

'The army is a political tool,' Ishai said, 'with which the Israeli government controls the territories.' After June 1967, some young men had refused to serve in the occupation forces. The army accommodated most of them with assignments to other duties. A few went to prison. That changed in 1982. Ishai had completed his three-year stint as a conscript and was near the end of his first year at the Hebrew University, when Israel invaded Lebanon. During the invasion, some serving soldiers and reservists met in Lebanon to form Yesh Gvul, but Ishai was not an original member. Later, his experience in Lebanon brought him in. 'I did serve in the war, yes,' he said. 'At the time, I could not believe they would use the army in such a manipulative way.'

Israelis of military age were at other tables in the university cafeteria. Most had served three years in the Israeli Defence Forces, then travelled abroad for a year, before coming to the university. They would be reservists until they were old men, spending part of every year in the occupied territories. Barely one in a hundred of them would resist the call to serve. After Lebanon, Menuchin Ishai refused and urged others to refuse. 'They put me in military prison Number Six,' he said. 'I was a member of Yesh Gvul and Peace Now. I had three or four days in prison. When I was in prison, there was a demonstration. Emil Grunweig [a Peace Now activist] was murdered by a bomb. When I got out of prison, my commander said he would change my unit, but my new unit would go to Lebanon.'

Ishai was back in prison and Yesh Gvul supporters demonstrated on his behalf. 'They had signs saying "Free Menuchin Ishai",' he said, raising his hands like a demonstrator. He appeared before a military court. His commanders asked him to apologize. They reached an Israeli compromise. 'The commander of infantry, Yitzak Mordechai,' he said, referring to a general who became a minister of defence, 'said he could not accept my refusal, but he understood it. He said I was part of the family. Then I commanded in boot camp for my reserve duty.'

Of the three thousand troops who signed the Yesh Gvul petition objecting to military service during the Lebanon war, he said, about 170 went to prison. During the first *intifadah*, another 2500 reservists put their names to a Declaration of Refusal. One hundred and eighty of them were put into jail. Since the beginning of the new uprising, Yesh Gvul counted more than three hundred soldiers who were called up and refused to assist the occupation. Of those, Ishai believed that fourteen had been imprisoned. The usual sentence was between fourteen and twenty-eight days. Some had served a second time.

'There is not much hostility from families or from other soldiers,' Ishai said, when I asked how people reacted to refuseniks. 'I know only about two out of four hundred who have had a problem at work. One of those was a teacher. For the rest, it's like, if you're man enough to go to prison, you're okay.'

Menuchin Ishai was a major and, at forty-three, had two years' reserve duty left. The number of days a reservist served depended on the army's need for men and on the willingness of the reservists to volunteer for extra duty. Sharon was using up reservist time quickly with the sieges and assaults on Palestinian towns.

'I met my battalion commander two weeks ago,' he said. 'I wanted him to know that I wouldn't serve in Lebanon and won't serve beyond the Green Line. He said he'd put me in prison for fourteen days. Fine. I said his predecessor put me in for thirty-five days and it didn't work. He was surprised. He asked me if my previous commanders knew about my beliefs. I told him, yes. In the end, he accepted.'

I asked, 'Why?' Ishai shrugged, as if to say, 'Who knows?' Looking for a possible explanation, he said, 'I'm older than him.'

Yesh Gvul was concerned about limits – the geographical limit of Israel itself and the limits beyond which conscience should not tread. He seemed proud when he said, 'In twenty years, we changed the limits of obedience. It is something very hard to convince the Israeli public.' The limit to obeying military orders – the border where duty to the state battled with conscience, morality, international law – had been set at Nuremberg. And being compared to the genocidal war criminals of Nuremberg was unacceptable to most Israelis.

Yesh Gvul operated a hotline and a website for regular and reserve soldiers. It provided legal help, and it fought the propaganda war inside Israel. 'We are not in the consensus,' Ishai admitted, 'but even the right uses our stuff on the limits of obedience.' Right-wing settlers said they would disobey any law that ordered them out of the occupied territories. Yesh Gvul soldiers went peacefully to prison. Radical settlers, with their own limits to obedience, said they would fight rather than return an inch of land to the Arabs. (In 2005, when ordered out of Gaza, they complained but did not fight.)

The border between Israel and the occupied territories was arbitrary, defying the landscape. But it was a fact, based on the disengagement line of 1949 and legalized under the first agreements between Israel and the Arab states. The United Nations recognized it, and most Israelis lived content on their side of it. Yesh Gvul had hung a green plastic sheet over a kilometre and a half of it to emphasize the demarcation between their state and that other, illusory state that should have belonged to the Palestinians. 'You remember Christo?' Ishai asked. Christo was the Bulgarian-born artist who draped the Grand Canyon, the Reichstag and the Pont Neuf. 'I took his idea.' Some time later, Ariel Sharon made the idea his own. Instead of hanging a green sheet, he built a cement wall that strayed from the 1949–67 Green Line. His 'security fence' put Israeli settlement blocs and much other Palestinian land on the Israeli side of a new line. At some points, the wall stole five miles of West Bank territory. A few villages, like Az-Zawieh, would be completely surrounded by walls and its people unable to reach their olive trees. The wall sealed Palestinian towns in ghettoes. Sharon swore the wall would stop the suicide bombers. If its sole function had been to exclude the bombers, it would have run along the Green Line – like Ishai's sheet.

Cement walls, ghettoes and an occupying army: these themes would have resonated in modern Jewish history even if there had been no Israeli state, no conquest of 1967. For some Israelis, Jewish independence required permanent occupation. For others, like Ishai, it meant clinging to justice. 'I'm looking at my children,' Ishai said. 'One was born here. My father was born in Argentina. My wife's parents live in Chile and the United States. My children have four grandparents in four different countries. My father is in Argentina. His family are in the Ukraine. It's the story of the travelling Jew. I'm Israeli. We feel part of this community. We have an ideological commitment to make this country behave better. Fighting to change this society is part of my identity as an Israeli.'

He was going to a demonstration on Saturday outside Atlit Prison in the north to support soldiers sentenced for refusing to serve the occupation. He believed in selective refusal: 'I'm a soldier and will be a soldier, but I am not going to do anything against humanity. This is a notion that the political establishment and the army are afraid of. They are not afraid of twenty pacifists a year. They are more afraid of the many who will fight for the country but not to occupy.'

The state reserved to itself the right to decide where, when and against whom its soldiers would fight. The United States had imprisoned the young men who refused to kill Vietnamese, while exempting pacifists from military conscription. Israel was no different. In both countries, the number of young men who opposed a specific war was never large enough to deprive the war machine of the bodies it needed. Ending an occupation, whether of Vietnam or the West Bank and Gaza, required a mass anti-war movement at home and a coherent strategy from the enemy that made it clear he was no enemy at all.

Ruth Lynn at Haifa University studied the background of Yesh Gvul's members. Unsurprisingly, most had university degrees and came from secular, Ashkenazi backgrounds. That was no longer the profile of the Israeli majority. Russian immigrants, religious Jews and Sephardim constituted most of the electorate and the army. It was easy for the government to portray Yesh Gvul as elitist. Yesh Gvul had assumed the educated elite's obligation to set an example.

A few months after I met Menuchin Ishai in the Hebrew University's cafeteria, a Palestinian blew it up. He killed five people, including himself. The bombing, as with all the others, did not change the terms of the debate over army service in the occupied territories. Some said the killings proved the army had to get tough in the territories to prevent terror. Others believed it proved the army should leave the Palestinians to govern themselves, thus removing the incentive to become a suicide bomber.

An Émigré Returns

Hanna Elias was an Israeli citizen. Born in Nazareth in 1957, he was the Palestinian Arab who had told me of his years as an undergraduate at the Hebrew University, 'Literally and meta-phorically, I couldn't breathe.' His graduate years at the University of California at Los Angeles were easier. I met him through Nidal Barham, an 'Israeli Arab' journalist I had hired to do research. Hanna, whose name meant John, from the Arabic Yohanna, was a film-maker. We met often in Jerusalem. His impressions struggled with themselves as they evolved into words and sentences. He criticized Arab society more than he did the Israeli one to which he would never quite belong.

'I inherited that fear of what it means to be an Arab in Israel,' he said. This was at our first meeting, arranged by Nidal Barham at the American Colony Hotel. To me, Hanna Elias looked like a Lebanese-American university student. Not tall, with clipped, dark hair, he had come into the lobby wearing an old duffel coat that he slung over a chair. He smoked and, like me, drank too much coffee. My friend Bernard Avishai, Canadian-American author of *The Tragedy of Zionism*, had written an article for *Prospect* magazine that analysed modern Israel as a land of five tribes: secular-liberal Ashkenazi founders, Sephardim, Russian, Ultra Orthodox and Arab. At about 20 per cent each, a combination of any three could constitute a democratic majority. Hanna was a part of the fifth, excluded by its non-Jewishness, yet included in all calculations in order to exclude it further.

Recalling that the Israelis had expelled the vast majority of Palestine's Arabs and subdued the rest, he said, 'I don't really respect the generation of my father, including my father. Why didn't they fight for their rights?'

Hanna grew up, the eldest of three brothers and two sisters, under martial law in Israel until he was nine. Then came the occupation of Gaza and the West Bank. Palestinian citizens of

Israel sublimated their identities. They learned Hebrew. They sought Israeli benefactors to shield them from the system's worst excesses. 'Every society has its Jews,' I. F. Stone wrote in his foreword to Fouzi Al-Asmar's *To Be an Arab in Israel*. 'Israel's Jews are its Arabs.' Many joined Israeli political parties, including Menachem Begin's Herut, or Freedom, Party.

Most of the Arabs from the Elias family village, Jish, ended the war of 1948 in Lebanon. They were still there in the refugee camp of Ain el-Helouie, the Sweet Spring, near Sidon. The Israeli army demolished the camp during its 1982 invasion, but the inhabitants rebuilt it as before. Each neighbourhood housed refugees from a different village in Galilee, and they kept their Palestinian accents.

'Nobody knows about Ain el-Helouie from my village,' Hanna said of the ones who had remained in the country. Jish became the Jewish Gush Halat. 'We are not a well organized society. We're tribal. They say, my tribe is good so I am good. But this is the worm that breaks the stick. Palestinians are diversified. They are well educated. But we carry this gene with us wherever we go.'

I wanted to know what he meant when he told me that he could not breathe at the Hebrew University. 'I remember that I had to go to the hospital,' he said. 'My limbs always ached. There was no diagnosis. For a year in the dorms' – the dormitories were segregated by race – 'a South African doctor checked me. We talked. Finally, he said, you have to leave. It was a kind of relief.'

After taking his degree in Middle East history and sociology in Jerusalem, Hanna studied film at UCLA. He made some short films and had just finished a rough-cut of his first full-length feature, *The Olive Harvest*. It was the story of two Palestinian brothers in love with the same woman. He planned to do the final edit in Los Angeles, where he would probably not stand out so much in his hooded burgundy sweatshirt and tennis shoes. Watching him tap his fist gently on the chair, I suspected he felt slightly out of place in both Israel and the Arab world.

'My grandmother is from Biram,' he said. Biram and Ikrit were two Maronite Catholic villages of the Galilee evacuated in October 1948. The Israeli forces had promised the people they could return at the end of hostilities, but the promise was not kept. The villagers, despite many appeals from the Vatican and the United Nations, became 'present absentees', Arabs absent from their homes but present in the state of Israel. A quarter of Israel's million plus Arab citizens fell into this category. In 1951, the Israeli High Court affirmed the right of the people of Biram and Ikrit, because of the army's 1948 promise, to return home. The army and air force then destroyed both villages, sparing only the Maronite Church in Biram – perhaps a gesture to Lebanon's Maronites, who were potential allies. For almost sixty years, there had been lawsuits and demonstrations. But only the dead returned, with army permission, for burial.

Hanna Elias was unique, in my experience of Palestinians, in condemning his own people for the fact that Biram and Ikrit's people remained in internal exile. 'I went to all the demonstrations, when I was young,' he said. Jish was almost next door to Biram. 'This is an indicator of the tolerance of Israel.' Israel tolerated the demonstrations, but it did not tolerate the restoration of the property. The problem for Hanna was that the Palestinians did not struggle for their rights. The problem, moreover, was bigger than the Palestinians.

'Look at the 1.2 billion Muslims in the world. Look at the one hundred million Arabs. We don't even have an animation industry. Humanly, we stink, because we do not show our children pictures of birds singing in Arabic.'

The rot, or the worm, started for him within the tribe and the family. 'I think we are fucked up because of the way we deal with women in our society. To slap a woman, and for your children to see that, makes you smaller and smaller. Every day, the Arab woman is not respected. It is a mentality. It's all related to a male mentality. Relations with women are based on fear.'

These flaws had nothing to do with Israel. For some Palestinians, it was wrong to show weakness to the enemy. To them, all faults stemmed from the *nakhba* of 1948 or the occupation of 1967. 'I can't blame Israel,' Hanna said. 'It's the same in Syria. And in Syria, there are no Israelis.' Male domination and fear within the family were the themes of Hanna's films and the core of his criticism of his people. If there had been no Zionists, no *nakhba*, no exile and no occupation, Palestinian culture as he saw it would still have been rotten. Its dominant figure was in that picture on the wall of the father, the chief, the king, the president, the general. 'How can you build a culture with people like this? You are supposed to believe you're no good.' He paused to stir the sugar in his tea. 'It's fear. Our fear of our fathers has made it so easy for the Israelis, so that one Israeli on a roadblock can control twenty thousand Palestinians.' (An Israeli friend of mine's son said he hated the power he wielded at checkpoints in the occupied territories. 'Daddy,' he said, 'when you're at the checkpoint, you are a god.' Perhaps Palestinians had trained their children too well to fear and to obey. It was a legacy of Ottoman rule, when family and tribal chiefs kept members in line rather than let the Turks do it for them.)

After finishing film school in 1991, Hanna knocked around Hollywood for six years. The movie industry did not welcome Arabs, especially Palestinian Arabs. He made commercials and promotional films, and he produced a few independent shorts. The big breaks, as for most other film-school graduates and Hollywood hopefuls, eluded him. In 1997, he returned to Israel. He stayed only four months.

The Oslo mood had opened possibilities for Palestinians and Israelis to work together. Despite the government and the in-creasing number of settlers, ordinary people were doing business. Hanna worked on an Israeli–Palestinian co-production of *Sesame Street*, *Shara'a Simsim* in Arabic. He directed live seg-ments with Palestinian children. Even that experience was dis-couraging. 'Two things I learned,' he said. 'All the boys are brats. The little girls are wonderful. The boys. Oh, the boys. They are little Arafats.' He meant little dictators.

He made a short film about his father, a man he had hated

as a child and longed to understand. His father, once a teacher, had become a farmer and merchant. In the film, Hanna took his father on a motorcycle to find a shepherd for his flock. Hiring the shepherd, however, was not its real purpose. Hanna did not tell his father his ulterior motive for making their odyssey through rural Galilee on a motorcycle rather than a car. For the first time since we met, Hanna was smiling. The smile was that of a mischievous boy. 'I wanted to impose on him,' Hanna said, 'the requirement to hug me. I am now the age he was when I was a child.'

Hanna had rented a house in the old city and I saw him every few days wandering from one quarter to another. He seemed like a man who did not belong, and he was discouraged in his work. Yet he was always interesting, always had some new thought and always had time for coffee. I introduced him to Albert and Madeleine Agazarian. The next time I saw him, he was pointing a digital camera at Albert near the Greek Catholic Church in the Christian Quarter. A Palestinian movie maker was documenting the wisdom of Albert Agazarian. At last.

One day, Hanna gave me a cassette of 'the very, very rough cut' of *The Olive Harvest*. The crew were Israeli. 'I had a crew available in the United States and France,' he said. 'I made a decision to use Israeli Jews. There is a crew of seven, all Israelis, behind the camera. To see Israel with them was an experience for the Arab actors. Why not? And it's good for an Israeli audience to see what a Palestinian director and an Israeli crew can do.'

For a man so disturbed about the soul of his society, he took unexpected pride in its artists and actors. 'The best actors in the Arab world are Palestinian,' he said. 'They are world-class actors.' The stars of *The Olive Harvest* were Mohammed al-Bakir and Makram al-Khoury, a Muslim and a Christian playing brothers. As 'Israeli Arabs', they did not appear in Egyptian or other Arab films. Hanna was furious at the whole Arab world. 'Why do the best actors in the Arab world have to work in Israel?'

Often he returned to the violence within. 'They say that if you see your father hit your mother, you will hit your wife. The Israeli who beats a Palestinian remembers how the Jews were treated in Europe. This is the link we need to break.' We would discuss the *intifadah*, a rebellion that caused him 'to disrespect both sides'. He wandered somewhere the politicians did not. 'The Middle East is going monochrome. When it becomes one colour, there is something wrong. Hamas is digging deep into our fabric. The problem of rich and poor is fundamental. The PA is getting the money and not giving any to the people. All these elements make people withdraw to their little zones, to their tribe. And the Christian tribe is vanishing.' And the Israelis? 'Israel is a strange tribe,' he said. 'For the last two thousand years, it did not trust any other tribe. You have to be extra careful, extra generous, to put them on a platform so they can communicate with you.'

In Los Angeles, he belonged to a Jewish–Arab dialogue group that met each month. The usual topic was Israel. Israel affected relations between Arab and Jewish Americans as much as it did Arabs and Jews in the Middle East. In Los Angeles, few of them talked. In Jerusalem, fewer still. 'There is no place here for the Israelis and Arabs to meet,' he said. 'You need to have an Israeli from Tel Aviv go to Qalqilya and give the people there a lecture on why Zionism is right.' I supposed the next step would be for an Arab from Qalqilya, if he could evade the checkpoints, to go to Tel Aviv and give a lecture on why Zionism was wrong. The difference was this: the Arab might find many Jews, Israeli or otherwise, who agreed with him; Israelis would not come across a single Arab who embraced Zionism's conclusion that he either did not or should not exist.

In the Think-Tank

The largest Israeli doves' group, Peace Now, published details of an aerial survey that discovered ten settlements that had not existed five months earlier. The Israeli 'Civil Administration', as the military government in the West Bank called itself, admitted that eight of the sites were settlements, but said that the other two were army bases. In the West Bank and Gaza, the army's primary role was to protect the settlements. The Population Registry at the Interior Ministry put the settler population of the West Bank – excluding East Jerusalem – at 207,513 on 29 June 2001. This was an increase of 4833 in six months, but it subtracted the settlers who had gone overseas or to stay with their families in Israel until Palestinian attacks ceased. Nor did it include the 200,000 settlers in Arab east Jerusalem.

Prime Minister Ariel Sharon had proposed a budget that reduced social welfare funding, and Israelis in wheelchairs staged vigils at the Knesset to beg their representatives to leave their benefits in place. The budget, so unpopular that it could not pass the Knesset, increased the amount spent in two sectors: the army and the settlements. Ze'ev Stornhell wrote in *Ha'aretz* on 16 November 2001 that 'settlers will always take precedence over unemployed, the sick, the single-parent family, the elderly living on social security and all of those who scratch out a living on the minimum wage'. The mechanisms of distributing state subsidies for education, medical care and social welfare were changing. Where the old Israeli welfare state had dealt with citizens as individuals, the new model was to distribute money to community leaders and institutions and let them take care of their own. It was state funding of the tribes.

'Tribalism is manifested in a welfare state that is slightly dismantled and channelled through tribes rather than direct to the citizens,' Moshe Halberthal told me one day at his modern office in Talbieh, a former Arab quarter of West Jerusalem. Halberthal taught philosophy and Jewish thought at the Hebrew

University. A friend of the writer Bernard Avishai, he was utiliz-
ing some of Avishai's insights into Israeli tribalism. 'Take Shransky, for example,' he said. Natan Shransky headed an extreme
right-wing party of Russian immigrants. I had met Shransky
on a speakers' platform in California in 1989, when we were
promoting our books. His was about his years as a 'Prisoner of
Zion' in the Soviet Union. Even then he displayed no empathy
for Zion's Arab prisoners in Israel. 'He's all for money channelled through his constituency,' Halberthal said. 'If you are a
new immigrant and you're a Shas member, you receive education, transport and hot meals. These are given to you, not on
the basis of reducing the income gap, but via channelling
through your religious-ethnic group.' Members of Shas, the
'keepers of the Torah', were mainly Oriental, or Sephardic,
Jews.

Born in Montevideo, Uruguay, in 1958 of an Israeli mother
and Polish Holocaust survivor father, Moshe Halberthal arrived
in Israel in 1966. He studied at the Hebrew University and at
Harvard. He had also been to Yeshiva and served in the army.
It was not an obvious profile. Yeshiva implied right wing. The
Hebrew University and Harvard pointed to liberalism. What I
liked about Israel was that nothing pointed in a predictable
direction. Natan Shransky had been imprisoned for his national-
istic convictions in Russia but felt nothing for nationalists, who
happened to speak Arabic, in Israel. Halberthal wore a black
kippa and had been a Yeshiva student and soldier, but he
opposed special privileges for religious Jews – like not having
to serve in the army and receiving state funds for religious
purposes. 'The money is not given based on your income,' he
said, 'but on who you are. If you are a settler, you receive more.
If you are a wounded soldier, you pay less tax.'

The mix of parties based on tribal allegiance, backed by state
funding, included Israel's Arab citizens. 'When you have a Shas,
an Arab party and an Orthodox party, politics cannot be guaranteed. Three of the five tribes have a coherent view of Israel:
the Russians, the secular Ashkenazim and the Orientals. The

other two, the Haredi and the Arabs, are different. The Haredi' – Haredi, or Haredim, were the ultra-Orthodox Jews – 'want a Jewish state but not democracy. The Arabs want the state to be democratic but not Jewish. The army takes people only from the three tribes.' He meant the secular Ashkenazim, the Sephardim and the Russians. 'The moment it arms the other two, it could create a situation leading to civil war.'

Where did the settlers fit into the tribal scheme? 'The settlers are in some ways a sixth tribe. They're another element. Theirs is a complicated demographic. The religious are the core ideological group, mainly Ashkenazim with a peculiar view of Zionism.' The tribal weakening of the state apparatus coincided with an assault on the founding fathers by the new generation of 'post-Zionist' historians. Halberthal connected the tribalization, if that is what it was, of Israel with a new appreciation of the Diaspora. David Ben-Gurion and many in his generation saw nothing redeeming in exile existence. His revisionist rival, Vladimir Jabotinsky, detested what he called 'the Yid' of Europe's shtetls and wanted an Israel that would bring Jews home to forge them into new Hebrews. His disciple, Menachem Begin, wrote in *The Revolt*, 'We fight, therefore we are!' In exchanging the ghetto's Yiddish for the Hebrew of a free Jewish commonwealth, Zionism would erase two thousand years of shame. But the new immigrants were no longer ashamed. The achievements of the Diaspora, they said, were not inconsiderable. Yiddish, the language that Zionist pioneers sought to extinguish, survived in Russia and among Israel's new Russian immigrants. The marks of exile would not go away, and some Israelis did not want them to. This was, in part, what was meant by 'post-Zionism'.

'Post-Zionism,' Halberthal said, 'means two completely different things. First, that Zionism succeeded in its goals. The whole idea that society must be recruited to this project is over. Second, it meant that Zionism is based on a primordial sin that de-legitimises the justification of Zionism and was a consistent history of cover-ups *vis-à-vis* the Palestinians. Yet post-Zionist historiography is a very marginal force in Israel.'

Halberthal believed that, however marginal, the post-Zionists were part of a wider attack on the legacy of Israel's founders. 'They are blamed for screwing the Palestinians, forcing the Haredim into secular nationalism and disrespecting the Orientals who came here.' The Haredim, the Sephardim and others dwelled in tribal enclaves. Their reaction to insults by the founders was to reject them and their Platonic ideal of the de-tribalized, Hebraized, secular Israeli Jew. Halberthal said that 'the founders' strong denial of Diaspora' allowed some to accuse them of neglecting European Diaspora Jews during the Nazi Holocaust.

The Israeli army functioned, in Halberthal's phrase, as a 'serious melting pot'. But two tribes would not melt: the Haredim and the Arabs. Both were exempt from compulsory military service, although some militant Haredim volunteered and Arab Druze were drafted. 'The basic institution of the Jewish democratic state is the army,' Halberthal said. Armies were not democratic institutions, but Israel's citizen-army was as close as any I had seen to having a democratic ethos. Officers did not isolate themselves from their troops, and rank did not guarantee respect. The men usually called their officers by their first names. Arguments between officers and men were normal. The late Israel Shahak had told me how, as a young recruit, he had once publicly assailed the then chief of staff, Moshe Dayan, without fear of reprimand. Dissidence and disobedience that in other armed forces guaranteed court martial sometimes prompted soul-searching, questioning and re-evaluation. The army's tragedy was not its admirable form, but the uses to which it was often put: seizing land for settlers; demolishing Palestinian houses and olive groves; shooting teenage demonstrators; committing political assassinations; dropping bombs on villages, cities and refugee camps; and occupying other countries. Worse still, its military justice system did not punish soldiers who committed war crimes, and officers would protect troops who shot journalists or unarmed children.

'The army, unlike in many other states, has a loyalty to the political process that is striking,' Halberthal said. The military's political colour blindness kept the state secure, although it was the tool that enabled the state to commit crimes against the Arabs. So many senior professional officers had become government ministers – General Sharon was prime minister, General Ben-Eliezer was minister of defence, another general was minister of culture and General Ze'evi had been minister of tourism – that the army had come to seem more master than servant.

As for Arab citizens of the state, Halberthal said, 'They don't want to be in the army, and the army doesn't want them.' In their many demands for equality as non-Jews in a state that defined itself as Jewish, the Arabs had never demanded to serve in an army that in 1948 expelled the majority of their compatriots. But 'discrimination' – in housing, land ownership, employment, education, provision of services – against Arabs was often justified on the grounds that the Arabs had not served in the army and were therefore not entitled to benefits reserved for veterans. Yet racial discrimination was no longer central to the Palestinian Arab's case against the Jewish State. At least, Halberthal detected this change among the 'fifth tribe' of his fellow citizens. The Arabs were moving from a 'discriminated-against minority to an occupied minority. This is a big shift. For Zionists like me, it makes the situation more complex. I can share their struggle on issues of discrimination, but not against the state. It has to do with identity. They are walking a very thin line.'

When Israel's Arab citizens demonstrated in the first month of the *intifidah* in solidarity with their fellow Palestinians, they crossed a line. They took sides against the state of which they were citizens on behalf of the people of whom they formed a part. Jewish Israelis crossed from toleration of their non-Jewish tribe to shooting fourteen of them dead. Israeli Arabs were shocked that peaceful marches against occupation could be crushed so forcefully, and they complained of other attacks by Israeli Jewish militants that the police ignored – all since the eruption of the *intifadah* in 2000. For Halberthal, as for many other liberal Israelis, the Palestinian Arab Israelis had gone too far: 'They were supporting almost openly a violent campaign against Israel.' Israeli Jewish activists had also marched in the streets and protested against military occupation of the West Bank and Gaza. The police did not shoot them. Every Friday night, Israeli Jews demonstrated near the prime minister's house in West Jerusalem against his policies, but they asked Arabs not to take part lest they offend Israeli Jewish sensibilities. In most other contexts, this would be called racism. I doubted that Dr Halberthal and other conscientious, tolerant Israeli Jews saw it that way. He was a husband, father and teacher. He taught a few Arab students. He believed in equality. But he had another belief: in difference. 'Arab society is ambivalent, because they would like to stay as Israeli citizens,' he said. 'They enjoy the fruits of a relatively free society, while using that freedom to question the legitimacy of the state.'

Many Jews questioned the state's legitimacy. Were Arabs forbidden to do so?

'I'm all for questioning the legitimacy of the state: but in the long term, they'd like Israel as a nation-state to disappear.'

We talked about the changes that Israel shared with the rest of the world: Americanization, accelerated disparities in wealth, the dwindling middle class, the retreat into tribal and religious laagers and diminishing state support for universal education. Not all of Israel's problems were specific. Halberthal told me he had taught a course on nationalism in political theory – not Zionism or Jewish nationalism, but the idea of nationalism. Nationalism was not old, and it was not always healthy. It was neutral on democracy. Yet to be a nation, its members had to believe they belonged to the nation. To be a democracy, he said, citizens had to participate in formulating the questions and determining the laws and policies that touched their existence. To be both democracy and nation, the losers had to believe they had lost in a fair contest. Malcolm X wrote that when the white man wins every time, somebody stacked the deck. In Israel, the Arabs lost every time.

'Democracies rest on civic participation,' Dr Halberthal said. 'They become non-democratic when voting percentages come down. Democracies want to have a non-violent procedure for adjudicating debates. Here we play high stakes politics. Both the right and the left see that the other puts the future of their children in danger. The right fears the left will sell out, and the left fears the right will bring war.' Neither left nor right had sold out, and both had taken the country to war. They were at war again in the West Bank to preserve all-Jewish townships, built by both the right and the left, on territory they had conquered together in 1967. Halberthal was wrestling with his conscience for a way to fix it without going to war and without selling out. So far, he had not found the secret.

The Artist and his Stones

Shlomo Vezzana looked exactly what he was – a worker and an artist, or a worker-artist. He lugged a big knapsack of pride everywhere, with the muscled arms and hands of a man who did not take abuse. He was the kind of man who deserved the epitaph that John Wayne wanted for his tombstone: 'He was ugly, he was strong and he had dignity.'

Israel's melting pot had not scalded Shlomo Vezzana. Born in Jerusalem in 1956 to two Moroccan Jews who met in an Israeli resettlement camp, he spoke Arabic like a Moroccan Arab and Hebrew with a better accent than the Ashkenazim who looked down upon their semi-Arab co-religionists. When we met for a coffee in the American Colony's courtyard, he joked with the Palestinian waiters. The coffee he ordered was Turkish. Later, we walked around Katamonim, his rundown immigrant neighbourhood. When he bantered with the Ethiopian and Oriental Jewish kids playing football, he did so as one of them. He was a guy who fitted in wherever he was. Crises of identity and self-doubt would not send him to a psychiatrist.

Lily Galili had told me to call him. Shlomo Vezzana was a

sculptor, she said, a painter, a Moroccan and a political trouble-maker. He had served in the army for four years, a year longer than conscription required. He had been a teacher and made documentaries. Her prediction that I would like him proved right.

'I make documentary films,' he said when we met at the Colony. English was difficult for him, but he made the effort to convey ideas that would have flowed in Hebrew or Arabic. 'I made a documentary about society and football. One guy in my neighbourhood was a star in the eighties, but he didn't know how to live with the stardom.' He stopped for a second, reaching for words in a language he knew but did not use much. 'Because he came to the position without any knowledge of what it means to be a star. Then he went down. He made too many mistakes. He was gambling. Now he lives with his wife and four children. All four are in a football team. He hopes that they will all be stars. But why? He hopes to get money. We have many football stars from poor places in Israel. It's an option you can achieve because you don't need an education or money. You just have to know how to play. The problem is that the media put it as an option for all poor people. As I understand it, it's not a real option.'

Through Shlomo Vezzana I saw in Israel's poor Sephardim the predicament I remembered of the 'white artisans' in pre-independence Rhodesia and the 'white trash' of the American South. The myth contended that these lower classes of the master race were the most hostile to blacks. But it was less race hatred than fear of descending to the level, the lowest rung, reserved for the defeated race. Sephardic Israelis, like Africa's poor whites *vis-à-vis* the blacks, emphasized distinctions between themselves and the Arabs that the educated, rich elite did not worry about. The Sephardim resembled the Arab underclass in more ways than poverty. They spoke Arabic at home. They ate Arab food. They listened to Arabic music. They looked like Arabs. They, or their parents, had grown up in Arab societies. For them to be accepted into the Israeli mainstream was hard. The Ashkenazim who founded the state identified with the dominant West and with European–American culture. They had founded Israel to solve the problems of European Jewry with no thought of the Sephardim – literally, Spaniards to denote the Jews who had been expelled from Spain in the fifteenth and sixteenth centuries *with* the Arabs and had remained in Arab lands. (Technically, Iraqi Jews – who had dwelled in Mesopotamia before the Arab conquest – could not be Sephardim. They were considered, along with the Sephardim, 'Oriental'.) For years, Israeli politicians and military officers came from the Western elite – often the liberal, kibbutz-educated cream of society. They claimed that Sephardi soldiers and policemen behaved more brutally to the Arabs because the Arabs had mistreated them in the lands they had left – Morocco, Iraq, Egypt, Tunisia, Yemen and Lebanon. Vezzana did not accept this. If the Sephardim were harsher towards Palestinian Arabs than the Ashkenazim, he said, it was to prove to the Ashkenazim that they were not Arabs. The other soldiers said the cruellest were Druze, who *were* Arabs. They, like African soldiers in Ian Smith's Rhodesia, had the most to prove.

Vezzana laughed at me when I asked whether his family had been oppressed in Morocco. 'Of course not,' he said. 'My mother was very rich there. My family came here because, in 1948, everywhere Jews lived and if communication went there, people understood they should come to the Promised Land.' His father had been a shoemaker in Casablanca, not rich, but he owned a shop and earned a good living. His mother's family, wealthy traders from Fez, took a steep step down when they made *aliya* and found themselves in an immigrants' camp. 'My father and my mother were put into a *ma'abara* camp, the "camp of passing". Five or six or eight years, this kind of passing.' What they passed to, he believed, was not much better.

In 1950 and 1951, about 350,000 Jews emigrated to Israel. Most came from the Arab states. Some, like Vezzana's Moroccan parents, believed the time had come to go to the Promised Land. Others were driven out by Arab regimes that punished their Jewish citizens, almost none of whom were Zionists, for the Arab defeat of 1948. Israel's reception of the Orientals was not as it had been for the Europeans. It did not put them immediately into confiscated Arab houses or build new towns for them. Instead, it opened 139 *ma'abarot*, transit camps where the Arabic-speaking Jews dwelled in plywood and canvas shacks. Often, more than one family shared a hut. It did not help that the 1950 winter was the worst on record, when snow fell even on the shores of Tel Aviv. After the *ma'abarot*, many of the Orientals were taken to Beersheva and Dimona in the Negev Desert. It was reported at the time that many of the Moroccans asked to go somewhere 'normal' rather than Dimona. They called it, with a slight change in pronunciation, *Dim'ona* – Hebrew for 'place of tears'. Dimona was also where the state placed its first nuclear reactor and its stock of nuclear warheads. Immigration fell to 24,000 in 1952, but many of the *ma'abarot* remained for another ten years.

Vezzana's parents met in the camp, where all classes of Oriental Jews – the merchants and the shoemakers – were brought to the same level. Conditions were primitive, worse than for European immigrants in the 1950s. Differences of class diminished in the camps, but a caste system awaited them on their release into Israeli society. And they were as near the bottom of it as anyone who was Jewish could get. Because Arabs were enemies, the Sephardims' Arabness was detested. 'Zionist ideology is anti-East,' Vezzana said. 'If the norm is anti-Oriental, you must forget the Oriental in your identity. If my mother dresses Arab and listens to Arab music and eats Arab food, it goes against my mother. But she is my mother.' The Sephardim took the worst jobs and lived in the most rundown neighbourhoods. 'For many years, they' – he meant the Ashkenazim – 'built a wall to keep their economic position and their culture. Culture and economics go together. If you push one kind of culture in the media, it gives a legitimization of how you share the resources of a society.'

Shlomo Vezzana was born in 1956, the second of five

children. It was the year Israel invaded Egypt and Lily Galili moved to Israel from Poland. His father went to work in a factory; and the family moved to Katamonim, built in 1965 as a fortress along the Green Line with Jordan. Vezzana was eleven when Israel conquered the West Bank and pushed the Jordanians far from Katamonim. He and his siblings studied in Israeli state schools, where Western education alienated them from their family. 'The school destroys what is in your house,' Vezzana said. 'Your family is a kind of enemy. It separates you from the centre of your life. It destroys families, of course.'

The Oriental culture itself was suspect in Israel, he believed. He told me about the Mimouna 'holiday of believing' that Jews had celebrated for centuries in Morocco. It was the last day of Pesach, Passover. 'At the end of Pesach, the idea of the Jews says we are equal,' he said. 'We got freedom from Egypt. In Pesach, we believe we'll be freed again with the Messiah. What happened? Pesach finishes, and still we are not free. It's a belief in next year. In the context of Israel, it is put as an ugly holiday because it does not come from Europe.'

He referred again and again to his mother. She was important to him in understanding, as it seemed to me, most aspects of his life. 'When my mother died, I go with death a long way to understand what it means to the living,' he said. 'I understood that I have something to say – not only to myself, to everyone, about death. It means life stops. What is the meaning of life? Where are these people going? All these questions that come to you make for intensive thinking. It means the mind grows because of death. It means that after you finish the pain, you must do something with it. You think what it means to be a man. Death comes to teach you something about life. This is what I am saying to the people, that death comes to teach you.' As an artist, he was trying to teach people, particularly in Katamonim, something about life and about bringing beauty from what the world called ugly. It was a difficult task, particularly when the newest immigrants – the Russians – also looked down on them. The Russians' arrival pushed the Orientals further down. 'Many functions in the society are taken by the Russians, and it means they don't need the Easterners. They don't need us.'

His wife was a young Oriental woman named Yael. They had one daughter and another child due in a few months. I met Yael at her dance class in a bomb shelter that had become Vezzana's studio. He managed to work there without much natural light, while people came to visit through his unlocked door. On one wall was a passage in Hebrew from Brecht's *Manifesto of Aesthetic Theory* that Vezzana translated: 'We are making something natural in such a way in order to make it clear later. We have to destroy accepted axioms so they don't need clarification.' He pointed to some framed photographs. One was of a damaged wall, the 'before' in a series of two. The 'after' showed the same wall repaired and painted white. A tree cast its shadow over its length. At least, I thought it did. 'When you put a white colour, the shadow of the tree comes to the wall,' Vezzana said. 'Without the wall, there is no shadow.' When he finished painting the wall white, he traced and painted the afternoon shadow of a nearby tree on it. He liked the fact that the shadow stayed on the wall even at night. 'One day after I did it, the people from the city came and took the tree away. Because the tree was dead.' The tree had gone and its shadow remained. Vezzana was a public artist. You were not likely to find his work in a genteel drawing room. To see it, you had to get out into the streets.

Katamonim was what Vezzana called 'a workers' neighbourhood' between Jerusalem and the settlement at Gilo. The government press office had badgered the American television networks into calling Gilo 'a Jerusalem neighbourhood' rather than a settlement. Although Gilo was built on land conquered in 1967, the government had expanded Greater Jerusalem's boundaries to include it. Under international law, it was an illegal settlement on occupied land. Israeli law said it was a neighbourhood. In the great contest between international law and Israeli propaganda, American television chose propaganda every time. Vezzana did not. He saw the money spent on Gilo and compared it to the neglect of Katamonim. If Gilo had been a 'workers' neighbourhood' like Katamonim, the government would not have paid people to live there and subsidized their mortgages. It was easy to tell the difference between neighbourhoods and settlements, and the difference was more than legal. Neighbourhoods were worse off. The settlement had Burger Kings and swimming pools.

'All you need,' Vezzana said, 'is to look at the earth and what you take for yourself and what you give me. Then I understand how you see me.' The state, he believed, did not see him at all. When it looked for a place to dump the waste dug out to make Gilo and the roads to it, it found Katamonim. Its residents woke one morning to see all the rubble the builders could carry at the edge of their neighbourhood. They mattered so little that the state regarded their home turf as a public dumping ground. Vezzana, however, turned the rubble against the state. He wanted me to see it and led me outdoors, past an old building that he said was about to be demolished, through open yards and chicken coops. A turkey and a few ducks pecked at the soil, and some boys were playing football on open ground. One side wore red, the other blue. The players were Orientals and Fallashas, Ethiopian Jews whose parents came to Israel in the early 1980s as part of Operation Moses that rescued about ten thousand of them from civil war. When the Fallashas reached Israel, the official rabbinate would not recognize them as Jews and required them to convert to Judaism. The Fallashas resented the decision, which they said epitomized their treatment in the new country. They and the Orientals were, like the scattered rocks Vezzana showed me, residue dumped far from middle-class eyes.

'They built the road and threw the stones here,' he said. Some of the stones were taller than a house, and it would have been impossible to remove them without the heavy equipment that had left them here. But something had happened to the rocks. They were no longer rubble. Vezzana had turned waste rock from a symbol of contempt to a triumphal monument, the rainbow gateway to Jerusalem from the West Bank. Over two years, Vezzana – with help from his neighbours – painted every boulder, every rock and every small stone a different colour. The largest rocks were vivid scarlet and vermilion, sapphire and saffron. The smallest were pink, each engraved with a black Hebrew letter. I thought of Usama Khalidy's bronze Arabic letters in Amman.

Did the colours mean anything? Yes and no, it seemed. He said, 'For example, the yellow. It's yellow for everybody. Also the green and the blue. It doesn't matter where you come from, rich or poor. It is universal language. Pure language. Because you are the ruler and you have a language. You have the newspapers and television. You put me in a position that is good for you, not for me. What can you say about yellow? Another source, but it's private. Years before I made it, my mother died. She had an eastern identity. Society defined her in a different way from the way I do. I had support from my mother. I say my feelings about my mother. But also about feeling the mother in society. For example, our society, because it takes the Western position doesn't like the Arab position. My mother is Arab, Jewish Arab.' To the Jewish Arabs, the colours and letters meant one thing, to the Ashkenazim – to whom the waste site was an eyesore – they meant something else.

Vezzana believed that the people of Katamonim understood immediately what he was doing. 'People gave me paint from their houses,' he said. 'Children in the school made a painting of the stones and brought it to me. I said, look, this is real education.' Like the Watts Towers in Los Angeles, a ghetto rebelled through art against the powers who denigrated a people.

What were the letters? 'Jewish letters are mystical,' he answered. Some meant peace, others strength, others the Bible. The stones were a rainbow, and the letters were the shadows of meaning that graced them – like the tree's shadow stuck to a white wall long after the tree had been taken away. 'As you see the tree,' he said, 'they are a kind of shadow. But you don't know their object, what made them. It's hiding. The object is secret. It is a kind of knowledge that makes a conversation, in a different way.' Children were playing hide and seek amid the rocks, while we climbed to the top.

'In the town, they know this is not easy to move,' he said, looking across to the Arab village of Beit Safafa. 'It's come to be a sign of Jerusalem.' He had taken a year to paint his masterpiece. He liked the fact that it confused most of those driving past. 'When you put colour on rooms, the function is understood,' he said. 'When you put colour on stone, you don't understand the reason. The function is hidden. What is it? It's not my room. Not my house. You are crazy. Why put colours on stones? It makes people think.'

Perhaps it was no accident that his political party called itself Hakeshet Itz Mizrach, the Oriental Rainbow Democrats.

'Know something strange?' Vezzana asked. 'All the cats born on this site are black. I have no black stones, but every cat is black. Generation after generation. Look!' As if on cue, a kitten padded from under a rock. I remained sceptical, until I saw another kitten. Then another. And another. And then a full-grown cat. All of them were jet black, not so much as a streak of white fur on any of them. Seeing my amazement, Vezzana said, 'The line between mysticism and bullshit is very fine.'

SIX

Gaza

'Gaza may best be described as in most respects the
southern counterpart of Damascus. It is a site of
abundant fertility on the edge of a great desert – a
harbour for the wilderness and a market for the
nomads; once, as Damascus, the rendezvous of
a pilgrimage . . .'
REVEREND GEORGE ADAM SMITH
The Historical Geography of the Holy Land (1894)

A Foreign Field

THE ALLIED CONQUEST of Syria commenced in April 1915,
when the French navy bombarded Gaza. France was to prepare
the ground for an assault by British and Commonwealth troops
of the Egyptian Expeditionary Force. The British, however,
would not be ready to attack for another two years, in March of
1917. In the meantime, the German commander of the Ottoman
defences, General Kress von Kressenstein, reinforced Gaza.
He built earthworks, trenches and barbed-wire barriers that
he manned with Turkish regulars and Palestinian Arab and
Armenian conscripts. Britain would fight three battles and lose
thousands of men to win the city.

The fall of Gaza in the west and of Aqaba to the east began
the Turkish retreat from Syria, the denouement to four centuries
of Ottoman imperium over its Arab subjects. The British paid
in lives to succeed the Sultan. The first battle of Gaza left them
with twice the number of dead as the Turks, the second with
three times as many. The British buried theirs in the Gaza War
Cemetery. My taxi driver did not know where the graveyard

181

was, but an old man at my hotel in Gaza City told him to look for it off the road to Erez opposite the Seven-Up bottling plant. Off we went through shabby lanes of light industrial shops in cold concrete with steel shutters. Gaza's bleak cityscape had been built on the cheap to utilize landless refugees who were so poor they worked for paltry wages and did not challenge long hours and dangerous conditions. Men in T-shirts without goggles welded iron bars together. Others loaded bottles and boxes onto trucks. If I wanted to remake *The Asphalt Jungle* in Palestine, I would have done it at the industrial edge of Gaza City.

Turning right from the highway and its warren of factories and flats, we came to an avenue of seventy new cypresses. The trees led to a stone arch at the cemetery gate. From the road, the *Makbar Ingleezi*, English Cemetery, had been as invisible as history. At the portal, it was the most beautiful place in Gaza. A five-foot wall enclosed Gaza's largest plot of green. Inside, all was in order. Every stone marker was a door planted at the head of its earthen bed, each the regulation distance from the next. One by one they lay, as one by one they had fallen. A small gleaning beside the great harvests of Flanders and the Somme, Gaza's dead had raised the stakes in Palestine. Until then, Palestine's acquaintance with European scales of butchery derived from folk tales of Napoleon's 1799 campaign and, before that, of the Crusades.

THE LAND ON WHICH THIS CEMETERY STANDS
IS THE FREE GIFT OF THE PEOPLE OF PALESTINE
FOR THE PERPETUAL RESTING PLACE OF THOSE
OF THE ALLIED ARMIES WHO FELL IN THE WAR OF 1914–1918
AND ARE HONOURED HERE.

Who were these men, who had given their lives to conquer the Holy Land again for Christendom?

The first tombstone I read was for 'Private F. J. Griffin, Wiltshire Regiment, 19th September 1918, Age 28'. Beneath a cross carved into his stone was the legend:

Gaza

Above the rest
This not shall swell
My Jesus hath done
All things well.

A sprinkler rained water on a corner of the grassy, foreign field that was forever somewhere else. Bougainvillea and rose bushes shaded the walls. Tombstones faced east, to the rising sun. Walking west, I read names and regiments from an imperial tableau: For King and Country, Royal Field Artillery, 8th Australian Light Horse, New Zealand Maori Battalion, King's Own Scottish Borderers, British West Indies Regiment, Argyll and Sutherland Highlanders, the Army Cyclist Corps, the Duke of Cornwall's Light Infantry, Royal Sussex Regiment, Machine Gun Corps, the Cameronians, First Cape Corps, Imperial Camel Corps, Thy Will Be Done. Boy soldiers in their teens lay beside Major R. W. P. Evans, Age 46, of the Welsh Regiment. Many were Unknown.

A smaller stone wall segregated a corner of the sacred ground. Ice plants grew atop a common grave for 'Twelve Musulman soldiers of the Indian Army'. Opposite, more boxed-in ice plants covered 'Twenty-five soldiers of the Indian Army', presumably Hindus.

The men had died in the three Gaza battles, the two that Britain lost and the last, when the Ottomans collapsed. A historian could date the 1917 battles from the tombstones, early March, 17 to 19 April and 27 October to 7 November. After that, the casualties stop. The British who died later were buried in Jerusalem on the Mount of Olives. Two additions to the First World War graves intrigued me: a Canadian plot for soldiers who died on United Nations duty, at least one man for every year between 1959 and 1966. Nearby were seven graves of Indian soldiers who died while serving with the UN Emergency Force between 1959 and 1964. They were honoured by words from the Bhagavad-Gita:

For certain is death for the born
And certain is birth for the dead.
Therefore over the inevitable
Thou shouldst not grieve.

Gaza had nowhere else as tranquil as this home for the dead.
The rest of the Strip consisted of battle lines between native and
settler, of towns and refugee camps that had so little space that
people slept six to a room, of streets where children played
because there was nowhere left for a park or a playground.
Some of Gaza's last Palestinian orchards grew right up to the
graveyard's southern and eastern walls. Factories poked above
the wall to the north; high, grey apartment complexes to the
west. It was a poor land, so arid that Palestinian farmers dug
twelve feet into the soil to plant the roots of their vines nearer
the falling water table. The necropolis was its opposite: vast,
empty, verdant and peaceful. I walked up the ranks of the dead
and back down again. When Britain planted its first casualties
here, open ground lay all around. No more. In 1948, the refugees came, doubling the population. After 1967, Israel added
settlers to the mix. The names, the Bible verses, the only solitude
in Gaza, shadows of tower blocks and tombstones, all of it was
a reminder that Britain's imperial deaths had achieved only a
century of turmoil.

I heard an engine and saw a tractor heading towards me. It
stopped. A tall Palestinian man, probably in his sixties, tanned
and healthy, set the brake. He marched up, extended a hand
and declared, 'How do you do? My name is Ibrahim Jarred,
MBE.'

I asked Mr Jarred how many men were buried there. 'Three
thousand five hundred and two,' he said. 'Thirty are not from
the World War, and fifty are not from the Commonwealth.
Seven hundred and eighty-two are unknown.'

Mr Jarred kept a fine garden, the grass, the bougainvillea,
the roses, the cypresses. He maintained the stone walls, the
monuments, the grave markers. If anyone deserved the honour

of membership of the British Empire, it was Mr Jarred. All that remained of that empire in Gaza lay within his walls.

Entry

Gaza was a two-hour drive from Jerusalem, through suburbs south past villages and fields, sites of famous battles and of expulsions from Latrun, Ramleh and Lydda. Then we came to a new place, new in that it had become a frontier post between the state of Israel and the pseudo-state of Palestine's southern district. It was called Erez, or the Erez crossing, or, to the drivers who were not allowed to drive their cars through it, fucking Erez. Patrick Bishop, a *Daily Telegraph* correspondent on assignment from London, and I had arranged for one taxi from Jerusalem to Erez and a connection to a Gaza taxi on the other side. In between, we lugged our bags into a Portakabin passport control with a separate counter for VIPs, potted plants and shiny vinyl sofas. One of the soldiers who stamped the passports of visitors – almost all of them from the UN or international media – was the son of a friend of ours, another British journalist. No Western journalists' children, as far as I knew, served in the Palestine Authority police or in Hamas.

Stamped in, we collected our bags and walked across the asphalt past the concrete blocks and gun towers, Israel's permeable ramparts that excluded from Israel all of Gaza's Arabs except those determined to murder Israelis. Among those kept out were: workers who used to make a living in Israel; women who wanted to visit their daughters or sisters during childbirth in the West Bank; farmers with fruit to sell; and students with university places in Bir Zeit and Bethlehem. At Erez, Israel had erected a wall that divided its citizens from those Palestinians who used to seek work or a way of understanding and living with Israelis. It did not stop the young men who were so desperate and lost that they strapped bombs to their bodies and accepted suicide in order to kill a few Israeli civilians or soldiers.

Of all the absurd borders that had defaced this land since the British drew them at the end of the First World War, this was the cruellest. How would a historian explain it in a century or so?

Why was there an Erez? Why was there a Gaza Strip? Before 1948, no geographer, historian or government had treated the area as a separate portion of Palestine. Gaza was a small city. Its daughter Delilah had tempted and tormented the Hebrew champion Samson, of whom Milton wrote in *Samson Agonistes*, '. . . wisest Men / Have err'd, and by bad Women been deceiv'd; / And shall again, pretend they ne're so wise.' Perhaps Jews had been warned off Gaza since Samson's time, no safer in the twenty-first century than in antiquity. The desert, orchards and villages near Gaza became the 'Strip' in 1948, the only corner of Palestine that the Egyptian army held after losing the Negev Desert and evacuating the Falluja pocket. A patch of non-Israeli ground to dump refugees suited the Israelis. Without it, Palestinian Arabs driven from their villages south of Jaffa might have been left within the Israeli state and thus reduced or prevented the Jewish majority. Israel conquered Gaza in 1956, withdrew in 1957 and occupied it again in 1967.

Israeli mythology demonized the Strip as a terrorist breeding ground, the land of Philistines who tempted faithful sons of Isaac to their doom. After the 1967 conquest, Gaza's youngsters resisted occupation. Unlike the West Bankers, who had been under strict Jordanian rule for nineteen years, the Gazans had access to weapons. The Israeli army responded with the standard methods for suppressing subject peoples. It demolished houses to clear wider roadways for tanks – as the French had removed large portions of Damascus in the 1920s to suppress Arab nationalists, as the American armed forces were in the same years doing to whole villages in Vietnam and as France had in Algeria. It assassinated suspected rebels, although not on the scale employed by US forces in Vietnam in the Phoenix programme that 'neutralized' more than thirty thousand suspected communists and nationalists. It employed collective punishment, torture and mass arrests. As in Vietnam and Algeria, the Israelis established a network of informers and collaborators, who were sometimes unreliable or personally motivated. The commander of the ruthless pacification of the Gaza Strip was General Ariel Sharon.

Sharon added a weapon to the arsenal of native subjugation that was novel in form rather than concept. While the Americans were attempting to fabricate a 'third force' between its corrupt South Vietnamese army generals and the Vietcong, Sharon financed an alternative to the nationalists and communists: Islam. The orthodoxy of the time, supported by Western and Israeli scholarship as well as by the CIA's experience of opposing Nasser in Egypt, said that Muslim ideologues were conservative and docile. The Saudi royal family was the model. It enforced Wahhabism, a strict fundamentalist doctrine, on a kingdom whose oil revenues were disrupting traditional society; and it supported American foreign policy and never threatened Israel with anything louder than a sermon. The CIA encouraged Islamic fundamentalism against the left throughout the Muslim world, and Israel did the same in Gaza. It founded an Islamic university. It arrested young men of Fateh, the PFLP, the DFLP and the communists, but it left the Muslim clergy untouched. Observant Muslims were expected to be 'good Indians', who would keep their tribesmen in order. It worked well, until Al Qaeda and Hamas prevailed over the secularists crippled by the US and Israel.

The Paediatrician

The Erez roadblock had not stopped the first man Patrick Bishop and I visited, Dr Abdel Aziz Rantissi, from sending youngsters to kill and die in Israel. His followers evaded the formalities of Erez. Rantissi's flat was in a new, rundown section of Gaza City, all unpaved roads and dust. The Hamas leader was one of the few Palestinian politicians I had met, apart from

Arafat himself, who took precautions against assassination. His apartment block was a concrete mess that looked as if it would never be finished, but two video cameras above its front door noted our arrival. Patrick and I said through a microphone that we had an appointment with the doctor. A young man, revolver tucked into his trousers, opened the door. He followed us up the stairs to Rantissi's apartment. No one frisked us, although that would have been a reasonable precaution. Perhaps Arab manners took precedence.

Rantissi, a man of middling height in his mid-fifties, invited us to sit on a sofa and drink tea or coffee. His beard and hair were short and going grey. Spectacles and a pen in his shirt pocket gave him a professorial but practical air, as if he were an engineer on a space programme. Although Israeli security people, and thus much of the media and public they influenced, regarded Rantissi and his colleagues as terrorist fanatics, he did not raise his voice. This was about two weeks after the New York and Washington massacres and during America's preparations to attack Afghanistan. I expected Rantissi to emphasize the commonality of Muslim grievances around the world, to show solidarity with Osama bin Laden and to denounce all those who oppressed the Islamic community. He didn't.

'America was not occupying another people,' he said. 'Islam does not accept what happened in America. We do not accept to kill Jews in America. But the ones here have come to take over our homeland, kill our people and destroy our homes. Look at the people who have been suffering for fifty-three years now. Look at the refugee camps. Look at the humiliation of the whole people. We say the occupation must end. The difference between here and America is wide.'

Patrick Bishop, who had to file a story that day, was interested in Rantissi's take on bin Laden. I was curious about Rantissi himself, his background, what motivated him to contest Israeli claims to the land with religion and suicide. Patrick was a good journalist, and I deferred to his need, as daily reporters say, to feed the beast.

'Until now,' Rantissi told Patrick, 'I don't believe bin Laden did it. America has no proof. I cannot imagine that bin Laden would kidnap people to kill them in a tower. America must look in other directions. If bin Laden did this, Islam would be against him. In the two towers, many Muslims were killed. All of them were innocents.'

Rantissi did not go as far as some other Palestinians had, displaying a morbid cultural inferiority, in absolving bin Laden and the Arabs who hijacked four American airliners on 11 September. They said that Arabs could not have done it. 'Only Mossad,' an otherwise reasonable Palestinian friend told me, 'had the capacity for an operation that sophisticated.' Yasser Arafat told a friend of mine the same thing, and my friend – among others – advised him to forget it. What had Israel done to the Palestinians – who numbered at home and overseas some of the best minds in science, engineering, medicine and the arts – that they doubted any Arab had the skill to fly an aeroplane into a building? Like the so-called self-hating Jews, some of them believed in racial stereotypes concocted by their enemies to demean them and to excuse their mistreatment of them.

Rantissi returned to the theme that his war was not the same as the one that had killed, as the media was then tabulating, six thousand unarmed people in the United States. 'Here, we are after occupiers, soldiers killing us. Israel says it has lost 175 people, but we've lost 700, more than 200 of them children.' The similarity was not between himself and bin Laden, but between Hamas and the Israeli army: 'What is the difference between a suicide bomb and F-16s hitting our buildings?'

Rantissi justified Hamas attacks on moral and legal bases, insisting that 'it is legal to defend yourself'. I answered that, despite his justifications, suicide bombing inside Israel was counterproductive: it killed innocents, and it turned otherwise open-minded Israelis against the Palestinians. Militarily, it achieved nothing. And, my final argument, it led to further Israeli repression and reprisals that killed more Palestinians.

'The Jews bombed the houses of the al-Saadeh family,' he

said, beginning a list of Israeli atrocities. 'Five of the family were killed. We had no reaction. The Israelis murdered Salah Darawazi, a political leader in Hamas. We had no reaction. They killed eight people and two children in Nablus. There was no reaction by Hamas. Then they killed Amar al-Hoderi, a student activist in Tulkarm. Four Israeli operations against us. Then the reaction by Hamas came with the pizza operation.' The 'pizza operation' was the suicide bombing at a Sbarro pizza outlet in West Jerusalem, that produced international condemnation of the Palestinians. Later, the American ambassador attended Sbarro's reopening. 'From the pizza operation until now, they have not assassinated one person from Hamas. We think our operation offered security. What you want is for us to accept to be killed in silence. There isn't any other method to stop Zionist terrorism.'

There was, of course, another method: accept the occupation. Rantissi was not going to do that, but he was wrong about the Israelis restraining themselves when he sent suicide bombers into Israel. Not long after we spoke Israel assassinated another Hamas activist. Later, Israel would assassinate Rantissi himself. Of all forms of resistance, why did Hamas choose homicide through suicide?

The founders of Hamas came of age as members of the Muslim Brotherhood, founded in 1928 by the Egyptian Sufi Hassan al-Banna. Although al-Banna died in 1949, a year after Egypt occupied Gaza, his message of Muslim reform and opposition to British imperialism influenced many of Palestine's newly displaced refugees. It did not take long for them to fight secular Palestinians and nationalists, who identified with Egyptian president Gamal Abdel Nasser. When a member of the Society of Muslim Brothers attempted to assassinate Nasser in October 1954, Nasser banned them and put hundreds in prison. In Gaza, they were marginalized by the more popular Arab nationalists. But they did not disappear.

Under the Israeli occupation, their fortunes reversed. Israel tended to favour them in disputes with the leftists and nationalists, who seemed the greater threat to occupation. When Palestinians applied to open a university in Gaza in 1978, the Israelis were given two proposals: for a secular institution, like that in the West Bank at Bir Zeit; and for a centre of Islamic learning. The military authorities opted for Islam. The Islamic University of Gaza opened in 1978. It required all students to spend their first year memorizing the Koran. The Israelis allowed the university to receive funds from the World Islamic Council, Saudi Arabia and Jordan. The Islamic University became a centre for the Muslim Brotherhood, which challenged Arafat's Fateh and the leftist Palestinians more than it did the Israeli occupier. Two writers who lived in the Gaza Strip in the early 1980s, Richard Locke and Anthony Stewart, wrote in their book *Bantustan Gaza* that when secular students were beaten by Muslim Brothers, the Israelis went to the hospital and arrested the *victims*.

Although the Brothers' priority was to convert Palestinians to their interpretation of Islam, they eventually came into conflict with the Israelis. It was then that some of them, including Abdel Aziz Rantissi and the blind, quadriplegic cleric Sheikh Ahmed Yassin, founded the Muslim Resistance Movement. Its Arabic initials were HMS, Hamas. In that year, the first *intifadah* began. 'In 1987,' Rantissi recalled, 'the Jews escalated their harassment of people here. They used to ask people to come out and lie on the ground, and they walked on their backs with their boots. They used to come to our coffee shop and tell old men to dance in the street. Our religion does not allow this. They ordered sons to slap their fathers in the face.'

Later, a Gaza psychiatrist told me that in a survey of three thousand young people during that *intifadah*, more than half – 55 per cent – had witnessed Israeli soldiers beating their fathers. The effect on a young girl or boy, seeing the father and protector of the family humiliated, was traumatic. Its effect on a society, on a generation, had yet to be measured. Said Aburish, a Palestinian writer in exile who was born near Jerusalem in Bethany, wrote about the deterioration of Palestinian society – a

traditional society, whose families were held together by patriarchs – when children lost faith in their parents. In *Cry, Palestine*, he observed that his young nephews, in and out of prisons
for demonstrating against occupation, stopped listening to the
cautious advice of their fathers.

'I have seen them,' Rantissi, seated upright on an old sofa
in his barely furnished apartment, said, 'order youngsters to spit
in their fathers' faces.' He claimed that the security services
recruited young Palestinians to inform on their families.
B'Tselem and other Israeli human rights groups had issued many
reports on the intimidation, blackmail and bribery – often with
promises of permits to work or travel – of boys and girls to spy
on their families and friends. The policy broke the bonds of
trust that held traditional society together. The reaction was the
murder, often on doubtful evidence, of hundreds of suspected
collaborators. In the first *intifadah*, Palestinians killed more of
their own than they did Israelis.

In December 1987 the unarmed uprising that the Palestinians
called the *intifadah* began. University students staged anti-
occupation demonstrations. Children threw stones at Israeli
tanks. Young women shouted abuse at Israeli soldiers. The older
generation lost control of its children. Rantissi remembered
driving his car through Gaza just before the uprising in 1987.
It was after dark. 'An intelligence officer stopped me and told
me to sit in the middle of the street. When I refused, he asked a
soldier to force me. He knew who I was. I sat there for an hour.
I had my neighbours' son with me. He beat the boy in front
of me.'

Rantissi could not protect the boy, the duty of every Arab
man. It was not long after this that he and other Muslim
Brothers formed Hamas. I wanted the details. Who had taken
part? Who had stayed out? Did that affect Israel's support for
the Islamic University? The *intifadah* had taken Yasser Arafat
and his comrades in their Tunis headquarters by surprise. At
first, as with the second uprising in September 2000, they did
not support it. Had Hamas decided to fill the leadership

vacuum? One thing both uprisings had in common was that Palestinians were reacting to the failure of their leadership to end occupation. Were the Hamas leaders doing any better?

Patrick Bishop, facing a deadline for that day's news, tapped his notebook. He did not need a history lesson. The interview was straying from what his editors and readers wanted, if they wanted anything. Bishop needed today's news, and today's news was Osama bin Laden. Rantissi was a bin Laden of Gaza. The past was for books like mine. Having been in his position, I sympathized. He needed a quote, a story. I wanted to understand. I was wondering about Rantissi. I understood a man with strong religious and political beliefs. I understood an educated man, who chose not to live in a more luxurious house. I understood a man willing to die for his beliefs. I did not understand men who sent youngsters, like his neighbours' son, to die for their cause. Maybe I had to go back to the beginning.

'I was born in Yibna,' he said. 'It's a little farming village between Tel Aviv and Ashdod. I was six months old when my family escaped to Gaza.'

When Israel invaded the West Bank and Gaza Strip in 1967, many Palestinian refugees crossed the Green Line and visited the villages, fields and houses they had last seen in 1948. Most had been destroyed by the Israelis, who demolished 385 Palestinian villages. Rantissi's had survived. Did he go back to see his family's house?

'I visited,' he said. 'Everyone in the area still calls it the Rantissi house. Jews from Yemen came to occupy my home. They have the same manners and hospitality as the Arabs. They let my mother into the house to see her room. I didn't try.'

The men never do. Israeli friends who have received visits from the original Arab owners of their houses told me that the women and children asked to enter. The men waited in the car or did not come at all. I asked Rantissi if he thought that, one day, he would get his house back. His answer was what every Israeli fears. In a soft, unemphatic voice that implied mine had been the stupidest of questions, he said, 'Yes.'

193

Rantissi would not live to return to his family's house. Hamas elected him as its leader, after Israel murdered Sheikh Ahmed Yassin. Rantissi swore to avenge Yassin. Then Israel murdered him as well. And other men promised vengeance for him.

The commander of a Japanese Kamikaze, suicide unit told the author Richard O'Neil in his *Suicide Squads: The Men and Machines of World War II Special Operations*, 'My men were not "war machines": they were young, they loved their country, and they took no thought for themselves. The spirit that inspires them stems from the warrior spirit of Japan; but, really, men of all nations are capable of summoning up a similar spirit. It isn't something that belongs to Japan alone.' Nor does it 'belong' to Islam. By the time I left Israel six months later, those who blew themselves up would come to include women, older men and secular people who could not bear to live under occupation any longer. In Lebanon, during the Israeli occupation, some of the suicide bombers were Christian. In Lebanon, the bombers succeeded: Israel withdrew. In Palestine, they were failing. The Israeli army was not leaving. It was coming back.

It returned to Ramallah, Jenin, Nablus and the other West Bank A Areas of Palestinian autonomy under the Oslo accords. It raided Gaza's towns and refugee camps. It attacked the Palestinians from the skies and on the ground. It assassinated the Hamas leader, Sheikh Ahmed Yassin, and then his successor, Abdel Aziz Rantissi. It demolished hundreds more homes in Rafah, along Gaza's border with Egypt. Then, in the spring of 2005, it pulled out of Gaza – just as it had in 1957. This time, it was not American pressure that forced Israel out so much as the cost of maintaining the settler–army presence in a corner of Palestine that most Israelis had never wanted in the first place.

I visited Netzarim, Gaza's largest settlement, in June 2004, shortly after Ariel Sharon announced his intention to remove all of Gaza's few thousand settlers. In the daytime, it was an encampment of women and children. The mothers sat knitting on benches, their heads modestly covered in scarves like pious

Muslim women, while their children played on the green lawn of a shaded park. Their husbands and grown sons were either in the Yeshiva praying or working in Ashkelon or Tel Aviv. They were traditional wives with large families, who lived in the cheap, American-style tract housing from the era in which they seemed stuck – the 1950s, when a woman's place was in the home and everyone worshipped together. Many of them were American, living on their new frontier and facing a new set of hostile natives. They did not believe Sharon would really make them leave. It was an electoral ploy, something to humour the Palestinians or a threat to the more extreme rightists in his coalition. Sharon was offering to buy the settlers out, the longer-term residents for hundreds of thousands of dollars. 'No money from all over the world will take people from here,' a young woman, Dina Abramson, swore to me. 'You can't sell your house and kids and belief, just for money.' Wearing a tight shift and sounding like an old-fashioned hippy, Dina said it was not her fault if the Arabs who lived beyond the Netzarim perimeter could not share her joy at living on the land.

A year later, they were gone. All of them. Palestinians nearby were allowed to walk again to the sea through what had been Netzarim and to swim. One young man drowned. Palestinian farmers took over the greenhouses that the settlers had not destroyed, but they could not send their produce to market outside Gaza while Israel blocked their way. Gaza remained a prison, now patrolled from outside the walls. The guards came inside only occasionally to quell a rebellion or teach a lesson.

In the autumn of 2000, Yitzak Frankenthal wrote a letter to Netzarim's settlers. Frankenthal was the founder of the Family Forum. On 18 October 2000, Frankenthal's friend and fellow bereaved father Roni Hirschenson lost his second son. His first son, Amir, died in a Palestinian bombing five years before. The second son, El'ad, killed himself that day – barely three weeks after Ariel Sharon sparked the second *intifadah* with his walk on Jerusalem's Temple Mount. El'ad's friend, David, had just been killed on military service, protecting Netzarim's settlers.

Its effect, combined with the loss of his brother, led to his suicide. 'Any sane individual knows that Netzarim will be evacuated when peace will be reached between ourselves and the Palestinians, just as Yamit was evacuated, just as the Sinai was evacuated,' Frankenthal's open letter stated. 'Why in God's mercy do you continue to inhabit this cursed place that has demanded so many lives? Where is your mercy for a mother who buried two of her children?' He went on, 'You really believe you are protecting the security of Tel Aviv, but this is just a myth. The citizens of Tel Aviv do not need your protection, what they need is protection from you.' He described the mourning of Roni and Miri Hirschenson, who had buried two sons in the cemetery on Mount Herzl. ' "Whose grave shall I visit first?" Miri Hirschenson asked. "Amir's or El'ad's?" Thank you, Netzarim's settlers, a straight red line is drawn from Netzarim to Mount Herzl. I have brought up my children to contribute to the country, and what did I get in return? Two coffins, two graves.'

Moving as Frankenthal's letter was, it did not impress the settlers. The totality of blood shed for Gaza, of money spent on Gaza and military time committed to Gaza impressed other Israelis. Whether to pay the price for Gaza or give it up was an internal, Israeli Jewish debate. The numbers of Palestinians killed did not come into it. Nor was Palestinian survival in the Gaza Strip part of the equation. The Palestinian had no voice in the Israeli debate. Israel left without discussion or negotiation, because Israelis had grown tired of keeping Gaza. Gaza discredited the more important settler movement on the West Bank. Gaza was a diversion of effort from the more important task of redeeming the land near Jerusalem and around the sacred towns of Israel's biblical past. How to dispose of the West Bank would also be an internal debate.

Fearless in Gaza

Ziad Abu Amr was a native Gazan, unlike the refugee Abdel Aziz Rantissi. The distinction in Gaza meant everything. Although neither the Gazans nor the refugees among them had any say over where they would find themselves after the *nakhba* of 1948, the refugees resented the wealth and undisturbed roots of the Gazans. The Gazans – not all of them – tended to condescend to people in the camps. Several men had told me, with pride, 'I am not a refugee.' Mohammed Dawwas, who worked as a 'fixer' and interpreter for Patrick Bishop and other foreign journalists, said, with the same pride, 'We never lived in a camp.' But he was a refugee. Mohammed Dawwas's father, a Muslim from a village near Ashkelon who lost his business and his orchards in 1948, arrived in Gaza without a home. A Christian business associate named Tarazi gave him a job and a house, sparing the family the indignity of the camp.

'I am a Gazan,' Ziad Abu Amr told Patrick Bishop and me in his office at the Palestine Council of Foreign Relations. Abu Amr, born under Egyptian military rule in Gaza in 1950, shared the admiration that much of his generation had for Egypt's president, Gamal Abdel Nasser. 'He's still popular here,' Abu Amr said of Nasser, who deposed King Farouk in 1952 and died in 1970. Abu Amr's office faced the Palestinian Legislative Council, a squat, white house of a parliament that had not been able to sit for a year. Nasser built it. 'Gaza is dense, small and poor,' Abu Amr said, 'but maybe there is some kind of consciousness here that they are destined to lead the Palestinian cause.' Al Fateh, the Muslim Brotherhood, the Palestinian Communist Party and Hamas sprang from Gazan roots. 'Gaza was the only place that was Palestinian, and in 1967 it was the first place to resist Israeli occupation.' What about the West Bank? He said that King Abdallah annexed the West Bank and made Palestinians into Jordanian subjects. Nasser never annexed Gaza, recognizing it as part of Palestine. Abu Amr believed that

Sharon's 'success in suppressing the resistance movement made him what he is today, as well as what he did in Beirut. This is why he thinks he can solve the problem militarily and politically.'

Major Ariel Sharon, commander of Unit 101 when the IDF created it in 1953, committed his first massacre of Palestinians in Gaza. Unit 101's mission was to prevent Arab 'infiltrators' from crossing the borders to return to their homes or to attack Israelis. Sharon, as he would do again and again, exceeded his orders. His 1953 raid on the Gaza refugee camp at Al Bureij left at least fifty Palestinian casualties. Sharon did not mention it in his autobiography. Unit 101's other major operation took place in October 1953 in the West Bank village of Qibya, sometimes transliterated as Kibbya, where Sharon's orders were to make a demonstration by dynamiting some public buildings. Instead, without warning, he blew up houses where families slept. Sixty-nine people died. Israel at first denied its forces were involved. Sharon wrote in *Warrior: An Autobiography* that the southern command's chief, Moshe Dayan, told him, 'Look, if it turns out to be too difficult, just blow up some of the outbuildings and get out.' Sharon's response, in his version, was, 'No. We're taking six hundred kilograms of explosives along. We'll carry out our orders.' He continued, 'The orders were clear. Kibbya was to be a lesson. I was to inflict as many casualties as I could on the Arab home guard and on whatever Jordanian army reinforcements showed up. I was also to blow up every major building in the town.' He claimed that his men searched the houses to make sure no one was inside, before he destroyed 'forty-two buildings and inflicted ten to twelve casualties – the home guards in the trenches above the village and the two soldiers in the jeep'. Later, he heard on Jordanian radio that 'sixty-nine people had been killed, mostly civilians and many of them women and children. I couldn't believe my ears . . .' He concluded that 'someone could have easily hidden in the cellars and back rooms, keeping quiet when the paratroopers went in to check and yell out a warning. The result was this tragedy that had happened.' Most Arab houses in the West Bank built before 1953 had no cellars. The army command did not discipline Sharon. David Ben-Gurion congratulated him for 'giving us the possibility of living here'. Two months later, Unit 101 and the paratroops were merged, with Sharon as joint commander. Foreign Minister Moshe Sharrett, shocked by the severity of Sharon's attack on Qibya, noted in his diary, 'I paced back and forth in my room perplexed and completely depressed, feeling helpless.' Not for the last time, the United Nations Security Council condemned Israel for Sharon's brutality.

'Today, the poor social classes have become more influential, as the old classes have demised. The resistance movement and the *intifadah* have changed the political and social order,' Abu Amr said. We were sitting at a long table, discussing Palestinians as if we were in a country at peace, where you could gather statistics and make peaceful redress to a government. But in Gaza at this time, Israeli settlers occupied 20 per cent of the best farmland and seafront. Israeli troops surrounded the cities and refugee camps, attacking them when ordered by General Sharon. The whole strip was contained within an Israeli wall.

'There was a lot of sympathy for Nasser,' Abu Amr said. Nasser did not nationalize private enterprises in Gaza as he had in Egypt. 'Only the Communist Party and the Muslim Brotherhood were subject to arrest. The Communists forgave him, because he was an ally of the Soviet Union. The Muslim Brotherhood never forgave him.'

The two themes – secular nationalism and Muslim fundamentalism – persisted in the rivalry between the PLO and Hamas, Palestine's armed successors of the Muslim Brothers. The Islamists were in the ascendant. 'There is a general trend in the Palestinian Authority to be like the Islamists,' Abu Amr said. 'These people think this will endear them to the people. I think this is a mistake, like Labour trying to be Likud.' Labour, which had built more settlements than Likud had, presented the Israeli public with a choice: its own hypocritical rhetoric of peace with settlement growth versus Sharon's straightforward commitment to war and settlements. The Israelis had chosen Sharon. Palestinians in Gaza admired Hamas and its more radical and better-educated sister movement, Islamic Jihad. Why choose Labour and Arafat, who talk peace and wage war, when you can have real warriors? 'In Muslim society,' Abu Amr explained, 'the propensities towards religion are very deep. It's also deep in Fateh. Most people pray, but not all are Hamas. All are brothers in prayer. I think this reservoir of religious sentiment is an undiminished asset in the Muslim world. You should have seen the Osama bin Laden interview on Al Jazeera. This is not a fool. He raised the right issues. He said the right words.'

Osama bin Laden had just appeared throughout the Middle East on Qatar's Al Jazeera Television. For the first time he spoke of Palestine. Like Saddam Hussein ten years before, he had not done anything for the Palestinians, but was cloaking himself in their flag to promote himself. Like Saddam, he raised Palestinian hopes. Like Saddam, he used the Palestinian cause for his own ends. And, also like Saddam, he delivered them nothing. If the Palestinians had had a country, had been allowed to prosper in peace, they would have told bin Laden to drop dead. Like anyone else, a Palestinian with a house, a mortgage, a job and a country was not likely to respond to demagogues who wanted him to blow himself up and kill unarmed people. But the Palestinians had nothing. They were drowning, and the lifebelt some of them reached for looked like Saddam or Osama bin Laden.

'I asked people,' Abu Amr said, 'even Marxists, and there was a great deal of admiration. Bin Laden was identifying issues that are important to Muslims: Palestine, Iraq, oppression, injustice.'

Abu Amr had taken his BA in English from Damascus University, then a masters in international affairs and a doctorate in comparative politics at Georgetown in Washington, DC. He looked like Patrick Bishop and me, spoke like us, had an education that was better than ours and was about our age. He looked as if he would prefer to drink wine and chase women with people like us than to take off his shoes, sit on a carpet and discuss the traditions of the Prophet with bearded men in turbans. Bishop asked about bin Laden's appeal.

'People need leaders, not preachers,' Abu Amr said. 'There are thousands of preachers. He's a man of action. In his interview, he suggested he was emulating the Prophet – going from Arabia to Afghanistan like the Prophet from Mecca to Medina. If he did the bombings in New York and Washington, he is a very capable leader. If he bombed the *Cole* and the embassies in Dar es Salaam and Nairobi, he is a different kind of leader – not a co-opted religious leader or sheikh of the court. If Muslims feel alienated, this is a saviour. If they feel weak, it is natural that they embrace a leader like this. Why do you think so many people supported the Iranian revolution? It was a source of elation and pride to millions of Muslims all over the world.'

And Palestine's own bombs? 'Even those who fought against suicide bombings said, "Screw the Israelis. They attacked us. They destroyed the peace process." When you are angry and frustrated, sometimes you are not rational.'

Abu Amr folded his arms when he finished an answer, closing one segment of the conversation and awaiting the next. When he spoke again, he unfolded them. There was frustration in both word and gesture, when he said, 'A few isolated intellectuals like us here say Western civilization and Arab civilization are two sides of the same coin. How can you sell that? People see the total opposite. They see Iraq bombed day and night.' Soon, they would see Iraq invaded and occupied.

Abu Amr's foreign education and relative freedom to travel to other countries set him apart from his people in slums and camps. He dressed like a Washington lawyer and would have been welcome as a professor in any Western university. Yet he stayed in Gaza. To him, Palestine was the prime symbol of conflict between Islam and America, between the world's powerful and its hungry. If the conflict were to be resolved, he believed, it would happen in Gaza. 'The issues that define the relationship,' he said, 'are here. This is not a local issue. It is important for hundreds of millions of people. Resources are the target. People feel they are being pillaged. The misery of people is linked to the external.'

We talked more about Osama bin Laden, who said that his father had paid for the restoration of the Al Aqsa mosque in Jerusalem, after an Australian Jewish fanatic had set fire to it in 1969. Bin Laden touched the destitute in a way that people like Abu Amr did not. 'I have a different mind-set,' he said. Abu Amr could discuss building a civil society and an effective democracy to one audience, while bin Laden had the ears of refugees who had lived for fifty years without running water in concrete and tin shacks. Bin Laden spoke to a people who were enduring Israeli bombardment and attending funerals almost daily of children shot by Israeli soldiers. No one in the United States was listening, in the weeks after the 11 September mass-acres, to calls for an understanding of Muslim frustration. Few people in the Gaza Strip heeded secular, reasonable thinkers like Abu Amr. Israelis listened to General Sharon.

Patrick and I had dinner in a kind of cafeteria with his interpreter, Mohammed Dawwas. All chairs except ours were empty, and drinking was not allowed in Gaza. The Palestinian Authority had not banned alcohol in its early days. Then some of the more exuberant Hamas activists burned a hotel that served alcohol *pour décourager les autres*. Discouraged they were. Our restaurant, however, didn't need discouraging. Its glass-fronted Coke cooler displayed all the colours of sweet drinks a Gazan could want. We ate an indifferent dinner, grilled meat and hummus, and listened to Mohammed complain about the ignorance of the journalists he escorted around Gaza. No doubt, I thought, he'd soon complain about us.

A few of the hotels, Mohammed said, kept alcohol in the mini-bars for guests to have in their rooms. Our hotel didn't, as I discovered when we went back to the Commodor (sic). It did have a television, on which New York's mayor, Rudolph Giuliani, was conducting a press conference with ex-president Bill Clinton. Giuliani warned that, while the city's rescue services dug for survivors beneath the wreckage, no one could live for two weeks buried without food and water. It was horrible. He estimated that 4333 people were missing and unaccounted for. That would have brought to seven thousand the total number killed in western Pennsylvania, Washington and New York. Pearl Harbor – in a remote colony where a couple of thousand sailors and marines died in 1941 – was less in comparison.

The Honourable Member for Khan Younes

Jawad Tibi was a physician and member of the Palestinian Legislative Council. He had been in prison. He had been tortured. He lived in the south of the Gaza Strip at Khan Younes, whose town and refugee camp featured among the bloodiest battlegrounds of the uprising. Several people in Gaza told me Tibi was an honest politician, a species H. L. Mencken said was impossible. His Gaza City office was in the Palestinian Legislative Council on Omar Mukhtar Street. Honest Tibi may have been; punctual he was not.

Security at the Legislative Council was, without exaggerating the point, somewhat less thorough than at the Israeli Knesset in Jerusalem. Small cubicles stood sentry at the two drive-in entrances, one on either side of the building's mock classical façade. A guard in one cubicle ignored a truck that roared past without pausing, and he stopped me only to exchange greetings. 'Hello.' Hello. 'How are you?' Fine. How are you? 'Welcome.' Thank you. That was the security check. The Council building dominated a long garden of palms, gardenias and power pylons. Level with the surrounding city, the Gaza parliament had been built on the orders of Egypt's President Nasser in 1957, the year that the United States forced Israel to end its first military occupation of Gaza. It functioned as the Egyptian military governor's headquarters and then, from 1961 to 1966, as the Palestinians' first parliament, the *Majlis at-Tashri'i*, or Council of Legislators. In 1966, when Egypt and the other Arab states delegated representation of all Palestinians to the Palestine Liberation Organization, the parliament closed. When Israel occupied again in 1967, the Council building became the head-quarters of its military governor and the Northern Gaza Battalion. They left thirty years later, when it became a parliament with as little independence of the executive as Nasser had allowed it in its first incarnation.

Inside, a man wearing an olive drab cotton shirt and trousers, like a soldier but without insignia, asked me what I wanted, offered me a metal chair next to his desk and went to look for Dr Tibi. Hoping that the telephone on his desk would not ring, I wondered why he hadn't used it to call Tibi's office. Then, I remembered, this was Palestine. If he found it more congenial to walk down the corridor than to call, he would take a walk. I surveyed the foyer. It had no bullet-proof glass enclosures for security people to hide in, no policemen at attention to impress visitors and no comfortable chairs. Newspapers and brown envelopes were stuffed into pigeonholes on one wall. The blades of a ceiling fan flushed shadows over the pages of a book I was reading. I almost fell asleep, which is what sane people did in the heat of Gaza at 2.30 in the afternoon.

The guard returned to say the doctor wasn't in, but would arrive soon. How soon? Soon. Would I like coffee or tea? He made tea and left again, this time to a little room nearby. He took off his shoes and knelt for afternoon prayers. I looked out of the doors of the Council at the modern, all-glass Palestine International Bank, and watched a gardener tending flowers in the parliamentary garden. The guard returned, without his shoes, and poured more tea. We talked about Lebanon, where I had lived and he had not been allowed to visit. He had not left Gaza, a forty-five-by-ten-kilometre north–south spit of sand. You could see the whole thing from any high building. You could also see the coastal villages from which most of Gaza's refugees had fled in 1948, places they would not forget until they were buried and their children would remember long after that. The only Gazans who had been outside the Strip were the few with enough money to travel overseas and the poor men who used to enter Israel as day labourers. The guard praised Lebanon's food, undoubtedly the best in the Middle East. Were the girls as pretty as they said? He dreamed of visiting Beirut, but had yet to go as far as Tel Aviv. He was thirty years old.

Dr Jawad Tibi arrived, fifty minutes late, and led me to a conference room on the ground floor. He did not waste time. In a business suit, with a businesslike manner, he jumped into conversation. Why was I in Gaza? What was I writing? What could he tell me? Across a long wooden table, he looked ready to open negotiations. 'I was born in Khan Younes on 5 May 1956, five months before the Israeli invasion.' From November 1956 until March 1957, the Israelis ruled Gaza and Sinai. The military governor was General Mattityahu Peled, who suggested Israel grant the Gazans limited self-government. Years later, he would be accused by his colleagues of treason for speaking to the PLO and calling on Israel to grant full independence to Gaza and the West Bank. But in 1957, Peled, like Ben-Gurion, did not want to withdraw. His daughter, Nurit, told me that her father had shouted in his sleep that Israel could not leave Gaza. Only a direct order from the president of the United States, Dwight Eisenhower, made Ben-Gurion relent. When Tibi was eleven, Israel invaded again. This time, it did not leave.

In 1967, Palestinian boys found small arms that the Egyptian army had, in its retreat, abandoned. They attacked Israel's occupying forces. Their resistance, small and disorganized, proved futile. Israel dispatched General Ariel Sharon, who in August 1953 had assaulted Gaza's Al Bureij refugee camp to quell the rebellion. In 1971, Sharon levelled large sections of Gaza's refugee camps. His forces built detention centres in the Sinai Desert for 12,000 Palestinians accused of resistance that Sharon called terrorism. In Gaza, Sharon perfected the methods of control that he would employ as prime minister thirty years later: house demolitions, sniping of demonstrators, curfews, closures of villages and refugee camps, shooting armed men and unarmed bystanders alike, arresting and torturing thousands of young

205

men. In Gaza, it worked. With the Palestinian population cowed, the Israeli army seized patches of land. Colonists fenced off the best beaches and orchards in the Strip and built houses. Israel took Gaza's electricity company and gave it to a private Israeli company. Tibi continued his studies under Israeli occupation.

He had supported Yasser Arafat's Al Fateh movement, a broad nationalist coalition that included as many devout Muslims as agnostics. Some of his friends had joined the Popular Front for the Liberation of Palestine and its offshoots, but Tibi was neither Marxist nor atheist. He left Gaza to study medicine in Egypt at Cairo's Ain Shams University and went on to graduate training in Syria and Bulgaria. In 1983, Tibi worked for the Muslim Foundation's Mokassed Hospital in Beirut. General Sharon, the subduer of Gaza, had just expelled the Palestinian commandos from Lebanon. Israeli forces occupied half the country. Some of Tibi's patients were victims of Israeli bombs. Others fell to internal Lebanese fighting, Muslims against Christians – sectarian violence that had never happened between Palestinians. In 1985, Tibi left Lebanon for Scotland to study surgery in Glasgow. His fluent English had a trace of heather.

When he returned to Gaza in 1987, the first *intifadah* was about to begin. The Israelis arrested Tibi a few months after his arrival. He spent the seven years of *intifadah*, from December 1987 to 1994, in a succession of Israeli prisons. The Oslo accords brought the release of Tibi and thousands of other Palestinians. He joined the staff of Gaza's Baptist Hospital and lectured in pharmacology. In 1996, the voters of Khan Younes elected him to the first Palestinian parliament since Nasser's experiment with restricted Palestinian self-rule. Tibi stopped practising medicine, but he helped in the hospitals when they received large numbers of wounded. Like many of his fellow legislators, he had the credibility of one who, like Nelson Mandela in South Africa, had emerged from prison preaching reconciliation.

A few Legislative Council members criticized Yasser Arafat's autocracy, demanded transparent accounting for the millions in aid and taxes that were disappearing and condemned the secret military courts and their summary executions. For their criticisms of Arafat, three Gaza members of the Council – Jawad Tibi, Dr Haidar Abdel-Shafi and Rifaat Najjar – never received permits from the Israelis to travel to committee meetings in the West Bank. Arafat ignored or attempted to intimidate the dissidents in parliament, even arresting some for speaking against him. The United States, which had a hand in creating the Palestinian Authority, did not praise the democrats in parliament for speaking up. Instead, America's inept vice president, Al Gore, came to Israel with praise for Arafat's new secret security courts. Gore had nothing to say about Palestinian civil society, the human rights groups that were coming into being in the West Bank and Gaza, the medical organizations and the training courses in democratic procedure. After seeing Arafat in Jericho in March 1995, Gore told a Washington audience, 'I know there has been some controversy over the security courts, but I personally believe that the accusations are misplaced and that they are doing the right thing in progressing with prosecutions.' It was at about that time that a security court handed down its first death sentence. Human Rights Watch concluded, 'These courts lack the most basic guarantees for fair trial, including the right of appeal, and have been responsible for most of the twenty-five death sentences issued under the Palestinian Authority.' Such courts would have been illegal in the United States, until George Bush introduced a similar concept into American jurisprudence after 11 September 2001. When the uprising began in the autumn of 2000, Israel prevented all Legislative Council members from travelling between Gaza and the West Bank.

Tibi said that, before the second *intifadah*, he had told Israeli audiences they could trust the Palestinians and told Palestinians to learn to live with Israelis. Among the Israelis with whom he worked, he said, was a man named Yitzak Frankenthal. Frankenthal had founded the Family Forum, a support group for those families who had lost someone in the wars. I made the mistake of asking Tibi whether he, like Frankenthal, had lost anyone. 'One?' he said. 'Four.' I wished I had not asked.

I had met Yitzak Frankenthal the year before, in some woods near Tel Aviv, on a Friday afternoon. A former businessman, he had worked for his family's Snow Crest Ice Cream, until they sold it in 1982. He then marketed devices that measured radiation levels in buildings. He sold that business too, when his son died. Frankenthal did not believe in small talk, and he was in a hurry. Shabbat, the Sabbath, was coming at sunset, when he would not permit himself to drive. We met in the woods to give him time to get home before dark. He was a heavy man, overweight but strong and tough. He was also thoughtful. He told me his story. His son, Arik, was a nineteen-year-old soldier in the tank corps. On 7 July 1994, he was hitch-hiking home. The Palestinians who gave him a lift turned out to belong to Hamas. They kidnapped him. Then they murdered him.

'Arik was a wonderful kid,' Frankenthal had told me that day in the woods. We were sitting at a picnic table amid trees donated by overseas Jews, who had sent donations rather than make *aliya*. Their gifts to the Zionist enterprise planted trees, supported hospitals and built settlements. The donors' plaques reminded me of an old joke that Uri Avnery, an Israeli writer and gadfly, had told me: 'Definition of a Zionist? A Jew who sends a second Jew to Palestine with money from a third Jew.' Frankenthal was the other kind of Zionist, the real kind, who lived amid the danger, who risked his life, whose commitment to the Jewish State did not waver, who sent all his other children to the army after his son was killed. Arik's death did not change his Zionism, but it did change something. 'He believed in the human being,' Frankenthal said of his son, 'and he wanted very much to find a peace solution between us and the Palestinians.'

Frankenthal mourned for the requisite seven days of religious observance, but I suspected the mourning would never end. On the eighth day, he said, he wrote to the then prime minister,

Yitzak Rabin, the foreign minister, Shimon Peres, and the army commander, General Ehud Barak. Other fathers had also sent letters, demanding blood, vengeance, eyes for the eye lost. Frankenthal, as a grieving father who had given his baby to the state, demanded more: 'a peace solution between us and the Palestinians to stop the hatred and the bloodshed'.

Rabin went to the Frankenthal house. They became friends. Frankenthal was in Oslo with Rabin when he accepted his Nobel Prize for the peace that never was. Then, in Jerusalem, other Israeli families who had lost children protested outside Rabin's office against what at the time was called the 'peace process'. Some demanded military action against the Arabs in the West Bank and Gaza. Others wanted the Arabs expelled or exterminated. 'So, I came on the same day to Yitzak Rabin's office,' Frankenthal had told me. 'I asked him to give me the list of those families who have lost their kids, because I would like to try to build a group of bereaved parents to support the peace process.' Rabin said there would be no other families like his. 'Yitzak,' Frankenthal answered, 'I think you are making a mistake, because I will find at least ten to fifteen people like me.' Frankenthal asked Rabin for the names and addresses of the bereaved, but Israeli privacy laws prevented their release. Undeterred, Frankenthal went to the library and read every day's newspaper from March 1977, when Likud leader Menachem Begin became prime minister, to March 1995, when his research was complete. It had taken him three months to come up with 422 families.

'I wrote a letter to 350 of them,' he had said. The letter asked their support for a Palestinian state in the West Bank and Gaza Strip. The Post Office returned one hundred letters that had gone to old addresses. Of the 250 letters that were not returned, Frankenthal received responses from forty-six. Two told him to go to hell. The other forty-four promised full support. The Family Forum was born.

The forty-seven families met. They talked. They consoled one another in ways that only those who had lost someone to political violence could. The movement evolved as part support group, part political activism. They grieved. They listened. They lobbied. They made trouble. If the real victims of Israel's 'war on terror' demanded compromise over the violent subjugation of an occupied people, what moral weight did the warmongers have to oppose them? The bereaved became a political force.

'Later on,' Frankenthal said, 'we thought, maybe, we are a strange people. Maybe, only we, the Israelis, would like to make a reconciliation, but maybe the other side doesn't want it.' Frankenthal was an Israeli army veteran. He was a religious Jew. He did not speak Arabic. Like most other Israeli Jews, he did not have Arab friends. But he went to the Gaza Strip. Gaza was a hateful wasteland to most Israelis. Its people had resisted occupation more than any other Palestinians. Poverty in the camps and towns rivalled that of certain parts of Africa. Population density – the numbers squeezed into square metres – was the highest on earth. It was so dangerous in the Israeli psyche that to say, in Hebrew, 'Go to Gaza' meant, 'Go to hell.' Frankenthal went into hell, but he did not find hell. He was welcomed. Through friends, he met 'a family who had lost a daughter, three months old. She was in her bed, and it was inside her house that they killed their daughter.' 'They' were Israeli soldiers, kids like his son; 'they' were his people. He did not say we, because he was becoming one of 'them', one of the Israelis who blamed Israeli deaths on the occupation rather than on the occupied people. He was becoming one of 'us', the fathers on both sides who had buried their children, the parents who learned that both Arabs and Jews had eyes, 'hands, organs, dimensions, senses, affections, passions . . . fed with the same food, hurt with the same weapons . . .'. He sat in a crowded Gaza refugee house, whose family, though as poor as any other, gave him tea, coffee and cakes. They listened to him speak of his son's death, and he heard them say what their baby girl was like before the soldiers shot her. 'So, I remember going out of their house . . . crying. Three months old. I remember meeting with bereaved Palestinian parents who lost a kid one and a half years old. Two years old.' Perhaps hardest for him was meeting the mothers and fathers of young men who had blown themselves up in order to kill the occupiers, to kill Israeli soldiers, to kill Israeli children. Frankenthal saw that they too mourned and they too wanted no more parents, on either side, to lose children. They joined him.

There were two conditions: that a family had lost an immediate member to Israeli violence and that they were prepared 'to make compromise with the dream, to be ready to make a peace solution with the Israelis'. The dream, for both sides, was impossible: that the other would disappear. The bereaved sought to substitute a reality in which Israelis left Palestinians alone in the Gaza Strip and West Bank, 22 per cent of their common homeland, and Palestinians ceded moral and legal title to the other 78 per cent on which Israelis had established their state before 1967. I asked Frankenthal whether he found Palestinians who had given up their dream. 'Yes,' he said, 'of course. Of course.'

The 150 Israeli families in the Family Forum welcomed into their ranks 120 Palestinian families. One of the Palestinians was Dr Jawad Tibi. That was why I had asked whether he had lost anyone.

'One? Four.' His tone was dispassionate, as if he were speaking of someone else. 'In 1967, I lost my brother Majdi in the Israeli shellings of Khan Younes. My brother Sharaf was in his last term at Bir Zeit University. On 21 November 1984, during a demonstration at the university, he was shot from outside by Israeli snipers. In 1978, my brother Assam was working as an engineer in Lebanon, and he died in an Israeli bombing. In 1987, my brother Rasmi was killed by an Israeli booby-trap bomb in eastern Gaza. He was thirty-two.'

That was the year the Israelis imprisoned Dr Jawad Tibi. Had he, as charged, been making a bomb? His eyes answered, with four brothers killed, wouldn't you?

Despite the defects in the Oslo accords, the first years after

211

1994 were hopeful. Palestinian leaders who had learned Hebrew in prison toured Israeli schools, universities, community centres and political think-tanks. Marwan Barghouthi, once the Fateh Youth leader in the West Bank, political prisoner and deportee who returned home as part of the Oslo process, shared platforms with liberal Israelis. Among those who appeared in public with Barghouthi was Labour Party justice minister Yossi Beilin. One side exhorted young Palestinian radicals to embrace Oslo and, with it, Israel; the other asked Israelis to accept that Palestinians had national rights. Palestinian and Israeli children, at least those from the middle classes who spoke English, sent their children to summer peace camps in the United States. It was the Palestinian–Israeli conflict's era of liberalism, when public relations substituted for reality. Pleasing words diverted the ear from gunfire and bulldozers. It was the age of President Bill Clinton, of smoke and mirrors, of conjurors, of promises, promises. An Israeli documentary film that dissected the period through the vision of Palestinian and Israeli children was called, appropriately, *Promises*. Jawad Tibi was not immune to the lure of the 'peace process' that had not addressed the causes of the conflict – despite losing four brothers, despite his years in prison, despite torture, despite the Israeli colony of settlers that he could see from Khan Younes. Over the seven years of Oslo and Palestinian Authority pseudo-rule, the Gush Katif settlements that blocked the Palestinians' path to the beach did not disappear. They grew.

Tibi met Frankenthal, who impressed him as a good man seeking the best for both peoples. Like Frankenthal, Tibi abhorred a future in which more Palestinians and Israelis buried their sons, mothers, brothers and husbands because they could not work out a deal. Both Tibi and Frankenthal knew that when either tribe lost a child in the biblical land of vengeance, the other would send a new donation to the graveyard. Tibi the physician, who had stanched the blood of wounded children in the first *intifadah*, may have known better than Frankenthal the consequences of renewing the struggle. Both were serious, both

212

were patriots loyal to their people and both wanted to do something to make peace. Both failed.

'When we met,' Tibi said, 'the Palestinian families saw that some of the enemy families were feeling the same pain. On the Israeli side, many who were proud of their sons found families who were also proud of their sons. After some time, they were . . . not friends, but nearly friends.' Nearly was closer than most of them had ever come. They toured Europe and America together to cultivate support – real support in money and clout – to make the illusory peace tangible. They tried, but a few hundred grieving families did not stop the cataclysm.

Tibi had not seen Frankenthal since the *intifadah* began in September 2000. That was a year earlier. The IDF would not let Frankenthal into Gaza, nor would it allow Tibi out. That was only part of the estrangement. 'Neither me nor Frankenthal,' Tibi said, 'we cannot do it now.' Meetings between Palestinians and Israelis had become a social and political taboo. With suicide bombers killing Israelis and Israeli soldiers shooting Palestinian children, the two societies had come to regard the decency of opponents like Frankenthal and Tibi as an irrelevance. I met Frankenthal again a few months later, in the basement office of his house in a Jerusalem suburb, and remained convinced of his integrity. Jawad Tibi, trapped like all other Gazans in the tiny strip and humiliated by aggressive settlers in his midst, no longer trusted Frankenthal and the other Israelis who said they were dedicated to peace. His faith was another casualty of the Oslo sham.

'The Israeli army destroyed sixty homes in Khan Younes,' Tibi said. 'If Frankenthal says something, says these people have children . . . If he brings blankets . . . If he says, we must share their pain . . . If he sends tents for the families who are sleeping in the rain . . . If he calls and says, "I'm sending rice or beans or trousers or university fees . . ." If he raised a fund to help, I could tell the people that the cruelty is just political and not from the people of Israel. But he did not do that.'

The second winter of the *intifadah* was about to begin.

Palestinians in Gaza had stopped believing in any Israeli's good intentions. They were doubting the *intifadah* as well. Some were writing in newspapers that the *intifadah* had ended. The mass, non-violent marches that I had seen during the first month – so like the *intifadah* of 1987 – had been suppressed with Israeli rifle and tank fire. Settlers and soldiers had shot young boys who threw nothing more lethal than stones at tanks, symbolic expressions of rage like the pebbles that Muslims on pilgrimage to Mecca cast at *Shaytan*, Satan. It was not long before Palestinian stones made way for rifles and, sometimes, crude mortar rounds. Perhaps the *intifadah* had ended and a war of independence – or, in the vernacular of the few leftists remaining in Palestinian ranks, a war of national liberation – was under way. If so, the reason was simple. The Israelis shot children who wielded placards and stones, so the children might as well shoot back. This produced greater Israeli repression and more Palestinian violence and harsher Israeli violence and . . . The global superpower had decided – and announced its decision – that it would stay out of the conflict. But it was not really out of the conflict. It furnished Israel with arms, money, diplomatic protection and the other means to build settlements and sustain the occupation. Staying out meant only that the Great White Father in Washington would not force an end to the escalating warfare or sponsor discussions on Palestinian independence.

Jawad Tibi could do no more than bind wounds and find shelter. His non-violence and cooperation with Israelis had been discredited. Still, he struggled. He asked a Palestinian member of the Knesset, a distant cousin named Dr Ahmed Tibi, to send 1500 blankets from Israel to help homeless Gazans survive freezing winter nights. His cousin was able to offer a tenth of that number. Jawad Tibi applied to the Israeli authorities for permission to import the blankets and hired a truck with his own money to carry them from the Erez crossing to Khan Younes and Rafah. 'Nothing was sent,' Tibi said. He looked down at his hands, palms pressed on the table. 'Peace cannot be just talking about peace.'

An Israeli soldier had recently killed the brother of Tibi's wife. This time, Tibi did not go to his Israeli friends in the Family Forum. 'If they sent condolences, then we could say it's not all Israelis. If they said, you have the right to independence ... They must do actions. I cannot reactivate it if they do nothing.' Jawad Tibi feared that those who buried their parents and children were becoming so numerous that both sides would heed only their gods of revenge.

On the day I met Dr Tibi, the American flag went back to the top of thousands of masts across the United States. The official mourning had ended. Action to avenge those for whom we mourned was beginning. New York held a prayer service in Yankee Stadium that I watched on the hotel television. Ignoring the political uses to which their suffering would be put by President George W. Bush, Jr, and by General Ariel Sharon, I felt, as all other Americans and many others did, for all of them – the widows and children, the cops and firefighters, the friends and lovers of the dead. The official grieving was over, the flag flew high and the world watched. When I woke up the next morning, the BBC World Service said the United States was presenting the dossier of evidence it had amassed against Osama bin Laden to its allies. NATO's secretary-general, the failed British politician George Robertson, said, 'Allies don't need evidence.' There was local news as well. Someone had shot a woman in the West Bank. She was a settler, and her assailant was undoubtedly a Palestinian.

Yasser Arafat announced he was on his way to Jordan to visit King Abdallah and to Syria to see President Bashar al-Assad. In the past he had visited their fathers, both of whose armies had crushed and deported his commandos – King Hussein from Jordan in 1970 and Hafez al-Assad from north Lebanon in 1983. Arafat would rather have met the Israeli foreign minister, Shimon Peres, but General Sharon would not allow the aged and discredited Peres to see him. Why not pop in on the Jordanians and the Syrians instead? There was no harm in encounters among the powerless to discuss new and more creative ways of doing nothing. The Arab duchies left by Britain and France had little governments with little armies that kept their peoples in line. Arafat's flaw, for which he was being punished, was obvious: he was not as good as the Hashemites and the Baathists at control. With Arafat unable – and later unwilling – to protect Israeli settlers from the people whose land they were stealing and whose liberty they curtailed, Israel did the job itself.

Day Trip to Khan Younes

On the road from Gaza City south to Khan Younes, almost everyone was a child. Imps in smocks of blue or grey, little girls with white fringe collars, boys leading their younger brothers, girls beside girls, boys and girls with canvas bags of books on their backs, little children holding the hands of other little children, hair brushed back and faces scrubbed to meet the grime of day, thousands and thousands of children's feet padding the dusty paths between their mothers' front doors and their schools: this was morning in Deir al-Balah, the largest town between Gaza City and Khan Younes. Gaza was a children's land.

The driver stopped his taxi again and again for children to pass on their morning procession. Some of them pointed their big, dark eyes at us and smiled. Gaza had a million people, and that morning they all looked as if they were under the age of ten. To you or me, they were beautiful youngsters, so innocent that they could laugh even in Gaza. To the settlers of Netzarim, who could watch the children of Deir al-Balah with binoculars from their watchtowers, they were not children. They were bombs waiting to explode. If Israel's border fences made Gaza a prison, then its settlements made it a lunatic asylum.

Deir al-Balah adorned itself in posters and spray-paint silhouettes: of hair salon models, of smiling couples enjoying Coca-Cola, of the Marlboro man, of the late Gamal Abdel Nasser, of the martyrs. The martyrs – in Arabic, *shaheed* – were the local boys and girls among the seven hundred who had died in the year's uprising. Before I left six months later, the number would double.

From Deir al-Balah we drove to the Israeli settlement at Netzarim. Like all settlements seen from an Arab road or town, it was a barrier of concrete and razor wire, watchtowers and free-fire areas, armed guards and tanks. From the little I could see of the houses beyond the ramparts, Netzarim looked empty. I asked the driver how many people lived there. 'Three families,' he said. In Gaza, the belief that most settlers had fled back to Israel proved that the martyrs' deaths had bought something. It may not have been true, but faith in its truth kept the *intifadah* strong in Gaza.

A silver tower on steel pylons rose from the plain, its viewing platform affording soldiers and cameras the early sight of any advance towards Netzarim's perimeter. The Arab houses nearest the settlement had been reduced to so much debris, smashed concrete, broken breeze blocks and rusting refrigerators. The houses still standing on the Palestinian side of the cleared area were halfway to rubble from rifle and tank fire. The residents, unlike some of the settlers, remained in their houses and on what was left of their fields. Unlike the settlers, they had no haven to retreat to. Some of those whose homes had been ploughed under lived in tents as near as they dared. Outside, women brewed tea on wood fires. Their tents too bore the signatures of bullets that may or may not have inflicted injury on those inside.

The road took us past a mile of solid grey wall on our left. At a red light, soldiers stopped us. Signs in English and Hebrew – nothing in Arabic – said 'Han Yones'. On our left was an army base, on the right Gush Kutif, the Kutif bloc of settlements along the sea. The soldiers checked the car and our papers. We were on the outskirts of Khan Younes. A sign announced in English, 'Palestinian Authority Area Ahead: Entrance is Forbidden'.

A hundred yards on, a Palestinian Authority flag drooped from an empty guard's kiosk. We were in Khan Younes, caravanserai of the biblical Jonah, an old town that found itself an appendage to vast camps of refugees. Despite the wars, the uprising, the occupation and the turmoil, Khan Younes, with its white stucco houses and banana trees, slept as it had for centuries in the nether desert between the civilizations of Syria and Egypt. Its streets seemed quiet. At that time of morning, the children were at school.

We reached Jawad Tibi's constituency offices in an old building shadowed by eucalyptus trees. Tibi's offices were, like those of the Palestine Liberation Organization in Beirut until 1982, at the top of bare and unwashed concrete stairs. In an anteroom, a half-dozen people were waiting for appointments. This time, Tibi was not late. I was. He introduced me to everyone – secretaries, the boys who made coffee, his constituents. We went into the office of the man he had invited me to Khan Younes to meet. Rifaat Najjar was big, stocky, shaved but with a thick stubble no razor could erase, a self-confident man whose rough hand took mine long enough to tell me he was stronger than I was. Tibi called him Abu Othman, as all Arab fathers became Abu, father of, their first-born sons. Like Tibi, he was a representative for Khan Younes in the Legislative Council. Unlike the refugee Tibi, Rifaat Najjar came from a Khan Younes family.

Tibi and I sat opposite Najjar, who was behind his desk. He said he was three years old when refugees reached Khan Younes from the towns and villages of southern Palestine. At first, there were no camps. 'In our home,' he said, 'a family lived with ours until 1951. Palestine is a small village. There are good relations between Palestinians here and there. The refugees in our house thought all the time they were going back to their house. Then, in 1951, the UN built shelters for the families.' It took those three years for more than 200,000 Palestinians to understand that Israeli leaders meant it when they said no Palestinian would ever return. For three years they lived as if they might go home any day – sleeping in schools, mosques, caves, tents and in the houses of families like the Najjars. In 1951, with the establishment of the United Nations Relief and Works Agency

(UNRWA), their status as refugees was institutionalized. Homelessness became, despite the annually renewed UN Resolution 194 ordering Israel to readmit them, permanent.

Abu Othman Najjar was fifty-six years old. He had been in Israeli prisons for twenty-four of those years. The political commitment that would send him to prison and later to parliament had begun in the Arab Nationalist Movement during the early 1960s. That was the era of Nasser, of the Algerian war of independence, of Britain's withdrawal from the Middle East and before Nasser's Arab civil war in Yemen and his military humiliation by Israel in 1967. Nationalism was a response to colonialism, British, French, American, Israeli. Rifaat Najjar's generation, the children of those who had lost Palestine to the Zionists, saw in nationalist ideology – secularism, socialism, democracy and Arab unity – a means to force all Arabs into the modern age and thus to challenge the results of 1948. Nationalism promised Arabs that they would – while America rallied Arabia's conservative, Islamic forces against them – depose the sheikhs and use their oil wealth to fight their primordial enemies: disease, malnutrition, ignorance and oppression. Arab nationalism, particularly with the charismatic Nasser as its spokesman, attracted the brightest young men and women of the Arab patrimony. A Muslim from Gaza was proud to work under a fellow Palestinian Arab, Dr George Habash, who happened to be a Christian refugee from Ramleh. They were all Arabs, all patriots, all on the right side of history – or so they believed.

During the Six Day War of 1967, Israel shattered Nasser's Arab nationalist premise. Its army expelled the Egyptians from Gaza and the Sinai Peninsula. Within a year, sixty thousand of Gaza's 385,000 people had fled – or were compelled by Israel to flee – to Jordan. Most of them were already refugees. Some who remained used Egyptian arms, particularly in the refugee camps, to resist the Israeli occupier. The Arab National Movement was reborn as the Marxist Popular Front for the Liberation of Palestine, and Rifaat Najjar was a charter member.

Within a year of the Israeli occupation of the Gaza Strip, Rifaat Najjar was in prison. Tibi and Najjar knew that I had been in Hizballah solitary confinement in Lebanon, but their experiences trivialized mine. Najjar spent the years 1968 to 1985 – from the age of twenty-three until he was forty – in prison. Two years later, he was inside again. The Israelis let him go in 1994, by which time he was forty-nine. That was the year of the mass releases, when Tibi and a few thousand others returned to their refugee camps and villages. It was a time when most of them believed that Arafat had done the deal, that the new Palestinian Authority was the framework within which they would build the independent state of Palestine and that war had ended.

I asked Najjar to tell me about prison. He resisted occupation and was captured. At the time, he was the age of my son George. You in the tranquillity of your home in independent and protected lands, ask yourself how you would speak of your young son if your country were occupied and he were arrested for shooting at the tank outside your door.

'In the beginning of detention,' Najjar said, 'we were tortured in varied ways.'

Tibi interrupted, 'We have many Mandelas.'

'In addition to physical torture, there was psychological torture. They left us without food. If we wanted to go to the toilet, it was very difficult. Some detainees did it in the cell. There were no toilets in the cell.'

My jailers in Beirut, when I had dysentery, had given me rolls of kitchen paper. They told me to crap on the paper. Najjar did not have paper.

'There was just a bucket. There was another bucket with water for drinking.'

Najjar's description of his treatment, told without anger, conformed to accounts I heard from released detainees when I first came to the occupied territories in the early 1970s and to reports by the United Nations and Amnesty International. At the time, Israeli spokesmen said the Palestinians lied and the human rights reports were motivated by anti-Semitic hatred. Some equated accusations of torture with 'blood libel' – the old, false charge that Jews in Europe killed Christian children at Passover to drink their blood. The *Sunday Times* broke a long Western press silence in 1977 when its Insight team published a detailed report on Israeli torture methods. The American media remained circumspect, but much of the European press picked up and developed the story. The secret – which had been no secret in Israel – was out.

When Menachem Begin became prime minister in 1977, he ordered an end to torture. Israel's first Likud prime minister happened to believe torture was illegal and inhumane. He had called Palestinians 'animals', who could be killed when they threatened Israel, but he believed that even animals should not be tortured. His successors were not as scrupulous. In 2000, the Israeli Supreme Court declared certain forms of torture – in the absence of legislation that permitted them – illegal. The decision so outraged one Likud Knesset member, Reuven Rivlin, that he introduced a bill to make Israel the only member state of the United Nations whose laws explicitly approved torture. At the time, I asked Rivlin whether his former party leader, Begin, would approve of his proposed law. His answer was rambling but instructive:

I really wonder what Menachem Begin would say. Probably, he would say to me, 'Mister Rivlin my dear pupil, you are all wrong. We could fight it better [without torture].' And I would have to convince him that, at the times that he was running the show, we were in a state of war with everyone. The boundaries of Israel were very closed. Now, we are living all together. We find guerrilla people, who really believe that they could go to heaven entirely by bombing themselves in the streets and the markets of Israel. Menachem Begin really fought with those guerrilla people, when they were acting as soldiers, although it was very terrible, terrible. And they were described as animals by Menachem Begin ... He really thought that everything could be done without any need of torture. But if people would tell him, 'Listen, this man we're standing in front of, he knows very well where there is a ticking bomb', he would say, 'Take the guts out of his body, and do whatever you can do in order to find out.'

When I asked Rivlin whether torture had ever stopped a bomb that was ticking, he insisted there had been 'thousands of cases'. However, he could not name one. There were thousands of confessions obtained through torture which sent Palestinians to prison. Rivlin, a night-club owner turned politician known to everyone as 'Ruby', became a government minister after Ariel Sharon's election in March 2001. His torture bill, however, failed to become law.

Rifaat Najjar recalled the prison regime. 'There was torture, beating with sticks and plastic and wire. And it was not just for information. They stripped us and left us naked. There was cold washing water in winter. With some prisoners,' Najjar hesitated at this shameful thing, 'they rammed sticks into their bottoms. They denied us sleep. They burned cigarettes into our skin. A youth called Abdul Wahab Masri, they put sticks up his anus.' Najjar stopped. Although he did not break down, tears were falling, many, many tears. 'He died.'

I put my pen aside and waited for him to continue. Tibi stamped out his cigarette. The three of us were silent. Najjar felt the tears on his face, and he wiped them off. 'There was some improvement after a forty-five-day hunger strike. That was in 1976, in October.' He stopped again. I saw that the death of the young man, Abdul Wahab Masri, had not left him. Without another word, he put his head down on his desk. We waited. Taking breath to compose himself, he looked up. He fought not to lose control, not to place himself back in the torture chamber where a boy had died. He wanted to tell the story as if he had not been there.

'After a month,' he said, 'we started the hunger strike again. For twenty-two days. At that time, we used to lie on the floor.

They gave us what they called three blankets, but they cut the blankets in four pieces. So, we had three pieces in summer and five in winter without pillows or mattresses. They gave us a piece of sponge to lie on, a half-centimetre thick. They improved the food and allowed us into an exercise area to walk, with our hands behind our backs, for a half-hour a day. They wanted to humiliate us. When they called my name, I had to answer, "Yes, master." These things decreased after the second hunger strike in Ashkelon.' After the boiling desert prisons of Beersheba and Ashkelon, they moved him to Nafha. 'The surprise was that the rooms there were completely of concrete and the door closed so completely that there was total darkness. There were two panels in the ceiling – ten centimetres wide – and covered in a screen for air. We were twelve to a room. The cells were not big enough for this number. We used to spread blankets on the floor to sleep as a group. You have to lie on your side. If I stood in the night, I cannot find a place to sleep again. This stayed until the big hunger strike in Nafha. That was in July 1980.'

Distracting himself from his words, from the experiences the words portrayed, Najjar was doodling. His pen described a series of arrows, all shooting out from an empty centre to make a kind of circle. With his other hand, he used a tissue to wipe his tears.

'They used to bring us food with insects or rats in it. We knew they urinated in the tea. They beat the prisoners. On day thirteen, they moved twenty-one detainees to Ramleh, to Beit Matsor. They took our clothes. They asked us to pass between two queues of their soldiers – about five hundred metres long. They beat us with sticks as we went past.'

His scribbling was filling up the page. The arrows were broken at right angles. He then put squares or boxes around the arrows, caging them so they could not get out. He spoke faster, to bring the story to a conclusion.

'The prisoners were beaten all the way to the end. This beating is on men who had not eaten in thirteen days. There was a medical team, who had warm water with salt and paraffin oil.

Then they shackled us to chairs. They put a tube into our nose and down into our stomach.' His cigarette fell from its filtered holder. He put it back and relit it. 'They put the salty water with the paraffin oil next to it and put a jug of about twenty glasses into each of us. It caused severe diarrhoea. In this action, three of us died: Ali Ja'atari, Abu Jamal Maragha and Rasim . . .'

He wrote 'Rasim' on the page and tapped the pen over it, trying to recall the family name. 'We think it passed into their lungs.'

Outside, a muezzin called from the mosque 'God is great.' His chant urged all of Khan Younes to prayer. Najjar remembered, 'His name was Rasim Halawa. It is symbolic of what happened. The ones who died are many. The ones who are crippled by torture are many.'

The 1980 hunger strike at Nafha ended on the thirty-fourth day.

Najjar put down his pen, pulled the cigarette from the holder and dropped it in an ashtray. He was exhausted. The muezzin finished the prayer. It was time for the funeral.

It was hard to tell where Khan Younes the town ended and Khan Younes the refugee camp began. Both were crumbling, crowded, dirt-poor. The two places mingled. Refugees had married town people and moved into Khan Younes, and Khan Younes residents had moved into the camp. The apartment blocks of town and camp, built side by side, had erased the frontier of fields that had separated them until the 1960s. Everything was grey. My shoes were grey with dust. The breeze blocks of the unfinished flats were grey. Grey roofs sprouted steel rods to await construction of the next floor in a society so squeezed that it could expand only into the sky. The half-paved road was dusted in grey cement powder. Jawad Tibi, Rifaat Najjar and I stood in a grey concrete avenue, awaiting a procession we could hear but not see.

From the direction of male chanting, at the crest of the grey road, came the first eruption of colour, a pinpoint of green. It came closer: a flag. It did not flutter on a staff or float above the procession. It was twisted like a cone. The green banner of Islam approached on the head of a boy, about eight years old. Like the peaked shrouds of the Confraternities in Seville during Holy Week, the hat stood two heads higher than the child who wore it. And it pointed the way for the hundreds of boys and men who followed. After the green hat came bursts of orange cloths, swaying like branches in a storm, held above the older boys. Their banners honoured a new martyr. More and more boys and men, all in work clothes, marched forward. Open pick-ups came next, with boys on the flat-beds shaking angry flags – the pure green standard of the Prophet Mohammed and the green–red–white–black stripes of Palestine. A thousand or more men, most chanting, some stunned, a few pointing weapons at the clouds and shooting, marched beside the trucks.

They passed us and went on to the cemetery, a square of untilled earth inside a grey concrete wall. At one end, beyond a dozen small stone markers, waited a shallow pit. They carried him – a sixteen-year-old boy named Nasrallah Jarghoun – through the doorless opening in the wall. Like all the other martyrs who had been killed by the occupying army, his fragile remains were swaddled in the flag of his non-existent country. I could tell which ones were his family. They were the men whose eyes were red with weeping, who did not chant and who waved no banners. Next to them were the only women, in black from neck to toe. They stayed as close to the boy as the mass of bodies permitted, clinging to him as he was brought to the grave. When a woman I took to be his mother cried out, a loudspeaker took over, praising all the *shaheed* who gave their lives for Palestine. Tibi whispered, when they placed the boy in the ground, 'His father was also killed by the Israelis.' I looked at the woman: her husband gone, now the son. Another boy – another son? – took her hand, but she didn't feel it, didn't see it. She beat her breast with the other hand and knelt in despair, watching her child as the men covered him in earth.

A short phalanx of children, some as young as seven, many

older than twenty, broke away from the funeral and marched up a hill at the edge of the camp. Najjar, Tibi and I followed them. We came to a new development of apartment buildings, grey concrete, four and five storeys, flat cubes with aluminium-frame windows. Their only decorations were holes: many were so small you could just poke your finger in, some big enough to drive through. Bullets and tank fire had left no gaps of more than a few feet, not a window unshattered. Yet people lived there. Women with babies went into the buildings, children played football behind them.

Above, on the hill towards which the boys were marching with their Palestinian flag as large as a bed sheet, an Israeli bunker, also of grey cement, protected the settlement. A few hundred yards separated the border of the settlement from the edge of the camp. What kind of mad world was this in which people were forced to live in refugee camps and other people chose to live next to them behind razor wire?

The boys carried the flag over the camp's only grass, a small playground like a baseball diamond. They marched through it and up to a wire fence that stopped them from reaching the bunker. 'There go our children,' Tibi said, resigned to seeing them risk their lives no matter what their parents said. Almost a hundred of them went closer and closer to the fence. From a distance, we could not see the faces of the soldiers in the bunker. The Israeli troops must have stared back at the children, who were staring at them. The Palestinian boys said nothing, and they did not throw stones. They just stared, their silence telling the soldiers and the settlers: leave, leave this place, leave us alone, go home. We waited. Nothing happened. We turned to walk back to the car, when we heard a shot. Then another. The soldiers must have fired at the sky, like the mourners in the funeral cortege. No one fell. The boys did not move. Another shot, no one panicked. They were still standing there, quiet and staring under their flag, when we drove back to Khan Younes the town.

We had lunch in Rifaat Najjar's office with the office staff and visitors. Someone cleared the newspaper tablecloth from the desk and took away the empty plates of salad, hummus, tahina, grilled chicken and kebabs. The others went back to work, leaving Tibi, Najjar and me. We were on our first cup of Turkish coffee when Najjar resumed his story.

'On the eighth day,' he said, 'they moved us to another prison, Jilmara. It was February, and it was very cold. There were two rows of soldiers. They took our winter clothes and gave us light clothes. They beat us, but not as hard as in Nafha. They pushed us into cells. On the sixteenth day of the strike, they called me by name. They took me to a hole, where some officers were waiting for me. They shackled me by my hands and feet. They blindfolded me. They told me to order an end to the strike. When I said, no, I cannot, they beat me very hard.'

He was drawing, not smoking. With closed eyes, he recalled the scene. 'They beat me for at least one hour. At the time, I heard someone crying. They brought him to the room I was in. They closed the door and went out. He was older than I was. His name was Yusuf Atallah. He asked the Israelis if he could use the toilet. At that moment, I was hanging by the shackles on my hands. My feet were not on the floor. An officer came and untied us and opened our eyes. They sent an investigator to us. Then they questioned me about breaking a window and trying to escape. It was the first time I had heard that.' The officer told him that they had found broken glass in a cell Najjar said he had not been in. Witnesses, fellow prisoners, were brought in to accuse him. Najjar had no defence. This was the world of secret police, of informers, of accusation and of terror. Broken glass in another cell meant you were trying to escape. The word of another terrified prisoner was evidence against you. When the Hizballah had held me in Lebanon, they said that a receipt that they found among my papers for coffee and drinks for half a dozen friends proved that I had held a meeting of local CIA agents. I did not know if they believed it or were tormenting me for sport. Najjar had no defence, but for twenty-four years he survived.

Amira Hass, one of Israel's finest journalists and the first Israeli Jewish reporter to live in Gaza, wrote in her book *Drinking the Sea at Gaza*, 'For Palestinians, serving time in the territories has played much the same role as the Palmach, the Jewish combat corps of pre-statehood days, did in Israeli society: a gruelling shared rite of passage that forged lifelong bonds among a sizable number of Palestinians ... Every day I meet someone else who had experienced late-night arrest, interrogation by Shabak [the secret police], detention without trial, or long periods in solitary confinement. Since 1967, 280,000 Gazans have passed through Israeli prisons, detention cells and interrogation rooms ...' Prison was a political experience that forged a national movement, but it was also a personal shock that killed some and left others physically or mentally disabled. Hass, who came to know many survivors of interrogation and solitary confinement during her years in Gaza, wrote, 'For all the talk of jail, however, most ex-prisoners say little about the legacy of trauma, precisely because the experience is so common and widespread, and also because Gazans rarely talk about the emotional aspects of their hardships.'

Rifaat Najjar had been in some of the worst Israeli prisons over twenty-four years: Ashkelon; the special Nafha prison that separated PLO leaders from the rank and file; Beersheva; and the Negev Desert prison camp, Ansar II, where prisoners slept in tents. If he had any animosity towards his captors, he did not tell me about it. Married with two sons and two daughters, he had worked as an administrator at the College of Science and Technology in Khan Younes. And, in 1996, the people of Khan Younes elected him, along with Jawad Tibi, to their parliament.

He and Tibi lamented the quality of leadership in Israel and among Palestinians. Tibi did not criticize Sharon as much as he did Shimon Peres, the Nobel Peace laureate. 'When you see Shimon Peres set a date three or four times to meet Arafat, he doesn't show up because Sharon told him not to. He should resign. He doesn't respect himself.'

Something disturbed them more about their own people, the

people for whom they had lost years in prison and on whose behalf unhealed wounds would wake them from sleep until they died. Tibi explained, 'The cat likes the one who chokes it. Our people like the whip-carriers. They like the one with stripes on his shoulder.' He put down his cigarette and tapped his shoulder with two fingers – to show a captain's rank. They let him and Najjar represent them in the Legislative Council, but they chose the tough men – Yasser Arafat, his Gaza security chief Mohammed Dahlan and his West Bank chief policeman Jibril Rojoub – to lead them. Why didn't Palestinians choose former prisoners, Arab Mandelas, men who lived in camps and resisted occupation?

'In Khan Younes,' Tibi explained, 'people will say, "Who is he to do this? What family is he from?"' Thirty-five years under military occupation, thirty-five years of prisons, thirty-five years of begging to be allowed to work for peasant wages inside Israel, thirty-five years of radical political education, and the tribal structure lived on. What family? What tribe? What religion? Not: did he behave with honour when the occupier tested him? Did he refuse to collaborate? Is he honest? The picture of the father's face, whip hand out of frame, hung in every house.

'It's not because they are afraid,' Najjar said. 'It's because they admire strength.'

What else could a people, dispossessed and occupied because of their weakness, look to? Had not the Zionist Jews of Europe done the same, after the Shoah shattered the anti-Semites' myth of secret Jewish power? They came to Palestine seeking protection from strong men – David Ben-Gurion, Menachem Begin – and ignored the compromisers like Martin Buber and Rabbi Judah Magnes of the Hebrew University. When contemporary Israelis felt – and the feeling could be wrong – vulnerable, they turned to General Sharon.

A young man brought glasses and filled them with tea. Abu Othman was weary from reliving twenty-four years of hell. Tibi too looked tired, from talking, from seeing another teenager buried, from thinking about life in the cage that was Gaza. He said I should leave before dark and asked how I would return to Gaza City. I would find a taxi. 'I'll go with you,' he said. 'I want to be sure I know the driver.' We drove to a vast round-about, where service taxis, cheroots, waited to fill with passengers. Ford Transits and other vans had replaced the old Mercedes I remembered from my first visits to Gaza. Tibi asked the drivers where they were going. Only one was willing to take me all the way to Gaza City that late in the afternoon. He was a big, friendly African Palestinian – there were many in Gaza – who leaned through the window of Tibi's car. Tibi asked, 'What is your name?' The man told him. 'Do you know me?' Tibi asked. The man shook his head. 'I am Dr Jawad Tibi, a deputy in the *Majlis at-Tishri'i*.' The man said, 'Yes. I know you.'

'This is my friend,' Tibi said of me. 'I want you to take him to his hotel and then let me know he arrived safe.'

Later, I read in Amira Hass's book a story that Abu Othman Najjar had told her about Ansar II prison camp. At six o'clock each morning he and the other prisoners had to kneel in the dirt outside their tents with their heads bowed during the long roll call. One Israeli soldier was caught smuggling coffee and cigarettes to the prisoners. The warders tried to force the prisoners to testify against him. Not one would do it, not one could be bribed or coerced, all of them kept their silence. They protected the soldier. It was something to be the friend of such men.

A Young Man of Business

Not everyone in Gaza was a former political prisoner, a politician, a freedom fighter, a human rights worker or a child. Many people had ordinary jobs or were looking for them. Some laboured in Israeli settlements, occasionally on land that had been stolen from their own families. Others worked in hospitals, schools, factories, shops, pharmacies, restaurants or hotels. A few Gazans still farmed, and a few more fished. Most stayed away from politics and violence, as far as they were able. A few were businessmen. Bashir Rayess was a businessman. Young, London-educated, savvy and an astute observer of the Gaza scene, he would meet me from time to time for coffee on the terrace at the Deira Hotel or at his house nearby.

After studying economics in Britain, Rayess returned to Gaza in 1993 to work for UNRWA as deputy of a refugee training project. He moved quickly to the private sector. 'Gaza was opening up,' he said of the first years of the Palestinian Authority. 'Jobs were everywhere. It was impossible to stay with the UN system.' He moved to the new Gaza Industrial Estate, whose sponsors included Shimon Peres and the then US ambassador, Martin Indyk. The estate offered Gazans employment making products that would be sold in or exported from Israel. The usual institutions – USAID, the World Bank and the EU – subsidized its construction. Investment came from Israelis and people Rayess called 'mega rich Palestinians'. He seemed impressed that the Palestine Industrial Estates Development and Management Company's paid capital was $185 million. Set on fifty acres near the Israeli border east of Gaza City, the industrial zone had its own water desalination plant, stand-by electricity generators, fibre-optic telecommunications and a fleet of 'sterili' trucks with transparent fuel tanks and other special features to ease Israeli border inspection. The sterilized trucks did not, as things turned out, help. 'Shipping from Ashdod Airport to Europe is cheaper,' Rayess said, 'than from Gaza to Tel Aviv.'

The procedure for sending goods from Gaza to anywhere else on earth meant going through Israel. Palestinians could not export or import direct by sea or air, because Israel would not allow it. Israel controlled Gaza's harbour, its airport and its border with Egypt. It required goods to reach the crossing point at Karni by six in the morning, which meant all-night loading. Then the wait began. Long queues of trucks laden with Gaza's citrus and flowers, its light manufactured goods, its dates and its handicrafts waited for hours, sometimes days. The Israeli security and Customs police made thorough searches and checked documents – driver's licence, truck registration, cargo manifests. The trucks, when allowed through Karni, disgorged their cargo just the other side of the border. There, drivers and porters loaded them onto other trucks. Some of the Israeli trucks went to destinations in Israel. Some went to the bridges over the Jordan, where security procedures were duplicated.

'Our economy is really distorted,' Rayess said. 'The cost of living is so high and the standard of living is so low because of our relationship with Israel. Gaza was always a trading centre. It's weak in agriculture and industry. Even the landowners had their land east of Gaza around Beersheba and north in Ashkelon. The land was better there. It was all lost in 1948.'

When Egypt occupied the Strip, Gaza became a free zone. Nasser did not interfere with its capitalists as he did with those in Egypt. 'Gaza had the best Persian carpets, the most beautiful crystal chandeliers. It was a golden time for Gaza. We were selling everything to the Egyptians.'

After 1967, Rayess said, Gaza stopped trading. The Israeli army controlled the streets by day, the fedayeen commandos by night. By 1971, Sharon's repression was working. But, Rayess believed, the economy had as much to do with the collapse of resistance as did the torture, detentions and destruction of houses. 'Sharon opened Israel to Gazan labour,' he said. 'Families went to Israel to work. A large family could earn $500 a day. The whole population of Gaza, including teachers, took jobs. Education was lost. People took jobs cleaning, farming, in construction and industry.' The money was good by Gaza's standards, but the conditions shocked Israeli workers whose trade union federation, the Histadrut, complained about the competition. Gaza workers had long daily commutes, because they had to be out of Israel by nightfall. Some employers let them sleep in the factories and warehouses where they worked. They locked them in. When there were fires, workers burned to death.

To allow Gaza's workers to produce for Israeli companies, Israel and the Palestinian Authority created the industrial zones – modelled on the American *maquilladores* factories on the

Mexico–US border. Native labour came in one side, finished goods went out the other. Israeli–Palestinian partnerships were formed to make furniture, clothing and plastics. The Israelis provided the design and marketing. Palestinian entrepreneurs invested in production. A captive labour force provided the work. Or did, until the *intifadah* began again.

Business and work in Gaza depended on what Israel needed, or believed it needed, for its security and its economy. When Israel sought to pacify the Gazans and depress Israeli wages, Gazans were permitted to work in Israel, albeit without the protections afforded Israeli workers. When Israelis felt threatened by Gazans in their midst and found it cheaper to let them work for Palestinian subcontractors in Gaza's borderlands, the workers moved there. When Israel wanted nothing to do with Gaza or its people, apart from occupying them and subsidizing Israeli settlers on Gaza's best land, they became wards of international charities. When Israelis grew weary of paying to protect a few thousand settlers from the people of Gaza by 2005, they pulled the settlers out.

Rayess blamed the Palestinian leadership for many of Gaza's woes. Between 1993 and September 2000, the Palestinian Authority had sufficient autonomy from Israel to put in place a body of commercial law to attract investment. It could have protected Palestinian workers and given Palestinian businessmen a fairer trading environment than they had known under direct Israeli occupation. It didn't. 'We blame the Israelis for 70 per cent of our misery,' he said. 'But what about the other 30 per cent?' Rayess said there was no rule of law under the Palestinian Authority, just as under the Israeli army. 'There is a difference between declaring a state and having institutions on the ground,' he said. 'Secret organizations control the economy.' The few government officials who exposed the ways in which Yasser Arafat's ministers were pilfering the PA treasury found themselves moved to new jobs, out of jobs altogether or in detention.

'They,' Rayess said of Palestinians in Gaza and the West Bank, 'cursed the person who threw the first stone of the first *intifadah*, because it brought the Authority.' Palestinians believed that the Israelis had signed Oslo and imported Arafat, at the time deprived of funding from the Arab oil states for his endorsement of Saddam Hussein's invasion of Kuwait, to quell the first *intifadah*. It worked for seven years. 'We still don't know where we're heading. We went down the road of Oslo. What did we expect? The Israelis stamped your passport and let you in? Come on, guys. My dad advised Arafat not to come back on these terms.'

Rayess was part of Gaza's establishment. Along with the Alamis, Shawwafs, Souranis and Tarazis, the Rayess family had the respect that came from long-time wealth and political influence that predated and would outlive Israeli occupation. He should have benefited from Arafat's administration, but he didn't. Almost no one did. He dressed like a British businessman visiting the tropics. He understood the commercial world outside. He knew that an order in which a few plundered the many would destroy itself.

'We had a leadership crisis,' he said. 'We have it in both the society and in the family. The structure has not been dismantled. My wife comes from a Bedouin family. Her grandfather would spend his own money solving other people's problems. He was the head of the tribe, and that was leadership. Now, they come and say, "Give me a thousand dollars, and I'll help you." People used to make someone a leader because he was good. Now, mukhtars are chosen by the PA for money.' Mukhtars were village or neighbourhood leaders.

Rayess saw the 'family and tribal society' breaking down. Israeli occupation had discredited the elders, who gave up their resistance, while young street kids risked their lives. One of the effects, he believed, was the fracturing of Palestinian cohesion. 'In the mosques, there are sermons against Christians. Why now? Why doesn't the Ministry of Religious Affairs do something about it? There are so many mosques now, more than schools or hospitals. Anybody can be a prayer leader. Most of the Gazans are annoyed. They grew up with Christians and like them. Christianity is part of our history.'

The Rayess family, good Muslims all, had a history with Christians. After the British occupied Palestine in 1918, they seized the Rayesses' house for the military governor. The Christian Tarazis gave them a new house. The connection went back further. Bashir's paternal grandmother's family, the Dahers, came from Nazareth. 'Most of the land of the Church of the Fountain', a major Christian shrine in Nazareth, 'was donated by Daher al-Omar, and he was a Muslim sheikh. There was tolerance. Now there is no tolerance. And it's not only between Christians and Muslims. No one tolerates anyone.'

We were on the Moorish terrace of the Deira Hotel. The sea lay untroubled in front of us. Prosperous Gazans were eating expensive dinners. They tried to live like the middle class in any other seaside town, with fresh lemonade and ice cream. In Gaza, they could not go anywhere else but home. They owned cars, some of them expensive, but they could not drive more than a few miles in any direction. They had houses, many with Persian carpets and crystal chandeliers from Gaza's golden years, but outside they saw the Israeli roadblocks and the Israeli helicopter gunships and the Israeli settlements. They sent their children to school, but they worried lest Israeli bombardment trap them and wondered what they educated their children for. A man could work his whole life, build a house, raise children, earn the respect of his peers and still have to ask a nineteen-year-old Israeli for permission to go to the beach. Or, as I saw more than once when Israeli troops rounded up scores of grown men, for a soldier's okay to piss. For Gaza to seem normal, you had to hold onto moments, forget the events of the day and refuse to imagine the humiliation waiting tomorrow. It was no shock that their children revolted – against Israel, against their parents – from 1987 to 1993. Now, they were doing so again. But there were differences between 1987 and 2001.

'In the first *intifadah*, we sent the Israeli people a message. We were suffering. Many Israelis felt abandoned. Many Israelis felt ashamed. They made a peace movement. This time, they are shooting at us. They think we are demanding Haifa and Jerusalem. The Israelis are confused and misled. We're the same people, and they're the same people as in the first *intifadah*. At that time, I'd argue with Israelis and they'd listen. This time, they say, "We offered you the best, and you started shooting at us." The Israeli public is not with us. It's not with peace. This time, it's more sour. It's going to take time to forget. People are after revenge.'

One aspect of the tribe remained: 'For fifteen hundred years, Islam could not destroy our tribalism. We want revenge. They want revenge. It's personal.'

The leaders, he believed, did not lead. They reacted. They made money. They prevaricated. 'What have they done on the ground to become a state? Zilch. Nothing. The country is not the flag only. During my Bir Zeit days, people would look at the flag and cry.' Israel did not allow Palestinians to display their flag before Oslo. 'Now, it's everywhere and no one cares.'

Later, I spoke to another man, a refugee and former political prisoner. He asked me not to quote him by name. Why not?

'Arafat can call me a traitor or a collaborator. People can come to my house at night and . . .' He did not need to complete the sentence. 'We need strong men. Everyone around Arafat is weak. I've seen him call Sha'ath *akh-sharmouteh*.' Nabil Sha'ath was an Arafat stalwart from Beirut days, a native Gazan and a minister in the PA government. *Akh-sharmouteh* means a whore's brother. 'I saw Arafat take off his shoe to him. He cannot do that to me. I have paid more for this country than he has.' The man still limped from Israeli torture, and he resented the fact that Yasser Arafat had reopened the interrogation centres where he had suffered for Palestine and its flag.

Morning by the Sea

On 25 September, two weeks after the attacks in America, I lay
in my bed at dawn listening to the sea. It was not more than a
ripple on sand, like a fountain in a Damascus courtyard. I did
not want to get out of bed, and I did not want to listen to the
news on the radio. I did both.

The BBC World Service ended my morning idyll with increased casualty figures for New York, Washington and Pennsylvania – nearing seven thousand killed. This was the *Maine*, Pearl
Harbor and Gulf of Tonkin all in one. And this was not an
accident, which is what Admiral Hyman Rickover concluded
had sunk the *Maine* in 1898. It was not a military attack in
a far-off colony, as Pearl Harbor was. Nor was it a Defense
Department fabrication, like the North Vietnamese potshot at
an American ship in 1964. This was real. It had happened in
the United States. The victims were thousands of unarmed men,
women and children. Someone, somewhere would pay.

'If you see the World Trade Center as an American,' a psychiatrist said to me later that morning, 'you will be shocked to
the core and traumatized. You want to defend your country.
Imagine. We are witnessing this for fifty-three years. In the last
year, Israel has killed – if this were America – the equivalent of
seventy thousand people in Gaza. We see this day in, day out.
We are living in a prison, but it's unprotected. The prison has
no roof. Imagine the uprooting in 1948. Imagine the internal
dispossession. All the trauma is affecting our mental state. This
is the main reason for breeding suicide killers.'

The psychiatrist was Dr Eyad Sarraj. He had long opposed
both the occupation and suicide bombings. His lush garden,
where we had breakfast with white napkins and fresh orange
juice, did not look like Sing Sing, Wormwood Scrubs or Le
Santé. Sarraj was a big man with a deep voice, and he reminded
me of Egyptian secular intellectuals I had known in Cairo.
We might have been in Zamalek, Cairo's leafy quarter on an

island in the Nile. He was wearing green shorts and a red golf shirt, attire that modest Gazans never wore in the streets. Dr Sarraj, who had founded the Gaza Community Mental Health Programme, was no suicide bomber.

'Sharon's strategy is simple,' he said, 'to provoke the Palestinians, so they will be continuously violent.' Palestinian violence, he believed, would enable Sharon to realize 'the Zionist project'. Far from preventing the expulsion of Palestinians, suicide bombing excused it. 'In the heart, Sharon still carries the Zionist dream. We Palestinians are traumatized and play into his hands. Sharon needs us to shoot so the Israeli public will be mobilized again in fear. If we stop, Sharon will provoke us.'

Dr Sarraj grew up with and in the Palestinian resistance. Born in Gaza, he had lived under the Egyptian occupation and admired Nasser, an Arab nationalist, a secularist, a democrat and a socialist – traditions in which Sarraj's generation was raised. Sarraj studied medicine at the University of Alexandria and psychiatry at the Maudsley Hospital in London. In Alexandria, he became president of the Palestinian Student Union. His equivalent at Cairo University in the early 1960s was Feisal Husseini, a Jerusalem aristocrat and son of one of the few Palestinian heroes of the 1948 war, the famous Abdel Qader Husseini. The head of the General Union of Palestinian Students in Egypt was a young man who was less secular than Sarraj and Husseini – Yasser Arafat.

'I met Arafat in 1964,' Sarraj recalled. At the time, Sarraj belonged to the Palestine Liberation Front, a short-lived rival to Arafat's Al Fateh. 'We had a discussion. Al Fateh was accusing Nasser of being pro-American. I said, "How can you contemplate fighting Israel without involving the host country? Israel will retaliate." He said, "Let them. We'll lose. Let them become refugees."'

Arafat did launch raids into Israel that had the effect of raising the temperature in 1967. He did not cause the Six Day War of that June, but he helped to bring it about. As he predicted, some Arabs did become refugees – Syrians in the Golan Heights,

Egyptians along the Suez Canal and more than 100,000 Palestinians whom the Israelis expelled from Gaza and the West Bank. When it was over, Israel occupied all of what had been Palestine under the British Mandate. Nasser, in the aftermath of that defeat, offered to resign. Arafat went on to become chairman of the Palestine Liberation Organization.

After his studies in London, Dr Sarraj returned to Gaza as a psychiatrist. He could not divorce the mental state of people from occupation and violence. 'The Arabs are a defeated people, morally more than on the battlefield,' he said. In 1977, Nasser's successor, Anwar Sadat, addressed the Knesset in Jerusalem. The peace he signed two years later at Camp David took the Egyptian army out of the Arab–Israeli equation. On the day the treaty took effect, Israeli prime minister Menachem Begin announced plans to build 150 new settlements in the occupied territories. Egypt, Gaza's protector and for centuries its cultural model, had betrayed the people of Gaza. In 1982, Israel invaded Lebanon and destroyed Arafat's PLO. Egypt did nothing. The PLO retreated to Tunis. Settlements expanded. In December 1987, Palestinians in Gaza and the West Bank rose against occupation, to the consternation of both Israel, which tried to suppress it, and the PLO, which tried to control it.

'In 1987,' Sarraj recalled, 'the Palestinians felt morally victorious over Israel during the first year of the first *intifadah*. Politically, it was hijacked by the armed men.' He meant the PLO. 'That was when I was convinced that only peaceful, democratic means would work. More Palestinians were killed by these armed men than by Israelis.'

The first *intifadah* showed young Palestinians that they did not have to be afraid of Israeli soldiers. Israelis too ran away and felt fear. They too bled. Thousands of Palestinian children threw stones at them, cursed them, laughed at them. The uprising made roads in the occupied territories unsafe for Israelis. It slowed the rate of settlement expansion. It threatened the dream of those Israelis who wanted to expel Arabs and replace them with settlers in order to possess all of the 'land of Israel'.

For all its success, the uprising had a debilitating effect on the Palestinians. 'Everyone is traumatized, to one degree or another,' Dr Sarraj, who had treated Gazans throughout the first *intifadah*, said. 'In the first *intifadah*, 55 per cent of three thousand children whom we surveyed witnessed the beating of their fathers. Forty-five per cent suffered trauma.'

In 1991, at the height of the uprising, Dr Sarraj went to Tunis to see Arafat and the other PLO leaders. He remembered a meeting with the head of the Revolutionary Council, Hamdan Ashour. Ashour told him, 'Get away from us. We are finished.' Ashour was right. The PLO was finished. The Palestinians were not. Then came the negotiations in Madrid, Washington and Oslo. Arafat abandoned the official talks at Madrid and Washington to sign up to Oslo.

'Oslo was a disaster,' Sarraj said. 'But, in Arafat's mind, it was something that could work. He could not be faithful to his strategy, so he lost the Israeli peace camp. There was so much corruption that he lost the trust of the Palestinians.'

The conversation was moving back to where it always did – to the leader, to the father, the tribe, the family. Like most Israelis and other Palestinians, Dr Sarraj, when he had done criticizing the enemy, condemned the flaws among his own. Israelis often confessed admiration for the strength of Palestinian families, the warmth they felt when Palestinians befriended them and the determination with which Palestinians educated their children. And Palestinians praised Israeli democracy: while admitting that Israel's democracy applied only to Jews, they said Arafat's democracy did not include even Arabs.

'Within any Palestinian faction,' Dr Sarraj said, 'there is no democracy. The leaders are tribal leaders. The head of the tribe cannot be replaced. People have to wait for him to die.' It was not only the Palestinians. He went on, 'I claim there are no citizens in the Arab world, because there is no sovereign country, no state of citizenry. The process of citizenry was stopped by the presence of Israel. The military took over the Arab world to face Israel. These revolutionaries have taken fifty years from the life of the Arabs. People are looking always for a hero to liberate them, or they don't mind if there's an earthquake. Now, all Arab leaders have no respect. People are afraid. The words "human rights" are not allowed in Saudi Arabia, Syria or Iraq. How terrified the people are.'

Sarraj had reason to be terrified himself. Arafat had arrested him three times after he joined other Palestinian intellectuals – among them the poet Mahmoud Darwish, the academic and political activist Hanan Ashrawi, Gaza's Dr Haidar Abdel-Shafi and Anis Qassem – to form the Palestinian Commission for Citizens' Rights. The Commission elected Mrs Ashrawi its first head. When her term ended, Dr Sarraj succeeded her. The job made a fight with Arafat inevitable. 'I examined all the files of people who were tortured or killed. I went to see him in May 1995. Do you know what he said to me? "I'm not a man of human rights. I ruled Lebanon with the Kalashnikov, not with human rights. I'm not going to rule here with human rights." I said, "Lebanon was a revolution. Here, we want to build a state." We had an argument. I was dragged out. They said, "How dare you argue with the president?"'

Arafat received encouragement from his 'peace partners', Bill Clinton and Yitzak Rabin, for his security state modelled on Israeli military occupation. The US sent as advisers to his police, not the American Civil Liberties Union, but the CIA. When Arafat established secret military tribunals, where defendants had no lawyers and could be executed within hours of a summary verdict, Clinton dispatched his vice president, Al Gore, to praise him for his commitment to fighting terrorism. The US did not neglect the financial incentive as well. Arafat was at war, not with Israel, but with Hamas and dissent.

Sarraj complained to Arafat and his security chiefs that interrogators tortured and killed suspects. 'I wrote to them all, saying we cannot tolerate this. I gave a press conference on torture and murder in December 1995. I was arrested that day.' Although he refused to sign a promise not to 'scandalize' the Authority again, he was released a day later. In a subsequent meeting with PA officials, he agreed not to publicize past torture if Arafat moved to prevent it from then on. However, for the next six months of Sarraj's silence, the PA continued the torture. In May 1996 he told the *New York Times* that the PA was 'dictatorial' and 'corrupt'. He was arrested again – this time, for nine days.

'I was treated well in the Police Department,' Dr Sarraj said. 'On the day of my release, I had another meeting with Arafat. He asked me, what exactly did I want? Someone at the meeting suggested I should be a minister, but I said nothing interested me but to campaign for human rights. He agreed to open the prisons to inspection and to stop the torture.' Afterwards, someone asked Arafat, on television, why he had arrested Dr Eyad Sarraj. Arafat said he had not arrested him. The attorney-general of the PA had arrested him. Arafat said he released him.

'I wrote to him and said we'd agreed to be honest. I said, "You ordered my arrest, not the attorney-general. Why lie? The issue is to end torture and end corruption in your authority." '

Sarraj was arrested again. 'The minute I arrived, at midnight, they beat me up. I was terrified. I thought they were going to shoot me. They put me in an underground cell.'

In May and June of 1996, while Sarraj was in custody, international activists – those bothersome people who send circulars and emails on behalf of political prisoners – campaigned for Dr Sarraj's release. They persuaded journalists to write about him and asked people to send letters to the PA for him. In June, Dr Sarraj remembered, a visitor came to his cell. It was Khalid al-Khidra, the PA attorney-general. 'He said, "I cannot go to my office. It's filled with all these faxes." ' Khidra and the chief of police suspected that Dr Sarraj had a secret mobile telephone. How else would the outside world know that the police had beaten him? Their suspicions were not far-fetched. Although Sarraj had no cellphone, many prisoners in Israeli detention centres did. Sarraj did not need a telephone. Gaza was a small society, in which released prisoners and sympathetic warders passed on information. Like most other political prisoners, Dr Sarraj received an education.

'In prison,' he said, 'Hamas people protected me. We played chess and talked with these young cadres. They were naïve, pure. They were all arrested before by the Israelis and tortured. What hurt them was to be arrested and tortured by Palestinians.'

I asked him about their motives.

'They are Arabs,' he said. 'Your honour and your dignity oblige you to take revenge. Otherwise, you are not worthy to live. It preceded Islam.'

That was the reason many Arabs, who hated American policy in the Arab world, understood America's reaction to the 11 September attacks. The United States, for its own honour and dignity, could not turn the other cheek. Revenge preceded Islam, and it superseded Christianity. And no one had made more 'reprisals' than the Israelis.

The secular Dr Sarraj and the young Islamic militants discussed their predicament for weeks. 'Because of the failure of Arab nationalism, they chose Islam. God is undefeatable. In Islam, those who die for God don't die. In the Koran, it says, "And don't think that people who die for God and Islam are dead. They are alive and looked after by God." Combine the political humiliation and defeat of the Arabs, and you have people who are ready to die. How can you fight a tank? How do you fight a Phantom jet? They have nothing to match that. This forces them into suicide.'

It was a generational divide, and Dr Sarraj was on the older, secular and discredited side of it. 'My generation believed in Arab nationalism,' he said. 'For the young, it's Islam. The commitment in my generation was very deep, but the commitment of Hamas is different.'

A senior officer in the prison threatened to charge Dr Sarraj with high treason. The penalty would be death. Then, as suddenly as Arafat arrested him, he let him go.

'Arafat is ambivalent,' Sarraj explained. 'He's not as ruthless as the rest of the Arab leaders. He has a one-track mind – to liberate Palestine. For him, the end justifies the means. For him, the arrests and the curtailment of freedom are okay.'

The day before we met, Dr Sarraj had published an article in the Arabic press that supported Yasser Arafat's call for a cease-fire. Palestinian suicide attacks were achieving little more than the escalation of Israeli reprisals. Sarraj said his article went on to tell Arafat that 'better than a ceasefire is to have democracy and allow people to choose their own leaders. But if I condemn Arafat only, people will say, "What about Sharon?" The problem is that dissent is treason. Palestinians will never liberate their land unless they are free.'

Dr Sarraj had considered this problem – or these problems – all his conscious life. They had been part of him at university, in his psychiatric practice, in his political activity, in his human rights work and in prison. His generation had rebelled against the feudalism and tribalism of Haj Amin Husseini. They tried nationalism. Their children were trying religion. What would be next? If the Palestinians had failed to keep the bulk of their homeland in 1948 or to end the military occupation of the rest since 1967, it was not for lack of nationalist or religious fervour. It was the lack of power. The Israelis had the Maxim gun, and the Palestinians had not.

Defeat led to introspection, and Palestine's intellectuals dissected the society and its flaws – political, historical, cultural, tribal. Mostly, it was the tribe – a source of strength as of weakness, something so deep that neither nationalism nor religion had washed it away. 'The tribal mentality,' Dr Sarraj said, 'starts in the home. The way you are brought up affects you immensely. My brother is secretary-general in the Ministry of Commerce. He is in his forties, but to this day he cannot smoke in front of my father. The tribal mentality is deeply rooted, almost in our genes.'

Dr Sarraj's house was a modern manifestation of the tribe. Like similar family houses in Cairo and Beirut, it had grown upward with each generation or each brother's marriage. In the villages, the patriarch's house spread out, as the son added a room for himself and his wife. When the patriarch died, the eldest son took his place and the adding went on. Thus did families with many sons become tribes. Thus did the father maintain his power and prestige. The Sarraj household had four storeys plus a basement that served as Dr Sarraj's office, a graceful structure in white stone where privacy was inconceivable.

Dr Sarraj believed that the Israelis too were tribal, despite their Western ethos, their democracy and their confrontational politics. 'They behave as a tribe, when the Palestinians shoot.' Although I saw a Palestinian society held together by the chief, the patriarch and the father, Dr Sarraj said I had misunderstood: 'We share with Israelis the characteristics of the mother. What kept the Palestinians going was the Palestinian mother, who had kept the society and family going because of her permanence and her affection. The functioning of the Israeli tribes is to do with the mother.' He spoke as a psychiatrist. 'The child's security is the mother and the house. The father comes third. To have a democratic revolution in our part of the world, there are so many challenges in the way we are brought up. In many cases, women here defend male domination. With all my democratic preaching, I practise tribalism.' He put down his coffee. His California shorts and shirt were a costume he could cover up, like 'democratic preaching'. He said, 'Look at this house. If I have a problem, I call my brother. If they have a problem, the whole clan comes together. To keep your roots, you have to function as a tribe. I try to preach democracy, but it's not easy.'

He practised tribalism and talked democracy. The young, who lived in the same tribal environment, preached religion. What was the difference?

'The Arabs have managed to contain Islam and use it to serve their way of life. Mosques are a way to practise this. You go inside and relieve your guilt. The rest of the week, you practise your Arabism. The preacher tells you a powerful message. The first ten minutes, he tells you how bad you are and you are going to hell. For the last ten minutes, he tells you how lucky you are to have this president, that God has sent him to save you. It struck me that I heard the same speech fifty years ago, but the preacher was praising King Farouk. He said, "You must obey him." The head of state functions as head of the tribe. This perpetuates tribalism. What kept tribalism here is that people never had a state they identified with or felt part of. The states were alien, enemies. We always learned to manipulate the system. My house is my house, but the streets belong to the Turks or the English.' In Gaza, I had never seen a dirty house or a clean street.

'The beach is littered with garbage,' he complained. 'These people are ready to die for Palestine, but they piss on it. It's because of centuries of alienation. The only thing that kept them going was the tribe.'

Was the tribe enough to sustain Palestinians in the unequal war with Israel?

'Everyone is traumatized to one degree or another,' he said. 'In this *intifadah*, the whole place feels vulnerable, because of the aeroplanes. You could see the rocket coming towards you. That kind of fear is generalized. Children perceive a threat when they see fear in the eyes of their parents. A three-year-old girl said to me, "Uncle, we are all going to die. The Jews will kill us." Children up to the age of fifteen are so afraid they wet their beds. Many of them have post-traumatic shock syndrome, flashbacks, depression, anxiety. They are bewildered. The worst is from children who lost their houses. Their security, I told you, comes from the mother and the house. In the last thirty years of occupation, more than 100,000 Palestinians have been arrested and tortured. This has left an impaired society. Thirty per cent of them suffer from psychiatric problems. Some are paranoid. Some are depressed. Some are violent. In prison, I overheard a Palestinian officer interrogating a man from Islamic Jihad. The Palestinian officer shouted at him in Arabic. Then he shouted at him in Hebrew. When he lost himself, he became his torturer. That is a case of identification with the oppressor.'

What could be done for such people?

'The best treatment is to allow people to express their feelings or to grieve. Then there can be understanding. Then you can have some immunity or protection.'

Dr Sarraj's Gaza Community Mental Health Programme had, by the time we spoke, treated 15,000 victims of violence. 'We fail in so many cases,' he said, 'either because their resistance is so high or, when they are helped, they are taken away again.'

The Gaza-born poet Waleed Khazar wrote,

> Our small mistakes
> Our spoiled mistakes
> Always rise before us.
> They shower
> And comb their hair
> And watch themselves a long while
> In our mirrors,
> And they may grow
> Before we wake, and become
> Beautiful.

Civil Society

One man in Gaza who knew the people taken in by the Israelis, released and then arrested by their Palestinian compatriots was a lawyer named Raji Sourani. Forty-seven years old, Sourani had received France's Rights of Man Prize from President Jacques Chirac. On the wall of his office in Gaza's Palestinian Centre for Human Rights hung a photograph of the impeccably dressed Sourani receiving recognition for his years of struggle from the taller Chirac, who had never struggled for anything more than money and high office. There were other photographs, other prizes, the Robert F. Kennedy Human Rights Award, dignitaries from the West, commendations from Amnesty International. I knew about Sourani from friends, and I had read about him in Amira Hass's book. A ferocious defender of the rule of law, he had challenged both the Israeli occupier and Yasser Arafat.

'We don't wait for victims to come,' he said. 'We initiate.' The eight lawyers at the Centre sought out the tortured, who were often afraid to speak lest they disappear again. The idea was to make Palestine a state, if ever it became a state, of laws and open institutions rather than what the PA was: the arbitrary rule of one man.

The Israeli military authorities detained Sourani in 1979 on suspicion of belonging to an organization that Israel had declared illegal. His interrogation lasted nine months, and he was not released until 1982. He was never charged, never put on trial. He resumed his law practice, representing prisoners and detainees against whom the only evidence was a confession made under relentless torture. They took him in again in 1986. And again in 1988. Between periods of imprisonment, the Israeli military governor would not permit him to travel to international law conferences, the United Nations or human rights symposia. Soldiers searched his house, found nothing to incriminate him and banned him from practising law for a year. When the Palestinian Authority succeeded the Israelis in Gaza, Sourani and others formed the Gaza Centre for Rights and Law. 'What I anticipated when the PA came was a marriage with the local culture,' Sourani said. 'But what happened was not marriage. It was adultery. Added to that, Israel and the Americans encouraged without limits to bring the devil out of the PLO. They made arbitrary arrests. They tortured like the Israelis. It was an American creation. The only thing about the PA that Al Gore praised was the State Security Court. At the end of the day, we were left with neither human rights nor security.'

The secret court that Vice President Gore admired came into being on 7 February 1995. Sourani declared in public that the court was illegal. On 15 February, the Palestinian police arrested him. There was an international outcry. Prominent Palestinian nationalists, including Feisal Husseini and Hanan Ashrawi, appealed to Arafat for Sourani. He was released, but the vilification began. 'They accused me of being corrupt. They said we had a hidden agenda. They called us lovers of occupation. On 1 April, they pressured the board to sack me. I know them all. They gave me the letter of dismissal like this,' Sourani said, his hand shaking. 'I went back to my private law office. The rest of the staff followed me the next day.'

They became the Palestinian Centre for Human Rights with a staff of forty-five. Many of those they represented belonged to Hamas. 'I'm not a big fan of Hamas,' Sourani said. 'They imposed the death penalty on me in 1988. But when the PA came, they began rounding people up – one thousand in one night. We were very critical of that. They restricted freedom of expression. In Israel, they call free speech democracy. Here, they say speaking out is against peace.'

It was difficult to tell whether Sourani was disillusioned or disgusted. All over the world, men and women, who had gone to the prisons of the colonial power, found themselves back in prison for demanding the rights that independence promised. 'Until the PA came,' Sourani said, 'I struggled against occupation and thought it was the hardest thing you can do. I discovered later that the struggle for democracy in your home-land is much more difficult.' Sourani and other Palestinians were struggling against both occupation and a semi-autonomous local constabulary that treated Palestinians with similar brutality.

'I was thinking all my life that, when the occupation ends, everything will be rosy,' Sourani said. 'But it isn't. Our experience with the PA is much tougher.'

Sourani said of the PA, 'They love what we do against the occupation. They circulate it. At the same time, they hate us when it comes to the PA itself. Our mission is to bring in the critical eye for the society.' Who else saw the misbehaviour of the PA and the Israeli military occupiers through Sourani's critical eye? Not Arafat. Not the Israelis. And, often, not the Palestinian people, who were victims of both.

Sourani lamented, 'Ninety-nine per cent of our people are in favour of the death penalty for collaborators.' Sourani opposed capital punishment for anyone, especially when sentence was pronounced by secret tribunals that had no rules of evidence. Israel had employed thousands of interrogators. Volumes of human rights reports from B'Tselem and other Israeli rights organizations recorded the methods Israel's Shabak employed to persuade people to cooperate: bribery, intimidation, blackmail, extortion and torture. The reports alleged that the authorities had threatened to kill or arrest members of a man's family if he refused to supply information. They recorded cases of sexual intimidation of young women. When the PA itself worked with the Shabak and the CIA, under agreements that Yasser Arafat signed at the Wye River Plantation, how could the PA hang poor people who were forced to do the same?

How did the State Security Court work? 'In simple terms,' Sourani said, 'Arafat says to them, "Execute that guy." And that's it. That is why the human rights organizations and the Bar Association cannot represent anyone before the State Security Court.'

Sourani had opposed the amnesty that the Oslo accords granted to all collaborators. He believed their cases should have been investigated and brought into an open court, but he did not believe they should die. That set him apart from the bulk of the population, to whom the concept of rights under law was a propaganda weapon against Israel and not a guide to the behaviour of their own leaders. Israel was an occupying, a foreign, power. Yasser Arafat was the chief of their tribe, the sheikh, the Ram ad-Dar, the father on the wall. What right did they have to question him?

'The question lies with us,' Sourani said. 'Can we make the change? I don't think it's in our genes. People without shoes in Indonesia can make a democracy. Why can't you do it here?'

Part of the reason was waiting at the Beach Hotel, where slick black limousines and bodyguards in leather jackets blocked the way. In the lobby, young men with light weapons lounged on sofas. The receptionist told me that Mohammed Dahlan, the PA chief of security in Gaza, was entertaining a Spanish representative of the European Union in the restaurant. If Palestinians could not have democracy, it was because they had handed some of the keys – the master key belonged to Israel – to men like Dahlan. Working with Israeli security operatives, Dahlan was the law in Gaza. Sourani's reports said that Dahlan confined people in the same buildings, cells and interrogation rooms that the Israelis had used and treated Palestinians no better than the Israelis had.

The detainees were called 'enemies of peace' or 'terrorists' for acting or speaking against the expansion of Israeli settlements, the secret courts, Yasser Arafat or Mohammed Dahlan. The crime with which they were charged most often – someone in the PA had read Kafka and Orwell – was collaboration with Israel. Who was not collaborating?

I walked across the road to Bashir Rayess's house. He was on the front porch, having coffee. His wife, a Ph.D. from a Bedouin family, brought us snacks. What did he make of all the suspicion, the treachery and the accusations of collaborating with the enemy?

'Who built these settlements?' he asked me. 'Arab labour. Arab contractors. Arab companies provided the stone and the marble. I work with those companies, and I know they made a lot of money.' He knew Arafat's cabinet ministers. One was the West Bank agent of an Israeli ice-cream maker. Another was a building contractor, whose company constructed settlements and the highways between settlements. He said that one of Ariel Sharon's ministers, who had been army chief of staff, had come to him a few years before looking for 'business opportunities at the Gaza Industrial Estate'. Palestinian businessmen hired ex-officers from the occupation administration for three or four thousand dollars a month as consultants to help them obtain Israeli permits to import, export and travel. 'What Sharon didn't like,' Rayess laughed at the thought, 'was that most of his military people were in business with the Palestinians.'

Collaboration went both ways. Rayess knew where the money went and where it came from, and that was part of the sordid story of occupation.

'When Palestinians and Israelis talk politics, it's a disaster. But in business . . .' Rayess said, shaking his hand and saying 'but in business' with an intonation that was almost Yiddish.

When I returned to the hotel, Dahlan and his security people were still there. I sat outside to write up my notes and listen to the sea. I watched Dahlan and his guests through the window of the restaurant. Someone in the hotel must have had a sense of humour. When Dahlan rose to leave, the piped music switched from Arabic dance to the theme from *The Godfather*.

Back to the Think-Tank

At the Palestinian Council on Foreign Relations, Dr Ziad Abu Amr considered my question and admitted that he did not have the answer to it. Rather than guess, he did something I had never seen done by a PLO official in Beirut or a bureaucrat in Syria or Lebanon. He made a telephone call to ask. Someone at the other end promised to look into it and get back to him. We had been talking for some time about my impressions of Gaza, mainly the thousands of children everywhere I went. Gaza had more children than ideas of how to feed, house and educate them within the walls Israel had erected around them.

'This scene,' he said, 'every time I see this, I pause. And I think. It has different significances. Where are they going to go ten years from now? I remember Gaza when it was like an orchard. I used to go to Manar, where you can see the whole of Gaza. You saw pockets of housing, and the rest was green. That was thirty years ago, when the population was three hundred thousand. Now, it's the opposite, and the green pockets are smaller every day.'

Where would people live?

'I'll tell you where they can live. When we have a Palestinian state, there may be a population redistribution from here to the West Bank, where there is more land.'

That was when I asked him the question he could not answer: what percentage of Palestinians in the West Bank and Gaza was under the age of eighteen? If I had asked Yasser Arafat, he would have snapped, 'Ninety per cent' or 'Twenty-five per cent' and dared me to contradict him. Abu Amr called the Central Bureau of Statistics. I didn't know the Palestinians had such a thing. Four months later, they wouldn't. The Israeli army would loot the Bureau's offices, steal its computer hard drives and vandalize its files. Until Israel's soldiers robbed the Palestinians of their documentary memory, Abu Amr and others relied on the Bureau for data to make their calculations. I waited to see whether the Bureau would call back.

'There is no space,' Abu Amr said. 'I'm crowded even in Gaza City. Before, I had to go to the West Bank to breathe. I had to go outside to buy a book, see a movie, be a human being. A person like me can find alternative ways of fulfilment. I read. I organize discussions. But, for ordinary people, there are no alternatives. There isn't much physical space.'

Gaza's population was 1.2 million, three-quarters of whom – 900,000 people – were registered as refugees. In the entire city of Gaza, there was one public park. There were no cinemas, no theatres, no concert halls, no space for entertainment or amusement. The Israelis closed the roads, but Hamas had closed the cinemas. There was tyranny from outside, and there was tyranny within.

Despite the fact that Israel controlled all access to, from and within the Gaza Strip and West Bank, Palestinians like Abu Amr proposed solutions. He had a Ph.D. from Georgetown and had been chairman of the Philosophy Department at Bir Zeit University. He was trained to think, and he had creative ideas to allay Israeli fears over withdrawal from the occupied territories, the administration of Jerusalem and the fate of millions of Palestinian refugees.

'The right of return?' Abu Amr said. 'The idea is very romantic. There is a discrepancy between the right of return and the way it's going to be implemented. The driving force now is nationalist. Once the national goal is achieved, it will be different. No one is saying they want to jeopardize the integrity of the Jewish State by exercising the right of return. I think the Palestinians would accept this solution.'

That would have meant some refugees could return, but not enough to leave the Jewish population as anything other than the majority they became when they expelled the Arabs in 1948. But what was the point in proposing any returns, when the Palestinians had no strength to change anything in Israel, the occupied territories or exile? Bashir Rayess had dismissed the solutions of Palestinian intellectuals with, 'Come on, guys. It's not like Palestinian tanks are rolling into Tel Aviv.'

Abu Amr insisted that Israel should seek solutions while it was strong. 'There are limitations of power,' he said. 'How much more can Israel's power grow? There will come a point where Israeli capabilities will grow very slowly, and the others will try to grow to come to that point. This is posing a dilemma for the Israelis. Israel always relied on its power to solve its problems.'

He seemed to understand the insecurity that Israelis, despite their relative power, felt as deeply as their Jewishness. But the Israelis needed to come to terms with 'shrinking' – giving up the Sinai Peninsula, withdrawing from Lebanon and discussing a retreat from Syria's Golan Heights. How much more could they lose – Gaza, Judaea and Samaria – before the Arabs demanded Haifa, Tel Aviv and the Galilee? 'The Israeli is like a man who lives in a palace, with lots of land,' Abu Amr said, 'and is asked to live in an apartment.' Israelis wanted the Palestinians to guarantee the apartment would be safe, while Sharon expanded the palace and took more land for moats, drawbridges and battlements.

The Palestinian Authority governed without sovereignty and abused 'democracy'. The Authority had not earned loyalty and respect. Abu Amr said he disagreed with both Arafat's Authority and the Islamists, neither of whom chose 'a democratic model – democratic and pluralistic, with the rule of law, separation of powers, freedom of the press and expression, a real democratic order'. Why? 'This may not be obtainable under these circumstances. This is what we should aspire to, like Plato's *Republic*. In the meantime, we can devise and improvise.'

The PA had too free a hand *vis-à-vis* Palestinians and no freedom when dealing with Israel and its settlements. 'When you are preoccupied with national struggle,' Abu Amr said, 'who cares who embezzled some money or didn't come to work?' Abu Amr saw both weakness and strength among his people. 'There is a thriving Palestinian civil society. Democracy is an integral part of that: transparency, accountability, freedom of expression. We have created a pluralistic and democratic culture. Palestinians have been through so much. I don't think they are going to be obedient, willing subjects in the future. They need to be rewarded after a century of struggling. We are grasping ideas from all over the world.'

Abu Amr had been elected to the Legislative Council. A hundred yards from his window, it stood forlorn and empty. General Sharon had begun to dismantle the apparatus of the PA, its ministries, its offices, its social services. The Council did not sit, and I wondered why it ever had. It was like a pretty girl walking by. When she disappeared around the corner, you thought as you drank your coffee that perhaps the street had been empty all along.

'Look at the history of the Palestinians,' Abu Amr urged me. 'This is not a stagnant society. It is not easy to subjugate the Palestinians. Nothing was stronger than this Zionist movement and its Great Power support. Look at what is happening. This is not the function of one individual. This is an aggregate of the rule of the people. This is the people.'

Abu Amr's telephone rang. It was the Central Bureau of Statistics. 'Write this,' he told me. 'Under eighteens in the West Bank, 51.2 per cent. In Gaza, 56.6 per cent. That means, overall, that 53.1 per cent of our total population are younger than eighteen.'

When the Statistics Bureau called back, it gave me hope for a moment that those tens of thousands of Palestinian children might have a chance. A month later, Israeli troops broke into the Bureau to seize its files. What the soldiers did not take they destroyed – depriving me of even that small hope for Palestine's children. The destruction of the Palestinians' records was another victory in the war on terror.

SEVEN

Jerusalem, from the West

'There are none of the natural conditions of a
great city.'
REVEREND GEORGE ADAM SMITH
The Historical Geography of the Holy Land (1894)

Yom Kippur

AFTER CONQUERING GAZA on 6 November 1917, the
British moved north up the coast and, ten days later, took Jaffa.
The Ottoman forces withdrew to the north and east to defend
Jerusalem. The German officer in command, General Erich
von Falkenhayn, counterattacked on 27 November to restore
a defensive line south of Jerusalem. General Allenby's forces,
marching along Roman roads through narrow defiles, suffered
heavy casualties. They nonetheless repulsed a last offensive by
the remnants of the Ottoman Seventh and Eighth Armies, which
included the German *Asienkorps*. The British and Commonwealth forces, outnumbering the Turks and Germans by about
four to one, penetrated von Falkenhayn's line. On 8 December,
the British 53rd Division of cavalry and artillery reached
Bethlehem. The Turks retreated, leaving Jerusalem open.

After he had captured Aqaba, Lawrence had gone to British
headquarters north of Gaza to see Allenby. 'While I was still
with him, word came from Chetwode that Jerusalem had fallen,'
Lawrence wrote in *The Seven Pillars of Wisdom*, 'and Allenby
made ready to enter in the official manner which the Catholic
imagination of Mark Sykes had devised.' Allenby invited Lawrence to accompany him on his ceremonial entry through the

257

walls into the holy city. Lawrence called it 'the supreme moment of the war'.

On Yom Kippur 2001, I walked, as General Allenby had, through the Jaffa Gate, past the old Imperial Hotel, into the old city of Jerusalem. The Jaffa Gate, the usual entry for European pilgrims, faced the port of Jaffa sixty kilometres to the west. Kaiser Wilhelm rode a horse through the Jaffa Gate on his state visit of 1898 with all the pomp that the Austrian emperor, Franz Josef, had avoided on his pilgrimage thirty years before. It was in Wilhelm's honour that the new Grand Hotel renamed itself the Imperial. Demonstrating the Christian humility that the German emperor had not shown, Allenby entered on foot. My reason for walking was less noble than Franz Josef's and Allenby's. I found it cheaper to walk than to take a taxi. And horses were no longer available.

Whenever I came into the Jaffa Gate, two or three shopkeepers approached to tempt me into their shops. I avoided them. When that proved impossible, I pleaded lack of time. One souvenir vendor was more insistent than the others – to the point of rudeness. I should have been more sympathetic. These men were near bankruptcy. The Christian Quarter mostly sold religious and secular tat, everything from olive-wood crosses to I ♥ Jerusalem T-shirts; and no tourists were there to buy. The Armenian Quarter had no shops, apart from a few groceries. The Muslim Quarter sold the basics to local people – meat, fresh vegetables, herbs, spices, shoes and clothes. The Jewish Quarter had a mixture of shops catering to tourists and locals. I headed for the Jewish Quarter along the Armenian Patriarchate Road and found myself at the edge of what had, until June 1967, been the Moroccan Quarter. It was now the open plaza of the Western Wall.

The sound: church bells. The view: a citadel's wall, man-high rocks at the base, decreasing up its sheer height to stones you could hold in your hand. It was the Wailing Wall, said to be the only remnant of the Temple built by the Roman–Idumean–Jewish King Herod. At its summit stood a vast and beautiful stone plaza that, after Mecca and Medina, was the most revered site in Islam. Muslims called it the Haram ash-Sharif, the Noble Sanctuary. Within its precincts were the Al Aqsa and Omar mosques, the latter also called the Dome of the Rock. If anyone had designed a city to encourage sectarian strife, he would be hard-pressed to beat Jerusalem's unique conjunction of Wailing Wall and Haram ash-Sharif. The more fanatical Jewish settlers in the old city longed to destroy the mosques and build the Third Temple to succeed Solomon's and Herod's. On occasion, enraged Muslims threw stones at Jews below, and Israeli police or soldiers fired on the Muslims in response. Rational city planners would have put the two holy places on separate hills beyond each other's artillery range. Or they would have redesigned the people.

A wooden screen set off a third of the Western Wall for women to pray. Women, though, outnumbered the men two to one. Some of the men and women pressed their foreheads into the wall without moving, like rocks themselves. Some bobbed back and forth, mechanical ducks pecking water. Others sat in folding chairs looking at the wall or reading holy texts. The dress code ranged wildly from kaftans with black hats to American 'leisure wear' with backpacks. The women wore bonnets like ladies at a West Indian church. One had a scarlet umbrella. One small group of women wore a kind of uniform, white linen nuns' habits, and sat with open books on their laps.

I found a chair behind the area cordoned off for the worshippers and watched them. They were white, and they wore black. Some men were bearded, others clean-shaven. Some clung to the rock face as if a tempest might sweep them away. It was not a wall or a barrier so much as a door, the opening to whatever they imagined God to be: infinity, mercy, justice, vengeance. Islam gave Him ninety-nine names for His many attributes, and they were not enough. My impression was that these devout Jewish women and men were, in their prayers, closer to whatever God was than I. I would always be outside the rope.

A young steward approached. With the cultivated manners

of a good *maître d'hôtel*, he said, 'Writing. Not in this place. Not now.' I put away my pen and notebook. He indicated some steps beside the police station at the back of the plaza, 'Over there. But not here. Not now.' This was the Western Wall of the lost Temple on the Day of Atonement. I left.

I went through the Jewish Quarter, passing scores of religious Jews on their way to the wall. In an open square, a sign on one large building said it was 'dedicated by Arnold and Ruben Cohen Martin and Thalia Resnick of Baltimore, Maryland'. I remembered meeting a Baltimore architect, Moshe Safdi, in Jerusalem in 1974. He was redesigning the Jewish Quarter, giving it the sanitized, quaint and American look it has had ever since. I asked him about vernacular architecture and involving the inhabitants in the design of their neighbourhoods. At the time, I had been reading *Gourna: A Tale of Two Villages* by Hassan Fathy, Egypt's great architect of indigenous forms. Safdi answered that he could not consult the inhabitants because they had yet to arrive from Russia. I told him I had just met a man who lived in the Jewish Quarter. In fact, he had been born there. His father and grandfather had been born there. Safdi could see where I was going and changed the subject. The man worked as a gardener at the Hebrew University. He was about to be evicted to clear the way for Safdi's new Jerusalem. Yes, he was an Arab. No, Safdi was not interested.

The Palestinian poet Salman Masalha wrote in his poem 'Wireless':

> . . . But hide and seek
> doesn't play well in the holy city.
> For God sees everything.
> And so do I.

On Yom Kippur in the Jewish neighbourhoods of the new and old cities, the streets were deserted and the shops shuttered. As on the Sabbath, no observant Jew was permitted to work or to operate machinery. Moreover, on the day when Israel's iniquities were purged, the devout were forbidden to eat, drink, wash, wear leather shoes or have sex. From sunset to sunset, they were to pray for the entire community – however wide they chose to apply that term – and ask God's forgiveness. In the Temple, when there was a temple, the high priests sacrificed a male goat and purified the precincts with its spattered blood. The daughters of Jerusalem were said to have worn white and danced in the vineyard. Some, as I had seen at the Western Wall, were still in white. None, alas, danced. 'For on this day,' the Book of Leviticus said, 'shall atonement be made for you, to cleanse you; from all your sins shall ye be clean before the Lord.' When darkness came, ending 10 Tishri in the Hebrew calendar, the people were free again to eat, drink, drive cars, wear leather shoes and make love. Jewish Jerusalem came back to life. Students strolled around Zion Square, traffic filled the Jaffa Road and the cafés in Ben Yehuda Street choked with cigarette smoke.

Yom Kippur was an ancient feast, about which the religious authorities disagreed. It may have originated with a slaughtered goat. When Joseph's brothers sold him into slavery, they covered his robe in goat's blood to convince their father Jacob that a wild beast had killed him. The day may have recalled their atonement. Yom Kippur may have derived from other events or earlier rituals, but it answered a need for forgiveness and renewal. Whatever the source of Yom Kippur, Jews in Israel and the Diaspora had celebrated it for at least 2500 years on 10 Tishri, which in 1973 fell on 6 October. That year, Israel nearly lost its first war.

The Anniversary of the Mosque

The next day was also an anniversary, but it was a first anniversary. One year before, on 28 September by the Western calendar, the mosque above the Western Wall received a visitor. In his worldview, he was not trespassing on the mosque that was there. He was asserting his right to enter the Temple that was not. To achieve his purpose, he took with him more than 1500

261

armed police. General Ariel Sharon's perambulation of the Noble Sanctuary ignited the dry kindling of Palestinian grievance that had been accumulating for the seven years of Oslo's false promises. The second *intifadah* and Sharon's campaign for the prime ministry had begun.

Early that morning a year later, I walked from Andrew and Emma Gilmour's house on the Hill of Evil Counsel to the old city. A day after Yom Kippur traffic was normal: that is, hundreds of cars were backed up, moving forward at a speed that allowed me to pass them on foot without strain. Many of the drivers were coming in to work from the southern settlement blocs and the East Jerusalem settlements that government spokesmen called neighbourhoods. Some Palestinian families from Abu Tor were taking their children to school. All of them were stuck together where the highway became a single lane above the Valley of Kidron. The road forked: to the left lay the new city by way of the King David Hotel; to the right was Arab eastern Jerusalem.

I went down to the right along the walls of the holy city. Inside the Jaffa Gate, most of the shops and cafés were closed. The streets were, as on Yom Kippur, empty. It was a Friday, Islam's holy day of rest and prayer, but the Christian and Jewish Quarters were deserted. The emptiness was more menacing than the day before. Police in dark glasses and carrying automatic weapons guarded every gate and every route between one sect's neighbourhood and another's. As well as the seven gates in the old city's external walls, built in 1536 by the Ottoman Sultan Suleiman the Magnificent, were many internal gates between quarters and at the many entrances to the Haram ash-Sharif. Approaching one of the smaller portals from the Muslim Quarter, I saw hundreds of people massed around some Israeli policemen. The police were blocking their way to the mosque complex. The day before, the government had announced on the radio and in the newspapers that no man under the age of forty would be permitted to enter the mosque for the Friday prayer. Worshippers from the West Bank and Gaza were already excluded from Jerusalem under standing orders imposed a year before. Some Jerusalem Arab men under the age of forty were demanding to go inside to pray. A few shouted, others pleaded; all were turned away. The police allowed women and older men through. Some young men, twenty or more of them, knelt and said their prayers in the covered road, while Israeli police cameramen recorded them on videotape.

I found myself caught in a stream of women and old men pushing through an opening in the police lines. I was over forty, so the police did not pull me from their midst. All the women were in long dresses and scarves, and most of the men wore keffiyehs. I thought they would lead me to an inner gate from which I could watch the Friday prayer. But the vaulted passage led to the middle of the Haram ash-Sharif. The magnificent golden Dome of the Rock shone only a few feet away. Thousands of people were already at prayer. I did not belong there, not that day.

Muslims say that the entire area, a stone surface surrounded by colonnades and enclosing two of Islam's most revered mosque buildings, is a mosque. I had been there many times since my first visit in 1972. During quiet political periods, the sheikhs of the mosque invited me to remove my shoes and sit with them within the Dome of the Rock to discuss religion. I was an agnostic throughout my late teens and twenties, and mullahs and rabbis alike intrigued me. It should have been obvious to me that I was looking for a way back to faith, and in those days our talks were cordial. Since then, Jerusalem's religious atmosphere had become more political, more extreme, more tribal. The Messianic Conquest of the West Bank by Judaism's fervent religious pioneers had fostered reciprocal Muslim versions of intolerance and extremism. I was treading on the new ground.

Along the shaded steps of the colonnade, women sat and listened to the prayers. Men below the age of forty were everywhere. They sat on stone, crouched on prayer rugs or stood in alcoves. I found an unoccupied stone step and watched Muslims prostrate themselves to the Almighty. A rumble of voices, deep and lulling, vibrated over the whole scene. '*La-allah il-allah*,' they chanted. 'There is no God but God.' Amid the beauty of their prayer, I was a fraud. Two excuses made my presence forgivable: I had entered by mistake; and, if there were shooting, as there had been the previous year, I would be a witness.

The prayer leader's voice echoed from loudspeakers across the compound. 'We are the believers,' the prayer leader said. 'God, give us your help.' I was the only person who was not praying. No one told me to leave or asked why I was there. The prayer leader stopped speaking, and the people waited in silence. All seemed well. Just then, the mobile telephone in my pocket rang. Set to the highest volume, it rang incessantly. I fumbled for it, but, by the time I got it out, the ringing had stopped. I turned the telephone off and put it back in my pocket. I sat down again. A mosque guard approached, and we exchanged a few words. No, I was not a Muslim. When he asked for my passport, I handed it over. We walked together through another gateway, and he gave my passport to the Israeli policeman. The policeman expelled me.

I went around to the Lion's Gate. More young men who had been excluded from the Haram were praying there. Camera crews filmed them. The service ended, and the exodus from the Haram began. There was no violence.

That evening I went to a reception at the French Consulate for two newly arrived diplomats. On a chaise longue under the vast ceiling of the upstairs salon, the *grande dame* of Franco-Palestinian society, Lela Shahid, was receiving. An effective spokeswoman for the Palestinians, she was the Palestinian Authority's ambassador to France. She was often on French television, where she condemned Israeli assassinations, bombings, closures and land seizures. Her more difficult task was defending the man she represented, Yasser Arafat.

Lela's mother, Serine, was visiting Jerusalem for the first time since the Israelis had occupied the eastern half of the city in 1967. I had known the family in Beirut. Serine was a Husseini, part of Arab Jerusalem's Muslim aristocracy. Her late husband was a Baha'i, a nineteenth-century Muslim sect that had been oppressed in Iran and sought refuge in Palestine, Lebanon and the West. Serine invited me to sit next to her and talked about her return to the city of her birth. I had rarely seen a woman whose sadness was as profound. She had gone to places she remembered from her youth. She had visited her relations in their old houses. Everyone had made her welcome. Everything, though, had changed. 'It's as if,' she said, 'we had never been.'

The Only Democracy in the Middle East

The morning news reported that the number of Palestinians killed by Israeli security forces in the previous twenty-four hours had reached twelve. During the night, the inner circle of General Sharon's government, the security cabinet, had convened for four hours. It announced that the Palestinians, who had not attacked any Israelis in the previous few days, had forty-eight hours to implement a ceasefire. Sunday in Jerusalem dawned bright. Emma Gilmour gave her three children and me breakfast in the kitchen and drove me to the Knesset. I had been there often to interview members of parliament. Today, I was a tourist.

When Israelis compared themselves to the states around them, they said that Israel derived its moral superiority over the Arabs from the fact that it was a democracy and no Arab state could claim the same. The Jews of Palestine wanted a state, fought for a state and, under the protection of Britain and later the United States, made a state. The majority of Arabs in Syria – whether in Jordan, Lebanon, Palestine or little modern Syria – had never wanted their mini-states, had not proposed them, had not waged war to create them and had not taken part in writing their constitutions or establishing their armies. Their states were fabrications of the French in Lebanon and lesser Syria and of Britain in Jordan and Iraq. France had used the Alawite minority in northern Syria as the officer corps of Syria's army. In Lebanon, it had entrenched tribal leaders of the religious sects, with primacy for the Maronite Catholics. Britain set the Hashemites of Mecca over the tribes of Jordan, as it did their cousins over the Arabs and Kurds of Iraq. Israel was conceived as a democratic enterprise in that it needed the cooperation of Palestine's and much of the Diaspora's Jewish populations to achieve their ends. The Arab states were established in opposition to their people's wishes. How could a colonial power create a democracy, with its implication of popular consent and involvement, in artificial states that their people did not want? The US was soon to attempt a similar endeavour in Iraq with predictably similar results.

The Knesset symbolized Israeli democracy. It had been built in West Jerusalem in 1966, the year that Israeli democracy was confident enough to lift martial law from its Arab citizens. Before that, the Knesset moved from place to place like the tents of the Children of Israel. Israel's first parliament convened in Jerusalem's Jewish Agency Building on St Valentine's Day, 1949. A month later, the Knesset met in Tel Aviv, the all-Jewish city on the sea. In 1950, it moved back to Jerusalem, despite international protests, and worked in the Frumin Building in King George Street, not far from the Histadrat and my favourite Jerusalem restaurant, Fink's. It remained there, in the heart of the Jewish city, for sixteen years. It was a time of Labour Party hegemony, of Knesset members who disdained neckties and imitated Ben-Gurion's studied proletarianism with their open-necked shirts and abrasive informality. The slow rise to bourgeois respectability began with the 1966 transfer to Giv'at Ram and the election in 1977 of the courtly right-winger in suit and tie, Menachem Begin.

The Knesset met on Mondays, Tuesdays and Wednesdays. On this Sunday morning I joined a queue of nine people for the official English tour. We handed a security officer our passports and walked through a metal detector machine as if for a flight. In a way we were departing noisy, violent Jerusalem for a democracy theme park in which all seemed well and, where not well, manageable. Passportless and scanned, our little group went from the reception building across a vast square towards a glass and concrete structure built in the time and style of the Los Angeles Music Center. The formidable security at the gate and the reception vanished once inside the Knesset itself. A young woman met us at the door to guide our tour. Everything was so relaxed I suspected I could have wandered on my own to any office I chose.

The guide's introduction explained the Knesset's biblical origins – from the ancient Grand Knesset of 120 wise men. The first Haknesset Hagdolah was established in the fifth century before Christ, when two of Israel's tribes returned from Babylon to the Promised Land. Elections, usually every five years, were by national party list. Any party receiving one and a half per cent of the vote won a seat. No party had ever achieved an absolute majority, and government was by coalition. The guide asked us to follow her into the council chamber to see its 120 seats with consoles for voting with red, yellow and white buttons. All the seats faced a stage, like a theatre, rather than one another, as in the British Parliament.

In 1957, the guide said, a madman threw a grenade in the Knesset at Ben-Gurion. The old man survived, but a bullet-proof partition was thereafter installed to separate the members from the public gallery. On the rostrum were three thrones for the speaker, the Knesset's secretary-general and 'a lady of stenograph'. The wall behind the speaker had been built to resemble the broken stones of the Western Wall that Israel conquered the year after the new Knesset opened. Waves along the wall, we were told, represented the Judaean hills that Israel also seized in 1967. The only other embellishments in the stark chamber were the national flag and a portrait of Zionism's Austro-Hungarian prophet, Theodor Herzl.

The guide told us that the current national unity government with twenty-eight ministers was so large that its table in the chamber had been extended. A few weeks before, the American president and 'his lady' had attended a special session. Among the invited guests were former prime ministers, judges, senior policemen, diplomats and 'the big rabbis'.

In another room, she showed us the Declaration of Independence in a tall glass case. It was not the copy, she said, from which Ben-Gurion had read at midnight between 14 and 15 May 1948. The signatures of the leading Labour Party, Jewish Agency, World Zionist Organization, Histadrut and Haganah men were there with one exception. Near the bottom of the third column of names was a space. In strictly alphabetical order, it should have been the signature of the Zionist champion, Chaim Weizmann. Ben-Gurion, our guide said, wanted to honour Weizmann by his absence. Weizmann, who had persuaded Britain to issue the Balfour Declaration for a Jewish National Home in 1917, was to be above politics, 'like the Queen of England', as she put it. What she did not say was that Ben-Gurion hated Weizmann and kept him not so much above as out of politics in the ceremonial job of president. Israel, she said, had no written constitution. The independence declaration had called for a constituent assembly to write a constitution by 1 October 1948. The assembly had yet to meet, and Israel governed itself under Ottoman, British and Knesset laws.

She led us down an open staircase to the Hall of Expositions in the basement. News photographs lined the walls, classic black and white portraits of founders, soldiers and politicians from the 1940s to the 1990s: Shimon Peres as a young man with a Haganah officer named Yitzak Rabin; one-eyed Moshe Dayan; Rafael Eytan; Yigal Allon; Ariel Sharon; and Menachem Begin. Begin, with his youthful moustache and a stylish cigarette, was standing in a 1953 picture next to Ben-Gurion's wife, Paula. A few years before, Paula's husband had called Begin a 'Jewish Hitler'. Among events depicted in the two photographs were the riots against German reparations to Israel in 1952: Jewish rioters and police near buildings aflame in the night. The pictures revealed hidden strengths and flaws in Israel's democracy. That political enemies met for debate in the Knesset and even socialized with one another confirmed that the country would not collapse from within. That Menachem Begin, who called Egyptian president Anwar Sadat in 1974 'an implacable enemy of the Jewish people', could meet Sadat in 1977 and sign a peace treaty with him showed that even an ideologue understood the advantages of neutralizing the Arab world's largest army. The photograph of angry Israelis burning buildings to protest against German 'blood money' confirmed tolerance of popular dissent. No Israeli policeman fired a shot at the demonstrators that night in 1952, the year that Egyptian police shot rioters who incinerated the physical symbols of British occupation such as Cairo's famed Shepherd's Hotel. Nor, in later years, would Israel's police fire on Orthodox Jews who threw stones at cars whose drivers violated the Sabbath. Nor did they fire on settlers, who sometimes fought police and soldiers with fists, stones and sticks. Israeli security forces never shot at Jewish demonstrators. That was strength. The weakness, the flaw, the hypocrisy at the core of that honourable democratic practice was that the same police and army shot and killed Arab demonstrators who had never dared to torch a building. When Jews protested, they exercised a democratic right. Arabs, whether citizens or subjects of the occupation, were a fifth column.

Bookshops, Cafés, etc

Most mornings I would find some café in which to have breakfast, read the newspapers and make notes. Sometimes, the place was the American Colony's coutyard, where I would forgo the newspapers for a talk with the bookshop's proprietor, Munther Fahmy. I had known Munther only two years, and during that time his business was never good. It should have been. His shop had the most extensive selection of Middle East books, both fiction and non-fiction, in Jerusalem. Diplomats, journalists and UN employees patronized him. Luckily, he said, he had made enough money in the United States to survive. His main passion was to reverse the trend in American and British public opinion away from Israel towards the Palestinians. Despite various unsuccessful schemes, he would not give up.

There was one café that I liked more than most on the old Bethlehem Road in a row of small shops in modest stone buildings. Its Israeli waitresses were attractive and its espresso was excellent. Opposite was the laundry to which I took a bag of clothes every week and from which I collected them pressed and smelling fresh the next day. The family that owned it, as well as the two Arab men who ironed shirts in an upstairs gallery, called me 'Glass'.

One morning, two older women were approaching the café door just ahead of me. Speaking Hebrew, they were dressed with as much style and taste as if they were meeting for tea and torte at Sacher's in Vienna. I opened the door and held it for them. As they passed, one of them said in perfect English, 'You're polite. I can see you're not Israeli.'

Around the corner from the café was an old bookshop that sold older books in English. Unlike Munther's, it had a range of novels, thrillers, children's books, classics, travelogues, mysticism, cookbooks and histories. Its choice of books on Israel and on Judaism was unusual and good. I picked up books by Abba Eban, Arthur Koestler, Amos Kenan and other writers from Israel's earlier days. The shop was a congenial mess of little treasures. The woman behind the counter was absorbed in a telephone conversation when I came in search of Ben Hecht's out-of-print *Perfidy*, about the trial of an Israeli politician accused of collaborating with the Nazis during the Second World War. The woman nodded to acknowledge my arrival, her eyes saying she was busy and I was free to have a look.

It was hard to concentrate on the books when her advice to some unfortunate man on the telephone was far more compelling than tomes on Mosaic Law and the flora of the Negev. 'You are letting these three women walk all over you,' she said in New York English. 'Go ahead. If you need it, it's your decision.' Pause. 'You're a grown man. See a psychiatrist. If you think it will help.' Pause. 'Norm. Norm. Norman, listen to me.' Pause. 'Norman! You can't let these women ruin your life. Norman, listen to me.'

I scanned the shelves, but my thoughts were with Norman. 'Norm. Norm. No. Now listen. You have to stop. Norman!' I thumbed some bestsellers from the 1960s, including a paperback of Leon Uris's embarrassing propaganda novel, *Exodus*. But I was wondering what was up with Norman. What was happening to him? Who were the three women ruining his life? Were they, perhaps, a wife, a mistress and a girlfriend? No, too Italian. Three girlfriends? His mother, his aunt and his sister? His wife and her mother and some friend of theirs? It was impossible to know who the three were, but I was listening, along with Norman, to the fourth. I wanted to take the telephone and tell him, 'Dump the women, Norman. Go to the shrink. And make sure he's a man.'

Histories

Albert Agazarian filled, emptied, refilled and tapped his pipe with the reverence of a priest consecrating bread and wine. The almost sacred veneration he showed his tobacco extended to ideas, books, family, history and language. We were having coffee in the Armenian Tavern, near his house in the ancient Armenian Convent of St James. Albert's earthy hands fiddled with the pipe, occupying them while his brain ran ahead.

As an administrator at Bir Zeit University, Albert had as one of his tasks liaising with the Israeli military authorities at Bet El. When Israeli troops arrested or shot a student, closed the university, banned a speech or impounded university supplies, it fell to Albert to intervene. He was a diplomat. As well as Arabic, Armenian and English, he spoke fluent Hebrew. And, most importantly for his Israeli interlocutors, he was not an Arab. That did not mean, however, that he was not a Palestinian. He was a passionate Palestinian patriot.

'The only people we Palestinians have to respect for suffering more than we have,' the Palestinian historian Tareef Khalidy had said years before, 'are the Armenian Palestinians.' The Armenian Palestinians were already – like European Jews – survivors of genocide when they suffered the *nakhba* of 1948 and military occupation in 1970.

Albert said, 'I asked one of the officers at Bet El, "When are you leaving this place?" He said, "When you kick us out." Then, in October 2000, I told him the process of kicking you out has begun.' Of course, the process had not begun. In the year's uprising, the Israelis had seized more West Bank land and built more settlement dwellings. A few settlers had given up and gone back to Israel or the United States, but far more Palestinians left for Jordan. Two years of repressing the revolt had accelerated what some Israeli writers called the 'slow ethnic cleansing' of the West Bank with the departure of some 200,000 Palestinians.

As the first year of the *intifadah* gave way to the second, Albert admitted he may have been wrong. Bet El with its military court, armed forces, officers, men and settlers still controlled life next door in Ramallah. Tapping his pipe on the table, he said, 'Now, on turning fifty, my prophet's licence has expired.' He still resembled a prophet, physically imposing with eyebrows that needed trimming and a goatee that didn't. When he looked at something, he looked at it for a long time and gave the impression that he saw more than I did. What he saw was time. Where he lived, within the walls of an ancient convent in a more ancient city, Herod was as real as Sharon, the emperor Vespasian as significant as the emperor Bush.

'Bush sent chills through this part of the world with the word "crusade",' Albert said. George Bush had just called his war on terror a 'crusade', a term his speechwriters came to regret. When the Crusading Knights conquered Jerusalem in 1099 during the First Crusade, they slaughtered every man, woman and child – Muslim and Jewish – in the name of the Prince of Peace. Albert continued, 'Look at the way Berlusconi denigrates Islam. Now, the way Israel played it is very dirty, saying that Osama bin Laden and Yasser Arafat are the same. What Israel is doing here is the climax of terrorism, state terrorism. What is this, bombing people with F-16s? Assassinating people? There is no due process. There is no evidence.'

Again, he patted the tobacco deep into the bowl of the pipe. The eyebrows danced and stopped. He puzzled over the goatee. His thoughts stopped somewhere on their forward course for him to say, 'This is breeding anger somewhere.' Another pause. 'They want to put the Palestinians in a box and crush them.' He struck a wooden match and sucked in the flame. The smoke and the thoughts drifted. We talked about the old city. Thirty thousand people, he said, lived within the walls. 'Even with the settlement of the Jewish Quarter and the fifty-three buildings Israel has seized in the Muslim Quarter, over 27,000 of the 30,000 inhabitants are still Palestinian.'

Ariel Sharon had seized a house in the Muslim Quarter over which he draped a fifty-foot Israeli flag. Did Sharon, I wondered, ever sleep in the old city? 'Never,' Albert said. I could see the brain dart sideways with the squeezing of the eyebrows. 'The man has no political programme. The people who ran the show from the beginning were the security establishment. Securitism is reflected at all levels. Life becomes impossible. And, now, the United States is imitating Israel.' Where was this going? He swirled the clean end of the match around the ash in the pipe. 'You know what this means? It means you are on your way down.'

Albert was in full flow. The empire swirled about the high, vaulted walls of the Armenian Tavern. 'Many people around the world condemned bin Laden out of fear of the United States,' he said. 'They cannot afford to risk the anger of this giant. But if the giant cannot bring in Osama bin Laden, this little bin Laden, he fails. Can the United States take Afghanistan? Yes. But can it occupy it?' He compared the collapse of that other vainglorious giant, the Soviet Union, to the potential implosion of another unpopular idea, globalization. 'In a way,' he went on, 'there is a spiritual emptiness in the world. I grew up in an age of belief in universal values. This emptiness is filled in the north with neo-fascists and in the south with ethnic cleansing and the rise of political Islam. The way political Islam develops depends on how the people in power deal with it.'

I tried, then Albert tried, to pay for the coffee, but the owner of the Armenian Tavern would not take our money. We went walking in the morning streets of the old city. Everyone who greeted Albert called him 'Doctor'. We came within sight of the Jaffa Gate, and I asked him why Allenby had chosen to enter the city from there. He said he had never thought about it. The Damascus Gate was for the local people, and pilgrims used the Jaffa Gate. It faced west. 'Did you know,' he asked, 'that it all started here?' He pointed at the Protestant Christ Church. The first consulate, Britain's, opened here in 1831. By 1847, seven more had been established – each claiming to protect one Christian minority or another. 'It began with the Egyptian invasion of Syria by Ibrahim Pasha and European meddling. This was the first Protestant church in Palestine.' Christ Church had been a joint Prussian–British venture to bring Protestantism to the Holy Land. Its first bishop was Michael Solomon Alexander, a Jewish convert from Posen whose mission was to bring other Jews to Christ. 'Go up to the roof,' Albert said. 'Look at this city, and you have the microcosm. Jerusalem faces east, to the mountains and the desert. But before the mountains and the desert, you have the tombs. All three religions have their tombs in the east. The city faces the dead, who rule this country. This is a necrocracy. In America, you look to the west and to future generations.' Albert pointed the stem of his pipe west. He swung it in the opposite direction, towards Al Aqsa, the Mount of Olives and the graveyards on the hillsides. He said, 'Here they consult the dead. Look at Feisal Husseini.' Feisal Husseini was a Jerusalem grandee and nationalist, who had recently died of a heart attack. His father was the hero of 1948, Abdel Qader Husseini. 'Now, Feisal is dead, and he has a son. His son will not think, what is good for my son? He will ask, what would my grandfather do?'

The Older Battle

I thought the days of Christians trying to convert the Jews were over, until I went to Mass in the Catholic chapel within the Holy Sepulchre on Sunday night. Many people had already told me of the Protestant fundamentalists who came from America to Israel to support Israel's colonization of the West Bank. Behind their agenda, shared by some within the Bush administration, was faith in the inevitability of the Last Judgement once all the Jews had been ingathered in Israel. So far, their fervour paralleled Israel's extreme settlers'. But they parted company on the outcome of the ingathering: the evangelicals prayed that, as the Judgement approached, the Jews would convert to Christianity. I put all this down to extremist brainwashing in that part of America that H. L. Mencken had called 'the hookworm and incest belt'. I was wrong. The Catholic priest in the Sepulchre chapel said in his sermon for the feast of Christ's baptism, 'Please, Lord, hear our prayer. Let us pray that the Jewish people in remaining loyal to their Covenant will recognize its fulfilment in accepting as the Messiah our Lord Jesus Christ.'

The Jews of Europe had put up with this sort of thing in the churches of Rome and Cracow for centuries, but I had assumed the Catholic Church had outgrown such nonsense. The Polish pope, John Paul II, had appealed for Catholics to understand Jews and Judaism and had declared anti-Semitism a grave sin. Still, there were priests who asked us to pray for the conversion of the Jews. I understood what drove Zionists from Europe to seek a land where they did not have to listen to the majority praying for their souls. I did not expect to hear that sermon in Jerusalem.

275

Digging in the Files

Israeli historians had been digging up the dead since the 1980s, disinterring the field reports and diplomatic communiqués that lay sleeping in the archives of the Haganah, the Jewish Agency and the government. The corpse of the founder, David Ben-Gurion, suffered most from their post-mortem scalpel. When one of them, the journalist-turned-historian Benny Morris, received a teaching appointment in Beersheva at Ben-Gurion University, the late prime minister's family protested. Morris told me that Amos Ben-Gurion, who lived in the United States, tried to stop the university from employing him. Ben-Gurion University was a backwater college in the Negev Desert. The respected Hebrew University in Jerusalem, Tel Aviv University and Haifa University would not offer him a post at all. He was off-limits, but he was rehabilitating himself with the right-wing establishment.

His first book, *The Birth of the Palestinian Refugee Problem, 1947–1948*, exposed much of the documentary evidence for what Palestinian historians had written since 1948: that the Zionists expelled the refugees. Morris, Simha Flapan, Ilan Pappe, Avi Shlaim, Tom Segev and others who came to be called the 'post-Zionist' or 'new' historians were undermining Israel's court historians. The orthodox account, taught in the schools, was that 700,000 Palestinian Arabs fled in 1948 at the command of the invading Arab armies. The documents showed the early histories to have been lies.

I had read that Morris now said Ben-Gurion's mistake was not expelling 700,000 Arabs, but leaving the other 200,000 within Israel's borders. The interview in which he first said that had surprised me. I had met Morris a couple of times, and I had reviewed his books favourably. I preferred to believe that he did not endorse ethnic cleansing. When we met for coffee in West Jerusalem's Gaza Road one morning, he did not remember the details of the interview that I had read. He did confirm the thrust.

'I probably said, if you are already expelling, Ben-Gurion did not expel enough,' he admitted. 'He left Israel with a huge time-bomb. If you chose a Jewish State, they should have done it. That is the logic of it.'

The logic was clear: partial expulsion was not enough to create a pure Jewish State. The minority might one day become a majority, or it might in a time of crisis launch an attack from within. Of course, neither eventuality had been realized. The higher Arab birth rate was offset by Russian Jewish immigration and a high birth rate among religious Orthodox Jews. And in the wars of 1956, 1967, 1973 and 1982, as well as during the *intifadah* of 1987 to 1993, Israel's Arab citizens had stabbed no knives into Israel's back.

Morris believed the Israeli Arabs were changing. 'Now,' he said, 'the Israeli Arabs identify with the Palestinian Arabs.' Did he think Israel would expel them?

'If you have an end-of-the-world situation,' he said, 'it could happen. It would have to be a war of survival. Without a war, you cannot do it – morally, technically . . .' I waited for another adverb, but it did not come. We were having coffee in one of those clean, bright cafés where Israeli liberals and leftists used to discuss politics. It was an open place, where the crowd might attract a suicide bomber.

Morris thought Yasser Arafat was 'stupid' and 'immoral' for shooting when Israel had been talking. While Israel talked peace, I said, it took land and shot Palestinians who resisted. 'It's not just the leadership,' Morris said. 'It's the people. The same people who were condemning land sales were selling land. Now, they help to build the settlements. Look, how do we know which ones to kill? Their friends are busy betraying them. You couldn't do that with the Hizballah in Lebanon. This is one of the reasons Israelis are contemptuous of Palestinian nationalists.'

Morris had a point. Dr Israel Shahak, one of Israel's most consistent champions of justice for Palestinians and a critic of Zionism, had told me the same thing a year before. Yet, to

Shahak, the weakness of Palestinian society did not excuse Israel's brutality. Shahak, who had died at home in Jerusalem the previous spring, had loved his country so much that he did not want it made ugly by treating Jews in one way and non-Jews in another. His first experience of that dated from his childhood in the Warsaw ghetto and two Nazi concentration camps.

Despite his harsh views on Palestinians and his sympathy for expelling them, Morris saw himself as an outsider, perhaps as a rebel. His credentials qualified him for something more engaging than a part-time position in the Negev. His thesis for his Ph.D. at Cambridge University was published in 1991. It dealt with the portrayal of Nazi Germany in the British press during the 1930s. After Cambridge, he became a journalist and wrote books on Israeli history. No Israeli university, however, would employ him. 'It was only after ten years, and five books and intercession by President Ezer Weizmann, that I got the job at Ben-Gurion,' he said.

Benny looked more like a street fighter, with powerful arms and a mess of brownish hair that needed a comb, than a professor of history. He did not rate most of his colleagues, who either concealed the historical record to sanitize Israel's past or had a leftist agenda with which he disagreed. Although clearly not a man of the left, Morris found himself classified with leftists as a post-Zionist.

'Most Israeli academics are against the new history, especially the older ones,' he said. 'If what we are writing is true, what they are writing is false.' The two historians he recommended were Avi Shlaim, who had just published *The Iron Triangle*, on Israel's consistent rejection of Arab peace offers, and Tom Segev, whose most recent book, *One Palestine, Complete*, told the story of Britain's Palestine Mandate that was unflattering at best to Zionism's pioneers. Shlaim was a professor at St Antony's College, Oxford. Segev was then on a fellowship at Rutgers University. Morris, meanwhile, lived in Jerusalem and drove to the Negev a few times a week to teach.

Morris was about to publish a book on John Bagot Glubb,

the commander of Jordan's Arab Legion during the 1948 war. His next project would be a new edition of his 1987 book on the expulsions of the Palestinians. 'There is a lot of new material,' he said, excited for the first time. I imagined him tearing through boxes of old army and foreign ministry papers to cast new light on old events. 'The new material includes Israel's responsibility for the problem, that there were more expulsions than I thought. Until the end of March [1948], there was no policy of expulsion. Things changed at the beginning of April. Paradoxically, the material also includes some Arab responsibility. The Arabs began sending out women and children by order of the Arab Higher Committee, the Arab Liberation Army and local commanders. From March of '48, they were sending children from Haifa and the villages along the coast. The depopulation began with women, children and old people. They had nothing to defend. This was a crucial factor in the demoralization of the Arab population.' Morris said this was the assessment of Haganah intelligence reports charting the daily movement of Arabs out of Palestine or from one region to another.

The Haganah reports offered more substance than the old lie about Arab radio broadcasts. It became an article of faith in early Zionist state histories that the Arabs left because the Arab states made appeals to them over the radio to flee the battlefield. The assertion ignored the fact, as Ilan Pappe wrote in *A Modern History of Palestine*, that one-third of Palestine's Arabs had been evicted *before* the Arab armies invaded in May 1948. The Israeli historians and politicians who blamed the Palestinian flight on these broadcasts concluded that the refugees were the Arab states', not Israel's, responsibility. Israel's United Nations ambassador, Abba Eban, told the General Assembly in 1957, 'The responsibility of the Arab governments is threefold. Theirs is the initiative for its creation. Theirs is the onus for its endurance. Above all – theirs is the capacity for its solution.' It was not a post-Zionist historian, but an Irish diplomat, Erskine Childers, who examined all Arab broadcasts transcribed by the BBC and an American monitoring unit for 1948 and stored in the British

Museum. Childers wrote in the *Spectator* on 12 May 1961, 'There was not a single order, or appeal, or suggestion about evacuation from Palestine from any Arab radio station, inside or outside Palestine, in 1948. There *is* repeated monitored record of Arab appeals, even flat orders, to the civilians of Palestine *to stay put*.' Childers noted that Damascus Radio threatened punishment for any Palestinian 'cowards' who left their homes. Although Israeli cab-drivers sometimes repeated the old myth about Arab radios, no serious Israeli historian any longer accepted it.

Ilan Pappe, one of its foremost scholars, wrote about post-Zionism, 'This movement represents a cultural view that strongly criticizes Zionist policy and conduct before and during 1948, accepts many of the claims made by Palestinians concerning 1948 itself, and envisions a non-Jewish state in Israel as the best solution for the country's internal and external predicaments.' Under Pappe's criteria, Benny Morris was no post-Zionist. He rejected the myths and lies of 1948, but he was committed to what he saw as the achievements of that war – including the ethnic cleansing of the Arabs.

When I was in London I asked another Israeli post-Zionist historian, Avi Shlaim, about Benny. Avi had written excellent books on Israeli history, particularly on its relations with the Arab states. He had supported the Oslo accords when they were announced, but he gradually saw their flaws. 'When you see Edward Said,' he said to me once, 'please tell him he was right about Oslo.' For a historian to admit a mistake was not easy, but Avi was scrupulous in his commitment to getting things right. On Benny, he told me, 'His shift to the right is emblematic of the Israeli peace camp. They say it's all the fault of the Palestinians and there can be no co-existence. Everyone says Oslo failed. No one says Israel didn't keep its part of the bargain. I'm appalled by his crass views. He was scrupulous in his use of sources. Now, he says Arafat didn't mean it when he signed Oslo. How does he know?'

Israelis and Palestinians were living a new phase of war that threatened an outcome as dramatic as that of 1948. The new *intifadah* was a conflict that Morris did not have to search the archives to understand. He and the rest of the new historians were watching it in what television producers called 'real time'. What did he make of it?

'I was surprised,' Morris said. 'I didn't think the IDF would sustain this for so long, which is something Arafat didn't understand. They're suffering more. It could go on like this, or it could explode.' I said it was already exploding, that Sharon provoked the Palestinians to violence. 'The one option that is not open under Sharon,' he said, 'is a unilateral withdrawal. If we did that, even if it were politically possible . . . going back would be seen as weakness.'

In common with most other Israelis and the prevailing views in the American press, he believed that the warfare that erupted in 2000 was Arafat's fault. In the summer of 2000, as they understood it, Arafat at Camp David said no to Prime Minister Ehud Barak's 'generous' offer of Palestinian independence in 95 per cent of the West Bank and Gaza. This version of events had hardened into faith, even in a historian as sceptical as Benny Morris.

'If that's how he responds to a 95 per cent offer,' Morris said of Arafat, 'we cannot trust them. Israelis now believe they want to kill us. You can only give them what you can afford to give, security-wise. The Palestinians can increase the number of Israeli deaths, but that has the danger of giving Israeli generals their heads. They could reconquer the West Bank.' Shortly after we spoke, the IDF did reoccupy the Palestinian A Areas in the West Bank.

'In September–October,' Morris said, 'Israel negotiated secretly, then publicly, in Taba. Clinton put proposals on the table. They gave Palestinians 94 per cent of the West Bank and a division of Jerusalem on demographic lines. Arafat refused. He said no to the Temple Mount and 94 per cent of the land.'

If that had been the case, and Morris knew there was no

document to prove it, why had Arafat rejected a solution that most of his countrymen wanted?

'He's unable, and they're unable, to abandon the grand vision of Palestine,' Morris said. 'He cannot sign on the dotted line and abandon the refugees in Lebanon.' Benny leaned back, away from the table where he'd pressed his elbows to emphasize his distrust of the Palestinians. There was something else he wanted to say. He was an Israeli, who had the natural fear that one concession to the natives might lead to others. He was also a historian, whose work would some day face the scrutiny of newer historians. I didn't ask him anything. He volunteered, 'Maybe they're like Jews in a sense. Jews didn't abandon the dream.' His eyes wandered around the café, and he didn't look at me when he added, 'We set a bad example.'

A couple of months later, I bumped into Benny in a supermarket in Jaffa Street on Jerusalem's west side. He had a trolley filled with groceries. His shirt was hanging out, and his hair was still a mess. It had been a bad week with a suicide bomber in Jerusalem and relentless Israeli attacks on the West Bank and Gaza. He was angry that the Israeli army was not doing more. 'They have to make an example,' he said. 'They have to go into Jenin and kill some people, arrest people, get everyone involved. They have to say to Arafat, "This is how it's done." It'll be up to him then.' Benny did not know whether the army would take his advice; in the months that followed, it did. 'How can Arafat have a dozen armed organizations? That's not how you have a state.' The Yishuv in Palestine had had three large armed organizations – the Haganah, the Irgun and the Stern Gang. They did not coalesce into one army until after the state was created. Everyone was setting bad examples.

EIGHT

Return to Gaza

'Occasionally Philistines penetrated to the neighbourhood of Jerusalem, or the Israelite raids swept to the
Gates of Gaza; but neither people ever mastered the
other's chief towns.'

REVEREND GEORGE ADAM SMITH
The Historical Geography of the Holy Land (1894)

The Same, but Worse

ABOUT SIX WEEKS after leaving Gaza I went back and took
a room at the Deira Hotel. While I had not minded the Western,
utilitarian styles of the Commodor and Beach Hotels, the Oriental luxury of my room at the Deira improved my morale. It had
a vaulted white ceiling, a vast bed on a massive stone platform,
a bath I could swim in and a sitting room with a divan for
guests – all open to the sea through Moorish arches. The other
hotels along the Gaza Riviera were functional. The Deira had
style.

Dr Eyad Sarraj came over on my first evening for coffee in
the hotel's bar. The Deira, like everywhere else in Gaza apart
from the United Nations' Beach Club, was still alcohol-free.
Eyad was tired. In my absence, the Israeli army had launched
more assaults on Gaza, especially on the refugee camps in the
south. He was going in the morning to visit two men whom the
Israelis had arrested. One was a physician with diabetes. Dr
Sarraj wanted to persuade him to end his hunger strike, a protest
that would be fatal in a short time.

Dr Sarraj stayed on for dinner. Nadia Sartawi, who was

283

visiting from Jerusalem, joined us. Only her French passport allowed her into Gaza. As an employee of the Palestinian Authority, she was still defending it against detractors. She said it was an embryo state that all Palestinians had a duty to nurture. Eyad Sarraj, an old friend of hers, did not see it that way.

'The biggest disaster since 1948 has been Yasser Arafat,' Eyad said. Nadia's father would probably have agreed with him. 'We have the organized, efficient and cruel power outside and the incompetent, useless and cruel one inside.'

In the morning, Nadia took me and her friend, a French journalist named Agnès Levallois, to the offices of the Palestinian Authority's minister of industry, trade and economy. Saadi Al-Krunz had refused to take bribes and tried to dismiss those in his ministry who did. He was having a hard time. Al-Krunz's background was typical Gazan. He was born in Falluja, the last pocket of Palestine outside Gaza that the Egyptian army had held in 1949. It was in Falluja that a young Egyptian army major, Gamal Abdel Nasser, had suffered his king's betrayal. Farouk's corrupt ministers had bought faulty surplus weaponry and failed to send supplies to their fighting men in Palestine. Nasser negotiated the withdrawal of his surrounded forces with Israelis who were nationalist, democratic and socialist and had thrown out the British. His 1952 revolution would attempt the same for Egypt. In the meantime, Palestinians who had not already fled the Falluja pocket were expelled to Gaza. Falluja became Kiryat Gat.

Al-Krunz grew up in Al Bureij refugee camp, site of Israeli major Ariel Sharon's first massacre of Palestinians in 1953. He attended UN schools, then universities in Cairo and Canada. He took his Ph.D. in mathematics from Indiana's Purdue University and joined Arafat's Al Fateh. In 1998, Arafat appointed him industry, trade and economy minister to replace Abu Ala, Ahmed Querei, who became speaker of the Legislative Council.

Al-Krunz may have had a typical Gaza background – refugee whose family made sure his education was good, nationalist who worked for the cause – but he was not a typical PA politician. His office was modest, in a rundown building near the Islamic University. He didn't wear a tie or gold jewellery. We sat on chairs in a circle, rather than across an imposing ministerial desk. He was a technocrat, the kind of man who, I imagined, would roll up his sleeves and dig in with the mechanics when he visited a factory. If anyone praised the PA, it was because a few people like him were trying to make it work.

What the PA had replaced in Gaza, Al-Krunz said, had been much worse. 'There was military rule,' he said. 'The tax expert was an officer in the Israeli military. He would put an arbitrary tax on a factory. It depended on the relationship between the owners and the Israelis. Many of the military officers were paid by the businessmen here.' Some Israelis said that Palestinian capitalists were corrupting Israel's army. Palestinians said Israeli officers extorted money from them in exchange for permits, licences, tax breaks and the possibility of exporting through Israel. 'The Druze were middlemen,' Al-Krunz explained, 'for their Israeli bosses.'

On the night the Israelis withdrew from much of Gaza in 1994, they placed the Palestinians under curfew lest they witness the lowering of Israel's flag. The PA moved into their empty offices the next morning. To the critics of Oslo, the old Israeli offices, prisons and police posts under Palestinian flags symbolized the new order. To the optimists, symbolism was less important than flying the Palestinian flag in a Palestinian sky, seeing Palestinian civil servants in a Palestinian administration and voting for Palestinian legislators in a Palestinian parliament.

Al-Krunz's task was neither symbolic nor political. It was practical: to make Gaza work. 'There were no telephone lines at the time,' he said. Gaza in 1994 had no airport, no harbour, no electricity for nearly half its people, insufficient water and sewage treatment, rudimentary medical facilities and nothing resembling an adequate road network. 'Take electricity,' Al-Krunz said. 'To be independent, we need 135 megawatts now. We buy 85 megawatts from the Israelis. I have a private generator here for my ministry. We are building a 160-megawatt power station, which is expandable, in a consortium of the American Enron company with Palestinian companies.'

Enron, before it went bankrupt in the United States, owned a third of Palestine's electricity network. Palestinian companies had a third, and the final tranche was in the hands of foreign investors. Why Enron? Businessmen said the American Embassy recommended the company to the PA. The Gaza electricity plant had been scheduled to start operation at the beginning of 2001. Israeli bombardment had delayed it indefinitely. Gaza continued to buy electricity from Israel, which cut the power for hours each day. Al-Krunz said that the American engineers he had contracted to work on the generator were still waiting in Israel for Israeli permission to enter Gaza. Soon, he said, they would give up and go home.

My cellphone rang. Taking the call outside on the stair-well, I heard the voice of an editor on London's *Evening Standard* asking me whether I had time to write an article. 'Tony Blair is in Syria,' he said. 'His wife is from Acton, the London suburb.'

'Cherie Blair is from Acton?' I asked, wondering what he was talking about.

'No, the Syrian's wife. Mrs Assad. She grew up in Acton. How about a piece on all these wives of Arab leaders who come from the British suburbs? It's a great story. Why are these Arabs all so attracted to British suburban women?'

I went over the wives of all the Arab leaders I could think of – Mrs Gaddafi, Mrs Mubarak, Mrs Saddam Hussein, Mrs Lahoud in Lebanon, King Fahd's many wives, the Palestinian wife of Jordan's King Abdullah. They were all Arabs. 'I don't think there are any others from British suburbs,' I said.

'So, you don't want to do the piece?'

I went back through the door, not into Al-Krunz's office so much as back to the Middle East, to the real problems of sur-vival to which the press in the Western world remained indiffer-ent. What were electricity shortages and poverty in Gaza compared to a jokey look at Essex girls in a sultan's palace?

Blair was in Syria, where the young, British-educated president embarrassed him with a lecture on the right of an occupied people to resist occupation. If Britain were occupied, would Blair lead the resistance or, like Pétain, sign the surrender? Blair, towing the British press along, would soon be in Gaza.

Agnès Levallois asked Al-Krunz about the Israeli–Palestinian joint ventures, capitalism's bridges to peace. There were to have been eight industrial parks, he explained. Since the uprising began, Israel had occupied or demolished seven of them. The only one left was the Gaza Industrial Estate that Bashir Rayess had described to me.

'According to Oslo,' Al-Krunz said, 'under what we call Israeli–Palestinian cooperation, we made industrial estates on the border to build partnerships between Israeli and Palestinian businessmen. These were Abu Ala and Yossi Beilin's ideas.'

'The new Middle East,' Nadia Sartawi said. Was she, at last, cynical about her boss and his Oslo process?

Among the many imbalances between Israel and the Palestinian Authority was trade. The PA, before the *intifadah*, sold $600 million in goods and services to Israel. At the same time, Israeli exports to the PA were $3 billion – five times as much. Even during the *intifadah*, Israel sold Palestinians processed food, soap, detergent and clothes with Hebrew labels. Palestinian exports to Israel had ceased. The debt to Israel was increasing, and Al-Krunz had no resources at his command to do anything about it. Nor could he prevent other ministers from stealing money meant for his infrastructure projects. When I left him, he looked tired – like a boxer who has just heard the referee count eight.

The Arabic word *samoud* described one of the qualities that the Palestinians most admired. Translated as 'steadfast', it referred to anyone who endured without complaint or collaboration. A people lacking the weapons and external support of their occupiers had little else. West Bankers with the education and money to live in the United States, Canada or Europe chose to be *samoud* when they stayed in their houses and suffered the strain of having all their fundamental choices made for them by foreign soldiers. During the first twenty years of occupation, from June 1967 to December 1987, most were *samoud* rather than rebellious or collaborationist. The Bar Association refused to cooperate with Israeli military courts because – as one Palestinian lawyer told me in 1974 – 'there is no law'. Most policemen resigned rather than work for the occupation, and there were serious – sometimes violent – debates over the line between survival and collaboration. To be *samoud* was the goal. To do the one thing that the Israeli settlers did not want: remain on the land.

Yasser Arafat appropriated the word *samoud* for himself, as if a public relations company had advised him which slogan would resonate in the market. It happened in the summer of 1982, after his commanders in south Lebanon had abandoned many of their fighters and their arms caches to Sharon's invading army. Arafat and the people of West Beirut suffered a three-month Israeli siege that entailed steady artillery and rifle fire, aerial bombardment, car bombs, denial of food supplies and chronic cuts of water and electricity. It was a disaster, but Arafat and his commandos held their ground for three months. In comparison, in 1967, the trained and modern armies of Egypt, Syria and Jordan could not resist Israel for even a week. Palestinian defeat, after a long siege and no help from the Arabs, became a propaganda weapon. When Arafat was exiled to Tunis, Fateh published posters that appeared all over the Arab world, including the West Bank and the Gaza Strip. Below a smiling Arafat were the words, 'In Beirut, you were *samoud*.'

Gaza's Grand Old Man

The one man in Gaza who was most *samoud* had been born in June 1919, a year after the British occupied Gaza and the last Turk had retreated to Anatolia. When Palestinians elected their Legislative Council in 1996, he received more votes than any other representative. People in his native Gaza and in the West Bank respected him because he, more than anyone else, personified that quality of being *samoud* that they all needed to survive – if not physically, then morally. His name was Haidar Abdel-Shafi.

Dr Abdel-Shafi received me in his office at the Palestinian Red Crescent Society, offered coffee and gave me a chair beside his desk. He was tall, gaunt and bald. In his dark suit and with the authority of experience, he made me feel I had come for a consultation. I asked him about Palestine's ills rather than my own. He was like one of those country doctors whose advice you would trust, because he had seen all the newfangled cures come and go. In Palestine's case, he had watched the passing of feudal leadership, of liberation, of fashionable socialism. His critical eye was now observing the children's fascination with fundamentalist Islam.

His father had been a custodian of the Islamic charitable foundation, the Waqf, under the Turks and the British. The son had done his elementary studies in Gaza and then gone to the Arab College in Jerusalem. He was seventeen when the Palestinians rebelled against British rule – then called the 'revolt' rather than uprising or *intifadah* – in 1936. 'It was a rebellion,' Dr Abdel-Shafi remembered. 'Palestinians had suffered from the beginning of the Mandate. The British Mandate itself was a violation of the right of self-determination. It can only be understood if you see that in twenty-five years, the British sponsored immigration that changed the balance from one Jew to eleven Palestinians to the point where there was one Jew for every two Palestinians. Secondly, there was the conduct of the Mandate. It accommodated only Jewish society. It allowed them self-rule and military training, while they denied both completely to the Arabs.'

And how did the Great Arab Revolt of 1936 to 1939 compare to the current *intifadah*? 'They were similar,' he said, 'in the lack of proper organization without defined objectives. They both made unnecessary mistakes. In fact, they make more now.

In the *intifadah* now, the Palestinians are affording the Israeli military forces easy targets.'

By the time Britain crushed the rebellion in 1939, disarming and crippling Palestinian society in the process, Haidar Abdel-Shafi was studying medicine at the American University of Beirut. He took his MD in 1943, the year British forces drove the Vichy French from Lebanon. He returned to Palestine as a general practitioner in Jaffa. During the Arab–Israeli war that began in 1947 and ended in 1949, Dr Abdel-Shafi served as a medical officer with Jordan's Arab Legion. After the loss of Palestine and the displacement of 750,000 people, Dr Abdel-Shafi studied surgery for five years at the Miami Valley Hospital in Dayton, Ohio. He returned to Egyptian-administered Gaza in time for the first Israeli invasion of 1956. When Israel withdrew in 1957, Dr Abdel-Shafi became Gaza's Director of Medical Services. Three years later, he told me, he resumed private practice. He did not mention something that is recorded in Palestinian history books: from 1962 to 1964, he was elected the first chairman, or speaker, of the Palestinian Legislative Council in Gaza.

In 1964, Dr Abdel-Shafi became a member of the first executive committee of the new Palestine Liberation Organization. Exhibiting the independence that characterized his political life, he was a vociferous critic and opponent of the original PLO chairman, Ahmed Shukeiry. It was Shukeiry who uttered the notorious and idiotic promise to 'throw the Jews into the sea'.

Then came the 1967 war. Shukeiry had not expelled any Israelis, but Israel forced thousands of Palestinians from the West Bank to Jordan. In six days, three Arab armies lost the Golan Heights, the West Bank, East Jerusalem, the Sinai Peninsula and the Gaza Strip. The Israelis occupied all of what, until 1948, had been Palestine, along with parts of Egypt and Syria. The IDF arrested Dr Abdel-Shafi and held him in a camp in Sinai's desert for three months in 1969 and a year later exiled him to Lebanon. He was allowed to return in 1972, when he established the Palestinian Red Crescent Society in association with the International Committee of the Red Cross. By then, Sharon had subdued all of Gaza. The PLO, meanwhile, had a new chairman.

In 1968, the young Palestinian commando organizations had joined the PLO. They took it over and named Arafat the 'spokesman', a post the wily Fateh chief turned into 'leader'. 'He is there till now,' Abdel-Shafi said, with what might have been regret.

What did Abdel-Shafi think of Ahmed Shukeiry? 'We don't like to discuss the character of those who have passed away,' he answered, or, rather, did not answer. 'He was at a loss for what to do. His temperament, he didn't give enough time to real thinking, how we could deal with our predicament. He was more inclined to move around and meet kings and heads of state and others.'

What about throwing the Jews into the sea? 'He never said it the way it was described. Shukeiry said Jews who came to Palestine under the protection of British arms were not Palestinian citizens and should leave.'

How did Shukeiry compare to Arafat? 'Well,' he said, putting his hands together, almost in what would have been prayer had he been a Christian, 'I say this openly and frankly. Our present chairman of the PLO, he . . .' Silence, then Abdel-Shafi's hands parted. 'He neglects . . .' He closed his eyes for a second, perhaps conscious that I was writing. He knew what he wanted to say. 'First of all, he is a real dictator. He insists on having his own way and on making all decisions. I speak openly about this. Presently, we are pressing him for the formation of a national unity leadership composed of representatives of all political forces, where we will have one decision that is respected by all parties and is reached democratically. I have been calling for this from the beginning of the *intifadah*.'

Second of all? There was no second of all. Nor third. Arafat was a dictator, and Abdel-Shafi opposed Palestinian dictatorship.

And the Palestinian Authority? 'I don't advise anybody to

participate in the PA in its present form.' To win Abdel-Shafi's endorsement, the PA would need 'an effective legal process, transparency, accountability. Then as soon as possible, it should make arrangements for general elections to elect a parliament.' There was an elected parliament, but Arafat – whose Fateh had a majority – had prolonged its life beyond its term.

Abdel-Shafi was eighty-three years old, and he wanted to rest. It was time for him to go home for lunch. He was too polite to end the conversation. Instead, he asked whether we could resume at three in the afternoon at his house in Charles de Gaulle Street.

Reunion with Dr Jawad Tibi, MP

I went back to the Legislative Council to see Jawad Tibi, by now one of my favourite men in Gaza. 'He's a foxy man,' Tibi said of Tony Blair, who was on his way to Gaza. 'The aim of his visit is strange. I think one who is the prime minister of a great state like Britain is strange to decide to visit Gaza. He's coming to the small country, to the small President Yasser Arafat, with something in his mind. He knows the Palestinian problem is central to all Islamic and Arab states. In order to undermine the efforts of the Islamic and Arab countries against their alliance in Afghanistan, he and Bush decide to play games relative to the Palestine issue. If there were justice in their minds, it would have been said before 11 September.'

We were in some kind of administrative office in an annexe to the parliament, where men and women came in to find papers in desk drawers and to chat. It was a busy place for a non-functioning institution, with telephones ringing and people typing at computer keyboards. It could have been an architect's office, where they were drawing plans for a Palestine that no one had commissioned.

If Blair had come to look good to the Arabs while the US was bombing Afghanistan, why should Arafat see him? 'Arafat,'

Tibi said, 'is receiving him because his hands are empty. He has no objection because he cannot reject anything.'

Tibi had come from Khan Younes to see me. The day before, he had watched as the Israeli army shot two young men – one in the neck, the other in the arm. Elsewhere in the occupied territories, six Palestinians had been assassinated by Israeli forces. While that was going on, Tibi was watching television reports of the American bombing of Afghanistan. If American television convinced its public that there was no difference between the Al Qaeda suicide bombers and Palestinians who fought against military occupation, many Muslims and Arabs were equating Israeli repression in the occupied territories with American attacks on Afghanistan. Blair's trip to Gaza would not change that.

'I'm a doctor,' Tibi reminded me. 'I feel it when I see these people pulled out of the rubble, in both New York and Afghanistan. I watch Jazeera Television, and I see these poor Afghans – even women and young people – being pulled out. But I do not see these pictures on CNN.'

The *International Herald-Tribune* published a *Washington Post* report that day: 'The chairman of CNN has ordered his staff to balance images of civilian devastation in Afghan cities with reminders that the Taliban harbour terrorists. In a memo to his international correspondents, Walter Isaacson said it "seems perverse to focus too much on hardship in Afghanistan".' Isaacson did not ask CNN to balance its coverage of civilian dead on 11 September with reminders that the US government subsidised Israel's occupation of the West Bank and Gaza, supported the Saudi monarchy's suppression of its people, supplied regimes around the world with weapons to devastate their populations and helped the Islamists who harboured Osama bin Laden to control Afghanistan. There was a certain imbalance in CNN's balance.

On the television in my room at the Deira Hotel, I had watched both Al Jazeera and CNN. Al Jazeera was supplying CNN with footage from Taliban-controlled towns where

CNN's camera crews felt unsafe. The Jazeera reports showed whole neighbourhoods demolished by the bombardments. Rescuers dug for survivors and corpses in hills of collapsed mud. Sometimes, they would unearth a foot or a torso. One of the diggers wept when he found a severed, bloody limb. I wondered who the dead one was to him – wife, child, friend. Later, CNN showed the same footage, but none of the body parts and no close-ups. They had edited the Jazeera video to use only the long shots of the rubble with a voice-over that spoke of 'alleged' civilian casualties.

The hacks who came to Gaza for the Blair junket were having lunch on the terrace at the Deira. I had eaten similar lunches with most of them in Beirut, Sarajevo, Cairo, Jerusalem and Baghdad. Usually, we had alcohol. In Gaza, there was no wine, no beer, no cognac with the coffee. But there were stories and gossip and complaints about an article one of them had written that predicted anti-Blair demonstrations in Gaza. No demonstrations were scheduled, and none took place. His paper had run his story of the impending protest that morning. So, we asked our colleague, how will you get out of this one? For an old Fleet Street hand, who had beaten bigger challenges, it was easy. His next lead would be: 'Demonstrations suppressed.'

In the afternoon I kept my three o'clock appointment at Dr Haidar Abdel-Shafi's house. It turned out that I did not need his address. All Gaza's taxi drivers knew the place, not as the white house on Charles de Gaulle street, but as Dr Abdel-Shafi's.

He invited me into a room whose drawn curtains blocked out some of the sun's heat. It was a traditional Arab receiving room evolved from the divan, lots of stuffed chairs and sofas for visitors. Today, I was the only visitor. The British prime minister would not be coming to this house. It had no guards, no security systems, no flunkeys awaiting orders. Dr Abdel-Shafi's wife gave us Turkish coffee.

Dr Abdel-Shafi had led the Palestinian delegation to the Madrid conference on the Middle East in 1992. He recalled,

'We went in hope that the US would adopt a balance of position as sponsor, especially in the aftermath of the war in the Gulf and the liberation of Kuwait from occupation.' In a way, the Arab–Israeli peace talks were Saddam Hussein's achievement. When he conquered and occupied Kuwait, he equated his occupation to Israel's. If Israel withdrew from the land it occupied in 1967, he would leave Kuwait. President George Bush, Sr, rejected what he called 'linkage' and what Arabs saw as equality before the bar of international law. To persuade the Arab states to participate in the war for Kuwait – Bush did not need their troops so much as their flags – he promised to bring Israel to the negotiating table. He would not, as with Iraq, order Israel to withdraw from occupied territory and grant the occupied population self-determination. Syria, Jordan and the Palestinian Liberation Organization went to Madrid to meet Israel face to face.

'Our hopes were frustrated,' Abdel-Shafi recalled. 'Our first demand was to halt settlement activity, violating the conference's terms of reference.' The Palestinians in the West Bank and Gaza had ended their *intifadah*, and they wanted a reciprocal gesture on settlements from the Israelis. If the discussions were on ending occupation, wouldn't more and larger settlements of Israeli colonists push that goal further away? Abdel-Shafi said that Bush's secretary of state, James Baker, agreed to suggest a settlement freeze to the Israeli delegation, who would not consider it. 'So, he tried to delay us asking for this, and we refused. We negotiated for twenty months.' Meanwhile, the talks moved to Washington. Secret talks took place in Oslo. Arafat did not tell Abdel-Shafi, Hanan Ashrawi and the other official delegates about the Oslo track until it produced an agreement.

'Three or four days before it was signed,' Abdel-Shafi said of the first Oslo accord, 'I was going to Washington for the eleventh round of talks. I stopped in Tunis.' The PLO's post-Beirut headquarters was in Tunisia. 'Arafat told me about Oslo. I read it, and I told him it was a bad agreement. I advised him to take time to revise the agreement. I saw Abu Mazen and Abed Rabbo' – Arafat lieutenants Mahmoud Abbas and Yasser Abed Rabbo – 'but there was nothing doing. As the Chairman wanted this, they all wanted it.' The only men in Al Fateh with the courage to question Arafat's judgement were two co-founders of the movement, men of his generation, who had been with him during his defeats in Amman in 1970 and Beirut in 1982: Salah Khalaf and Khalil al-Wazir, called Abu Iyad and Abu Jihad. Israel had assassinated them both.

From the beginning of the Madrid negotiations, Abdel-Shafi's strategy differed from Arafat's. 'As chairman of our delegation,' he said, 'I was calling for suspending our participation so we could decide where to go. How could we negotiate when Israel went on building settlements? After the sixth round, I was disassociating myself. But there were demonstrations in the Gaza Strip. One of our weaknesses is that people support the people in power. This is our misfortune.'

Abdel-Shafi in Gaza and Hanan Ashrawi, a respected professor at Bir Zeit University, had to hold out over settlements. They lived under occupation, in the Palestinian homeland, and witnessed the steady confiscations of their neighbours' property. If it continued, there would be nothing left to discuss. Arafat was in Tunis, and his PLO was almost bankrupt. The Arab oil states had stopped their subsidies when he supported Saddam Hussein in Kuwait. His loyal followers in refugee camps did not have the money to compensate the PLO for its losses. He had to pay civil servants, diplomats, pensions, commandos and the widows and orphans of martyrs. Between his organization and the land, he chose the survival of the organization.

'The Oslo agreement did not address the settlement issue,' Abdel-Shafi said. 'Surprisingly, this did not seem to faze Arafat.' I looked at this old and tired man. I had seen him years before in Gaza, and I had watched him on television when his face betrayed his reaction to Arafat's secret manoeuvres that conceded Palestinian rights at Oslo. All that Abdel-Shafi predicted then had come to pass: Israeli settlers had taken more territory, built more concrete houses and dug more roads across Palestinian farmland. They had uprooted thousands of Palestinian olive trees, and they had restricted Palestinians to ever smaller zones between settlers' roads. Abdel-Shafi, like Professor Edward Said in New York, had seen it coming.

Yasser Arafat saw something else. He saw the leader of the Palestinian people, himself, taking part in a photo opportunity at the White House in September 1993. Posing with the president of the United States and the prime minister of Israel, he believed its implicit message that the three men were equals. That was more than any Palestinian leader had ever been granted, although Arafat did not achieve equality between the Israeli settlers and the occupied Palestinians. Abdel-Shafi and Professor Said made one other prediction: when reality under the agreement wiped away the memory of the White House tableau, the people who were losing their homes, their land and their livelihoods would explode.

Was Dr Abdel-Shafi in despair? 'It's not a hopeless situation,' he said. 'If we can engage in proper organization . . . if we heed basic issues . . . if we have a proper dispersal of public money . . . if we divide responsibility . . . if we can prevail on ourselves to do these basic things, it would be the beginning of Israeli worry about the future. With our disarray, why should they worry? If we can wear out the Israelis with our ability to understand the situation, they know that they cannot sustain themselves. We are more able to withstand deprivation.'

Palestinians often asked me, as an American, how long Israel would survive without American money, American arms and American power. Palestinians survived, they said, without help from anyone. They were – not that they had a choice – *samoud*.

I asked Dr Abdel-Shafi whether the Palestinians had ever had good leaders. 'No,' he said. 'Our leadership in the Mandate period was primitive: heads of families, who were always in conflict. The main failure is the PLO, which did not study the past and so continued to make serious mistakes.'

Dr Abdel-Shafi called again and again for a leadership of

national unity. Should it, I asked, include the Islamic fundamentalists? 'It won't work without them.' And Arafat? Why would
he share power? 'He should not see it in terms of his interests.
He should start thinking in the interests of the Palestinian
people. The people with Arafat are captives of their personal
interests, and they don't want to sacrifice them.'

Putting the Islamists into the limited self-rule government of
the PA would limit their options for, as Abdel-Shafi saw it,
self-destruction. He opposed the Islamists' suicide–homicide
strategy. 'We should confine our military actions to the defensive,' he insisted. 'Killing Israelis conveys the wrong impression
to the world. If we defend ourselves against settlements and
the uprooting of trees and organize ourselves to endure these
difficulties, we can defeat Israel.' Abdel-Shafi was relying, as the
South African majority once did, on the conscience of the world.
'We must make it clear to the world that we have legitimate
demands, that we are engaged in a defensive battle with a
superior force. We can face Israeli pressure in all its forms and
sustain this. This will influence the attitude of the democratic
world. Palestinian society will be more respected.'

How would Dr Abdel-Shafi hold back the anger of the young
men who heeded the call of Hamas and Islamic Jihad? His own
father, after all, had been a religious leader. Sheikh Moheiddin
Abdel-Shafi belonged to the Higher Muslim Council under Haj
Amin Husseini, another leader who failed the test of protecting
his people. As custodian of religious endowed properties after
the First World War, Sheikh Moheiddin moved from Gaza to
Hebron. There, he oversaw Muslim charities and the Great
Mosque where the Patriarchs of Israel – all of them prophets
within Muslim theology – were said to be buried. Dr Abdel-Shafi
spent two happy years of his childhood in Hebron, where he
lived among its ancient Jewish community. The flat opposite his
family's belonged to Jewish friends. 'I remember, as a child, the
rabbi, called Abu Yusuf, came often to visit us,' he said. 'Every
Saturday morning, the woman from the flat opposite would
knock on our door and ask me to light her kerosene lamp.' A

Gentile like young Haidar Abdel-Shafi, who performed work forbidden to Jews on the Sabbath, was called a Shabas-goy. 'I liked Abu Yusuf, the rabbi,' he said.

The Abdel-Shafis returned to Gaza in 1928. A year later, their Jewish friends in Hebron were massacred. His father condemned the killings, and the ten-year-old Haidar Abdel-Shafi was 'very disturbed'. The Hebron massacre of 1929 symbolized to Jewish settlers Arab fanaticism and, something new in Palestine, anti-Semitism. The American journalist Vincent Sheehan, who was writing in Palestine at the time, recalled in his book *Personal History*, 'Hebron was one of the four holy cities of Judaism, and had had a small, constant Jewish population since medieval days. There were no Zionists at all; a more innocent and harmless people could not have been found in Palestine; and many of them were Oriental Jews, and all were religious. They had had nothing to do with the Zionist excesses, and had lived in amity with their neighbours up to that day. But when the Arabs of Hebron – an unruly lot, at best – heard that Arabs were being killed by Jews in Jerusalem and that the Mosque of Omar was in danger, they went mad.' Hebron's Arab rioters murdered sixty-seven Jews, most of whom had lived there all their lives. Ben-Gurion called it a 'pogrom', a view not shared by Israeli historian Tom Segev. 'Unlike attacks on the Jews of Eastern Europe,' he wrote in his history of the British Mandate, *One Palestine, Complete*, 'the authorities did not initiate the Hebron riots, and the police did not simply stand aside.' Hebron's more responsible citizens resisted the rioters and hid Jews in their houses. Segev wrote that the Zionist Archives preserved a list of 435 Jews, more than two-thirds of the Hebron community, who were saved by Arabs. In all of Palestine, the 1929 death toll was 133 Jews and 116 Arabs.

Recalling that shameful day, Dr Abdel-Shafi said that some of the Muslim Hebronites tried to rescue his friend Abu Yusuf. I asked what happened to the rabbi. Dr Abdel-Shafi said, with sadness, 'He was killed.'

Balfour Day

I left Gaza on Balfour Day, the anniversary of the declaration by Britain's then foreign secretary, Arthur Balfour, that promised Palestine to European Zionists. Palestinian Authority police in smart uniforms, some of pure black and others camouflage, stood at attention along the route from Gaza town to the Erez crossing. A few shouldered American M-16 rifles, but most had only wooden clubs to beat back rioters. There were no rioters, no civilians shoving for a look at the prime minister from Great Britain, no one showing any interest at all. There were just children, everywhere children, walking and running, oblivious to the impending arrival of the august visitor.

At Erez, Israeli troops would not allow anyone to leave Gaza until Tony Blair had passed. I waited by a block of concrete. Fifteen minutes later, a procession of Land Rovers and limousines, like a funeral cortege, approached the Israeli inspection station. They did not pause for the stamping of their passports, but they did change security guards. Blair's Israeli escorts stopped at Erez until his return, and a detail of Palestinian security men took over. The Palestinian and Israeli guards seemed to be on good terms. After all, the rebellion had only recently interrupted seven years of cooperation between them under the Oslo accords.

The cars fired up and drove in single file through the last checkpoint. I saw Blair in one of the Land Rovers, smiling just in case anyone on the roadside waved at him. No one did. He went on in his long, protected cavalcade through the squalor of Gaza City and its slums into which thousands of Arab inhabitants of British Palestine had been dumped in 1948. He said later that he delivered a message to Yasser Arafat: control the terrorists. It was a fitting way to recall Lord Balfour's Day.

NINE

The Desert

'– the Negeb, translated *The South* in our version,
literally Dry or Parched Land.'
REVEREND GEORGE ADAM SMITH
The Historical Geography of the Holy Land (1894)

A Secular Shrine

DAVID BEN-GURION BELIEVED the desert would redeem
Israel. In 1949, the Negev Desert was half the state's land area
and held about 1 per cent of its Jewish population. By making
the sands blossom, Ben-Gurion intended to settle millions of
Jews. It was to a kibbutz in the Negev, Sde Boker, that he retired
to write his memoirs and to work with its young idealists
at their daily chores. Thousands of Israeli and Diaspora Jews
made the pilgrimage to Sde Boker to see the great man, but
most did not emulate him. Life in the remote wastes appealed
less than the cafés of Tel Aviv and the politics of Jerusalem.
Fifty years after Israel's conquest of the Negev, its two growth
cities, Beersheva and Dimona, looked as desolate as the landscape around them. Most of their inhabitants were Oriental and
Russian Jews – poor, badly educated and without connections
to obtain jobs in the fertile Galilee or along the Mediterranean
shore.

Of all the areas conquered during Israel's War of Independence, the Negev fell most easily. In March 1949, while Israel
and Jordan's King Abdallah were negotiating a Negev ceasefire,
two Israeli brigades made an unopposed dash south through
the desert to the Red Sea. They occupied Umm Rashrash near

301

Aqaba and hoisted a home-made Israeli flag to claim all of the Negev for Israel. From 10 March 1949, the Negev and access to the Red Sea were Israel's.

The message that Israel's young warriors sent from Umm Rashrash adorned Ben-Gurion's modest bungalow at Sde Boker. 'The Negev and Golani brigades present the Gulf of Eilat to the State of Israel.' Ben-Gurion's elation was evident in his diary entry of the next day: 'This could well be the greatest event of the last few months, if not of the entire war of liberation and the conquest. And not a drop of blood was spilt.' He also wrote, 'The Negev is the only wide space where a non-mixed Jewish population is possible.'

To look at what Ben-Gurion called the 'conquest' from a Zionist perspective, without regard for its effect on the prior inhabitants, is to see a heroic tale of rebirth. Think of it. For two thousand years, a dispersed and exiled people waited to return to the land they believed God had promised their ancestors. The twentieth century created the conditions for success: a new colonial power inclined to settle European Jews among primitive *indigenes*, idealistic Jewish youth willing to become pioneers on collective farms and the murder of 5.1 million Jews proving the Zionist case that the *goyim* hated and wanted to destroy all Jews. The Gulf of Aqaba becomes the Gulf of Eilat, Beersheba is Beersheva, the Negeb the Negev. The Arabs, their legacy and their names are erased. History as told within this schema begins, not in Palestine where mostly Arabs, along with a few Armenians, Samaritans and Jews, dwelled; but in Paris, where Theodor Herzl observed the Dreyfus trial, and Basel, where the Zionists held their Congresses. On this telling, the Arab does not exist. The Jew of the Diaspora will cease to exist. The 'Yid' that Zionist pioneers detested was an aberration, albeit of two thousand years, between the heroic if suicidal exploits of Bar Kokba in the first century and of Yosef Trumpeldor in the twentieth. Trumpeldor's death fighting Arabs in the early years is remembered in Zionist folklore for his final words: 'It is good to die for your country.' Erasing the Arabs and their language was a side-effect of the central project: to wash away the deformities of the ghetto, restore Hebrew and impose a national amnesia upon the Exile. It would also prevent the annihilation of Jewry by its greatest enemy: assimilation into other national or religious cultures. (Herzl himself had once proposed mass conversion to Christianity as a solution to the 'Jewish problem'.) The new Hebrew nation would forget Yiddish, Klezmer music and money-lending. The Arabs lacked even the dignity of being the target of the enterprise that displaced them and washed away the names of their cities, towns, villages, hamlets, hilltops and rivers. They were minor obstacles to Judaizing Eretz Israel, the Land of Israel.

It was easy to share this vision in the Negev, where few traces of the native presence remained and where the triumph of Ben-Gurion's work was heralded at his home and in his tomb – both shrines to the man and to the Israel he was instrumental in creating. To understand Israel, even a little, you have to let go for a few hours the belief that all men are equal. You must forget that Arabs were in the land, that they resided there for centuries and that they belonged to a world culture. Instead, you must walk where Ben-Gurion made history and listen to Ben-Gurion's words.

The first of his aphorisms that I saw at Sde Boker had been engraved in a marble slab beside the yellow brick road from the car park to the wizard's bungalow. Block Hebrew and sans-serif English characters proclaimed, 'It is in the Negev that the creativity and the pioneer vigour of Israel shall be tested.' A yard away, on a silk screen between two stumpy olive trees, pioneers posed with horse and covered wagon. They were the young Jewish socialists, who had severed themselves from the *shtetl* and rabbinical control to settle a wild land that their prophet, Theodor Herzl, called old–new land. The wagon, drawn by four ponies across the Negev plain, was almost life-size. To an American visitor like me, the message was that Israel's forebears were like mine. They risked their lives in a hostile physical environment and triumphed over nature and savages. We will not return North America to the Native Americans and they will not give this land back to the Arabs.

Sde Boker was established in 1952, when seven ex-soldiers from the Haganah's elite and recently disbanded Palmach unit settled there. The covered wagon image dated to the 1950s, when the Palmachniks were breeding horses to pull ploughs and carts on Jewish farms near Jerusalem. Ben-Gurion stopped there on his way from Eilat, when he opened its port, and promised the kibbutzniks he would return. A year later, he came to live with them. In 1961, when Israel imported small tractors from Germany, the kibbutz lost its market for workhorses and turned to agriculture and research. The covered wagon was a misleading symbol. Sde Boker's pioneers had come in the twentieth century in cars and trucks and well supplied with money to realize their dream. Ben-Gurion ensured that a pipe would carry water south across the desert to Sde Boker and more than forty other Negev settlements. The settlers had problems with the Bedouin, whose grazing land had been confiscated. Yehoshua Cohen, a kibbutz member who was said to have assassinated United Nations mediator Count Folke Bernadotte in September 1948, settled the Bedouin problem with force and threats of greater force.

Another marble slab on Ben-Gurion's Via Felicia read, 'It is written: "Whoever seeks wisdom, south he shall go."' It did not say where this had been written, but most Israelis, Jewish and Arab, had ignored it. They had also turned away from Ben-Gurion's admonitions to live on the land, to grow their own food, to work within the collective of the kibbutz and to practise socialism. He was nonetheless revered as the Founder. His counsel, like George Washington's against foreign adventures and entangling alliances, was forgotten amid the patriotic uses to which his legacy had been put. Every Israeli prime minister, including the ultra-capitalist bulldozer Ariel Sharon, longed to be likened to Ben-Gurion.

Like Ben-Gurion, Sharon kept a house in the desert. Ben-Gurion's was a bungalow, like a California farm worker's shed from *The Grapes of Wrath*, shaded by eucalyptus and roofed in terracotta. His house belonged to the collective. Sharon was a rancher, Texas-style, with a large private spread that an army salary alone would neither have bought nor maintained. Yet the corpulent cowboy shared with the socialist man of the people the vision of a land with as many Jews and as few Arabs as the world would allow.

Evidence of Ben-Gurion's contradictory nature decorated the house: proletarian chic furniture; testimonials from the *goyim* to the Jewish exclusivist; a lavish library with scores of books on religion and reincarnation for the professed agnostic; and, in the bedroom with his single bed, a photograph of Mahatma Gandhi with Ben-Gurion's tribute: 'The moral strength of the East is perhaps embodied most of all in the great Indian leader Mahatma Gandhi, the outstanding man who is heading the war for independence ... and the weapon of this commander is non-violence.' In 1917, the year Britain occupied Jerusalem, Mahatma Gandhi wrote, 'The Palestine of the Biblical conception is not a geographical tract. It is in their [the Jews'] hearts. But if they must look to Palestine as their national home, it is wrong to enter it under the shadow of the British gun ... They can settle in Palestine only by the goodwill of the Arabs.' Ben-Gurion seemed convinced that he was, like Gandhi, an anti-colonial rebel. The self-image required a memory lapse: an imperial power, Britain, protected his nascent white-settler state until the settlers were ready to sever the tie to their sponsor. After Israeli independence, Ben-Gurion supported the white settlers in Algeria and the 1956 Anglo-French imperial invasion of Egypt. His successors would ally themselves against anti-colonial natives in Ian Smith's Rhodesia. They would also give succour to apartheid South Africa, where Gandhi had begun his struggle against racism.

Ben-Gurion had admirers, even in the enemy camp. The great historian of Arab history Albert Hourani met him in Jerusalem in 1942. 'I saw Ben-Gurion, whom I liked enormously,' Hourani told Nancy Gallagher in her book of interviews with Middle

305

East historians. 'He invited me to spend most of an afternoon talking with him. He talked expansively with great vision of the future. I have never thought badly of him since then. I had the impression of a man of integrity. You always knew where you stood with him. You may not have liked where he stood, but at least you knew.'

In 1946, Ben-Gurion told the Anglo-American Committee, whose report would lead the United Nations General Assembly a year later to propose dividing Palestine into Jewish and Arab states, 'We don't want to say that this is our country because we conquered it, but because we made it, we remade it, we created it.' Yet it became the Zionists' country because they conquered most of it in 1948. As with his attempt to remake the Negev into a population centre, Ben-Gurion could not convince a majority of the world's Jews to live anywhere in Israel. That did not mean failure. Enough did come – in waves from Europe, the Arab countries, Russia and the Americas – to create a country like no other. And Ben-Gurion was right when he said, 'We shall not return to what we were.'

A young woman sitting in the shade next to the house offered to help me. A kind of Ben-Gurion worship radiated from her, a vestal virgin at his temple. She gave me a pamphlet on the life of the man who was born on 16 October 1886 in Russian Poland and came to the Promised Land twenty years later. There was a website, she said, with all his papers on it. There were many other places in Israel associated with his life, most of which she wrote down for me.

The full shrine was a trinity – house, museum and, a few miles away, tomb. Ben-Gurion had lived in spartan simplicity – bare floors, cheap chairs and tables, a kitchen with no elaborate gadgets. The opulence, if any, was confined to his study, where shelves and the surface of a long table were awash with books – in Hebrew and in English, histories, biographies of secular Jewish heroes like Spinoza and Einstein, treatises on mathematics, evolution, genetics, language and philosophy. It was to this room that Ben-Gurion retired in December 1953 to write his version of Israel's history. It was a short-lived retirement. In February 1955, the government called him back as defence minister. The following November, he became prime minister again. During the thirteen months at Sde Boker, he maintained close contact with his military acolytes – among them Moshe Dayan, Yigal Allon and Yigal Yadin – and undermined the authority of his successor, Moshe Sharrett. Within a year of his restoration to the prime ministry, Ben-Gurion had invaded Egypt and the Gaza Strip in collusion with France and Great Britain. He retired again in 1963, after Israel had withdrawn from the Sinai and executed Adolf Eichmann for crimes against the Jewish people. He returned to Sde Boker, where he finished *Israel: A Personal History*. He served in the Knesset until 1970, three years after the Six Day War completed the conquest of Eretz Israel.

The longer I walked through the house and the museum, itself another modest desert shack, the more intimate Ben-Gurion's life seemed. Here were the relics of little David Gryn of Plonsk, the photographs of him and of his world: the Plonsk synagogue, the wilds of what would become Tel Aviv, the Turkish law student in Thessalonika who aspired to membership of the Ottoman parliament, the young trade union leader on the hustings, the statesman declaring Israel an independent state on 14 May 1948, the grand old man with fellow leaders of his time – Eisenhower, Adenauer and De Gaulle. In the museum were displayed his Parabellum pistol, his delegate's card for the fourteenth Zionist Congress in 1925 and British pass number 0948 that exempted him from the curfews of 1936. In one glass cabinet was an old reel-to-reel tape of his voice reading the Declaration of Independence. An album of battle maps was inscribed to him by former army chiefs of staff, among them Yigal Yadin, Moshe Dayan and Yitzak Rabin, and dated, according to the Hebrew calendar, 7 Tammuz 5723. In the house and the museum were frequent references to his wife, Paula, whose single bed in her own bedroom was identical to his. He had met and married Paula Munweiss in the United

States in 1916, when the Turkish government exiled him and his colleague, Yitzak Ben Zvi.

Paula lay buried beside him, in a grave of her own with a separate tombstone, on a forlorn plaza above the desert plain. Its solitude reminded me of another grave, in the Matopos Hills of what became Zimbabwe, of another founder, Cecil Rhodes. His white Rhodesia endured for almost a century. Although Paula is mentioned, again and again, the tomb and the memorabilia did not say much about her beyond the fact that she was beside him at important moments. And she was beside him still, the girl from America, who bore him two daughters and a son. She died in either 1964, which is what the chronology in Ben-Gurion's book said, or 1969, the date etched into her tombstone. Ben-Gurion lay next to her in an identical sarcophagus, side by side, like twin beds, closer than the two beds in the house.

Ben-Gurion had lived to see a state that, when he reached Ottoman Palestine in 1906, must have been one of the least likely possibilities to be realized in the twentieth century. He presided over its birth and nurtured its childhood. He had witnessed its expansion in 1967 and had outlived his only formidable Arab nemesis, Gamal Abdel Nasser, who died in 1970. Then, in the year of Israel's first military retreat, from the Suez Canal under the Egyptian assault of October 1973, he died.

In *Israel: A Personal History*, Ben-Gurion wrote, 'The first immigrants endured the trials and tribulations that always confront pioneers. They fought the forces of nature, the perils of the desert, hostile neighbours, malaria, the lack of water; the difficulties of putting down roots in a land that is both loved and desolate; of unifying tribes from distant corners of the earth and creating a renewed national identity.' The pioneers beat the forces of nature, the perils of the desert, the hostile neighbours and the malaria. Lack of water remained critical, and the neighbours within the renewed land were hostile yet.

David Ben-Gurion became the archetype for Israelis of the fighting Jew, the new leader who took them from the *shtetl* and the ghetto into the Promised Land. He was fierce, he was courageous and he did not grovel to the *goyim* the way many community leaders in Europe's Diaspora had. He was a devious, cunning political operator who outfoxed the British, the Arabs, the Israeli communists and his fiercest enemies in Menachem Begin's rightist Herut party. If Palestine's Arabs had had a leader like Ben-Gurion, who knew both his society and the modern political world, their history might have been happier.

After the Haganah expelled most of the Arabs from Palestine in 1948, Ben-Gurion said of the Arab refugees, 'They must be harassed continuously.' In *1949: The First Israelis* Tom Segev wrote that Ben-Gurion asked Jewish National Fund head Yosef Weitz to study ways of driving the refugees, who might try to return, from the borders of the neighbouring states. The evening before I drove to Sde Boker, I read in Segev's book that the Foreign Ministry reported on the refugees to Ben-Gurion, 'Some will die but most will turn to human debris and social outcasts and probably join the poorest classes in the Arab countries.' Weitz's 'Transfer Committee' and the Middle East Department of the Foreign Ministry were right. The Arab leaders who promised the Palestinians they would return to their villages, most of which were erased from the map by Israeli bulldozers, lied.

An Inn in the Desert

The day before I came to Beersheva, someone set fire to the office there of an Arab Knesset member. MK Taleb As-Saneh had already reported a death threat against him from an Ortho-dox Jew. The spokesman for the national infrastructure minis-ter, a Russian immigrant named Avigdor Liebermann, said that 'some Arab MKs want to serve the country and be a part of it, others just want to destroy it'. As-Sanaa himself told the *Jerusa-lem Post* that the arson attack on his office exemplified 'the failure of Israeli democracy' and was the result of 'incitement of the right-wingers and the Israeli media who fan the flames'. Beersheva police did not apprehend the arsonist.

The first thing I saw when I drove into Beersheva was the glass office tower of Ben-Gurion University. It stood next to a modern hospital, where an old Bedouin woman in a long, embroidered dress limped from the door of the emergency entrance. The seven wells that Allenby occupied as the rear base for his assault on Gaza had become a city – not a beautiful city, but a city nonetheless. Ben-Gurion had driven off most of the Bedouin, who still lurked in encampments nearby and had a weekly market that attracted, when they were not fearful, tourists from overseas. Beersheva's Jewish immigrants from the Arab countries and from Russia lived in identical small houses with identical small gardens. Driving through the city, I heard on the radio that a plane from Tel Aviv to Siberia had fallen out of the sky and into the Black Sea. The passengers, who must have been in the main Russian Jews, were all presumed dead. Was it a bomb or an accident? If an accident, would the fury at the incompetence of Russia's airlines be as great as at a murderer? (It was an accident.) There was local news as well: Israel raided Gaza, and a Palestinian, dressed in an Israeli army uniform, shot people waiting at a bus stop in Afula.

I checked into the Desert Inn Hotel amid the dunes at the edge of town. An attractive Russian receptionist whose blonde hair modestly concealed her ample breasts gave me a key and apologized that there were no porters. Upstairs, my monastic bedroom had two rock-hard single beds and a small table. The bathroom, the size of a small cupboard, offered only one postage-stamp-size bar of soap. For Beersheva, this was tall cotton. The guidebooks said the Desert Inn was the best hotel in town, and it probably was. It was more Russian Black Sea resort on sand than a replica of its older namesake in Las Vegas. Two large swimming pools attracted fat, squat women unashamed of their corpulence and their bad Hebrew. They bounced in the water with their children, and they luxuriated in foaming hot tubs. The cafeteria was a legacy of the kibbutzim, a communal eating hall favoured by most of Israel's provincial hotels. Hotel restaurants from Dan to Beersheva must have been designed by the same utilitarian mind: suffocating ceilings that anyone could touch without stretching, long trestle tables against bare walls, cold-drink dispensers, stacks of plastic trays and wax paper napkins in holders that looked like visitors from the era of Stalin, Eisenhower and the automat. I thought this was the sort of thing the Russians were escaping, yet here they were in their hundreds at communal tables eating boiled meat and stale bread that they had grown up with beside the River Moskva. Perhaps it was nostalgia, like Americans seeking make-believe 1950s diners.

After my communal dinner in the hard light of the cafeteria, I went to the bar for a brandy. The bartender, an Arab born in Beersheba, gave me a Cognac filled to the brim of a Coke glass. So far, I was finding Beersheva discouraging and dull. Did he know of anything a visitor should see or do here? 'Nothing,' he shook his head. 'There is nothing here.'

In the morning, the BBC World Service reported that Egypt's President Hosni Mubarak, the absence of whose portrait was one of the few aspects of Beersheva life that I found agreeable, had placed a wreath at the tomb of his predecessor, Anwar Sadat. It was the twentieth anniversary of Sadat's assassination. The BBC reminded listeners that two of the defendants in the trial of Sadat's killers, led by the army officer and Muslim fundamentalist Lt Khalid Islambouli, were in an American prison for the 1993 attack on the World Trade Center. They had, the radio said, shot Sadat at a military parade.

Sadat staged annual military parades to commemorate his only triumph during eleven years as Nasser's unpopular successor: the assault on the east bank of the Suez Canal and the destruction of Israel's 'impregnable' Bar Lev Line. For three years before that 1973 war, he had pleaded with the United States to open discussions with Israel on the withdrawal of its forces from the Sinai Peninsula. Israeli occupation, apart from its effect on Egyptian pride, deprived Sadat of two major sources of income: fees for transit of the Suez Canal and revenues from Sinai's offshore oil that the Israelis were, illegally, lifting. Richard Nixon's secretary of state, Henry Kissinger, ignored Sadat. Egypt, he calculated, was too weak and demoralized from its 1967 defeat to threaten Israel. It could be discounted. So it was, until the Egyptian army attacked on Yom Kippur in 1973. At the same time, Syria launched an armoured offensive through the Golan Heights. Thanks in large measure to General Ariel Sharon's seizure of Egyptian territory on the west side of the canal and his encirclement of Egypt's Third Army, Israel managed not to lose the war. But it did not win. It found itself having to negotiate with Sadat after all. The sixth of October was the anniversary of Sadat's victory and, something he had not anticipated, his death. Almost every day was an anniversary – of a battle, of a terrorist attack, of a retaliatory raid, of a war, of an assassination. There were not enough days in the calendar to accommodate them all.

The Anthroposophists

The sixth of October 2001 was an anniversary for me, too, of my first day as a journalist. In 1973, ABC News in Beirut conscripted me to cover the Arab–Israeli war. Twenty-eight years later, it was the first day of my friendship with the Levy family. Juwal Levy, the young Israeli I had met on the *Nissos Kypros* with his Danish wife Anne Marie, roared into the Desert Inn's car park like a knight astride his armoured stallion of a motorcycle. I threw my bags into my Dalla rented car and followed Juwal's motorcycle to Kefar Rafael. I met his mother, Orna, and the youngest of his three sisters, Noam. Later, I would meet his grandmother, Eva, at her Jerusalem flat. On several occasions she gave me tea and cakes as if we were in the cosmopolitan Vienna of her youth. She would show me photographs of her late husband, Mike Levy, with Ben-Gurion and the rest of the Labour Zionist pantheon and tell me of their life together. At one of our teas, I met Juwal's two older sisters, Dania and Elijah, with Elijah's German husband. In Tel Aviv, Juwal's Uncle Shimon would show me the university, invite me to the theatre and take me to lectures by Palestinians. And, some time later, I would return to Kefar Rafael to meet Juwal's father, Udi, who had written the standard book on Petra and the Nabataeans. He would drive me to that other great Nabataean city, Shivta, in the middle of an Israeli army firing range in the Negev.

The sixth of October was a good day to remember. We went out of Beersheva (or Beersheba) to the desert that the city was swallowing. We turned at the Kefar Rafael sign onto a short track and came to an iron gate. An unarmed security guard came out of his post and slid the gate open. Leaving the car and motorcycle, we walked into an oasis. Kefar Rafael's shade and tranquillity were rare in Israel. Udi and Orna Levy had settled there in 1981 to build Kefar Rafael. It was not part of the great Zionist experience, neither a kibbutz to redeem the land for the tribe nor a settlement to stake a claim to more Arab land. Like the Levy family, it was something original, better than politics.

Juwal and I walked onto a shaded common, where a few adolescents sat cross-legged on the grass. The grass was a six-pointed star, with a single-storey house nestled in every angle. One family lived in each house, and with the family lived six or seven young people in the family's care. They had come as children from their own families, who were ill equipped in temperament or wealth to provide for them. Yet the families who sent their afflicted children to Kefar Rafael were not abandoning them to an institution to be fed, clothed and caged. Living with a family like the Levy parents and children, they received something closer to a healthy existence than they might have anywhere else. At Kefar Rafael, they were called villagers. The villagers had been born with Down's syndrome and the other maladies for which many are killed before they are born.

'I think for a child,' Juwal said, 'it's a perfect place to grow up because it has the right values.' It was not, however, a place to remain. Juwal had moved to Denmark. He was twenty-four. His sister Elijah, two years younger, lived at Kiryat Tivon in the Galilee with her husband. Dania, the second sister, was in Sweden. Juwal suspected that Noam, the nine-year-old youngest sister, would leave when she finished school.

Children's photographs were jammed into crevices between books on the many shelves that comprised most of the Levys' furniture. Udi was travelling. That left Orna, a surprisingly attractive woman with a trailing braid of fair brown hair, her son Juwal, his Danish wife Anne Marie and Noam. Noam was a small replica of her mother, the same endearing face and smile, eyes that did not quite open but seemed to register everything from some secret hiding place. She watched us so intently that I did not realize, until we had lunch in the little garden behind the house, that she did not speak a word of English.

Udi and Orna Levy were born in Jerusalem in the same year, 1952, and married in their early twenties. Like his older brother, Shimon, Udi Levy served in the Israeli army during a war. Shimon's was in 1967, Udi's in the Sinai in 1973. After the war, Udi and Orna moved to Dornach, Switzerland, where Juwal was born. They became anthroposophists, followers of Rudolf Steiner. Orna said Steiner had a 'holistic approach, to see man as a whole, and believed in therapy by doing. It was better to let some people work with horses than to pump them full of medicine.' Kefar Rafael was one of about three hundred anthroposophical therapeutic communities worldwide, one of two in Israel. The other was at Hardouf in the north. Kefar Rafael was, they said, like a kibbutz. 'Staff members meet in a circle to make big decisions,' Anne Marie said. 'Everyone must agree.'

'They have no normal problems,' Juwal, who was the most cynical about Kefar Rafael, said. 'If a dog barks, it's a big issue.' Later, he said, 'If you do not follow what they say, it does begin to look like a sect.' The others insisted it was not a sect, despite some resemblances, and not a kibbutz, despite other resemblances. The families who worked in Kefar Rafael took no wages, as in a kibbutz, but each had its own kitchen. All were *havarim*, fellow villagers or friends. They grew almost all their food without pesticides or artificial fertilizers, and the food was kosher. All the *havarim*, in accordance with Steiner's teaching, were vegetarian. The most important aspect of Kefar Rafael life, however, was caring for those least likely to have a near-normal existence anywhere else. 'You live close to the people that many of us do not want to be with,' Juwal said, one of his rare confessions of the strength of the place.

Kefar Rafael was like a kibbutz in community, simplicity and dedication. It was like one as well in the frustration and boredom it engendered in its children, most of whom left when they came of age. The main difference was that the kibbutzim existed for themselves. In the early days, kibbutzim provided a military mass to protect kibbutzniks from the peasants they had dispossessed. Kefar Rafael existed to care for children. It nurtured them into adulthood with no more chemical interference than the *havarim* permitted their plants.

Lunch was a difficult collation, for a carnivore like me, of cheese, bread, tomatoes, cucumber and olives. The only drinks were juice and water. Afterwards, we walked through the compound. The half-dozen family houses were like Arizona bungalows on the fringes of a golf course, more or less identical, with sloping roofs catching the shade of eucalyptus branches. Orna and Juwal showed me the bakery, laundry, silk workshop, olive press and the kitchen where they made jams to sell and the shop that sold them along with home-made shawls and scarves. Outside the circle of houses and workshops, we came to the farm – orchards of olive, avocado, pear, lemon and orange. The trees produced fruit that was larger than normal, all organic, none with their genes engineered in a laboratory. Families, volunteers and villagers alike, worked on the farm's 80,000 square metres. High-pressure pipes reached deep into the desert for water. Ancient wells that gave Beersheva its name and attracted Allenby in 1917 to make it his forward logistical base kept Kefar Rafael green.

Noam followed Orna, Juwal, Anne Marie and me on her

bicycle and listened. Some of Kefar Rafael's twenty-five young volunteers, most from Europe, were playing guitar on the grass beside the vast trunks of squat palm trees. This was their day off. Almost all of the charges were at home with their real families, where for two days and a night they would be cared for by their mothers or sisters who may or may not have understood what Down's syndrome, spina bifida and oxygen deprivation at birth meant. When I returned later to Kefar Rafael to meet Udi Levy, it would not be a day off. The children would all be gathered for dinner. If the desert bloomed anywhere, it bloomed there.

I drove out of the centre without Juwal as motorcycle escort. The guard rolled back the iron gate, and over the first rise in the road a Bedu youth rode a tall, sleek Arab horse up and down the dunes. His face was hidden in a *keffiyeh* as protection from sand kicked up by the horse's hooves. The young rider galloped, his back as stiff as a cavalry officer's, towards the town of Beersheva. He and the mare shared a joy in movement. I went on, past the town, to its southern fringe. There, his people dwelled in hovels of tin or corrugated iron or plywood, shaped like the black tents of their desert ancestors. Camels grazed on weeds, and goats stood still in barren wire pens. Children looked too tired to play. An old woman sat beside a small wood fire while a kettle came to the boil. The land over which their forebears had wandered had been fenced off, built upon and claimed by Ben-Gurion's children. The Bedouin had been moved, again and again, to less convenient corners of the sands. No desert bloomed here.

Later that day, at a Visitors' Centre for tourists in the new town of Matzpeh Ramon, I would read a long account of the desert's history that concluded, 'But in the Negev, the days of prosperity always come to an end.'

Wandering Tribes

From Beersheva, I spent days traversing the desert: Nabataean ruins, the Dead Sea, a kibbutz, the great Ramon crater and the charnel house of Israelite militarism at Masada. It was a lonely time, when I lost my travel writer's passion for company and curiosity about the human landscape. What compelled me – as on no other part of the journey through Greater Syria – was death. My thoughts were born of solitude, the condition of the desert traveller. I wandered over the stones where Roman swords pierced Jewish flesh, where Nabataean farmers pressed desert grapes into wine, and through a crater so vast it looked as if the moon had crashed into the Promised Land. The distinction between body and soul seemed unimportant here. When the one rotted to sand in the Negev furnace the other carried on. My loss of interest in the living had an irreversible side-effect: guilt. The purpose of my trip was to record what the people were like, why Jews came to this land, why Arabs struggled to remain, what the two peoples had done and were doing to make each other what they were, to listen to them. To travel through Israel, or Palestine, in the early twenty-first century was to bear an obligation to understand. I was dreaming.

It was at the kibbutz of Ein Gedi on a hill above the Dead Sea that I lost the guilt. Desert solitude was preparation. This part of the land more than any other was filled with omens – from the prophets, the wanderers of forty years, the forty days and forty nights before the final ministry, baptism by heat in a dead place. George Adam Smith, whose observations of the Holy Land in the late nineteenth century omitted the people who lived there, wrote of Ein Gedi, 'The oasis burst upon him [the desert traveller] from one of the driest and most poisoned regions of our planet.' From the kibbutz that early Zionists planted in what had been a Bedouin oasis, the night-time Dead Sea looked as if life might lurk beneath its placid surface. The sight of the moon above the Jordanian bank of the Dead Sea in absolute stillness hinted at the reason people come here; why the place itself – the silent, dead landscape – was necessary in a country whose tribes squabbled even during the quiet centuries while they awaited conquest by the great empires of the more fertile and populous east and west. Prophets, madmen, monks and misfits needed this desert for momentary retreats into sanity. The Essenes came here to escape the doctrinal and temporal disputes of the Israelite priesthood, and Christian anchorites followed them. The desert was where, T. E. Lawrence wrote, man first heard the wind, *hawa* in Arabic, utter the name of God, *Yahweh* in Hebrew.

There was no people so dead, so forgotten by those who came after, as the first desert-bloomers, the Nabataeans. I had seen their greatest achievement, the metropolis at Petra in Jordan's Valley of Moses. In the Negev, I went to another in the chain of fortified cities that protected their trading route from Yemen to Gaza. It was called Avdat. The achievement, as at Petra, was impressive. When the Arab tribes who became Nabataeans settled along the invisible road between Muscat in modern Oman and the Mediterranean, they preserved customs that allowed them to survive in the desert. Wine was forbidden, and they were not allowed to build permanent houses. Later, they surrendered to settlement; and they refined wine-making and house-building into their most valued arts. At Avdat, the houses were free-standing stone – unlike Petra's, which were carved into rock. The Nabataeans here made effective use of the Roman arch, of wine cellars and of cisterns that gave them enough rainwater for public baths and private gardens. Each house had alcoves in the walls to store chinaware. The residue of plates and wine jugs proved them to have been among the world's finest ceramic-makers. Nabataean nomads, like the ancient Israelites, became the most avid urbanites.

When Pompey conquered Syria for Rome in the first century before Christ, a garrison of two thousand soldiers settled at Avdat to guard the trade route. Muscat exported incense, the vital ingredient in the rituals of all ancient religions – Roman,

Jewish, Nabataean. The Nabataeans controlled the trade in the mystifying aromatic. When they and the Romans converted to Christ, their churches relied on the obscuring effects of the burning powder. The fragrance of the same incense was used by Levantine women for less spiritual seduction.

From the top of Avdat's Roman tower, sentries saw so far along the desert horizon that they would have two days to ready themselves for an attack from any direction. They would also have seen the caravans of spices, of whose bounty Avdat's merchants would claim a share in exchange for wine, pottery and cloth. I saw wadis that were so desolate, apart from a tenacious acacia or palm, that Nabataean vineyards seemed an impossibility. Yet the grapes that fed the giant wine presses and filled the clay barrels had come from somewhere. The wine had gone, the vineyards and the Nabataeans with them. The Nabataeans abandoned their cities in the sixth and seventh centuries. It was the dawn of Islam, whose pure monotheism required neither ritual nor incense. Its ethos, like that of the pre-civic Nabataeans, proscribed wine. The Nabataeans lost their refined sensibilities, sensuous courts, steam baths and fierce defence of a system of hidden water wells, forts and cities over thousands of miles. Their cities – like the Byzantine dead cities on the northern Syrian plain – were depopulated in a short time. But the people did not die from war, massacre, famine or plague. The Nabataeans dispersed to their nomadic rooflessness, leaving their descendants to wander the desert or confined to tin shanty towns.

A few miles from Avdat, I came to a narrow wadi with no more soil or water than any of the ground around it. Yet row upon row of vines shrouded the tiny ravine in fresh leaves. I went into the vineyard to ask how it had been accomplished, but no one was there. Netting covered the plants, and channels along the hillsides guided whatever rainfall there was to a cistern to irrigate them. This was, as I read in the Avdat tourist centre, how the Nabataeans had done it when they became farmers. The sight of the vineyard, which I took to be the work of one of those iconoclastic Israelis who hated the money-grasping modern world, made me hopeful. The Israeli farming that Ben-Gurion foresaw for the Negev was modern – bringing water from an already depleted River Jordan and its aquifers, growing tasteless tomatoes in water baths inside plastic greenhouses, spending millions to grow food that grew easily and cheaply elsewhere. Someone had gone back and seen how it was done before hydroponics, genetic engineering and chemical fertilizers. When I had a glass of wine that night at the Ramon Inn, I toasted this heroic wine-grower.

I stayed for a couple of days in Matzpeh Ramon, a town that grew up around an encampment for the workers who built the highway through the Negev to Eilat in the 1950s. Matzpeh Ramon stood on the ridge above a crater thousands of feet deep, down millennia of rock formations and bedding planes. The crater, Makhtesh Ramon, was as dead as any place on earth – forty kilometres of sandstone. A hundred million years ago, it was a lake. The ridge was, like the Judaean summit at Jerusalem and the peaks of Mount Lebanon, a watershed between the desert and the Mediterranean. The water that fed the green slopes of Lebanon evaporated before it touched the Ramon floor. Guidebooks said that anemones and tulips thrived in the spring. In the autumn, the only living things I saw were sprigs of marjoram between the rocks and wormwood that the Bedouin used as medicine to cure stomach pain. A plant or animal had to be tough to find water, food and shade. There were said to be leopards, desert rats, sand partridges and vultures. They had one advantage over creatures elsewhere in the Negev: they did not have to contend with artillery and tank fire. Makhtesh Ramon was a nature reserve off-limits as an army firing range. Fifty thousand years ago, hunters and gatherers, who left flint tools and not much else, lived in the crater. The Israelites under King Solomon made the ridge above the crater their southern frontier, and it was left to the Nabataeans to traverse the deadly land in their caravans and then to settle and build. Makhtesh Ramon lay on the spice route from Felix

Arabia via Petra to Gaza, until the Romans built roads that left Makhtesh Ramon to lie fallow until, in turn, Christian monks retreated there and built churches. They too departed.

I sat at the edge, knowing that a fall would leave me a minute or more of undisturbed contemplation before my body hit the earth like a meteor. Waves of inhabitants and sojourners had left the plain untouched. Its sands had stayed out of the violent march of mankind's history. In a way, I thought, sitting there while the wind flapped my clothes, I too was standing aside from a moment in that same history. This was the time when the world's new and only Rome prepared to smite its attackers and avenge what it said were seven thousand American dead. The crater looked like one of the dry Afghan valleys the American armed forces would soon assault. Makhtesh Ramon – and I with it – stayed aloof from the approaching drama. It was quiet, undisturbed, lifeless. At that moment, my only fear was that some unseen hand would come from behind and push me into that alluring abyss from which I would not return. Someone dropped a plastic cup. It floated in the currents of air, down and up and down again, until it gathered speed and smashed onto the rocks.

A Deadly Sea

Before dinner at the Ramon Inn, CNN broadcast silent pictures, using an infrared lens, of night firing over Kabul. The Pentagon confirmed that the fight for Afghanistan had begun. Military experts were educating Americans on the geography of Afghanistan, and the simple people of Illinois and Oregon were becoming familiar with the names Jalalabad, Herat, Kandahar and Kabul and the differences among Pashtuns, Tajiks, Uzbeks and Baluchis. In Matzpeh Ramon, it was 6.45 p.m., in Afghanistan, 9.45, and in Washington nearly the moment for a noontime statement from the Commander-in-Chief. George Bush announced he had ordered the attacks with his close friends, the British.

Speaking from somewhere called the Treaty Room, perhaps the place where he ritually tore up the treaties his administration had sworn not to honour, he looked into a camera and said, 'The United States is a friend of the Afghan people.' I had heard the head of the Voice of America make a similar announcement to the Libyan people in 1986, on the night that US warplanes bombed Tripoli. 'We are a peaceful nation,' Bush continued. 'The only way to pursue peace is to pursue those who threaten it.' The war had a name: 'Operation Enduring Freedom'. Five minutes after the president began his speech, he concluded, 'Peace and freedom will prevail. Thank you. May God bless America.' He was wearing a red tie, a white shirt and blue suit.

The war raged on from the heavens: Kandahar Airport destroyed, Jalalabad bombed, the Taliban radio station disabled. CNN experts spoke of the impressive array of cruise missiles, smart bombs and guidance systems. I turned to the BBC. Tony Blair, in another white shirt and blue suit – the tie may have been blue or funeral black, it was hard to distinguish – was speaking live from Downing Street, almost like a president, almost as if this were his war. Regarding the Afghans, he said, 'They chose to side with terror.' As pious as the leader of the Free World himself, he swore 'to do all we humanly can to avoid casualties'. Perhaps confusing the Afghan crusade with the previous Anglo-American war, that on drugs, he claimed that 90 per cent of all the heroin on Britain's streets came from Afghanistan. So that was it, still the war on drugs. How convenient to battle the twin demons – terrorism and narcotics – in one little war. Strange, some might have said, that America's Northern Alliance allies were the largest opium producers in Afghanistan. 'We are a peaceful people,' Blair said, echoing President Bush and forgetting the previous five centuries of British wars around the world. 'We have no choice . . . We will not let up until our objectives are met in full. Thank you.' He did not say, 'God bless Britain' or even 'God Save the Queen'. Next up was the Taliban's consul-general in Pakistan, who said,

'We are ready for Jihad.' He called the bombardment of his country 'a terrorist attack'.

An hour later, the BBC reported that the city of Mazar-e-Sharif was also under attack. More maps to show viewers where Mazar-e-Sharif was. Then an announcement from the Taliban government: after two hours of bombardment from B-52s, B1-Bs, Tomahawks and the rest, Osama bin Laden was still alive. I turned off the television.

The dining room and bar of the Ramon Inn were a change from the claustrophobic, windowless cafeterias of the kibbutzim and traditional Israeli hotels. Windows on all sides opened to Matzpeh Ramon's streets. It was like a good modern hotel anywhere else, not much character but pleasant. Children ran amok while their parents had dinner on this holiday weekend. No one was speaking about Afghanistan. I took a table near some indoor plants and read the menu. I asked the waitress why she had pinned three badges – the British, Israeli and American flags – to her blouse. 'It's for my languages,' she said. 'Hebrew and English.' She pointed to the Israeli and British flags. And the American? 'That's just an extra.' Did she know that the USA and Britain were bombing Afghanistan? 'Yes.' She was not interested. 'We are the ones who are going to suffer. The Muslims always blame us.'

In the morning, I listened to BBC radio's account of the night of bombing. The Taliban claimed the bombs had not done much damage. Then I succumbed to morbid fascination and watched CNN again. General Pervez Musharraf, the self-declared president of Pakistan, was speaking from Islamabad. He compared terrorism to a tree. Last night's bombardment was like blowing off the leaves. Eliminating Osama bin Laden and Al Qaeda would cut off a branch. He said the task was to go to the roots, the deprivation that fed resentment. When he finished, the newsreaders on CNN, the BBC and Sky summarized and analysed his speech. None of them mentioned his final point about deprivation. On CNN, Cristianne Amanpour, an Iranian-American correspondent whom I knew and liked, said the root problem was Israel and Palestine. Al Jazeera broadcast an epistle from Osama bin Laden, who spoke of crimes against Muslims in Pakistan, Iraq and elsewhere. He did not say what he had done to improve the lives of Muslims anywhere. He did not say how his actions had lessened their deprivation, why he had provoked an American attack and provided General Sharon with another excuse to attack Palestinians as part of an American war on terror. Osama bin Laden was helping Palestinians to achieve what the Zealots of ancient Israel had for the Jewish people, their utter defeat.

The desert was a place, as the ancient Israelites from Egypt discovered, for wandering – even for forty years. It was not a place, despite Ben-Gurion's hopes, to live. The Nabataeans had tried for as many centuries as their culture could endure it. The Bedouin crossed it when they were free to, but reserved their longest passages for the green, watered fringes. I roamed in my Dalla Rent-a-Car from Beersheva to the Dead Sea, Sde Boker to Avdat, Ein Gedi to Masada, Matzpeh Ramon to the Makhtesh below.

Along the Dead Sea was an ugly stretch of beach, where the salt corroded everything and someone had built a hideous spa complex. I tried to swim, but the salt defeated me after half an hour. I had to lie on my back on the water's surface almost as if I were on an operating table. The salt stung, and the buoyancy made it impossible to swim. I tried a gentle backstroke, afraid that splashing or turning onto my stomach would let the deadly water burn my eyes. When a child bashed the water with his fists, a drop found my eye. The only reason I did not drown him was that he'd float back up immediately. The smell of the Dead Sea was, well, the stink of death. Perhaps our association of sulphurous fumes with eternal damnation came from this place, deep within a cavity in the earth's face. This was where Sodom and Gomorrah had been damned to brimstone by the Almighty. Reverend George Adam Smith wrote, when he came here, 'Nature, when she has not herself been, by some convulsion, the executioner of judgement, has added every aggravation of horror to the cruelty of the human avenger or the exhaustion of the doomed.' He called the desert around the sea 'one of the driest and most poisoned regions of our planet'. That much had remained constant since the late nineteenth century. Mark Twain in 1867 found the place depressing. He wrote in *Innocents Abroad*, 'Where Sodom and Gomorrah reared their domes and towers, that solemn sea now floods the plain, in whose bitter waters no living thing exists – over whose waveless surface the blistering air hangs motionless and dead – about whose borders nothing grows but weeds, and scattering tufts of cane, and that treacherous fruit that promises refreshment to parching lips, but turns to ashes at the touch.'

The saltwater was a kind of medicine that, appropriately, hurt. I got out, had a cold shower, rubbed myself in Dead Sea mud, showered again and lazed in a freshwater pool with the other masochists. I was reborn. My skin was like a baby's, my sinuses excavated. A couple next to me – a man and woman in their sixties – said they came from Jaffa every week to take the waters. They extolled the attractions as if they worked for the Dead Sea Tourist Board. He was tall, thin and muscular. She was short, fat and fair. Both spoke English, Hebrew and Arabic. I could not tell whether they were Jewish or Arab. He complained about the Arabs and Jews who did not know how to make the best use of the Dead Sea's healing powers. She nodded.

There was a kind of ritual, the couple said, to Dead Sea bathing that hardly anyone else knew. First you went to one of the indoor sulphur pools to prepare your skin. Very important, he said. She agreed with a quick flick of the head. You showered and went outside. A little tram took you to the shore. You went down the ramp into the sea with your sandals on. Very important. She agreed. If you cut your foot in that water, it would heal very quickly but would sting like hell. Then you floated for an hour on your back. You could bring a book if you got bored. Never put your head under water, but rub water into your hair. The water was good for the hair. He was bald.

When you came out, you showered and took the tram to the mud pond. There, you covered your whole body in the thick mud. Even your head and hair. Even, he whispered, your balls. Leave it on to dry, then wash it off in sulphur water and come into the pool to relax, as we were doing. The spa's pamphlet called the Dead Sea 'ideal for relaxation and re-energizing'.

Relaxed and energized, I drove up to the Ein Gedi Kibbutz to check into its guest house. The kibbutz stood in a hillside oasis above the Dead Sea, an ancient site that had belonged to the Arab Rushaideh tribe. 'The verdure and water, strange and sudden, with the exhilaration of the view across the sea, produce most generous impressions of this oasis and tempt to exaggerate its fertility,' Reverend Smith wrote. He thought that Ein Gedi, where he stayed with the Rushaideh, was 'large enough to sustain an army'. The Crusaders had built a convent in the oasis, but the only buildings were the bungalows, communal dining hall, recreation centre and farm sheds of the Ein Gedi Kibbutz.

The receptionist at the Ein Gedi Guest House informed me that a night in the kibbutz's functional discomfort cost 550 Israeli shekels, more than $125. 'The Dead Sea is the most expensive place in Israel,' he said, 'and it's high season.' High season? October? Israeli children were at school. In October, the Dead Sea was one of the hottest places on earth. No tourists had come to Israel since 11 September, and all the new hotels along the Dead Sea Riviera were empty. Ein Gedi, if its car park were an indication, was itself short of visitors. And this otherwise sensible and polite receptionist was charging $125 a night for a dreary room in what looked like a 1950s motel on Route 66 in the American Midwest. Was this kibbutz socialism? I did not say any of these things, but he detected my unease and lowered the price to 440 shekels – still more than $100. He gave me a key and a page of instructions, more like the rules and regulations of a prison than a hotel. At the top, it warned, 'The Guest House Dining Room is self-service'. Everything was 'self-service', American euphemism for no service. Carrying my suitcases, I made the long walk from the car through the oasis

grounds to Room 66 – that is, the sixth room in Bungalow Six.
As I searched, mistaking one identical white hut for another, I
thought again about the price. On my advance, I would not
survive a month in Israel. I let myself into a cement cell with a
single bed beside a tiny window. There was an iron in the closet,
more self-service, and a television set in the corner. I read that
Friday dinner-time was from 18.15 to 20.30 and 'The Dining
Room is *Kosher* under the supervision of the local religious
council. Therefore, it is absolutely *PROHIBITED* to remove
dishes from the dining room or bring dishes or food into the
dining room.' Why would I bring food *into* a dining room?

The answer to the question was in the dining room. There,
amid hordes of hungry guests, loomed vast metal serving dishes
of what masqueraded as food. Some people ladled the stuff onto
plates, but the lumps of whatever it was were buried so deep in
red or brown sauces that I could not make them out. With my
newly opened Dead Sea sense of smell, I did not try. Platters by
the wall offered rice, boiled potatoes, carrots, courgettes, let-
tuce, cheese and stale bread. I took a plastic tray and a couple
of plates and made do with green salad, hummus, some sort of
dry meat and tap water. It reminded me of the *Nissos Kypros*,
whose cooks had the same disdain for the human taste-bud.
The dining hall was daring in its 1960s spartan functionality.
Unlike every other building, it was round. I suspected that the
Reverend Smith had done better – for price and nourishment –
with the hospitality of the Rushaideh. The dining hall closed its
doors at 8.30, but the bar had opened fifteen minutes earlier.

The bar in the reception building was no larger than a closet,
so I sat in the lobby with my Gold Star beer and Tom Segev's
1949: The First Israelis. It was hard not to be discomfited by
his account of the expulsions of the Arabs, the looting of their
property and the twisting of the law to make sure that even the
Arabs inside Israel would not receive back their houses, their
furniture, their linens or their family jewellery. Some Arabs in
Israel in 1949 attempted to lease their old property from the
new Israeli owners, but the Ministry of Finance advised that

'our office does not lease the lands expropriated by the government to the present absentees, so as not to weaken our control over the properties in our charge ... the government should make the legal definition of "absentee" match the normal construction of the word's meaning, i.e. a person who is absent.' 'Present absentee' was a term Israel employed first in 1948, the year George Orwell wrote *Nineteen Eighty-four*, to describe those Palestinian Arabs who were out of their houses but in Israel. Absent absentees were the refugees in Lebanon, Syria, Jordan, the West Bank, Gaza and Egypt. Neither absent absentees nor present absentees got anything back.

I walked through the 'international botanic garden', as the receptionist called it, past an old baobab tree. My room was the last in a long line of huts. On its deck, I unfolded a small table and set a chair behind it facing the sea. That morning, when I had floated on it, the Dead Sea surface was the bright turquoise of the evil-eye talisman that the Bedouin wore. Tonight, without the moon, it was as dark as it was dead. Moses, Jesus, the Essenes and the monks came to the Negev or the Judaean deserts to find their souls and listen for the voice of God. This would be my last night alone in the wilderness before I resumed my journey among the rival claimants to this tormented land. I did not want to go into the room, where an air conditioner set impressively into the wall did not work. But outside the Ein Gedi mosquitoes found my sea-fresh skin too tempting to resist. Facing a choice between malaria and suffocation, I went in.

I should not have, but I turned on the television. CNN was showing a protest in Gaza. Two Palestinians were killed. CNN did not give their names. The policemen who shot them were also Palestinian. The victims had taken part in a demonstration against Yasser Arafat for turning over Palestinian suspects to Israel. The Palestinian Authority, following Israeli precedent, declared the street where people were marching 'a closed military area'. The shooting by the Palestinian Authority police of its people did not impress the Israeli prime minister, General

Sharon. He said it was insufficient for him to permit his emasculated foreign minister, Shimon Peres, to meet Arafat. In other news, both Sharon and Peres endorsed the American bombardment of Afghanistan.

The Gorgon's Head

At Ein Gedi, breakfast was, if not served, then available at seven in the morning. It was not as bad as dinner, but that did not make it good. Tea bags with lukewarm water and something we used to call bug juice, a kind of Kool-Aid or squash, were the drinks. The buffet featured bread rolls, processed cheeses, cucumbers and cold meats. A young Chinese man was clearing tables, and another Chinese scraped plates in the kitchen. So much for the original kibbutz commitment to 'Hebrew labour'. After breakfast, the radio transmitted more Afghan news: the night-time bombing of Afghanistan's towns would from now on be followed by more raids in daylight. It meant that the Taliban had no anti-aircraft guns left. The Northern Alliance Afghans would soon go into combat for the Americans and for themselves. With US air cover and the destruction of the Taliban's heavier weapons, losing would be difficult.

Osama bin Laden appeared on the television again in a videotape sent to Al Jazeera. His appearances were becoming so frequent I suspected he was auditioning for his own regular programme. 'I swear by God the great,' an interpreter's voice said in English over bin Laden's Saudi Arabic, 'that those who live in America will never taste security and safety unless we feel secure in our land and in Palestine.' CNN allowed two Arab journalists, Hisham Melham of Beirut's *As-Safir* and Raghida Dergham of *Al-Hayat* in London, a rare bit of airtime – on their international broadcast. Miss Dergham said, 'The Osama bin Ladens of this world hate the Arabs as well. Their view is that we should have a Taliban regime.' Mr Melham, a distinguished Lebanese reporter, emphasized bin Laden's cynicism: 'Unfortunately, he has taken up some legitimate causes like Palestine. But he has never done anything for Palestine. He is exploiting the deep sense of despair.' Next came a commercial followed by news from the world of sport.

As I drove beside the Dead Sea, I was thinking about something else Raghida Dergham had said: 'Osama bin Laden thinks he is attacking the new Rome.' In the Middle East, opponents of the old Rome had made their stand – as the Taliban was then in the Hindu Kush – atop a cliff more than 1300 feet above the plain where I parked. The Arabs called the table-top mount *Es-Sebbeh*. To the Jews, it was Masada. In both languages it meant 'fortress'. Masada was one of the most impressive sites of the ancient world, both as a physical testament and as an idea. At the roof of a dry land, Masada held water enough for an army; 40,000 cubic metres of rainwater – channelled from dams that sent flash floods into hand-chiselled caverns. On the rocky surface there were vegetable plots, grain storage for livestock, public baths and a king's palace. The king was Herod, one of the greatest builders and most cunning statesmen of the Roman world. Herod built the fortress at Masada to withstand a siege, either by Jewish Zealots who despised his collaboration with Rome or by Cleopatra who coveted his suzerainty over Palestine. In the modern era, Masada was preserved as an Israeli shrine to the idea that death was preferable to foreign occupation, a concept some Palestinian Arabs had also absorbed.

If ever a stronghold looked impregnable, it was Masada. An enemy had to approach it up the steep eastern face along a switchback path that the Jewish historian Flavius Josephus in his *On the Jewish War* called the Serpent. The only alternative was to construct a road on the western side where the great rock met the foothills at a depth of only four hundred feet. Along either route, attackers would have to breach Herod's solid rock walls. On first sight, it was unimaginable that any ancient army could conquer Masada. Yet two – Jewish rebels under Eleazar ben Yair and the Roman Tenth Legion – succeeded within seven years of each other.

For the modern tourist, a new cable car was a more practical means to the summit than the long trek up the Serpent's Path. Masada was as big as any ancient village, but its twenty-three-acre surface was designed for a last stand. Once you retreated here, you could hold out for a long time. But there was nowhere else to go. You had to hope your enemies gave up and went home. Rome was no such enemy. An Israeli guide was telling an American family, 'You talk about this bin Laden. The Zealots had a rebellion against the Romans. They controlled the whole of Europe from Scotland to Palestine, now Israel.' Clearly, the Romans impressed him more than the Americans, and the Zealots more than bin Laden. The Zealots and the Taliban had one thing in common: they were not especially popular with their own people. 'For the Jews,' the guide continued, 'it was a question of religion. For the Romans, it was a question of ego.' Ego won.

Masada was, as Josephus described it, 'encompassed with valleys of such vast depth downward, that the eye could not reach their bottoms; they were abrupt, and such as no animal could walk upon, excepting at two places of the rock, where it subsides, in order to afford a passage for ascent, though not without difficulty'. Masada had captured the imagination of some Israelis, and it repelled others. Its solitude was emblematic of the way many Israelis saw their country – alone against the world. The story was as dramatic as the place. It occurred at a time of rebellion throughout the Roman Empire. The Germans fought Roman tutelage in the West, and some Jews sought independence in the East. Early in the Jewish *intifadah*, in AD 66, rebels seized Masada from its Roman defenders. It was there that they made a final stand after Jerusalem fell to Titus, son of Emperor Vespasian, four years later. The Romans then conducted, as the Americans would soon in Afghanistan, 'mopping-up' operations. Masada, where no great battle took place, was one of many. The only source for the events at Masada is Josephus, a Romanized Jew whose original name was Yosef ben Mattityahu (Joseph, son of Matthew). He was a brilliant writer, who had himself sided first with the rebels and then with the Romans. By the end, he sought to reconcile the two.

The Roman procurator in Judaea, Flavius Silva, set out to capture Masada in AD 72 from the Sicarii. These Jewish rebels took their name from the *sicarius*, or dagger, hidden under the cloak when assassinating fellow Jews at the Temple. The Sicarii, Josephus wrote, 'first became barbarous towards those allied to them, and left no words of reproach unsaid, and no works of perdition untried, in order to destroy those whom their contrivances affected'. From Masada, the Sicarii raided the Jewish settlement at Ein Gedi, stealing supplies and killing seven hundred people. With the looted provisions and those that Herod had left, they waited out Flavius Silva and the Tenth Legion. But Silva would not wait. He constructed a ramp to the walls, often under fire from the Sicarii above. With his catapults supplying cover, Silva's engineers finished the bridge that carried his army into the fortress. The Romans set fire to the wooden gate the Sicarii had erected behind the walls, but the winds blew the fire first back towards the Romans. Josephus wrote that the Romans retired for the night and 'resolved to attack their enemies the very next day'.

During the night, the real drama in Josephus's story took place. One leader, Eleazar ben Yair, knew 'what the Romans would do to them, their children and their wives, if they got them in their power, [so] he consulted about having them all slain'. He delivered a speech to 'the most courageous of his companions' in which he said, 'We were the very first that revolted from them, and we are the last that fight against them; and I cannot but esteem it as a favour that God hath granted us, that it is still in our power to die bravely, and in a state of freedom, which hath not been the case of others, who were conquered unexpectedly.' He said that their defeat 'was the effect of God's anger against our manifold sins, which we have been guilty of in a most insolent and extravagant manner with regard to our own countrymen; the punishments of which let us not receive from the Romans, but from God himself, as executed by our own hands ... Let our wives die before they are abused, and our children before they have tasted of slavery; and after we have slain them, let us bestow that glorious benefit upon one another mutually, and preserve ourselves in freedom, as an excellent funeral monument for us.' Some of his men took up the call to suicide with enthusiasm, but those 'who were most effeminate' fretted for their families. Eleazar delivered a second, more emphatic oration to persuade the waverers. Josephus quoted him at length:

> And why are we afraid of death, while we are pleased with the rest that we have in sleep? And how absurd a thing is it to pursue after liberty while we are alive, and yet to envy it to ourselves where it will be eternal! ... it is by the will of God, and by necessity, that we are to die; for it now appears that God hath made such a decree against the whole Jewish nation, that we are to be deprived of this life which we would not make a due use of. For do not you ascribe the occasion of our present condition to yourselves, nor think the Romans are the true occasion that this war we have had with them is become so destructive to us all: these things have not come to pass by their power, but a more powerful cause hath intervened, and made us afford them an occasion of their appearing to be conquerors over us ... Let us pity ourselves, our children, and our wives while it is in our power to show pity to them; for we were born to die, as well as those whom we have begotten; nor is it in the power of the most happy of our race to avoid it ... God himself hath brought this necessity upon us; while the Romans desire the contrary, and are afraid lest any of us should die before we are taken. Let us therefore make haste, and instead of affording them so much pleasure, as they hope for in getting us under their power, let us leave them an example which shall at once cause their astonishment at our death, and their admiration of our hardiness therein.

When the Romans breached the burned gates in the morning, they found 960 Jewish corpses – men, women, children.

Josephus recorded that 'they came within the palace, and so met with the multitude of the slain, but could take no pleasure in the fact, though it were done to their enemies. Nor could they do other than wonder at the courage of their resolution, and the immovable contempt of death which so great a number of them had shown, when they went through with such an action as that was.'

How did Josephus know what Eleazar ben Yair said on that final night? The only survivors were two women and five children, who had hidden in 'caverns under the ground' until the slaughter ended. One of the women or children may have related the tale to Josephus or to someone else who relayed it to him. He may have imagined it or represented it as he thought it should have been. Josephus himself had been a rebel in command of Jewish forces at another debacle, the defence of Yopatapa (or Jopatapa) in Galilee in AD 66 – at the beginning of the revolt. There, the defenders had also chosen suicide, although Josephus argued against it: 'It may also be said that it is a manly act for one to kill himself. No. Certainly, but a most unmanly one: as I should esteem that pilot to be an arrant coward who, out of fear of a storm, should sink his ship of its own accord.' He acceded to the majority, who cast lots to decide the order of deaths. Josephus was last. When the rest were dead, he surrendered to the Romans. He witnessed, as a Roman himself by then, another mass suicide at the fortress of Gamla (or Gamala) in the Golan Heights a year later. At Gamla, the Jewish defenders leaped from the walls to kill themselves rather than surrender.

Josephus's account of the Jewish revolts against Rome is one of treachery as much as of nobility. The rebels, not unlike resistance movements in other times and places, killed their own as often as they did the enemy. The rebellions led, not to independence, but to the forfeit of autonomy; not to freedom, but to exile and slavery. The tragedy reached its culmination at Masada. Masada captivated poets and film-makers of the twentieth century, although the dead there – 960 – were few compared to the

40,000 said to have died at Yopatapa and the 9000 at Gamla. Yet it may not have happened as Josephus told his Roman readers in his Greek text. Josephus wrote an earlier version, in Aramaic, that he dispatched to the Jewish community in what is now Iraq. The Aramaic text has not survived; but a fourth-century Latin manuscript purporting to be based on a Hebrew text that Josephus may have written did. This 'Sefer Yossippon' version – translated back into Hebrew in the tenth century from the Latin text discovered in southern Italy – differs from Josephus's Greek account. In both stories the men kill their womenfolk and children. In the Greek version, the killings were merciful, to save women and children from slavery. In the Hebrew, the killing was ritual sacrifice – *lekorban oleh leratzon lifnei hashem*. The Hebrew version said that, after the ritual slaughter, the men went out to die in battle with the Romans.

In a lecture entitled 'Masada as a Cultural Experience', part of a series sponsored by the Jewish Agency, Zvi Howard Adelman observed a pattern in Josephus's Greek renderings of the suicides at Yopatapa in AD 66, Gamla in 67 and Masada in 73. The tales may have been literary tropes, in each of which 'the Jews are holding out in a high place on a precipice, they continue to add walls, the Romans below, led by Vespasian and Titus, are attacking their position using conventional weapons, siege engines and battering rams, and massive construction to build ramps . . . The variable in each case was Josephus himself, which in turn affected his discourse. At Yopatapa, he realized all was lost and wanted to save his life, both arguing against suicide and forming a suicide pact with the Jews who had trapped him. At Gamala, which he himself had originally fortified, he reported the events as a Roman observer.' By the time of Masada, he was in Rome living on an imperial pension. Adelman contended that Josephus by then wanted 'to isolate in the minds of his [Roman] readers the disruptive element among the Jews and then to literally excise it forever. This way he could tacitly offer the Romans a de-zealotized picture of the remaining Jewish population of Palestine, which had been presumably led astray by these tyrants and now was willing to live with the Romans in peace'. Some of Palestine's surviving Jews preferred not to live in peace under Roman rule. They rebelled again in 119 and, most destructively, under Bar Kokba from 132 to 135 – after which the Romans forbad Jews to live in Jerusalem. Masada was by then forgotten, and the Talmud did not mention it. In fact, the Talmud condemned the Sicariis' allies, the Zealots, as *baryonim* – boorish or savage – for their treatment of fellow Jews. The six-year revolt from AD 66 to 72 and those that came after were at least as disastrous for Palestine's Jews, who would live in exile for two millennia, as the Palestinian Arabs' second *intifadah* was proving to be for them.

Fr Jerry Murphy-O'Connor, that indefatigable Dominican scholar, studied Josephus and the stones at Masada. 'Josephus's account becomes utterly incredible from the moment he has the Romans retire once they have breached the wall,' he wrote in *The Holy Land*, the standard archaeological reference. 'Even though night had fallen, it was Passover and there was a full moon. In any case they would have driven home the attack, as Vespasian did at Jopatapa. This means that there was no time for Josephus's scenario of heroic suicide . . . Josephus the Jewish apologist invented the speech of Eleazar to lay the blame for the war, not on the Jewish people as such, but on a minority of violent revolutionaries, the Sicarii.' Fr Jerry added that Flavius Silva's 'brief and standard textbook operation merited no mention in Roman records. The inexperienced Sicarii had posed no significant resistance.'

The site was rediscovered only in 1838 by two American travellers, Smith and Robinson. In 1894, the Scotsman the Reverend George Adam Smith thought it worthy of a detour on his Holy Land exploration and wrote, 'Masada is the Gorgon's head magnified into a mountain.' In the 1920s and 1930s, Zionist socialist youth climbed to Masada's top to study its ruins and meditate their significance. A wider audience among Jewish colonists discovered it in 1927, when a Russian immigrant, Isaac Lamdan, published his epic poem 'Masada', part of which reads:

Masada shall not fall again!
Stumble? Surely, we will go up!
Ben Yair will be revealed,
He is not dead, not dead!

The Jewish National Fund bought the mountaintop in 1938, but Ben-Gurion was not enthusiastic about it. In 1946, he cabled back from Paris to a meeting of his Mapai party, 'Neither Vichy nor Masada.' No collaboration, no suicide. General Yigal Yadin supervised important digs at Masada from 1963 to 1965, and most of the artefacts on display during my visit dated from that time. Among them were shards with names, including 'Ben Yair', that may have been the lots cast on that final night. Yadin's diggers found skeletons of about thirty people who may or may not have been the defenders of Masada. The state gave them an official funeral and buried them on a hill near Masada, but cynics said the dead were probably Byzantine monks who set up there in the early Middle Ages. The Israeli army held torchlit parades up the mountain, where recruits took an oath that ended, 'Masada shall not fall again!' After the conquests of holy sites in the old city of Jerusalem and in the West Bank in 1967, Masada did fall again – from official favour. The army cancelled ceremonies there, and tourism had declined even before the Palestinian *intifadah* and the massacres of 11 September 2001.

Masada remained a kind of Alamo to some Israelis. At both, all the defenders died. But that was the only similarity. The siege at the Alamo began rather than concluded the fight for Texan independence. The Texans died fighting to delay the Mexicans' advance north. Masada's is altogether a less hopeful story. The defenders, in the authorized version, chose to kill themselves rather than negotiate or fight to the death. The rebellion was already lost, and resistance was futile. The Hebrew University historian Benjamin Kedar wrote, 'The rock on the shore of the Dead Sea is a dead end, a cul de sac, a dramatic curtain-fall. He who tells his soldiers of the armoured corps at the swearing-in ceremony on the heights of Masada that it is owing to the heroism of the fighters at Masada that we are here today, is both deluding himself and deluding others.'

Isaac Lamdan, the depressive poet who tried to graft the Masada ideal onto Zionist consciousness, never visited the scene of his epic. It was said that his poem inspired the Jewish rising in the Warsaw ghetto against the Nazis. Some said that the new state of Israel had acquired a 'Masada complex' – a willingness to destroy itself rather than compromise. Six years after the birth of the state, Lamdan, like Masada's defenders, killed himself.

TEN

Jaffa and Suburbs

'In close commerce with Jerusalem,
Joppa [Jaffa] was infected with the fanatic patriotism of
the latter; as there were rebels and assassins there,
so there were rebels and pirates here.'
REVEREND GEORGE ADAM SMITH
The Historical Geography of the Holy Land (1894)

A Viennese Library

I FIRST MET GABY ALDOR IN 1974, when she and her
husband, who had been her English professor at the Hebrew
University, were living in an old Arab house in Jerusalem. She
was an actress, and I more or less fell in love with her. Circumstances favoured friendship over romance: I was twenty-three,
she thirty-two; I lived in Lebanon, she was Israeli; she was
married with a baby daughter; and she did not let me touch her.
We conducted a long-distance correspondence, as illicit as it was
innocent, via my father in California because no mail passed
between Israel and the Arab states. We used to meet and talk
when I came to Israel from Beirut or, later, London. All young
men need an older woman as confidante and adviser. Mine was
an ideally sage and sexy Israeli artist. When she was not acting
in Israeli films and plays, she wrote – stories, plays and dance
criticism. Her husband had died, and she was married again to
a dedicated and engaging Israeli physician, Dr Arie Bass. They
moved to the upper floor of an Arab house in Jaffa, a beautiful
old palace built around a courtyard in Ottoman style, replete
with flowers in tin pots. The other apartments into which the

building had been divided after the 1948 Arab–Israeli war belonged to Jewish refugees from Iraq and a large family of Palestinian Arabs.

Gaby once told me the story of her father's return visit to Vienna, when he was eighty-three. She had often said Israel meant nothing to him. He was neither Zionist nor anti-Zionist. 'He doesn't even know why there is an Israel,' she used to say. They flew together to Austria on a pilgrimage to the family house he had not seen since the Anschluss in 1938. When they reached the *belle époque* apartment building in Vienna's centre, her father stopped dead. As courtly in coat and hat as any Austro-Hungarian grandee, he just stared at the flat in which he had grown up and to which all his memories were tied. She took him closer, but he would not go inside. She entered alone. That was all she told me. Later, she wrote to me, 'We stood downstairs in the courtyard, and my father pointed at the apartment where they lived. A woman came down and looked at us with suspicion. My father said he lived here once. She was not impressed, only more cold.' More than anything else in the house, she said, the old man missed the library. The books were his lost treasure. Were they still there? The Austrian woman said that, when she moved in after the war, the books had already gone.

A year or so later, in the gentrified upper-floor restaurant of an Arab stone house in Jaffa, Gaby told me about another family who went looking for their abandoned home. Following the peace treaty with Jordan in 1994, many Palestinians visited the houses they had left in 1948. They could not claim them back, but they wanted to see them. Or, they thought they did. One evening, two women from Amman came to Gaby's house. 'They send the women,' Gaby explained. 'The men are too proud.' Like her father. The older woman said she had grown up in the house, and her daughter was seeing it for the first time. They inspected room after room, each redecorated many times since their family's departure, Gaby watching as if she were a tenant. Finally, the mother asked, 'Where are my father's books?'

The epochs of comfortable houses with large libraries, for the Jews of Vienna as for the Arabs of Jaffa, were lost to the generations born since their respective catastrophes – for Vienna's Jews, 1938; for Jaffa's Arabs, 1948. The arid plain that is Palestine must have been an unsatisfactory reality for a child dreaming of the Vienna Circle, Freud and Wittgenstein, Sachertortes and *Le Nozze di Figaro*. And the desert camps beyond the Jordan Valley were no substitute, in the imaginations of refugee children, for Jaffa's orchards, water bubbling in courtyard fountains and waves caressing the shore.

Gaby Aldor was sensitive to the parallels between her life and that of the Palestinian daughter from Amman: fathers who would not enter their old houses, the realization that the past would not be reclaimed and the libraries would not be reassembled. She was aware as well that the hostility of the Austrian woman in her father's house mirrored her own to the previous owners of hers. Her response was to write a play, *The Lane of White Chairs*, about an Arab house in Jaffa to which a Palestinian refugee named Taher returned when the Jordanian border opened. 'He came in with a burst of anger, as if he were continuing an argument cut off a short while ago,' Gaby wrote. 'But the argument he was continuing was actually fifty years old.' Taher was searching for treasure, hidden in a box that he had buried underneath the house when his family fled the Jewish onslaught. His quest disrupted the lives of everyone, Israeli and Arab, living in what had been his house. By the end of the play, he unearthed, not gold, but a childhood toy. He knelt on the floor to play with it, happily.

The Lane of White Chairs opened in 1997 at the Theatre Festival in Acre, another Arab coastal town emptied of its Arab inhabitants in 1948. Its cast included both Arabs and Israelis. The production was a testament to the vibrancy and self-assurance of an Israeli civil society able to confront the most disquieting, and often denied, aspects of its past. But the confrontation with the unsavoury aspects of the story – the ethnic cleansing of Arabs from their homes and the brutality of military occupation – had yet to change the realities. Israelis might confess what they had done in 1948, but the state would not make amends. They could acknowledge the wrongs done under occupation since 1967, but the state did not end the occupation.

After *The Lane of White Chairs*, Gaby performed in another play with a mixed Arab–Jewish cast. Its theme was an aspect of Israel's relationship with its indigenous population that was as troubling as the ownership of land and houses: torture. Arab victims of torture played themselves, but the producers could find no torturers willing to do the same. Israeli actors, some of whom had served as soldiers in the occupied territories, played the interrogators. The production was to be the kind of Truth Commission that neither Israel nor the Palestine Liberation Organization was likely to sponsor. It won good reviews from Israeli critics, but it did not end the torture. The Israeli High Court had already done that, for a brief period between proscribing it in 1997 and the eruption of the second *intifadah* in 2000.

Before dawn on my first morning back in Jaffa, the muezzin's *salah al fajr* – morning prayer – woke me. In the flat below, a radio blasted the Arabic news from Kol Israel. That gave way to an even louder news bulletin in Hebrew from a car outside. In both languages, I heard the same word, Gaza. Something had happened in Gaza. My eyes were closed, and I hoped the muezzin and the duelling radios would stop and let me sleep again. More cars drove into the narrow road below my room for the daily commute from Jaffa to Tel Aviv. Lying on a single bed in the extra room at Gaby and Arie's flat, I opened my eyes. Above loomed a ceiling higher than a basketball court's, solid wood planks carved into painted cornices, as in Tuscany. Outside on a promontory, the minaret that woke me went silent.

At that hour it was a long walk to an open café. The first I came to was a rendezvous for the early morning people – street sweepers, van drivers and workers – who ate at tables on the pavement. I ordered a Turkish coffee without sugar in Arabic, and the Arab proprietor answered me in Hebrew. I wandered on through the old port town that was for centuries the Westerner's gateway to the Holy Land. Jaffa had been Jerusalem's harbour, the western edge of its *Jund*. It was also the southernmost bead on the string of Levantine ports that marked Greater Syria's Mediterranean shore: Alexandretta, Latakia, Tripoli, Beirut, Sidon and Haifa. When Israel opened a new commercial port at Ashdod in 1965, Jaffa – the world's oldest regularly used port – was reduced to a marina for small yachts. Old houses that survived property developers, a breed as destructive in Beirut as in Jaffa, had become slums for Arabs and Jews alike. The rich lived in new palaces and villas, quaint and sanitized copies of the slum dwellings. Most of Jaffa was Israeli Jewish and working class, but there were also the kinds of artists who would have colonized Greenwich Village, New York, in the 1950s.

Amos Kenan, in his novel *The Road to Ein Herod*, wrote, 'Old Jaffa, of course, is home mainly to artists and intellectuals – but the kind of artists and intellectuals who had not been squeamish about taking over the homes of the city's former inhabitants, the ones who fled by sea in 1948. Anyone who can live in a house whose previous owner is now a refugee is someone who can be relied on, someone who won't turn traitor.'

Later that morning, Gaby took me to rehearsals at Jaffa's Arabic-Hebrew Theatre in the cellar of the Ottoman-era Antiquities Museum. The new play was *Exile at Home*. The characters – each on his own stage set – addressed the audience rather than one another. The director, Igal Ezrahy, let the actors improvise parts of their monologues, making them co-writers. Gaby played an Israeli tour guide in Berlin. Drawing on her Viennese origins, she dredged up turbulent passions about German culture and Jewishness. Another actress, Rauda Saliman, was playing her own uncle, a Palestinian farmer from Ein Hod, in heavy work boots and army surplus trousers. In what must have been her uncle's leonine roar, she said that his niece, herself, 'was not raised properly and became an actress. Each time she is on television I switch to another channel. Well, she used to come here and say, "How can you work the land which used to be yours? Have you no shame? Where is your honour? The Jews expelled you and took your land, and now you work for the Jewish boss. And you never told him the land was yours." And I say to her, "The most important thing for a man is to work his land. All the rest is of no importance." Besides, I told my boss these are my fields. And he said, "Go to Yemen, and take all the land I had there. I give it to you as a present." And we laughed, and I prepared us another cup of coffee.'

The other characters were immigrants and Arabs, the elixir of peoples that constituted modern Israeli society. The play that I heard parts of that morning was not obviously political. It dealt with longing – an Egyptian Jewish woman who fed Egyptian food to her children in Israel and yearned for Cairo; a Russian immigrant family from Uzbekistan who did not care where they lived as long as it was not Uzbekistan or Russia; Gaby's Israeli–German–Jewish–Berliner, tormented by identities; an Arab man who returned from the dead to see his village mosque become a nightclub. 'It is as if,' the dead man said, 'someone had taken your synagogue and turned it into a whorehouse.'

Not far from the theatre was St Peter's Catholic Church, a Franciscan Baroque ornament on Kedumim (Ancient) Square, Jaffa's main tourist plaza. It stood on the site of an old Crusader fortress, Napoleon's headquarters in 1799 for his abortive conquest of Syria. In 1830, Benjamin Disraeli stayed at its hospice of St Nicholas and St Joseph. Posted on the church door were matrimonial banns for Alvaro Astoquiza and Luz Trujillo of Colombia and a young couple from Poland, who would soon – like Perseus and Andromeda – wed in Jaffa. There were no banns for Christian Arabs, probably because so few remained. Thirty Filipino tourists studied the late nineteenth-century church and its Crusader foundations, the women carrying parasols and a few of the men in baseball caps. Outside, four young Indian men sat on a bench. I didn't see any Arabs or Israelis. The plaza itself was polished stone, worn by millions of footsteps, smoother than the rough rock art galleries and restaurants on its fringes. The spirit of old Jaffa had been exorcized. It had once boasted a lively fish market. Artisans used to bang out pots and pans, and women boiled marmalade from Jaffa's lemons and oranges. But no one made anything here any more. Kedumim Square was the wax mannequin of a town whose insides, its people, had been surgically excised. It was a restoration project – Boston's Quincy Market, London's Covent Garden, Les Halles in Paris – Disney's Orient. It sold copies of artefacts from the ancient past, its faux quaintness a backdrop for tourists to pose before as they did at Big Ben and the Eiffel Tower.

The Tanner's Well

When Disraeli came to Jaffa on his Levantine Grand Tour in 1830, he met 'Damien, the descendant of an old Venetian family but himself a perfect Oriental'. The future British prime minister called Jaffa 'a pretty town', where he found 'the most delightful gardens of oranges, citrons and pomegranates, the trees as high and the fruit as thick as our English apple orchards'. Macmillan's 1910 *Guide to Palestine and Syria* dismissed Jaffa: 'A few hours will amply suffice to see everything of interest in and around Jaffa.' To reach a place the *Guide* recommended, I passed a number of others that the *Guide* did not mention. Plaster casts of Napoleon, one arm outstretched, pointed the way to a Visitors' Centre discreetly buried underground. There was an old house whose explanatory plaque stated: 'In 1740 the first Jewish hostel in Jaffa was established here, which included a synagogue and a mikve. The synagogue reopened in 1948 by Libyan Jews is still in use.' In use, but closed. On I went, past Ali Baba's carpet shop and the Ilana Goor Museum where I had an excellent lunch later. Finally, at the bottom of a steep climb, I came, as St Peter the Fisherman once had, to the house of Simon the Tanner. Peter, also called Simon, had a vision while sleeping on the roof of the house that legend placed here. He saw 'fourfooted beasts of the earth, and wild beasts, and creeping things, and fowls of the air' that a voice ordered him to kill and to eat. Peter refused, saying he had never eaten anything 'common or unclean', meaning not kosher. The voice said, 'What God hath cleansed, that call not thou common.' The new sect thus accelerated the momentum away from its Jewish beginnings. The Apostles would from then on accept Gentiles into their ranks – 'but God hath shewed me that I should not call any man common or unclean'. If not for the dream on Simon's roof, Christians would, like Jews and Muslims, forgo pork chops and bacon. Christianity became, instead of a Messianic branch of Judaism, its rival and, later, its persecutor.

Simon was gone, as was his tannery. Christopher Zakarian and his family had succeeded him. The Zakarians were Armenians, who had migrated from Persian and Turkish Armenia three centuries before. Christopher Zakarian, a spry man of eighty-two, opened the door hesitantly. The house, he said, was no longer open to the public. When I explained I was writing a book, he relented. Two Israeli military policemen were camped in the foyer, their light weapons, rations and walkie-talkies incongruous in the domestic setting. One ordered me to write my name and address in a book. Mr Zakarian apologized. 'When somebody comes to visit me here, he has to sign.' The soldiers resumed speaking to each other in Russian, and Mr Zakarian took me to the courtyard in the middle of his house. 'Private on these premises,' a notice advised visitors. 'Do no photograph please.' The garden had clay pots in the flowerbeds and a covered well, both standard in the Levant. What was unusual was the vast lighthouse, its rounded foundation occupying much of the courtyard. Mr Zakarian was used to it. His family, he said, had operated and guarded it for two centuries. 'The lighthouse is no longer used,' he lamented, 'because the port is no longer used. It's only for tourists now.'

I wondered about the Israeli security men. Were they protecting the house from tourists? No. Some of the more enthusiastic young worshippers at the mosque next door, the Jama'a Butros, or Peter's Mosque, had attempted in 1998 to expand into Mr Zakarian's property. The lighthouse and an ancient well took enough room. If the mosque moved in, there would be no space for the Zakarians. 'I don't like them,' he said. 'I had no problems for fifty years. All the time we helped tourists and pilgrims to visit the house. I am an Armenian Christian. We were the first Christian kingdom, in 301, before the Byzantines.' He said the militants tried to break into his house two or three times, and the soldiers came to stop them. Mr Zakarian did not seem fond of the soldiers either. 'Nobody protect me. God protect me.' If Jewish settlers claimed his house, as they had many in Hebron, the soldiers would have protected the settlers from him.

Someone must have protected him. His was one of the few Jaffa families to survive intact in its own house in 1948. 'My grandfather opened the door to give people water to drink,' he said. 'Until 1900, this was the only water.' He was born, he said, in December 1919, after the British had occupied Palestine. He worked as a mechanical engineer repairing Mercedes-Benz cars for a German firm in Jaffa. During the Second World War, the British interned him as a German employee. They then hired him as a mechanic for the RAF in Ramleh. He repaired engines for the British until they withdrew in 1948. When the first Arab–Israeli war began, he stayed at home in Jaffa. Most of the population fled under attacks by the Jewish forces. The Zakarians were lucky. It may have helped that they were Armenian. 'My boss with the British army,' he said, 'he knew I worked in the lighthouse. He wrote and asked if I'd like to work in Oman on the Trucial Coast. I took his letter and went to Jordan to the Iraq Petroleum Company. So, I worked three years there and came back to Israel.' In the meantime, he maintained oil rigs in Bahrain, Dubai and Qatar. 'When my father asked me to help him here, I took sick pay. It took me one year to fix the lighthouse.' At the time, the light was fired by paraffin and he turned it mechanically. When the port closed, he and the lighthouse retired.

He showed me his British Palestine passport, issued in Lydda in 1945. 'It was accepted in the Arab countries until 1950,' he said. His full name was Krisdasdar Michel Zakarian, and there were ornate visa stamps from Jordan, Qatar, Bahrain and Lebanon. Mr Zakarian, the mechanical engineer, believed in miracles. After all, St Peter stayed in a house that once stood here. Peter's host, Simon, had tanned animal skins with water from his well. What was more, St Peter performed a miracle in Jaffa: he brought a seamstress named Tabitha back from the dead. 'All the Christians come from here,' he said, meaning that Christianity took form with Peter's vision on the roof. 'The Holy Spirit come to St Peter here. I will tell you something. When I was a boy, the neighbours have a child sick. We have no doctors. They bring him here to wash him. They come three times in the week – Friday, Saturday, Sunday. Then I see the boy was praying with us. I ask my mother why they come to wash him three times. She said they came for all the holy days – Christian, Muslim and Jewish.' It was a time when the line between folk religions was not so well drawn by politics as it would be later. In Syria, I remembered, Muslim women prayed for fertility in the Christian shrine of St Takla. Mr Zakarian said he too was saved by a miracle. It happened when, as a child, he had an extremely high fever. One night, he saw a man with a white beard waving incense, praying and walking three times around his bed. Mr Zakarian told his mother, who gave him a glass of water from the ancient well. The fever left him.

Mrs Zakarian brought us tea. We sat talking between the disused lighthouse on one side of the garden and the well-used mosque on the other. He was squeezed between the useless past and a threatening future. Who would take over the house when he went? 'Until now,' he answered, 'the first child got the house. But I don't want it that way, because my first is a girl.' The Zakarians had four grown-up children, and the only son lived in Jaffa. One of the girls, the youngest, was sitting in the garden with us. She had moved to California and did not mind that the house would go to her brother. I suspected the Pacific Ocean appealed more to her than sharing a house with Israeli soldiers and foreign tourists beside Islamic fanatics to watch a lighthouse that did not work. Yet, somebody had to do it.

Dear Hill, Spring Hill: The First All-Jewish City

'Jaffa has a history and a stirring one,' Mark Twain wrote in *Innocents Abroad*. 'It will not be discovered anywhere in this book.' Nor in this one. Contemporary Jaffa survived as a trendy and rundown dormitory for its upstart neighbour down the hill, Tel Aviv. Where Jaffa was an ancient Arab town of dark stone, Tel Aviv was born in 1909 as a pure Jewish city of bright cement. Tel Aviv, founded near a hill called by the Arabs Tel Habib, was the secular, financial capital of Israel. Jerusalem was merely the political capital that most countries did not recognize, because the UN stood by its 1947 resolution making it an international city. Jerusalem traditionally was where old Jews went to die. Tel Aviv was where the young came to live. If there had been no triumph of political Zionism, no state, Tel Aviv would still have been one of the great cultural and commercial centres of the Levant.

One night in Tel Aviv, friends introduced me to a young Israeli woman who took me on to a nightclub. We danced and, in the natural order of things, went back to her house. I moved in with her for a while. She was a late sleeper, and I used to go out early to idle in Tel Aviv. I became a boulevardier in the cafés of Sheinkin Street, where I read the newspapers and wrote up my notes. The waitresses were, for the most part, gorgeous. Tel Aviv's espresso – once unheard of – was as good as Rome's. My favourite café for reading and appreciating the waitress was the Bialik on Allenby Street. A few young men, undoubtedly home on leave from the army, carried rifles. There were almost no Arabs. Along eucalyptus-shaded Chen Street, old central European exiles, men and women, passed their morning on stone benches talking, reading or playing chess. At Steimatzky's, the W H Smith of Israel, a long shelf held books by or about

Edward Said. Israelis could read works by America's leading Palestinian intellectual in English or Hebrew, but Palestinians in the occupied territories could not. Yasser Arafat had banned some of his books, when Said criticized him for brutality and selling out his people.

Walking from Allenby Street towards the seafront one morning, I stopped at a shop selling 'used books'. I could not ignore the dusty ground-floor attic, where the shelves ran ten feet up to the ceiling. An old salesman, maybe the proprietor, told me where to find 'arte, philosophia, novella and historia'. There was a familiar smell of old Penguin paperbacks by Galsworthy, Angus Wilson, Somerset Maugham and other Englishmen popular here during the Mandate. I found Theodore Dreiser's *Life, Art and America* in a 1976 edition from the Progress Publishers of Moscow – foreword in Russian, the rest in English. Price: twenty shekels. There were old histories of Israel from the days when the Zionists were still calling it Palestine. I picked up an Edwardian tome called *The English Marriage* for Emma Gilmour. When I took the books to the counter, the man added up the prices and said, 'Seventeen five.' Seventeen five? I handed him a hundred-shekel note, and the change was twenty-five. An April 1975 issue of *Playboy* lay atop a mouldy stack beside the cash register. He said the 'collector's item' cost ten shekels.

I walked to the beach, where hotels straight out of old Miami rattled in the wind. Waves, gripped by a gale, splashed the rocky breakwater. It was too stormy for sunbathers, but hardy souls made their way along the sand, dodging pools of water and retreating when the waves advanced. Some were Russian, others Romanian workers on their day off. Two men in bare feet scanned the wet sand with what looked like a vacuum cleaner. One in a yellow slicker worked his metal detector with the determination of a Cornish wrecker. Along a pebble-dash beach path, an old man in a red back-to-front baseball cap wheeled a shopping cart.

On this beach in the 1920s, young Jewish girls from Austria and Germany donned skimpy dresses and danced, amusing

Jewish labourers and outraging the rabbis. Among their number was Gaby's mother, whose photograph on a Tel Aviv beach I had seen in her house. The old Arab men of Jaffa, if they had seen this far to the new city, would also have been scandalized. They did not want their daughters infected by the modern contagion of female freedom. Arab notables, already afraid of losing their homes and lands, wondered whether their children would defy them – as many socialist and secular Jews did their fathers. Their workers might organize and demand rights, like the Jewish workers did. Jewish and Arab women noticed the wind stirred by the dancers on the beach. But there would always be men – policemen, mullahs, rabbis – to keep everyone in his or her place. And there would always be rebels. Tel Aviv intruded on traditional Arab – as well as Jewish – life. It symbolized revolution. For that, it was despised less by the Arabs of Jaffa than by the rabbis in Jerusalem.

I went on a Tel Aviv tour one day with Didi Remez, the young spokesman of Peace Now. The Likud hated Peace Now, which came into being to protest against the Israeli invasion of Lebanon in 1982. To the right wing it was the incarnation of decadent, outdated liberalism. Arabs and Israeli leftists distrusted it for compromising with state orthodoxy. Didi was what I would call a good guy – droll, open-minded and committed. He was also young and physically fit, the picture of the 'new Jew' Zionism was meant to create on fertile Palestinian soil. His grandfather, who had been the first commander of the Israeli air force, would have been proud of him. He had taken Peace Now in a more radical direction by setting up Settlements Watch to report on the settlers, the acres they stole, the olive trees they uprooted, the Palestinians they harassed and the houses they built. His research gave the outside world a picture of what the settlements were doing to the Palestinians. With the settlements, there would be no peace. Not now. Not ever.

Didi had recently moved back to Tel Aviv from Jerusalem, whose increasingly religious ambience he found suffocating. Tel Aviv was the last redoubt, Didi said, of the secular, young, off-beat, sometimes gay, irreligious Jews who placed themselves in the tradition of their secular Zionist fathers while renouncing their sins and their crimes. He showed me where the opera house had once stood. An American shopping mall called Opera Tower had replaced it. He loved the older buildings, the few that survived. 'This was the old municipal building, City Hall,' he said. 'This was the poet Bialik's house.' Nothing lasted long in Tel Aviv. City Hall, headquarters of Tel Aviv's legendary mayor Meier Dizengoff, in the 1920s, had become a museum. Hayyim Nahmam Bialik's white stucco house was a cultural centre. Tel Aviv had named one street and a roundabout posthumously for Dizengoff and another street, in 1924 while he was still alive, for Bialik. Already known for his Yiddish poetry, the Russian son of a Talmudic scholar was one of those who fashioned modern Hebrew out of the biblical language that had lain moribund for almost three millennia. He became the laureate of political Zionism, who – like other Zionist pioneers – had only contempt for the exilic intellectual traditions of the rabbis. In 'On My Return', he wrote,

> You have not changed, you're antique old.
> There's nothing new, I think;
> Friends, let me join your club, we'll rot
> Together till we stink.

Bialik broke from the 'antique old' in the new air of Tel Aviv, where he lived at 22 Bialik Street for a few years before moving to Ramat Gan. He died in Vienna in 1934. From Bialik's time to the present, poetry – like archaeology, sport, humour, religion, family, painting and just about everything else – has been politically charged. When the Education Ministry recommended in 2000 that the Palestinian poet Mahmoud Darwish's poems be added to the Israeli curriculum, right-wing Knesset members dissolved into a frenzy of fury and disgust, and the religious Shas Party threatened to abandon the then Labour coalition. Darwish himself doubted young Israelis would be swayed by his verse. He said that Bialik, whose poems he had studied in the Israeli schools of his youth, 'did not change me into a Zionist. He did not even get me to like his poems.'

Didi had already introduced me to the Café Bialik, where we ended our tour and flirted with the waitress. Why did he involve himself in politics, especially left politics when the country had shifted to the right? 'When I was young,' he said, 'it was kind of a family thing. My brother and I began going to demonstrations against the war in Lebanon. We were twelve or thirteen.' Didi's brother Ari was two years younger than he was, and both had served in the army. And both were doing more than attending demonstrations. Why? 'What did it for me was my army service. I was a career officer with six years in a combat unit. I joined at eighteen and was in the airborne infantry from December 1988 to December '94. I served in Lebanon and the occupied territories. One of the last things we did was to hand over to a Palestinian commander in the Gaza Strip.' When he left the army, he did what most Israeli kids did: he went backpacking. Many went to India. Didi chose South America. He had spent four years of his childhood in North America, when his parents were studying at Brandeis University. Both his grandmothers were American. His father, Gideon Remez, returned to Israel to work for Radio Israel.

After Didi started Settlements Watch, he spent most of his time in the occupied territories. He made Arab friends, he said, and he got to know some of the settlers. He came across people he called 'hilltop grabbers' – those who answered Ariel Sharon's call after Oslo to 'grab every hilltop'. They differed from the old-style settlers. Like him, they had done their army service and gone backpacking. 'They are New Age fundamentalist Jews,' he said. 'They put their existence above the existence of the state. Many of them had their New Age experiences in India. Now, they sit around the rabbis the way they used to with the gurus. They have a strange sexual relationship with the land.' He said they huddled up on the hilltops in cabins and rode bicycles, armed hippies. 'They'd stop me and put their bikes on top of my 4×4 and take a ride. It would make me die inside. Their rabbis say there is no such thing as Arab-owned land. They say, "We're going to kick him off the land and take the olives." They are kids with such utter conviction.' Unlike their New Age counterparts in India or America, they were not pacifists.

The New Age settlers were a minority, however. 'The majority of the settlers are lower-middle-class Israelis enticed by the local vision of the American dream,' Didi said. We drank coffee and watched people coming in and out of the café. Most of the young Israelis were smoking cigarettes, and the girls wore tight jeans or short skirts. But for the cigarettes, we could have been in Los Angeles. The other difference was that these kids were intelligent and well informed. It was hard to say that about the youngsters in smoke-free Starbucks outlets in the city of my birth. (When I was visiting a few years ago, I'd asked a professor at UCLA the difference between his California students and those he'd taught in New York. 'Let me put it this way,' he answered. 'Things are so bad out here that even the Jews are stupid.') 'I was brought up on pioneer values,' Didi said. 'Pioneering was a pragmatic enterprise. We discussed real world issues of the survival of a nation. The settlers are not pragmatic.' Since the *intifadah*, the settler worldview had been in the ascendant. The left in Israel had believed Oslo was a genuine end to conflict, but they – like the Palestinians – had been taken in by lies and public relations. The *intifadah* came as a surprise, although Palestinian critics of Oslo had predicted it all along. 'People took the *intifadah* as a personal betrayal.' The situation before the *intifadah*, he believed, was no different from the years before it. There was no betrayal of the left by their Palestinian friends. The Palestinians simply lost hope.

During his time in the army, Didi said, he'd had bad experiences with the settlers. They tended to take advantage of the troops protecting them, often provoking Arabs to attack or taking land that the army then had to defend. Settlements, he came to believe, were inimical to building a Jewish and democratic state in Israel. 'There's no shame,' he said. 'The ultra-Orthodox say they are against peace because it will lead to

Israel becoming a normal society. The damage they are causing to our institutions is fundamental. It is the issue of a pioneer elite, which I happen to belong to, and the mistakes it made and which we are still paying for.' One of the mistakes, he believed, was holding on to the West Bank and Gaza. He believed his world, Israel's secular Jewish world, was contracting. He looked around the Café Bialik, at the beautiful waitress and the young men with glasses of beer, and said, 'All we have left is this little ghetto in Tel Aviv.'

I met Gaby for dinner that night in Neve Zedek, the oldest part of Tel Aviv. She had come from a dance performance she was reviewing at the Suzanne Dellal Centre. She was irritated. It was not the dance, though. It was the speech afterwards by the minister of culture. 'Was the speech any good?' I asked. 'No.' Did the minister know anything about dance? 'He's a general. In the late 1960s, he killed Palestinians in the Jordan Valley.' She did not think that qualified him to disburse Israel's decreasing cultural budget. After a good Italian dinner, she walked me through old Tel Aviv. Sixty families built the first houses here as a garden suburb of Jaffa. Like Jaffa's, the original Tel Aviv houses were solid stone. Their style was called 'Eretz Israel', a blend of Arab and Bauhaus. More Bauhaus. In the central square was a mural of the city's 'founders', the respectable burghers who broke ground on the few acres of sand that became the world's first 'all Jewish' city. When the next wave of residents came, they built beside the hill that the Arabs called Tel Habib, Dear Hill or Lovers' Hill, and named it Tel Aviv – Hebrew for Spring Hill. This was what Didi Remez called the 'heart of Tel Aviv'. Around the silent square, white Bauhaus flats brooded over a world that was retreating into its own ghetto. Overwhelming them were fanatics and settlers who hated their liberal dream as much as they did half-clad women dancing on the beach.

'There's an old man who lives in the little hut there,' Gaby said, pointing at a plywood and cloth hovel. 'He pretends to keep an eye on the cars, and we give him money. He tells stories.

I don't know if they are true, but they're stories. A young man was listening to him, and the man offered him a drink, whisky or vodka or something. The boy said, "No, thanks, I don't drink." And the man said, "Then, go away."' She liked his spirit. Poor, drunk and proud. There were too many poor now, she said, more than ever. 'Jews do not let other Jews die. There is always enough food for everyone. That's what I thought. Then I read that last winter, old people froze to death in the street.'

Something went wrong. During the election campaign between Ehud Barak of Labour and Ariel Sharon of the Likud, Sharon had come to the opening of an art exhibition. Gaby doubted the general liked modern art or had ever been to a play or a concert. Still, he came. She saw him – 'fat, imposing, pushing his way in' – as the Arab-killer of Qibya and Sabra-Shatila. Perhaps she had been drinking. She didn't say. Each time Sharon started to speak, she booed him. Her booing got louder and louder. Her friends – the artists, the dealers, the connoisseurs, the liberal elite – said nothing. She was furious, and she was not a woman whose fury I would choose to rouse. When Sharon left, her friends said, 'Good for you.' She told me, 'They're cowards.'

Walking through Tel Aviv that day with Didi and that evening with Gaby, I recalled an Arab man who had told me there was nothing admirable in Israeli culture. From his point of view, the Israelis were conquerors. They had taken his land. They kept him in financial misery. They arrested his family. Policemen stopped him because he was Arab. The Israeli municipality would not pave the road outside his house, and the government did not provide his children with schools equal to those for Jewish children. If I had been him, I too might see nothing to redeem the cruelty. But, to me, there were things and people to respect. There was Jeff Halper, the university teacher who threw himself in front of bulldozers when the army demolished Arab houses. There was Gideon Levy, who every week in *Ha'aretz* told the story of one more Palestinian's agony under occupation.

There was Amira Hass, who had lived in Gaza and the West Bank to report the truth about Israeli abuses of Palestinians. There was Uri Avnery, who even in his eighties wrote, marched and preached against the harm Israel was doing to Palestinians. There had been Israel Shahak, the Hebrew University chemist and Warsaw ghetto survivor who relentlessly challenged the state over its treatment of Palestinians. There was Daniel Barenboim, who – with Edward Said – had created a classical orchestra of Arab and Israeli youngsters who played around the world. There was Ehud Ein Gil, who organized and defended Palestinian and immigrant labourers against exploitation by Israeli employers. There were the historians – Tom Segev, Ilan Pappe, Avi Shlaim – who unearthed the truth about Israel's history and confronted Israelis with it. There was Didi. There was Gaby. And yet, Israeli liberalism made its capital in a city whose people – disparate as they were – belonged to the same dominant race and religion. The Arabs, the natives, the Other lived elsewhere – in mixed cities like Jerusalem and Haifa or in their own villages. In Tel Aviv, liberals discussed the Arabs, but they did not see them.

One Sunday evening, I went to the Polish Mass at St Peter's Church in Old Jaffa. The pews were filled with Polish workers, men in heavy boots and leather jackets, women in waterproof coats. Israel was filling up with Russian immigrants, many of whom were not Jewish, and labourers from Poland and Romania. They came from the lands of vicious Christian anti-Semitism. Yet, to avoid giving jobs to Arabs from the occupied territories and to keep the Arab population within Israel a permanent minority, they were importing peasants and workers from the realm of the pogrom and the blood libel. Someone had told me one Russian Christian group maintained an anti-Semitic website in Haifa that urged Russians to kill Arabs *and* Jews. The *Jerusalem Post* had just reported the latest population data from the Central Bureau of Statistics under the headline, 'Jews are 81.1% of population'. The Jewish population included 'immigrants not registered as Jews ... An estimated half of

immigrants coming today are halachicly [according to Orthodox rabbinic law] Jewish.' The other half were not. Fear that
the Arabs, 1.2 million of whom were citizens, might outbreed
Jews had led government ministers and Knesset members to
propose everything from forced sterilization to mass expulsion.

In the taxi on my way back to Tel Aviv, the driver asked me
where I came from and stretched his arm next to mine. 'You are
very white for California. I'm very black. Good for women.
Thirty years ago, I go to Finland. Not like here. Women have
hair like this. Blonde. Stomach like this. Flat. Girls very white.
They love black. Three times a night fuck. You? You meet friend
now? Man or woman? Here. Have this.' He opened a plastic
bottle and shook out some black powder. 'Put in nose like this.
No? It's good. Like viagra. Homeopath viagra.' I declined. 'No?
Very good. Make hard.' He put some on his tongue. We were
passing some nightclubs in a neighbourhood that was as seedy
as an orchard. 'Ha, la,' he said. 'Hommous.' Hommous? I had
no idea what he was talking about. He pointed at two men
getting out of a car. 'See. Hommous.' Maybe it was taxi-driver
code. A Chinese man at the corner waved. The driver stopped,
they argued in Hebrew and we sped off. What was that about?
'The Chinaman, he say it's too expensive.' The Chinese man
was right. The driver charged me thirty-five shekels for what
had been a fifteen-shekel trip an hour earlier. Before he drove
away, he tried to sell me his homeopathic viagra for another fifty.

I had dinner in Sheinkin Street with the Israeli girl whose
house I was sharing. I told her about the taxi driver and his
conquests in Finland. She remembered him. 'Did he tell you he
had two lesbians fondling each other in his back seat?' Maybe
I should have bought the viagra. After dinner, the news on the
radio was all about a ship that Israel had seized on the high
seas. The army said it was loaded with weapons for Yasser
Arafat. A few days later, the girl asked me to move out. Our
romance, if that is what it was, had run its course. I moved to
the Cinema Hotel and roamed Tel Aviv alone. My happiest
hours were in the Ben Yehuda Market and the Café Bialik.

The Last Warrior

The doors on the seventh floor of the Tel Aviv apartment block had no numbers that I could see, but one of them sported more bumper stickers than an old Ford pick-up in Oklahoma. These were not in English and did not say, 'Gun Outlaws/Don't Outlaw Guns' or 'Honk if you love Jesus!' They were Hebrew appeals to Israel's conscience: fight anti-Arab discrimination, resist the occupation and stop Sharon from turning the country into a military state. There was no doubt which door was Uri Avnery's.

Avnery had been fighting causes all his life. His unlikely beginning as a radical was in Menachem Begin's Irgun in 1938. He was fifteen. In 1944, he quit over his comrades' racism against Arabs and their use of terror. During the 1948 war, he fought and was twice wounded as a commando in Samson's Foxes. He became a journalist with *Ha'aretz*, leaving when the paper would not publish his reports on the mass seizure of Arab land. His next venture was a dying family magazine, *Haolam Hazeh*. *Haolam Hazeh*, whose name meant 'the world that is' as opposed to *Olam Haba* ('the world to come'), became under Avnery's stewardship a radical populist weekly. He annoyed someone. The offices and presses were bombed, and the staff were injured. When Avnery published early reports of Ariel Sharon's infamous massacre in the Arab village of Qibya in 1953, thugs attacked him and pointedly crushed his hands – his writer's hands. (Syrian intelligence had made a similar symbolic demonstration against a Lebanese magazine editor, Selim al-Laouzi, in the late 1970s. But they murdered al-Laouzi and burned his writer's hands in acid.) Avnery was fearless. Before his hands recovered, *Haolam Hazeh* was back in business damning the government. He ran for the Knesset in 1965, won a seat and served through three parliaments. He left the Knesset in 1983, a year after the invasion of Lebanon and his controversial visit to Yasser Arafat in besieged Beirut. Avnery had

359

already begun a dialogue with the PLO's London representative, the urbane and much respected Sayed Hammami, in 1974. Avnery was nearly arrested for meeting with the PLO, but Hammami was assassinated. So too was his next Palestinian interlocutor, Issam Sartawi. Mutual recognition was not on the official agenda.

Gaby Aldor had told me Avnery was one of the handsomest men of his generation, and his fine features still marked him as a healthy and well-bred German gentleman. The hair and the trim beard had gone snowy white before I met him thirty years before, and his physique was still that of a tennis player. Gaby remembered attending political protest picnics that Avnery organized in the mid-1960s. 'He's very courageous,' she said, 'but very egocentric.' He was one of a group of activists and intellectuals who used to congregate at the Café Kasit in Dizengoff Street, where Gaby too imbibed 1960s radicalism. 'I never go there any more,' Avnery sighed. 'They all died.'

We were talking about Gaby and the picnics of forty years before from either side of a huge coffee table. Behind Avnery were political posters and campaign souvenirs that made the flat look like a well-heeled graduate student's. Despite the memorabilia, he was not wistful about the past. His life pointed to the future: creating a Palestinian state, ending Israeli land seizures and making a place where children were not murdered. Noticing my American accent, he laughed at America's imperial pretensions. 'America reminds me of an old Jewish joke,' he said. During the war between Russia and Turkey, a young Jewish boy was drafted into the tsar's army. His mother went with him to the training camp to make sure he was warm and had enough food. 'My son, be careful,' she said. 'What should I do, Mama?' he asked. 'Here is what you do. You just go and kill one Turk. Then you have to rest. You kill another Turk, and you rest. Kill another Turk, and rest again.' 'But what if a Turk tries to kill me, Mama?' he asked. She was outraged at the suggestion: 'Why should he try to kill you? What have you done to him?'

Avnery did not think much of the foreign press corps in Israel. He complained that none of them covered anti-government demonstrations and protests in which he and his organization, Gush Shalom – Hebrew for Peace Bloc – played a prominent part. The largest protests, he believed, deserved international coverage. The Western press wrote that the Israeli opposition movement was dead, but it was unlikely to die while Avnery lived. 'Sooner or later, the foreign journalists here all become agents of Israeli propaganda,' he said. 'The government can deny them access, or it can give them scoops.'

Almost before we had sat down, he'd had a go at my accent and my profession. Fair enough. His accent was German, and he had spent most of his life as a journalist. His wife Rachel made us tea and left her husband to talk. He loved talking. I could not write fast enough to keep up. Rachel, like Uri, was German Jewish. They had just returned from Sweden, where they had received the Alternative Nobel Peace Prize. I doubted they qualified for the real Nobel that had gone to the likes of Henry Kissinger and Menachem Begin. They enjoyed Sweden. 'Both Rachel and I are from northern Germany. We are predisposed to a cold climate.' He'd been born in Beckum, Westphalia, in September 1923. His father left Germany in 1933 when Adolf Hitler took office. 'Being Zionists, my parents chose to come to Palestine,' he said. His father's decision had defined his life. Had the family gone to the United States, there would have been no Uri Avnery. Helmut Ostermann, as he was called in Germany, would have been unlikely in New York to exchange his name for one in Hebrew. But in Mandate Palestine, taking a Hebrew name was part of reclaiming identity. Of becoming a new man, a new Hebrew. But what fascinated the young Helmut about the country when he arrived in 1933 was its Arab mystique.

'We landed in Jaffa,' Avnery recalled. 'Actually, one didn't land in Jaffa, because it never had a real port. Arab boats brought us to shore. Jaffa was an Arab town. Everything was different – the smells and the noises. There were horse-drawn carriages. It was very exciting.' He compared his recollections as a ten-year-old German Jewish boy with those of David Ben-Gurion, who had arrived in Jaffa twenty-five years before. 'Ben-Gurion wrote how disgusting it was. It was the same with Herzl. He came in 1898. He didn't like Palestine at all. He took the same attitude as Mark Twain. He hated religion, the religious Jews and the heat. That was despite the fact he came in September. He came only to see the Kaiser, against his wishes. He wrote in his private diary awful things about Palestine. He wrote that Jerusalem was dirty and disgusting. In a letter to a friend, he said Palestine was not a country for Jews. Jews were Europeans. He fled on the first ship, skipping Jaffa on the pretext he was going to be assassinated.'

Avnery dragged me through the terrain of Zionist history. 'The Zionist movement was founded by people who'd never been in the country. In 1897, at the First Zionist Congress, out of two hundred or so delegates, only one or two had been here. Zionism was founded by people who had no knowledge of or liking for Palestine. Their interest was to get the Jews out of Europe. One of the basic facts of the conflict is that the Zionist movement had an impact on the history and inhabitants of Palestine, but the Zionist movement was formed without any consideration for Palestine.' Hadn't Theodor Herzl written *The Jewish State* as a programme for remaking Palestine? '*Der Judenstadt* was written in 1896,' he said. 'It really means *The Jew-State*, not *The Jewish State*. Before that, when he conceived the idea, he wanted to do it in Argentina. Before he published that booklet, he became convinced the Jews, especially religious Jews in Poland and Russia, would not follow him to Argentina. Palestine is not mentioned in *The Jew-State*, except in one chapter.' The British offered part of East Africa for Zionist colonization, a proposal that split the Zionist movement for a time. Only the biblical appeal of the Holy Land, however, would rally religious Jews to the cause. Even then, most of them resisted Herzl's call. Some even declared him a blasphemer for putting a temporal state ahead of the Messiah. The Zionists had to convince not only their fellow Jews, but an imperial power to protect their colonies – first the Kaiser, who was uninterested, and then the British, with whom they were successful. 'There is one sentence that signifies everything,' Avnery said. 'Herzl wrote, "In Palestine, we would be part of a European wall against Asiatic barbarism."' Asiatic barbarism then, Asiatic communism in the 1950s and 1960s, Asiatic terrorism in 2001. 'The word "Arab" does not appear once in the book. With all his detailed proposals, he did not mention the Arabs.'

In contrast to what was taught in Israeli schools, Avnery had no admiration for Herzl. 'He was an ordinary Mittel-European of the time for whom non-Europeans were not real human beings,' he said. 'Zionism was not extraordinary. What was extraordinary was building a country about which he knew nothing and about whose inhabitants he knew even less. This is in the genetic code of the movement. They had contempt for the Palestinians, from the beginning to today.'

He thought the early Zionists either did not notice or deliberately ignored the similarities between Arabic and Hebrew. 'If Arabic and Hebrew were written in the same script, they could read each other. It's interesting that Jews from the Arab countries pronounce Hebrew correctly, but they are ashamed of it. They actually try to get rid of their correct pronunciation. You can have a rich Ashkenazi woman with a Yemenite housemaid, but the housemaid envies the landlady and tries to imitate her accent. It's absurd.'

His father came to Palestine as a wealthy banker. The wealth did not last. 'People who brought £1000 were exempt from the quota. The idea was that a poor country could not absorb so many immigrants. Our parents lost all their money within one year. Commercial morality is very low here. They were cheated left, right and centre. They went from rich to poor within a year.' After spending their first six months losing money in Haifa, they moved to Tel Aviv. The family were so poor that Avnery left school at the age of fourteen. He took jobs as a radio technician, a private detective and a lawyer's clerk. By the time he entered the National Military Organization, Irgun Zvai

Leumi, in 1938, he had a colourful curriculum vitae. Why had he joined the Irgun? 'They were the rulers of this country,' he said of the British, 'and we wanted to get rid of them.' The Haganah was more cooperative with the British in the 1930s, particularly during the Arab Revolt. Some Haganah operations against the Arabs took place under a British officer, Captain Orde Wingate. Wingate, a Christian Zionist, established the Jewish Special Night Squads to attack Arab rebels and villages. Without British protection, there would have been no Zionist colonies. Labour Zionists led by Ben-Gurion believed they needed the British to protect them from the Arabs until Palestine's Jewish community, the Yishuv, was strong enough to defend itself. About 1500 Haganah men disagreed.

The dissident Haganah militiamen formed the Irgun and sought the sponsorship of Ben-Gurion's enemy, the Revisionist leader Vladimir Jabotinsky. Irgun's military commander was David Raziel, and his deputy was Avraham Stern. Avnery joined them. Working in a solicitor's office, Avnery knew the British and the Arabs of Jaffa. 'The fact that I came to know Jaffa at a young age explains why I saw the Arabs as human beings.' As an Irgun member, he was working against both the Arabs and the British. He quit after five years. 'When I left the underground, it was nearly impossible to leave. It was at the time of a big split. Psychologically, it was very difficult to leave such an organization. Your whole life is concentrated – danger, a sense of purpose, an ideology. It becomes your life. I sometimes think it's like a monk leaving holy orders. I felt a complete break in my life. I was nineteen. It led to a profound personal crisis. But it was also liberating. You become independent. You realize you could think for yourself. It gave me an understanding for life of how such an organization works. I applied it to how Al Qaeda, the Taliban, Fateh and Hamas work.'

In October 1939, the Irgun leadership called a truce in its war against Britain because the British were fighting the greater threat – Hitler's Nazis. Avraham Stern refused to go along and formed the *Lochmei Herut Israel*, or Fighters for Israel's

Freedom, popularly known as the Stern Gang. 'Avraham Stern said that while Britain was weak, it was the time to attack. He contacted the Nazis for help against Britain.' Avnery may have had a personal reason for not wanting to fight the British during the Second World War. His only brother, Werner, had volunteered for the British army. He served as a commando in Ethiopia, where Orde Wingate also fought. Werner died in action as a British soldier. At the end of the war in 1945, Irgun rejoined the war against Britain. Its 'heroes', as Menachem Begin called them, escalated terror attacks on both the British and the Arabs. Irgun hanged British non-commissioned officers, blew up the British headquarters in the King David Hotel and terrorized Arabs throughout the country. 'The underground put bombs in Jaffa, Haifa and Jerusalem,' Avnery said of three cities that contained, not coincidentally, Palestine's largest mixed populations of Arabs and Jews. He accused men of his generation of selective amnesia about their pasts. 'Quite a few of them are unable to apply their experiences to others,' he said. 'Yitzak Shamir spoke about Arabs as if they were on a different planet.' Shamir, long before he became prime minister, had been an assassin and follower of Stern. 'When I was in parliament, Begin didn't stand my making this comparison in a debate on the death penalty. I interrupted him: "You more than anyone else should know that the death penalty serves them. It gives them martyrs."' Britain had given the Irgun a martyr when it hanged Irgunist Shlomo Ben-Yosef for attacking a bus filled with Arab civilians in 1938. 'Begin looked at me in sorrow,' Avnery said. 'He said, "Mr Avnery, are you comparing Arab terrorists to our freedom fighters?" I had joined Irgun because the British executed a member of the Jewish underground. I know why young Palestinians join Hamas and Islamic Jihad.' Israel, in the event, did not adopt capital punishment for Arab terrorists; but extra-judicial executions of Arab suspects later became normal procedure.

Avnery's first two years in the underground were during the Arab Revolt of 1936 to 1939, when Britain used massive force and methods that Israel would replicate in the West Bank and Gaza – house demolition, assassination, torture, collective punishment and curfew. Avnery thought the Arab Revolt was badly led by Haj Amin Husseini, 'who killed everyone who did not agree with him. The Arabs were left without any leadership.' When the British under Major General Bernard Montgomery suppressed the revolt in 1939, the mufti left Palestine for Iraq. The British invaded Iraq to suppress a pro-German military coup in 1941, and he moved to Berlin. Haj Amin's presence in Germany reinforced the notion among Zionists that Palestine's Arab leader was as anti-Semitic as the Nazis. Haj Amin seemed to believe that Germany was his natural ally – ignoring the role Nazi anti-Semitism played in driving Europe's Jews to seek refuge in Palestine and thus to displace the Arabs. A later generation of Palestinians, many of them living in the West, came to understand that European and American anti-Semites were their enemies and sympathetic Jews could be allies. 'From 1936 to 1939,' Avnery said, 'more Arabs were killed by Arabs than by the British or the Jews.' Palestinian leaders then, as later, placed tribal quarrels ahead of their people's survival. Nine years after the revolt collapsed, the problem was the same. 'The crisis in 1948 was that there was no leadership,' Avnery said.

'Arabs don't understand the very real Jewish roots of Zionism,' he said. 'They think it was invented by the British for the oil.' A little later, he made a similar charge over Israeli impressions of the Arabs. 'Butros Ghali told me, when he was acting foreign minister of Egypt, "You Israelis have the best Arabists in the world. They know everything, and they understand nothing."'

Avnery's recollections of 1948 belonged to an unabashed veteran of the good fight. The name of his unit, Samson's Foxes was 'a kind of collective decoration. It came from the Bible, Samson and the forty foxes and torches in the vineyards. We were in the same area.' (According to the Book of Judges, Samson took revenge on the Philistines because his Philistine father-in-law gave his wife to Samson's Jewish friend. As with

Delilah later, Samson's life was an object lesson to Jewish men not to stray from Jewish girls. 'And Samson went and caught three hundred foxes, and took firebrands, and turned tail to tail, and put a firebrand in the midst between two tails. And when he had set the brands on fire, he let them go into the standing corn of the Philistines, and burnt up both the shocks, and also the standing corn, with the vineyards and olives.') Avnery's Foxes were a 'mobile cavalry'. 'We used to mount two machine guns on jeeps in imitation of the Desert Rats,' he recalled. 'We didn't have tanks then. Today, you couldn't do it.' Avnery fought against the Egyptian army at the siege of Falluja, where he was wounded. The two sides agreed a temporary truce to bury their dead. The Israeli commander, Yigal Allon, dispatched an Arabic-speaking Yemeni Jew to negotiate. The Yemeni, a friend of Avnery's, was Yeroham Cohen. 'Egypt sent Major Gamal Abdel Nasser,' Avnery said. 'They became friendly. At one meeting, Abdel Nasser was depressed and said, "We will not come out alive." Cohen said, "You have weapons and drive. You will come out alive."' When the two sides held armistice talks in 1949, one of the Israeli delegates told Nasser that Cohen's wife had had a baby girl. 'Abdel Nasser sent him sweets from Groppi,' Avnery said. Groppi was Cairo's most fashionable chocolaterie. Had Avnery met Nasser? 'Abdel Nasser was wounded in an engagement where we got decorations. It was during some fighting at night. So, we were never properly introduced.'

When young Egyptian army officers staged the July 1952 revolution, Avnery said, *Haolam Hazeh* supported it. 'My idea from 1945 on has always been there is an Arab nationalism, and we should win it as an ally. First, as an ally against colonialism; second, to ally ourselves with the region.' The revolution's nominal leader was General Mohammed Neguib, but Nasser was its secret instigator. 'Cohen told me Neguib is nonsense. The man to watch is Nasser. I published this first in 1952. Later, *Time* magazine wrote the same thing. In 1953, Nasser invited Yeroham to meet him in Cairo. The fool, he went to Moshe

Sharrett.' Sharrett had just succeeded Ben-Gurion as prime minister. 'Sharrett forbad him to go. I believe we could have made peace with Abdel Nasser right at the beginning. He made contacts, but they came to nothing. Then we had the Lavon Affair.' Israeli defence minister Pinhas Lavon had approved, without informing Sharrett who was conducting secret talks with Nasser, an underground network in Egypt. The spy ring, mainly of Egyptian Jews, detonated bombs in British and American institutions, including the American cultural centre. The purpose was to derail the bourgeoning relationship between Nasser and the United States as well as Anglo-Egyptian discussions on British withdrawal from the Suez Canal Zone. Unfortunately for Lavon and his agents, they were caught. The Egyptians hanged two, Moshe Marzouk and Shmuel Azar, in 1955. 'Nasser couldn't pardon them after hanging a Muslim brother.' After the Muslim Brotherhood had attempted to assassinate Nasser in 1954, he executed some and imprisoned hundreds of others. Muslim opinion in Egypt would not have sanctioned death for fellow Muslims and clemency for Israeli spies.

A year later, Israel invaded Egypt in collusion with Britain and France to punish Nasser for nationalizing the Suez Canal. 'We attacked it very strongly, mostly because of the coalition with the British and the French,' Avnery said. 'I wrote a story about an Israeli tank lost in the dark. It joined a column of Egyptian tanks. At first light, it realized its mistake but was destroyed. This is what happened to us. We found ourselves in the wrong column with the French and the British. *Haolam Hazeh* supported Nasser.' In 1956, supporting Nasser would not have endeared the magazine to the government and much of the population. The magazine struggled on without government advertising, the mainstay of other Israeli publications. 'I always liked the guy,' he said of Nasser. 'He preserved the dignity of the Arabs after their defeat, but he did some very foolish things before the 1967 war.' Nasser asked the UN to remove its peacekeepers from the Sinai and closed the Straits of Tiran, precipitating Israel's six-day conquest of the Sinai, Gaza, the West Bank,

East Jerusalem and the Syrian Golan Heights. Nasser accepted blame for the catastrophe, but the Egyptians would not let him resign. 'Such a good speaker. He got carried away. He got the masses excited and couldn't stop. *Haolam Hazeh* picturing him in a positive light got everyone upset. Ben-Gurion always called him the Egyptian dictator. In Hebrew, it's even worse. He was always the tyrant. Ben-Gurion was afraid of him. Ben-Gurion was an old man. He had an idea of what Arabs should look like – small, dark and humble. There was this dynamic, young and fascinating person that everyone was interested in.'

Rachel reminded Uri that they had to leave for a demonstration. It sounded like they went to protests every evening. I asked how they met. 'After Qibya, I was attacked by some people and they broke my hands,' he said. I asked who had attacked him. 'Sharon's soldiers, I suppose.' He shrugged, as if to add, 'Who else?' 'I didn't use my hands for some time. Rachel moved in with me to help me. After five years, we married. Forty-nine years? My God. We're very close together, because we believe in the same things.'

Avnery was nearly eighty. He protested and demonstrated and wrote splenetic essays every day. Was it time to rest? 'I can't dream of taking time off.' He had just organized what he called 'a successful conference on war crimes'. Gush Shalom worked with Palestinians more than Peace Now did. It was less fearful of offending anti-Arab Israelis. Avnery, like Jeff Halper of the Committee Against House Demolitions, was often to be seen confronting Israeli bulldozers at Palestinian doors. He had even supported the 415 Islamists whom Yitzak Rabin deported to southern Lebanon in December 1992. It was in Lebanon that the Palestinians of Gaza and the West Bank received help from Hizballah, who introduced them to suicide bombing. International pressure forced Rabin to readmit the Islamists nine months later. 'After the 415 came back, they invited me to a mass reception,' Avnery said. 'We were there among five hundred sheikhs, and we were very well received. I wore this in Gaza.' 'This' was the Gush Shalom emblem, a pin with the crossed flags of Palestine and Israel. Avnery the secular Jew among the zealous Islamists of Hamas made for an interesting picture. Maybe there was hope.

I told him I had seen Benny Morris and was going to Haifa to meet Ilan Pappe, two of the new or post-Zionist historians. Avnery was part of Israeli history, and I assumed their revision of the old history would appeal to him. 'I've got a prejudice against history and historians,' he said. 'When you read history about events in which you've taken part, the spirit of the times isn't there. Writing about past times in which you had no part, you get the facts. It is like an X-ray of a beautiful woman. The picture is true, but . . .'

Was he frustrated that things went worse, not better? 'Never,' he insisted, looking at Rachel for confirmation. 'It's one advantage of being able to look back over fifty years. Fifty years ago, the concept of the people of Palestine wasn't accepted by ten people in the whole country. On the fifth day of the Six Day War, I wrote an open letter to the prime minister calling for the immediate establishment of a Palestinian state. At that time, it sounded crazy, but today 80 per cent say there can be no peace without a Palestinian state.' He admitted that conditions for the Palestinians under siege in the occupied territories had reached new lows. 'People say it's darkest before dawn. The closer we come, the more the differences of opinion become radicalized. I wouldn't say the outcome is guaranteed. There is a possibility of a second *nakhba*. Minister Avigdor Liebermann said he wants to expel all the Arabs, including the citizens of Israel. The danger is there.'

Rachel was urging him into his hat and coat for that night's outdoor rally. He complied, but went on talking. 'I've done three big biographical essays on Sharon. He is a very serious person. I know him well. He wants to destroy the Palestinian people. For this reason, he wants to destroy the Palestinian Authority and Yasser Arafat.'

Sharon was doing a thorough job of reducing the Palestinian Authority and Arafat to insignificance. Their institutions were being systematically dismantled. The Israeli army bombed their police stations, attacked their media centre, looted their statistics bureau and rendered their ministries impotent. Arafat himself was confined to his West Bank headquarters in Ramallah. The reason Sharon gave was that Arafat was responsible for attacks on Israelis. Arafat blamed Palestinian violence on the appalling and repressive conditions in the occupied territories. His rationale had a precedent. In 1945, the British High Commissioner had called Ben-Gurion to his headquarters on the Hill of Evil Counsel to protest against the murders of British soldiers by Jewish extremists. Ben-Gurion said that 'the Jewish Agency completely dissociated itself from the murderous attacks on Government and army establishments on Thursday night . . .' But Ben-Gurion blamed Jewish terrorism on 'the policy pursued in Palestine by His Majesty's Government on which the primary responsibility rests for the tragic situation created in the country, and which had led in recent weeks to bloodshed and innocent victims among Jews, Britons and others'. Arafat, who would soon die, might have been reading from Ben-Gurion's script.

After the Cleansing

Lydda lay ten miles south-east of Tel Aviv, but the two cities had spread and sprawled and swelled so that their outskirts were almost intertwined. The road from one to the other offered no relief from urban grit. You noticed two changes as you came into Lydda from Tel Aviv: its people looked poorer, and about a quarter of them were Arabs. A century ago, Lydda was an important link in the Jaffa to Jerusalem railway. In ancient times, it had changed hands among Canaanites, Israelites, Greeks, Arabs, Crusaders and Arabs again. For a few weeks in the summer of 1948, Lydda became an inland refuge for Arabs fleeing Jaffa and the coast, doubling its population to sixty thousand. The extra thirty thousand took shelter in mosques, churches, railway buildings and the army camp that the British had recently evacuated. In mid-July, a Haganah column under then Major Moshe Dayan entered Lydda. 'Moshe Dayan led a jeep commando column into the town of Lydda with rifles, Stens, and sub-machine guns blazing. It coursed through the main streets, blasting at everything that moved,' wrote the *New York Herald Tribune*'s correspondent, Kenneth Bilby. 'The corpses of Arab men, women, and even children were strewn about the streets in the wake of this ruthlessly brilliant charge.'

A young medical student at the American University of Beirut had just arrived to join his family in Lydda. Forty years later, he recalled the events in an interview published in *The Nation*. His older sister, the mother of six children, was suffering from typhoid. He went to the clinic, despite the curfew, to find medicine for her and remained to treat the wounded. He left when informed that his sister had died. 'Outside I saw terrible sights,' he remembered. 'Dozens of bodies lay in pools of blood, old and young had been shot. Among the dead, I recognized one elderly man, a neighbour who had a small falafel shop and who had never carried a gun. The Israelis were killing defenceless, unarmed people indiscriminately.' He went on,

> When I reached my sister's house, I found that they had already buried her body. Almost at once the shouting and gunfire arrived at our neighbourhood. My mother and the small children of my sister were very frightened. Everyone was ordered out of the house. Israeli soldiers banged at the door shouting, 'Get out! Go to King Abdallah!' We were herded like animals, rounded up and searched. You can't imagine the savagery with which people were treated. Everything was taken – watches, jewellery, wedding rings, wallets, gold. One young neighbour of ours, a man in his twenties, not more, Amin Hanhan, had secreted some money in his shirt to care for his family on the journey. The soldier who searched him demanded that he surrender the money, and he resisted. He was shot dead in front of us. One of his sisters, a young married woman, also a

neighbour of our family, was present. She saw her brother
shot dead before her eyes. She was so shocked that, as we
made our way toward the village of Bir Zeit, she died of
shock, exposure and lack of water.

The young physician would abandon medicine for politics
to restore his people to their homes in Lydda and the rest of
Palestine. Dr George Habash, a Greek Orthodox Christian,
became an Arab nationalist inspired by Gamal Abdel Nasser
and then the Marxist head of the Popular Front for the Liberation of Palestine. In the late 1960s and 1970s, PFLP commandos
crossed from Jordan and Lebanon to wreak havoc in Israel. His
spokesman, after a particularly brutal raid in which foreign
visitors and nuns were murdered, said, 'Palestine is not a tourist
attraction.' Habash himself remained sensitive to his people's
suffering under occupation and in the refugee camps, and his
loyalists were said to be among the bravest detainees in Israeli
prisons. When the Israelis assassinated his successor, Abu Ali
Mustafa, in the West Bank, the PFLP responded by killing
Tourism Minister Rehavam Ze'evi. The roots of the Israeli–
PFLP war went back to Lydda in 1948.

Tom Segev wrote in *1949: The First Israelis* that Yitzak Rabin
asked Ben-Gurion what should be done with the inhabitants of
Lydda and its sister village, Ramleh: 'According to him, Ben-
Gurion responded with a gesture which Rabin interpreted as
indicating expulsion. And that, he said, was what happened in
Lydda: the people were marched to the border. Ramleh learned
the lesson and its inhabitants agreed to leave of their own
accord, on condition that they be given vehicles to take them,
and this was done. These details were to be included in Rabin's
memoirs, but were barred from publication in Israel.' Dan
Kurtzner quoted direct from the diary in his biography, *Soldier
of Peace*. Rabin wrote, 'Ben-Gurion would repeat the question:
"What is to be done with the population?", waving his hand in
a gesture which said: "Drive them out!"'

Lydda's trail of tears to the Jordanian lines in the West Bank killed many of the weakest, particularly small children and the old. Palestinians would refer to it as the 'death march'. Israeli troops harassed them on the way, and the July heat intensified their thirst. When the UN mediator Count Folke Bernadotte found the survivors three months later in a camp in Ramallah, he wrote, 'I have made the acquaintance of a great many refugee camps, but never have I seen a more ghastly sight than that which met my eyes here at Ramallah.' Bernadotte had bravely resisted the German evacuation of Sweden's Jews during the Second World War, and he was sympathetic to Europe's Jewish refugees. He was nonetheless assassinated by Yitzak Shamir on 17 September 1948, a day after he proposed that the Lydda and Ramleh refugees return home and their villages become part of an Arab state.

Lydda's Arab railway employees lived in a separate cantonment and were permitted to remain to restart train services. Fouzi el-Asmar, whose father worked on the railways, wrote in his beautiful memoir, *To Be an Arab in Israel*, about the day the trains resumed operation. It was a Sunday, and the Israelis allowed Lydda's Christians to take the train to church. When the few Muslims still in the city shouted, 'Traitors!' at the Palestinian Christians, his father explained to him the principle of divide and rule. His first sight of the town since its evacuation confused him: 'Now there was not a soul in the whole of the desolate town. The shops were closed and the doors of the houses open. Our footsteps were the only sounds we heard, and for the first time I felt fear without being able to explain it. I asked myself time and time again, "Where are all the people who were here? So many Arabs had lived in these houses. Where are they?"' Later, the wife of his Uncle Elias told him of her forced march to Ramallah. 'It was a ten-hour walk, and we did not have water or food. Many died on the way. Abandoned children were seen wandering around crying. There were some who urinated and drank their urine. I felt that I could not go on, that my strength was gone and without the help of my son, I would have died on the way.' Fouzi Al-Asmar, who became a poet and wrote for Uri Avnery's *Haolam Hazeh*, scrounged a living picking cactus fruit to sell in Tel Aviv. It was in Tel Aviv's central market 'that I first heard the words "dirty Arab". I remember how much I was hurt. I left my stand and went to the public toilet and sat down and cried.' He was eleven. Twenty years later, he would be placed under administrative detention and go on hunger strike to demand that the government charge him and grant him a trial. His lawyer, who also went on hunger strike, was Sabry Jiryis. It was Jiryis whose wife died when the Palestine Research Centre was bombed during the Israeli occupation of Lebanon.

Lydda was strangely forlorn for a town beside prosperous Tel Aviv. Litter on the streets had been ignored by the municipality, but not by the wind that strewed it everywhere. What shrubs there were needed tending. Some shops were boarded and abandoned, as in the poorest neighbourhoods in the United States. Most of the Jewish population were from Morocco and other Arab countries. I was looking for the town's former chief engineer, Aref Muharib. He had worked for the Interior Ministry's building department, and he was going to explain how Israel's property laws worked. He lived in Shaneer, called locally the 'Arab ghetto'. It would not be difficult for me to know when I reached Shaneer, he told me over the telephone. It began where the paved roads ended. Aref Muharib lived in a small bungalow with his wife and two young sons. Like almost every other house in the ghetto, his was built illegally.

'I built this house in four days,' he said. 'It was very risky. We built it during a Jewish holiday in 1994.' He had to get it up and move in before the authorities, who rarely granted building permits to Arabs, knocked it down. He succeeded, and he taught other building contractors how to build before anyone noticed. 'When it's finished, they give up. If you live inside, they cannot destroy it – according to Israeli law. I feel I did something good to my community with this.'

The sitting-room carpet – woven into fields like those around Lydda before 1948, with an old shepherd beside his flock and birds hovering between the pine trees – was as vivid as the neighbourhood was drab. Outside were neither meadows nor sheep, only miles of urban neglect. Muharib and his wife laid a coffee pot, cups, dates, nuts and pretzels on a coffee table. During the long, drizzly afternoon, I was one of many guests. His nieces came to visit, as did a few neighbours. Muharib had the bearing of a man respected in his community, a modest alderman who had their trust. He sat in a stuffed chair. While he spoke, the wind howled and blew eucalyptus leaves against the window. He offered me a Time cigarette and lit one for himself.

He said that of Lydda's 70,000 people, 22,000 were Arabs – almost as many as the 30,000 of 1948. Muharib's family were not from Lydda, although he had been born there in 1959. His father came from Bassa, later Netanya, in the Galilee. In 1948, his father's family fled from the Israeli army to Jaljulia, then under King Abdallah's Arab Legion. Jaljulia was part of the Triangle – Jaljulia, Taibeh and Barqa – that Abdallah ceded to Israel in 1949. 'In 1949, my parents came under Israeli control. They tried to move them. The agreement with Abdallah said the residents can stay, but they were not residents. Some of them went to Qalqilya. My father refused, and they put him in a car and threw him beyond the border. He came back illegally and hid, as did my uncle. After the war finished and the situation was calm, they went to the military ruler and asked to go back to their house in Bassa.' The house in Bassa was no more. The family petitioned for the restoration of their land, but as 'present absentees' they had no rights before the court. They were offered land in Lydda. 'They gave them 10 per cent of what they had. It was one dunum for every ten dunums lost.' A dunum, the standard unit of land measurement from Ottoman times, was about a quarter of an acre. He was granted thirteen dunums that had been stolen from other Arabs. Did he feel guilt?

'All the time, my father said, and I say, that if they come back, we'll just give it back to them as a gift. At the time, taking another Arab's land hurt.'

Who lived in Lydda? Muharib said that, as well as railway workers, the government had allowed hospital staff to remain. The few Arabs left in Lydda in 1948 were concentrated in one corner of town. 'In this place, there were five or six families. The Arabs had gone from thirty thousand to one thousand. The soldiers came. There was looting everywhere. The city was stripped. In 1950, I think, they brought newcomers. They ran away, because it was scary. They were Oriental Jews. So, the Israeli authorities brought to Lydda Arabs who had stayed in places where Israel didn't want them. A big group came from Majdal. The Jewish didn't like to be here, so it was empty. By the mid-1950s, more Jewish were coming and it became a Jewish city. From that time, they made a huge effort to destroy any symbol that said this city was empty. They destroyed the Arab houses. By the 1970s, the Arabs were a small minority. People started to immigrate from the Negev – Bedouin looking for jobs. It became a retail outlet for Tel Aviv. There are cheaper shops here, telephone and computer outlets. Until now, this immigration is going on.' That immigration was increasing the Arab numbers in Lydda, even as the Jewish population remained static. While the state focused on settling the West Bank, parts of Israel were becoming Arab again.

Muharib stood when his little boys came in. He held their hands and introduced two shy brothers, three-year-old Bashar in pyjamas and Mohammed, eight, in jeans. The boys were polite and quiet, not quite understanding their father's English. When they eyed the pretzels, he told them to wait until dinner. Their mother called from the kitchen, and they disappeared.

He said Mohammed was studying at a local primary school, one of five in Lydda. But there was only one secondary for both Lydda and Ramleh. He himself had gone to Haifa for his secondary education at a Greek Orthodox high school. Afterwards, he took his B.Sc. in engineering at the Haifa Technion. Also called the Haifa Institute of Technology, it had been founded in 1924 and was one of the best in Israel. Muharib worked as a civil engineer and then for the Interior Ministry dealing with building laws. 'I quit in 1996 because I felt they used me. I couldn't change the situation. Their policy is bad. They discussed planning, and I couldn't change it. They tried to use me to justify the policy, because I'm Arab. So, I quit. Also, I believed I would do better privately. And I was right.' As a private contractor, he was making more money building houses, for Jews and Arabs, than he had as a civil servant.

I asked why the roads in this part of Lydda were unpaved. 'There is discrimination against the Arab. This city is ruled by the Jewish community. It's worse inside the mixed cities: Ramleh, Jaffa, Haifa, Acre and Lydda. Arabs in the mixed cities have two kinds of discrimination: from the central authorities and from the local authorities. It makes the situation worse than in the Arab towns. If I lived in Taibeh, for example, I would face only the one. Here, the city does nothing. Even the road you see, we did it by ourselves.' The road had been levelled and packed down, but the rain was even then turning it to mud. The asphalt streets were in the Jewish neighbourhoods. 'There is no garbage collection. The sewers we did ourselves. A few years ago, there were no sewers. Four or five years ago, our project connected it to the city sewer network. They didn't like it, but we did it.'

As if to emphasize his point, the electricity went off all over Shaneer. The sky was already dark with clouds, and rain pounded the roof. The only light in the sitting room glowed at the tip of his cigarette. Muharib did not comment on the chronic power cuts. He inhaled the tobacco smoke and said, 'They want to get us out of Lydda.' Where did they want him to go? 'The Triangle.' Wasn't that the place his father had been expelled from? 'Yes. The Israelis see us as trouble-makers. They would rather we just disappear from here. They started a policy in the mid-1970s, when the Arabs stopped being a very little minority. So, in the mid-70s, they decided on a strategy to make life in the Arab neighbourhoods very tough. They stopped maintaining the streets. In Lydda, it's very extreme, very obvious. That's why the situation here is the worst. They thought, "If you make their lives hard, they will go away." The result was the opposite. Living here is cheap. Lots of people from the south came, because it's cheap. More and more Arabs came.'

Had any Arabs moved from Lydda to the Triangle? 'Very few. Once, the local authority here gave a grant. If you sell your house and go to the Triangle, they gave you $10,000. There was no legal way not to let the Arabs live here. Contractors who built the houses don't sell to Arabs the first time. An American company, Coldwell Banker, is a realtor here. But after the first sale, you can buy them second-hand. When an Arab buys, prices go down. Jews don't want to live near Arabs, because they are racist. Jewish settlers in the West Bank go to live between the Arabs. Here, they don't want to be near them.'

He thought Israeli Jews were afraid: 'The Jewish community here is struggling to keep this place Jewish. They don't have the money to move. House prices went down 50 per cent. So, they talk about bringing Jews here to solve their problem. All the time, they talk about Arabs building here. Every Arab house is illegal. So, in the last few years, illegal houses are 100 per cent of what was built.'

Were the Israelis trying to preserve the Jewish majority in Lydda? 'They send more Jewish newcomers,' he said. 'They cannot do anything. They cannot put people in cars and send them away. Beginning in the mid-nineties, Jewish people started running away from Lydda. At that time, two cities were built near Lydda – Modi'in two kilometres to the east and Shoham. The richer people left. Every Jew who stayed feels he's stuck here. The situation of this city is very bad. There is a lot of crime, mainly in the Arab neighbourhoods. There are no jobs. Unemployment is estimated at 60 per cent among the Arabs here. Some people are talking about Lydda as an Arab city again. There is drug dealing. When you were coming here, you saw taxis. Most of them are carrying drug consumers. At night, the shooting here is more than in the West Bank. The police ignore the Arab neighbourhoods. It is more convenient for the police if drug dealing and crime stay in the Arab neighbourhoods. It's like America. If crime spills out to the Jewish neighbourhoods, they act.'

Why did he stay and raise children in this atmosphere? 'Sometimes, I think . . .,' he paused, as if he didn't want to finish the sentence, then went on, 'to live in another place. It is very hard for the children, but it's not so bad. There are a lot of good people here. But you get tired of living in this kind of neighbourhood with no streets, nothing.'

Lydda looked dead on my drive in. What was there to do in the evenings or with the children? He said there was one community swimming pool that Jews and Arabs used in the summer. There was not much else. 'In this city, we don't have a cinema. We don't have restaurants at night. After nine o'clock at night, you see only a kiosk selling cigarettes. There is no city centre. It's not a city. It's not even a village. If you want to go to a restaurant or a cinema, you don't do it here. When I was a kid, there were five cinemas.' The night before, he and his wife had gone out to a restaurant for dinner – in Jaffa.

'I don't belong to any party,' he said. 'I run a struggle against the city council about building rights. I had a group here that helps people whose houses are destroyed. Two times we built houses again when the city destroyed them. The first time was in 1988, when I organized this group. After they demolished the house, we built it again. And they didn't touch it. The other time we did it, in 1999, they shot at us. They shot me with rubber bullets. Fifteen of us were shot. One Arab Knesset member, Azmi Bishara, was shot too. We built the house again, and they didn't touch it. We broke that policy. It is your basic right to have a house. After that, the Arabs aren't afraid any more.'

Lydda, or Lod, was next to Israel's international airport named for David Ben-Gurion. Planes landing at night woke people up. The airport was a gateway for drugs that Muharib said came from Egypt and Lebanon. 'There is cooperation among Arab and Jewish drug dealers and the police. I had a big fight with the police. One year ago, our group decided we cannot fix this place without getting rid of the drugs. We don't have addicts in this place, maybe five. But we have maybe fifty drug dealers here. We decided to get rid of them. We gathered about four hundred people for a meeting that took a decision.' The residents decided to close the neighbourhood to people from Tel Aviv coming to buy heroin and cannabis. 'We made road-blocks. If he is resident or visiting here, okay. If he is a drug customer, we don't let him in.' In a few days, they had prevented more than three hundred cars from coming in to buy drugs. 'They used to sell about twelve thousand *jura'a* – units – of drugs a day. The first day, it was down to less than one thousand. In a few days, all of them closed down.' He cracked a peanut shell to punctuate their triumph, but then he told the rest of the story. It did not have a happy ending.

After that, the police became involved. 'It's not legal, this thing. So, the police invited us, all the group. They asked us to stop this action. We refused. The other day, they arrested a few of our people. We heard from the drug dealers that the police contacted them indirectly, so they can keep dealing. So, I know now that I'm not facing the drug dealers. I'm facing the Israeli police. After that, the police came to my house. They knocked on the door. They sat here, where you're sitting.' I wondered whether he had given them coffee and sweets, as he did his other guests. He said that police intelligence officers ordered him to leave policing the drug trade to them. 'We were stronger than the drug dealers, but when they knew the police were on their side, they decided to break us. Ten or so of them gathered and said we have to fight back. Together. Before, they were separate. They opened again in May 2000. They asked for a meeting with us. At that meeting, I knew we had lost the war, because they were united.'

I told him a similar story about east Los Angeles, where a Jesuit priest – Fr Greg Boyle, who was my cousin by marriage – worked with the local community to put a stop to drug dealing. Residents set up similar roadblocks. Beverly Hills limousines confronted signs saying, 'If you came here to buy drugs, go home.' Someone took video pictures of the buyers to give to the local media. The mainly Latino community's success lasted until the organizer's house was firebombed.

Muharib said Lydda was not like Los Angeles. 'In Los Angeles, this is a deteriorated society. There is drug dealing. There is prostitution. But the society here is not deteriorated. We still have families. Social relations are good. We are not talking about a situation where society has collapsed. There is no prostitution. There are only drugs and violence connected with drugs. Other sides of society are normal. We are poor, but not so poor. Sometimes you feel there is a hidden hand that wants this society to collapse. You never have proof, but you feel it. This is a Muslim society, and religion protects them.'

He became philosophical, and his words hinted that there was no peaceful compromise between the two peoples of Israel and Palestine. 'We don't feel that the Jewish community is superior. Mostly, we feel we are better than them. Here, we feel we have a culture. We are living in a situation. They are stronger than we are, but we never give up. This situation will be fixed. It will not stay like this. They never convinced us that their culture is better. I don't think they have solid values like other communities. Sometimes you make a culture and it's shining, but something inside is not right. I can give you an example. I can take you to a drug dealer's house and show you a beautiful family and house, but this thing is not right. The basic thing is wrong. I think this culture is the same. It's not enough to build a culture with aspects you see from the outside. The basic thing is not good – to come from the other and then to build democracy and culture. They stole something, and this culture is based on an illegal culture. They have nice restaurants, streets and buildings, but this is not the most important thing. I think this is what our struggle is all about.'

The historian Dee Brown wrote that Native Americans saw the white man as a passing phenomenon and believed the land would revert to what it was for them to dwell in freely again. It was perhaps a dream, like Muharib's. 'To be an Arab in this country is not easy. You believe this is fake. This thing has to be changed. As a human being, I cannot agree with the injustice. But you see the discrimination everywhere, and you cannot agree with it.'

Wasn't it better to live as an Arab citizen of Israel than as a Palestinian refugee in the Arab countries? 'People in Lebanon and Syria are, I think, the worst off. People in Israel are in the best situation. But the Israeli people want people to conclude that Israel is good – to prove that Israeli society is better. First, we are not refugees. The Jewish people are refugees. I'm living on land that my father gave me. I'm not looking for legitimacy from Israel. Israel is asking me for legitimacy. I have the right to be here. Israel doesn't have that feeling. Israel all the time wants us to recognize it. They want us to say they were right in 1948. I'm ready to compromise on everything, but not to cancel myself. If we live well here, it's not because Israel wants us to. It's in spite of their desire. It's because they don't want us to be here. The refugees are still Arabs in an Arab country, but we are still residents in our homeland. I don't feel a minority here. If I open the television, I see twenty Arabic stations and one in Hebrew. We live in an Arab ocean. Maybe the Jewish people feel a minority here. I think there is something wrong with their culture. It may seem racist, but I'm not talking about Jewish – I'm talking about Israel. It's fake. It's not ugly in buildings, but ugly in values. They have Jewish and goy. This is a very strong idea. These are their borders. Jewish and goy. In my culture, this is not strong. You can live with the other. You can accept his values. You see this mixed city. There is no reason I don't have a street to get to my house. I'm not fighting this state. I'm not an enemy. I'm a citizen. I pay taxes. It's a matter of money. Not a matter of ideology.'

When I left, Muharib came outside to show me a route to the highway that avoided the worst of the mud and holes. I got lost, and some kids helped me out of the mud. They spoke Arabic, but they could have been Jewish or Arab. I wondered if the day would come when it wouldn't matter.

ELEVEN

The North

'Their fidelity, often unreasoning and ill-tempered, was
always sincere. "The Galileans," according to the
Talmud, "were more anxious for honour than for
money; the contrary was true of Judaea." For this cause
also our Lord chose His friends from the people; and it
was *not* a Galilean who betrayed Him.'
REVEREND GEORGE ADAM SMITH
The Historical Geography of the Holy Land (1894)

Baring All For Strangers

GABY ALDOR TOOK ME north to Ein Hod in search of the
Arab actress Rauda Saliman's Uncle Fawzi, the farmer who
laboured on what had been his land. We could not call ahead,
because the old man had no telephone. The farm was in a valley
near the coast road south of Haifa. It was not impressive, many
acres of scrub, some eucalyptus and a barn. But for a Chihuahua
puppy which snapped defiantly when we got out of the car, the
place was deserted. We looked in the barn, where a partitioned
corner functioned as a bedroom. A man's clothes were neatly
stacked on shelves. We searched the fields. A Chinese farm
worker, who spoke neither Hebrew nor English, somehow convinced us that Fawzi had left for a few days. The last thing we
saw was the cooking stove on which Fawzi must have made
coffee for himself and his employer from Yemen, as Rauda had
done in the play. '"Go to Yemen and take all the land I had
there. I give it to you as a present." And we laughed, and I
prepared us another cup of coffee.'

It was almost dark when we reached the hilltop above the

384

Bay of Acre. Two promontories marked its boundaries, Haifa in the south and Acre in the north. The annual theatre festival had closed Acre to cars, so we parked and took a shuttle bus to Acre's Crusader castle. On board, two teenage Jewish girls – faces tattooed in washable blue and midriffs wobbling like rice pudding – cooed in Hebrew at a Palestinian baby. Israel seemed almost like a normal country at such moments.

We alighted near the fortress, where open white tents, as at a medieval joust, hawked sandwiches, souvenir clothes, glass-bead necklaces, shoes, popcorn and fortune telling. The canvas arcade led to a breach in the castle walls. Acre's castle was in the throes of restoration. Concrete appendages had been added to some of the old stone houses, and the streets were slowly being swept clean and made quaint and sterile for the American tourists who were not coming anyway. Within the formidable walls, Teutonic Knights had held out longer than any other Crusaders against the combined forces of Islam and the natives of Palestine – Muslims, Christians and Jews – who had tired of the foreign presence. The Knights returned to Europe, especially to Poland and Germany, and became part of the history of European anti-Semitism. The citadel they left behind was as formidable as any in the Mediterranean with its vast chambers and forbidding ramparts. It survived sieges by Richard the Lionheart in 1191 and Napoleon in 1799. Part of it became a prison in which, famously, the British interned Jewish 'terrorists' and from which many escaped. When the British left, the Israeli government turned the prison into a mental asylum (anyone who fought against Israel must have been mad).

Acre castle's last indignity had been its transformation into a museum and heritage centre. The majority of Acre's populace were Jewish and lived outside the city walls. The old city, the original seaside town in and around the fortress, remained Arab. Its native shopkeepers sold tat, including Chinese-made 'I ♥ Israel' T-shirts, to Israelis and the occasional foreigner. From rows of identical outdoor restaurants with plastic garden chairs and tables, they served inedible Palestinian food that would have shamed their mothers. Most of the Arab boys cut their hair short to look like Israelis on military service. They swaggered like America's ghetto elite, young gang bangers blasting canned music – Arabic, Hebrew and rap – so loud from their shops and their cars that ancient stones vibrated and old ears throbbed. Strings of Christmas lights above lent a festive look to the night. Promenading families – indistinguishable from one another by race or religion – strolled past the useless shops and foul eateries and the make-believe world of Arab–Israeli theatre.

Theatrical folk were converging for plays, concerts, recitals, lectures and readings in little corners where Templars had fought Christendom's final battles to hold onto the Levant. Palestinian boys sat in front of their fathers' shops, luring visitors to buy. On a bench outside one café, several policemen were eating kebabs. 'It's a good thing to see policemen sitting down,' Gaby said. 'That's how I like to see them.'

A dozen doors within a walled garden led to secret alcoves, where the knights once lived or stored their armour and victuals. The vaults had since become merchants' warehouses and, for the festival, retreats for various theatre companies. The Jaffa Arabic-Hebrew Theatre's supper club was done up like the Coconut Grove. Golden palm trees adorned a makeshift stage, and a big piano dominated the room. Gaby's Arab and Jewish troupe hugged her and took us to a table. A three-piece band – Wisam Aram on tambourine, Elias Habib on drum and Nazar Francis on *aoud* – played Arabic music. Apart from a few traditional singers like Feyrouz and Oum Kalsoum, Arabic rhythms were too repetitive to my ear. The young men were good musicians, but the dirge went on and on. As it did, I needed more and more to drink. I was hoping they would finish, until an American woman mounted the stage. That was when I yearned for the band to return. She said, 'Jazz is the music of freedom. It is the music that is banned by repressive regimes.' I was wondering why she had brought up jazz. The three Arab youths had not been playing jazz, and jazz was not banned. I'd heard it played in Israel, Syria, Jordan, Lebanon and Iraq.

Maybe it was banned in Saudi Arabia, but then most things were. Before we could figure out what she meant, she introduced another American woman named Leslie. Oozing the inexplicable overconfidence of the American female abroad, she quoted Elie Wiesel. Gaby whispered, although everyone else heard her, 'How embarrassing.' If there was one thing most Israelis could not bear, it was being lectured to by Americans on the Holocaust.

Leslie became, if anything, more embarrassing. 'I live on Hudson Street in New York,' she said. 'On 11 September, I was in a bar on Hudson Street. Someone came into the bar and said, "Why are you still open? You should be with your families." And the bartender said, "But this is our family, and we will remain open." And I hope you'll remain open too.' How could they close? A country isn't a bar. If the Bosnians and Lebanese remained open for years of disruptive civil war, why would Israel consider shutting down for a few suicide bombers?

Where was the Arabic band? I prayed for their return. Leslie prolonged her pep talk to the Israelis on terrorism that was – as she saw it – similar in its little way to the big terror that struck America. At long last, she introduced an American guy named Arnie Lawrence. Sporting a western hat with a lion of Judah pin, a huge western cow's-head belt buckle and khaki workshirt, Arnie Lawrence was the perfect 1960s country star. He reminded me of one of my favourites, Kinki Friedman of Kinki Friedman and the Texas Jewboys. But he was not a country singer. He played saxophone with the Arab band, and he wasn't bad. In fact, when the boys played with him, they weren't bad either. Better than the women's homilies. They played a few sets that brought the room back to life, but Leslie restored the sepulchral mood. She sympathized with the 'children in this part of the world' and their struggle with psychological effects of terror. No one could have misjudged an audience more. The Jaffa Arabic-Hebrew Theatre was not part of the war on terror. Its role was to break down the prejudices that made terror inevitable. The troupe and their fans had come to think about things other than American propaganda. The next speaker did not disappoint.

He was a writer, whose Hebrew novels – Gaby told me – were beautiful. His name was Salman Natour, and he was an Arab about my age. Gaby said he was a Druze, once a communist and still a firebrand irritant to the government. Natour came onto the stage like a man who had entered the room by mistake. He could have been a truck driver or factory foreman, who could handle himself in a fight. Gaby translated his sonorous Hebrew for me.

'I'm proud of the normality of the Middle East,' he said. 'I wrote a book about Beisan, which is 75 per cent Moroccan Jewish, people I call Arab Jews.' Beisan had been the Arab village of Beit Shan until 1948, when its people were expelled. In 1974, Palestinian commandos from Lebanon staged a savage terrorist attack there. Its name resonated with Arabs and Israelis, although for different tragedies. 'Ten years ago, I was told that Arab Jews there hated Arabs. It is not true. They don't hate the Arabs, and they don't hate Arab culture. There is a difference between what you sing in the bathroom and what you sing in the living room. The song of the bathroom is the true music.' When the Ashkenazim were not listening, he said, the Moroccans sang in Arabic. As an Arab among them, he had felt no race hatred. He told us about one Jewish woman from Beisan, who was killed when Arab youths stoned her car. He talked as well about two other women, Ilham and Esther. Ilham was an Arab, and Esther was Jewish. They were both twenty-one, and they were both about to be married. They did not know each other. But they died on the same day, a week before their weddings. 'I wrote a story about the childhoods of these two girls who were killed before they could become brides. The story was "A Marriage in the Sky". I tried to tell the story to the girls' mothers, but neither mother wanted to hear the story of the other. But the moment Esther's mother listened to me, she spoke differently about the other mother.' Finally, the two women met. Afterwards, neither mother allowed her daughter's

death to be used for propaganda. The tragedies were personal.
The point was not that Palestinians murdered Israeli brides or
that settlers did the same to Arab girls. The injustice was that
any girl should be murdered for politics.

Outdoors, in a Tuscan piazza bounded by two-storey stone
houses, a play called *The Dresses* was about to begin. Gaby and
I found chairs at the edge, beside a house whose Arab family
watched from the balcony. The cast was one actor, Ghida Adon,
who played different Palestinian women: one driven from her
village in 1948; one who had gone insane; a girl in Beirut's
Shatila refugee camp who had hijacked an airplane and languished in prison; and that most tragic of all heroines, a woman
in love. Each dress she wore – the villager's embroidered black
gown, the refugee's rough cotton shift, the lover's gown –
defined the character and became the story. Ghida spoke in the
northern Palestinian accent of the Galilee, preserved still by
refugees in Lebanon. Not all her Israeli audience would have
understood the words, but her body did most of the talking.
She could have mimed the whole play, and we would have
understood. The motifs were familiar – flight, exile, fear, despair
– to everyone there. It was a story of exilic Palestine – not her
Palestine of the minority who stayed. The audience went silent
when she left the stage. It took time, perhaps a minute, to absorb
what she had done. Then all the Israeli Jews and Arabs, even
the children on their balconies, were out of their seats cheering.
It was real make-believe.

It was worth making believe, acting out the hatreds and confusion and torment and resentment that lurked in all hearts,
stating the obvious that was not spoken in polite encounters in
the more unreal world offstage. The truth was that the people
in the audience were at war with one other. An actor could
scream it from the stage in the middle of a plaza, where those
watching were the actor's neighbours and enemies. That audience did not want war. The Israelis watching Ghida Adon had
long ago admitted that crimes were committed, that wrongs
were done and that amends should be made. They did not want

to hate or to oppress. They wanted to live without harming or being harmed. The Arabs there, although in their country, had relations in Lebanon or Syria – cousins, aunts or brothers who had escaped the war or who happened to be away when the fighting began. The exiles were part of the patrimony, and they were missed. But even the most conscientious of the Israelis in the audience did not want them back from their wretched refugee camps, could not imagine being swamped by an Arab majority and would not abandon their self-government as Jews. It was an impossible dilemma, and both sides were aware of it – even the best and most loving among them. If there was catharsis that night, it did not end the tragedy.

The beautiful Arab actress who played a young woman captured, tortured and raped by Israeli soldiers screamed the torment of all Arab women who lost their home, who'd been sent into exile, who saw their men's manhood robbed by the armed usurper, who had suffered and who continued to endure. Ghida Adon relived her people's and her own anguish on a wooden platform outdoors in the centre of old Acre. For an Arab woman to act in public, to change her dresses and to bare her soul in front of strangers would have been impossible in the traditional Arab society that the Israelis swept away in 1948. The old men in the pictures on the wall would never have allowed it. That too was the Palestinian Arab tragedy. Not all that was removed was good, and not all that came was bad.

In Jaffa, another Arab woman had enacted the drama of her Uncle Fawzi. It was a tale anyone could understand. After I saw that play, Rauda Saliman told me another story. It was about her life rather than her uncle's. Her family and society, itself beset by the dominant society around it, had conspired to keep her in her place as they saw it. Rauda's suffering derived from neither loss of land nor citizenship as a non-Jew in the Jewish State. Her husband, with whom she had no children, had taken a second wife. Her destiny, as her husband saw it, was to remain at home with him no matter whom else he married. If the younger woman had children and Rauda did not, her life in the house would be intolerable. Rauda went to court to request a divorce, and her own family testified against her. Duty to husband and father required her to accept the new wife, but Rauda had come too far. She had worked in a modern world. She had read too much. She could not go back, and the past would not let go. There were many plays to be written, many tragedies and many prisons.

That night, Israeli soldiers invaded northern Gaza with tanks. They killed six Palestinians and wounded six others. The assault followed an attack by Hamas militants, who shot and killed two Israeli settlers. Vengeance had been as swift as in Joshua's time.

An Abnormal City

Gaby returned to Jaffa, and I retrieved my Dalla rent-a-car for the drive to Haifa. Theodor Herzl had declared Haifa a 'city of the future', perhaps because it did not have much of a past. The British constructed its port, over the resistance of the sheikhs of Acre, long after Herzl's death. As the sheikhs feared, Haifa eclipsed its older northern rival and Jaffa as well. Its development, even as a Jewish city, had little to do with Zionism. The first Jews to move outside the city walls were Orientals who built houses south-west of the town walls in the late eighteenth century. Geography rather than architecture accounted for Haifa's charm. Terrace upon terrace of banal white houses ascended from the Mediterranean through groves of umbrella pine to the summit of Mount Carmel. The Levant presented no more magnificent view than from Carmel north along the shore to Acre and Lebanon.

'Happy peoples are like innocent women,' the writer said. 'They have no past.' He was talking about Haifa. 'That is why she is a normal city. She has no past.' Sami Michael had fled to Haifa from Iraq, not because he was Jewish but because the Iraqi government of 1948 was planning to arrest him for being a communist. His flight took him first to Iran, where he lived for a year. Because the Shah's Iran was no more hospitable to communists than Iraq was, Iran's Communist Party, the Tudeh, helped him to reach Israel. When he arrived, Sami Michael was twenty-three years old. A tall, dark-skinned lad with only a year of university behind him, he was drafted into the new Israeli army. He still spoke Arabic. When he got out, he worked for the Israeli Agriculture Ministry as a hydrologist. It took him six years after he got the job to qualify by correspondence. 'I started to work in the hydrology department without knowing anything,' he admitted. He said he worked for twenty-five years in the field, 'body work, not mind work', every morning. At night, he wrote.

His second wife, Rahel, was away, and Michael took me into his kitchen. Did I want coffee? More importantly, did I want Turkish coffee? He pulled down a brass pot and set it on the fire. While he stirred the coffee powder, I commented on his view from Mount Carmel. 'Mount Carmel?' he asked, smiling. 'In Israel, they call it a mountain. It's a hill.' Sami Michael – Michael was pronounced the Arabic and Hebrew way, Mikha-el – had the healthy look of an outdoorsman rather than a writer. His blue plaid shirt gave the impression he'd been chopping firewood. A bald head and professorial glasses lent him a kindly, avuncular look. I felt I could ask him for advice on my love life, and he would not put me wrong.

'I am sure normal people built Haifa,' he said. 'The first mayor was Arab. He was accepted even by the Jews. Arabs and Jews, like the religious and the secular, live together here really peacefully. There's no tension. You can go to the Arab part and feel at home. Where we are here, Arabs live among us.' His flat was in a new apartment block with huge windows over the Mediterranean. The building, like the neighbourhood, had a mixture of Arabs and Jews. 'You can travel through the most religious parts of Haifa in your car on Shabat without any problem,' he said. In Jerusalem's Mea Shearim, religious Jews hurled stones at any car they caught driving on Shabat. 'Maybe it's the sea, the mountain and the greenery.' Haifa's hills opened to the sea and all its influences. Jerusalem's Arab and Jewish ghettoes enclosed themselves in stone and opened their doors and their minds to nothing. In Israel, Haifa's normality was anything but normal.

Russians were adding to Haifa's diversity. In parts of the city, Russian shop signs outnumbered those in Hebrew and Arabic. 'The Russian streets are also the Arab streets,' Michael said. 'They live peacefully together, which means Russians kill Russians and Arabs kill Arabs.'

Michael wrote about Arabs, Jews, Sephardim, Ashkenazim and Russians in his novels, children's books and plays. His first novel, *All Men are Equal, but (Some are More)*, appeared in 1974. Highly praised for his Hebrew style, Michael wrote in Arabic when he arrived in 1949. 'It was only after twenty-five years that I published my first novel in Hebrew. I started to write in Hebrew when I learned to think in Hebrew, to dream in Hebrew and to love in Hebrew.' His degree from Haifa University was in Arabic literature rather than Hebrew, and I asked him why he didn't write novels in Arabic. 'Who would read me in Arabic?' he asked. The Arab states would undoubtedly ban him as an Israeli and a communist, and most Arab publishing houses didn't pay royalties anyway.

Growing up in Baghdad in the 1930s, he had studied Hebrew for Torah class until he was thirteen. 'In Baghdad,' he said, 'no one spoke Hebrew.' He was suspicious of the Baghdad Zionists whose propaganda for a Hebrew nation repelled him. He had a love for the Baghdad he remembered. His Baghdad had vanished, abracadabra, long before. 'The Jewish community in Iraq is the most ancient in the world,' he said. 'Nebuchadnezzar took the elite of Jerusalem's Jews to Babylon, not as slaves, but to help him build the empire. They were especially important in finance and so on. We felt we had more time there than the Arabs – thirteen centuries. Our Arabic is spoken with Hebrew, Chaldean, Turkish, Indian and English words. The Muslims spoke the Arabic of the Saudis. Many waves of cholera epidemics killed the Muslims. Jews and Christians had better conditions and left the city during plagues. Generations of Muslims died and were replaced by waves of Bedouin. Our Arabic was more ancient than the Arabs'.'

The first return to Palestine came when Persia conquered Jerusalem and invited the Jews back. 'Only the *meshugga'im* came back,' he said. *Meshugga'im* was the Hebrew plural of the Yiddish word for lunatic. 'Babylon was richer. Who comes from the US and Britain to Israel? It's the same thing. At the beginning of the last century, the British Empire occupied Iraq. The Zionist movement gave a choice, and the choice of our fathers was to be in Iraq. The Zionist movement in Iraq was very weak and died by itself. The government didn't even feel the need to ban it. The Second World War started, and there was anti-Semitic propaganda in Iraq. They hated Britain as the occupier of Iraq. The Zionists leaned towards Britain. Through that, they began to hate Jews. It started in 1936 and '37. The mufti fled to Baghdad. He did a good job inflaming anti-Jewish feeling. Young Jews asked what they were going to do. Some became Zionists. Most came to the decision they were still Iraqis.'

Judaism's ancient roots in Babylonia made its Jews what Michael called 'Iraqi Iraqis'. He said, 'We spoke Arabic. We lived in an Arabic way. We dreamed in Arabic. It was a special situation when the Zionist movement became allied to the government. The communist Jews became enemies. Until 1947, there was no law forbidding the Zionist movement.' The Communist Party, however, was outlawed. The worst period was during the army coup of 1941 that made Rashid Ali Gailani prime minister. The putschists asked for German help to expel Britain. Iraqis took revenge on those, including the Zionists, who had collaborated with the British occupier. 'It ended in a pogrom,' he remembered. 'Nearly two or three hundred Jews died. I was outdoors when it happened, when they killed Jews in the streets. Since I was black, they thought I was a Muslim and no one touched me. They entered homes. They raped women. They looted stores. It went on for one night and a whole day. They looted, raped and burned the poor part of the Jewish community. The better-to-do Jews were defended by the Iraqi army. I think this is why the rich and the middle-class Jews became communists and the poor were influenced by the Zionists.' He said that, after the British returned and restored order, the Zionists were afraid to leave their neighbourhoods. 'Because of that, they did not know anything about the Middle East.' I asked how communist and Zionist Jews saw each other. 'We didn't fight each other,' he said, 'like the communists and Zionists in Europe.'

Despite the 1941 pogrom, he said, most Jews remained in Iraq. Those who opposed the government, like Sami Michael, found allies among the Arabs. 'I was sitting in a café,' he said. 'The waiter came and said the café was encircled by the police. He defended me and gave me the opportunity to jump over the wall. People saw the communists as heroes. The cry "I'm a communist and I'm in danger" was enough for everyone to help you.'

Baghdad at the time was 20 per cent Jewish. 'We had a financial and intellectual stamp on Baghdad,' he said. 'The banks closed on Shabat, not on Fridays. This situation continued until 1947. Everything changed for the worse for the Jewish community when the United Nations voted to divide Palestine and build a Jewish State. For the first time, the Zionist movement was regarded as an enemy and a law was passed against the Zionists.'

His father had been a wealthy textiles importer. The family lived near Bab Sharki, the eastern gate, in a quarter called Bataween. He had loved Bataween. Baghdad's richer Jews were, he said, secular – as were most Christians and Muslims. Baghdad had only one Yeshiva for 120,000 Jews, and Bataween had no synagogue. It did have, he said, thousands of beautiful villas. He sounded wistful. I had been to Bab Sharki, I told him. Haifa looked better to me. 'Okay,' he said, 'I have the sea.' Would he go back to Baghdad? 'I am afraid,' he said. 'If you love something and you go back, you want to see it with the people you knew. All of my Arab comrades were killed, in the prisons, in the wars. It would have no meaning without my friends.'

Israel's creation at the expense of Palestine's Arabs in 1948 made Jewish life in much of the Arab world untenable. Zionists claimed to represent all Jews everywhere, something many Jews of the Diaspora rejected. Arab leaders, stung by defeat in Palestine, took the Zionists at their word and made scapegoats of the Jews in their midst. 'After 1948,' Michael said, 'Jewish existence became impossible in the Arab countries. After the defeat of the Arab armies, the only revenge they could have was against their Jewish communities. They expelled Iraqi Jews from their professions. The newspapers published atrocious propaganda. The first Jew hanged in Baghdad was named Adas. He was a millionaire, neither a communist nor a Zionist. It was as if to say to the Jews, "We do not want Jews here who are not even communists or Zionists." The existence of the Jewish community was in danger. They filled the prisons. I think the same thing happened in other Arab countries. We became a part of Israel, whether we wanted it or not.'

For the Iraqi Jews who remained after 1948, life grew worse. Bombs planted by Zionist agents, as in Cairo, led to a reaction against them. Then, under secret arrangements between Israel and senior Iraqi politicians, Jews were flown out in their thousands to Israel. When the Baath Party took power in 1963, one of its first actions was to hang two Iraqi Jews on dubious charges of subversion. By then, only a few hundred remained. 'Nearly all of the Iraqi Jews came here,' he said. A few of the richest, like the Sassoons and Saatchis, had already moved to Britain.

'The Zionists planned to bring ten or twenty thousand Iraqi Jews here, no more. That was what Ben-Gurion told the Zionist organizers here. He told them he didn't want a flood of Iraqis here, because they look and talk like Arabs. But there was a deluge. Only 10 per cent stayed. Another 2 or 3 per cent went on to England, Canada, France and the US.' His own family emigrated after he did. His father, mother, five brothers and three sisters came to live in Ramat Gan near Tel Aviv. His father died there aged ninety-two, but his mother was still alive. He said she was one hundred years old.

Even the wealthiest Iraqi Jews suffered financially when they left. 'Most smuggled money here through the Iraqi government and the Israeli government,' he said. 'The Iraqi government took their fortunes illegally. The Israeli government did it legally. It took a 40 per cent tax to allow money in. The worst thing was that they said one Iraqi dinar was worth one Israeli lira. But the dinar was worth four Israeli lira.'

Michael married a woman of Russian origin born in Palestine. They had a daughter and a son, both of whom were grown up and lived nearby. He said they were completely Israeli. After his divorce, he married again. Had it been difficult for him to adapt to Israel? 'Yes, of course,' he said. 'First of all, to be a refugee. Then to lose your mother language. To lose your way without home, without profession, without friends. To come to a country that regards your language, your colour and your traditions as enemies. To be seen as inferior. They are European. We are Asian. To manage with these problems, when you haven't a penny in your pocket, was difficult. And when you come also without their political views, it's difficult. They regarded you like a traitor. Many communists here were defeated. The strange thing is the racism against Eastern Jews was crystallized in two opposite centres – the very Orthodox and the Communist Party. The party was still very European.' He worked for the party's Arabic paper in Haifa, *Al Ittihad* (Unity). *Al Ittihad* later became independent, and he continued writing for it until 1995. He had also translated the Arabic novels of Neguib Mahfouz and Yusuf Idris into Hebrew. As president of the Association for Civil Rights in Israel, he could be seen like Uri Avnery protesting at injustice in Israel and the occupied territories. His last demonstration had been at Hebron two years before, when Benyamin Netanyahu put the whole city under curfew to please a few hundred settlers. At seventy-six, he did not want to demonstrate any longer. Sami Michael was a writer, known as a political and literary essayist in Arabic and as novelist and playwright in Hebrew. It was a precarious balance.

'To become a writer in Hebrew without a Zionist ideology offended the literary class in Israel. They did not like it.' His first novel, *All Men are Equal, but (Some are More)*, dealt with Israelis who were not Zionists and with citizens who were not Jewish. 'It brought the Arab not as a servant, but as an intellectual. It brought the Eastern Jew to the centre of the plot, especially those who were not Zionists.' When the book was published in 1974, the critics were harsh. 'It broke like a bomb, a social bomb, at this time. An Eastern Jew was taking his place in the literature of Israel. Wow. Israel divided into two camps. One side hated me. The other . . .' Who was on the other side? 'Not even one. Especially the leftist writers. They call themselves left, but they live for the prizes that left writers get outside and inside Israel. The best kept silent.' He said one critic, a historian of Hebrew literature, wrote, 'Sami Michael hates his people. His writing is shallow.' Nonetheless, his books sold in Israel and found an audience in translation abroad. 'The public put me on the literary map against the will of the literary establishment.' He mentioned that Israel had been created by a writer, Theodor Herzl, although no one ever said he was a good writer. 'Zionist ideology is grounded in Hebrew literature.'

Another novel, *Water Meets Water*, treated Israel's romanticism about its past. 'All Israeli literature,' he said, 'looks romantically on Israel when it was small. That means, before the Eastern Jews came to Israel. They look on it as paradise. I tried through this novel to find who killed this compact, beautiful, romantic Israel. A beautiful, young, fragile girl in the novel represents that Israel. She is raped in the army by the commander of her platoon. After that, she is killed by him. Her name is Ina, a love name for Tina, small. When I wrote this, I had in the back of my head a quote from Avi Shlaim, the iron wall.' Avi Shlaim, a post-Zionist Israeli historian at Oxford, had also been born in Baghdad. His recently published history of Israel's relations with the Arab states, *The Iron Wall*, took its title from Vladimir Jabotinsky, who wrote in 1923, 'We must either suspend our settlement efforts or continue them without paying attention to the mood of the natives. Settlement can thus develop under the protection of a force that is not dependent on the local population, behind an iron wall which they will be powerless to break down.'

To Michael, iron walls were antithetical to Jewish tradition: 'Through the ages, the Jewish people were excellent at diplomacy. They had a tradition of conciliation. Problems were not solved by fighting. The Israeli population before 1948 has huge achievements by using this tradition of concession. We lost this ability when we built a strong army. Using the army is quicker than using traditional Jewish methods.'

Israel was born in conflict with the Other, and he believed it perpetuated clashes within. 'One of the left thinkers said this state was founded by one people and is now populated by another people. Israel was founded by East European Jews. They have a deep experience of fighting each other. Two synagogues led by rabbis who are like saints, they fight each other. There is a fierce conflict between Zionists and communist Jews. They brought this tradition of conflict to Israel. Jews from the Arab world did not have this. We regarded all of us as Jews. We did not fight. We did not give names of the other side to the police. But they did it in Eastern Europe. The Baghdadi Jewish community was guided by two bodies, religious and civil. They worked in harmony. They ran schools. They gave help to the poor. But it was not like that in Eastern Europe. Eastern Europe put its stamp on this country. Remember, Yitzak Rabin was killed not by an Arab, but by a Jew. In a whole generation in Iraq, I heard of only one Jew killed by a Jew. Here it is horrible how many Jews are killed by Jews. Sometimes, a simple discussion in the Knesset looks like a fight among mentally ill children.'

Why had he become a communist? 'I went into the Communist Party for two reasons: because I was a Jew and because I lived in a dictatorship. There were no citizens' rights. I dreamed of living in a democratic society. I believed communism was the peak of democracy.' His association with the Iraqi Communist Party began during the Second World War, when he was a teenager. 'The only power that stopped Hitler was Russia. I became a communist because I was a Jew in a very hard situation. We succeeded. We built a very powerful underground in Iraq. It was the strongest Communist Party in the Middle East.' Although the party resisted militarists in Iraq and supported the deprived in Israel, it could not hold him for ever. 'Year after year, I felt I was wrong. The last decision came after reading an article in English in the Soviet Union, in *New Times*, that praised military dictatorship in the Third World. It said the army was the most advanced progressive force. And I do know what the army means in the Third World. They are killers. It shocked me.' He quit the party in 1955.

He poured me more Turkish coffee. We might have been in an Arab coffee house, where political discussion was fuelled by caffeine and tobacco and could go on all day and night. He was thinking out loud as he sipped the cup, musing on democracy, nationalism, Zionism and communism. Michael's imagination darted around problems, unwilling to settle on absolute truth. I suspected that the absolute truths of the party, as of religion, drove him away. 'Nevertheless, after all we said,' he confessed, 'Israel is still a very democratic country for the simple reason that Jews cannot live inside a dictatorship. Jews are very individualistic. The Jewish religion gives the opportunity for the Jew to question or even the right to argue with God. Job argued with God. Why? In the centre of the Jewish religion, you have the right to ask why. You can't stand dictatorship. Jews among themselves have a deep feeling they are equal to each other. You see it inside the army. The most simple soldier can stand before the commander-in-chief and ask why, why should I do that?'

His childhood in Iraq did not prepare him for his experience as an Israeli conscript. 'When I served in the army, after two months, I had to stand at the gate of the camp with another soldier who was born here. We heard two motorcycles. Then a big car. I saw Ben-Gurion. Coming from Iraq, I started shaking.

The other soldier said, "Hey, Ben-Gurion, Paula is inside."'
That sense of equality, he said, did not extend to non-Jews.
Israel was, in that sense, half a democracy. Uri Avnery had
written that you could no more be half a democracy than half
pregnant.

When Michael settled in Israel, he felt as much Arab as
Jewish. 'I was in a foolish position when I came to Israel and
saw how the Arabs live here,' he said. 'I remembered how Jews
lived in the final days in Baghdad. I defended Arabs and most
of my readers thought I was Arab. The only reason they didn't
put me in prison was because I was a Jew.'

I said something about Israeli history and the newer versions
of it that came closer to his point of view. 'That's the problem
with Israel – too much history,' he said. 'I don't like history.
One of the reasons people hate each other is because of history.'
He talked again about Haifa, the city without a history. He told
me that his friend, the late Emile Habibi, had wanted to write
a novel based on Haifa's Arab history. Habibi was an acclaimed
short-story writer, Arab Palestine's Jorge Luis Borges. Like
Michael, Habibi had lived in Haifa and been a communist. His
most famous novel, a true comedy of tragedy, was *Tales of Said
the Pessoptimist*. He died in 1996. When Habibi first mentioned
he would write a historical novel, Michael said, 'Please, don't.'
Habibi eventually abandoned the idea. 'Why? Because he found
out Haifa was originally a fishing village of Jews. I told him,
"I'm so happy to hear it."' He smiled, still happy to hear it.

'A friend of mine who lived in Haifa moved to Nazareth,' he
said. 'Before dying, he asked to be buried in Haifa. And he made
them write his epitaph: I AM STAYING IN HAIFA.' Michael
laughed. 'I have Haifa. It's so beautiful.'

Not long after we met, I read an interview with him in the
New York Jewish newspaper *Forward*. He was quoted as saying,
'When I write about a Jewish character or an Israeli character,
I write as a Jewish writer. When I describe an Arab character, I
write as an Arab writer about Arabs. So, for me, the Arab isn't
the other one – he's myself also.' Sami Michael was also himself,

as a Jew, an integral part of the world's culture. He told *For-ward*, 'I would say Jews are the barometers of a civilization. When a civilization is developing, it invites Jews to come in. And when a civilization is deteriorating, it begins to oppress the Jews. The one who is a stranger to, say, German history, is Hitler – not the Jews. He's the one who betrayed German culture.' My old landlord in Tuscany, the novelist Gregor von Rezzori, told me he hated Germany for what it did to the Jews. He detested the killing, but he also despised Hitler and his insane associates for destroying Europe's universalist civilizing influence. It was not surprising that his magnum opus was called, with all the irony von Rezzori could bring to bear, *Memoirs of an Anti-Semite*. I thought he and Sami would have liked each other.

Another Haifa Writer

I checked into Haifa's Dan Panorama Hotel for $180 a night. Its lobby was empty on Shabat eve. For the benefit of religious Jews, the lift stopped automatically at each floor so they would not have to perform the work of pressing buttons. Like almost every other building on the slope of Mount Carmel, this one looked out over the water so far you thought you could see Cyprus. Perhaps that was what I was paying for. It certainly wasn't the tiny, airless room.

Salman Natour's office was downtown in the Media Centre for Palestinians in Israel. The evening had gone dark, and only a few people were working late. Natour let a few of the younger workers sit in on our talk. I wanted to know more about the two murdered brides he had spoken of in Acre. The Jewish girl from Beisan was Esther Ohanna, and the Arab was Ilham Abu Zarour of Nablus in the West Bank. He lit an L&M and leaned into his chair. 'It was in 1983,' he said. 'Both girls were twenty-one years old. Both were killed a week before their wedding. The girl from Nablus was killed when she was coming back with her mother after visiting relatives in Jerusalem. Esther was killed with her boyfriend while they were going from Beersheba to Jerusalem to invite her relatives and friends to their wedding.' Settlers killed the Arab girl, and Palestinian boys killed the Jewish girl. 'I met Ilham's mother in Nablus in 1983, one week after Ilham was killed. The mother in Beisan, I met in 1990, seven years later. The mother from Beisan hated the Arabs very much. She took part in demonstrations against Palestinians with Kahane.' Meir Kahane was an American rabbi, who founded the violent Jewish Defence League in 1968, emigrated to Israel, attacked Arabs, won a Knesset seat on a platform of expelling all Arabs and was assassinated in 1990. 'When I went to her house, people in Beisan said she would not welcome me because she hated Arabs. But I went, and I told her I wanted to publish the story of her daughter. In the beginning, she told me how she hated the Arabs because they killed her daughter. When I asked her if she was ready to meet the Palestinian woman, she said she couldn't. She said that Palestinian mothers brought many children and sent them to the street to throw stones to kill Jews. When she told me the story of her daughter, she said the same words that the mother from Nablus said about her sorrow: her daughter was killed one week before her wedding.' He said it in such a way that either girl might have been his daughter.

Natour gave Esther's mother a photograph of Ilham Abu Zarour and told her the story of her death. 'After that, she began to tell me how they lived in Morocco – in Casablanca. She talked about the close relations between Jews and Arabs in Casablanca. They lived in the same buildings, in the same squares. On the religious holidays, they visited each other. She told me also that a few weeks after her daughter was killed, some Palestinian workers were working near her house. It was July, very hot. She said one of the workers came to her house and asked for water.' The woman could not decide if she should give water to an Arab, because Arabs had killed her child. 'She said, "After that, I thought and I said to myself that the water is from God and it is for all of us." And she gave him water and told the worker that every day when he came to work he would find three or four bottles of cold water for him and his friends. I asked her if she was ready to meet this woman from Nablus, and she said yes.' He left the two women to call each other. I asked him why he had not arranged a meeting, and he said that he had gone to Beisan only to write a book about the Sephardim.

Over two months of daily visits, he met most of the people there – Moroccan, Algerian, Yemeni and Iranian. He remembered meeting a Sephardi poet, Emmanuel ben Sabo, who in 1983 had been driving with other young soldiers to Lebanon. 'In Galilee, there was an accident. Their big car and a small car crashed. In the small car, a child and a man were killed. The soldiers called for help. An ambulance and the police came. A girl soldier came. When she saw the accident, she asked who the victims were. The poet said they were Arabs, a child and his father. The Jewish girl asked, "Arabs?" Yes. Her reaction was, *Mashallah.*' An Arabic term also used in Hebrew, it meant roughly, 'As God wills.' Natour went on, 'If they're Arabs, it was okay. This man who was religious and very fanatic said that when he heard her words, "I lost my God, I couldn't accept that a Jewish girl could say such a thing about a child and his father." He couldn't sleep. He wrote six or seven poems. One was titled, "*Mashallah*".'

Emmanuel ben Sabo signed his poems with the Arabic pen name Khamis Tutunji. Natour explained that Tutunji was a Palestinian taxi driver, murdered by Jewish settlers near Ma'ale Adumim in 1985. The newspapers wrote that the police knew who the killers were but would not prosecute. It was then that ben Sabo from Beisan adopted the name of the Palestinian from Silwan. He sent his poems to the Hebrew daily *Ma'ariv*. 'The editor thought he was from Silwan,' Natour said. Silwan was a hilltop village in the West Bank. 'He thought a new Palestinian poet was writing in Hebrew. He published the poems. Other Hebrew newspapers published this new Palestinian voice.

Emmanuel ben Sabo finally wrote a letter to the editors saying, 'Khamis Tutunji is Emmanuel ben Sabo from Beisan.' A *Ma'ariv* reporter asked him why he had masqueraded as a Palestinian. 'He said it was because the settlers killed this driver, and this was his empathy and his solidarity with the family of this driver.' Natour met ben Sabo and published his poems in *Al Ittihad*. One of them was dedicated to Tutunji's sister. In the poem, he called her Nadia. He told Natour he chose the name Nadia because it was popular among Palestinians. 'On the day I published my interview with him, I got a telephone call from a girl. She said, "My name is Nadia, the sister of Khamis Tutunji. I am calling to thank you." I asked if she were ready to meet this man, and she said yes.' Tutunji's father, mother, sister and other relations came to Haifa to meet ben Sabo. 'Tutunji's mother said this was the first time she had gone out of her house since Khamis was killed. She said Emmanuel ben Sabo is like my son. After the meeting, Emmanuel ben Sabo shook her hand. The father said to his wife, "Kiss him. He is like your son, so kiss him." And she kissed him and invited him to Silwan.' Natour said his book on Beisan was filled with similar stories. The people there convinced him that the Sephardim did not hate the Arabs. He believed they were Arabs. Jewish Arabs.

Natour himself was an Arab Arab, although privileged among Arabs in Israel because he was a Druze. 'There are no Druze refugees,' he said. Druze had fought on Israel's side in 1948, loyalty the Jews appreciated and other Arabs called treason. Loyalty had one reward: no Druze were expelled. 'Inside Israel, there are about eighty thousand Druze,' he told me. 'They live in sixteen villages.' His village was Dalliet al Karmel in the hills east of Haifa. He had studied in Haifa, become a journalist on *Al Ittihad*, which made him its cultural editor, and begun writing books. His first book was published in 1971. After that, he wrote twenty-four more in Arabic and one in Hebrew. The Druze dwelled one step down the ladder from the Oriental Jews and one up from the rest of the Arabs of Israel. The Arabs of the occupied territories weren't even on the ladder. For the

Druze in Israel, identity had become a preoccupation. 'Most Druze think of themselves as Arab and Israeli,' he said. 'Only a few think of themselves as Palestinians. It comes from the education. The schools in Druze villages use the Israeli curriculum that teaches them all the time that they are not Arabs. Their education is to prepare them to serve in the army. The schools have many programmes with the army. The education is also very Zionist. Students have no meetings with other Arab students – only with kibbutzim and Jewish schools.'

The Druze, like Jews in Israel, were subject to conscription. Natour had been in the army, and he had also been in prison. 'Service in the army is like a machine to change their minds. I know how it works. In training, the target is an Arab. They say, "One Arab comes to kill you. How would you defend yourself?" It's also in the media. They write about the Druze and the Arabs. The government says to the Druze, "You are different from the Arabs."' The Druze, however, were as Arab as any other Arabic-speaking community in the Levant. They adhered to a syncretic version of Shiite Islam based on the teachings of eleventh-century mystics, including one called Darazi who gave his name to the faith. Central to their belief was that the last Fatimid Caliph in Cairo, Al Hakim, was a hidden imam or incarnation of God. Strict Sunni Muslims regarded the Druze as blasphemers. When the ruling Sunnis persecuted them a century later, they stopped accepting converts and became more or less a distinct people. They spoke Arabic and, perhaps because the secrets of faith were revealed to only a small group of elders, were almost all secular. A little more than a half-million of them lived in Lebanon, Syria, Jordan and Israel. Only among the Druze of Israel was there confusion about identity.

Natour had written a novel about Druze in the army, *You are the Killer, Ya Sheikh*. 'It's about two relatives,' he explained. 'One is from Israel, one from Syria. The one from Israel discovers that, in the war of 1973, he killed the brother of his wife.' He said there were similar tales in reality. I asked whether, as some Israeli officers told me, the Druze were more brutal than other soldiers to Palestinians in the occupied territories. 'I think it's not true,' he said. 'I'm sure there are Druze who are killers and criminals, but no more than the others. I investigated this in the first *intifadah*. The border police committed crimes against Palestinians in the West Bank. People think most of the Israeli soldiers are Druze, because they know Arabic. They put the Druze at checkpoints. People think the Druze occupy the West Bank and everyone who speaks Arabic is Druze. But it's not true. There are Muslims, Christians, Bedouin and Sephardim who speak Arabic. In the first *intifadah*, somebody told me there were sixty thousand Druze serving in the West Bank. I said, "How many Druze do you think there are?" "Half a million," he said. I said there were only seventy thousand Druze in all of Israel.'

Natour had been a communist until 1995, when he quit the party to concentrate on his writing. 'I am a writer,' he said. 'I write novels, short stories and plays for the theatre. I also write political, social and cultural critiques.' He had translated Hebrew poetry and David Grossman's *Yellow Wind* into Arabic. He had also been imprisoned for his political activities. He called his three interrogators at Atlit Prison 'the good, the bad and the ugly'. The good and the bad were the usual nice guy–hard guy combination that all police forces and most kidnappers employ, but the ugly one was new. Natour recalled his big hands and his first questions, 'Who do you think you are? A big philosopher? A big hero? You won't leave this place alive.' Natour believed that his Israeli citizenship would probably protect him. The man also said, 'We can shoot you, but it's a waste of a bullet. Some day, when you are driving your car, a big truck will come and crush you.' Natour said his answer was, 'I know you are a strong state and have the atom bomb and tanks and I am nothing. But you do your job, and I can do mine. I know that after forty-eight hours I'll go back to my family if I live.' That was in 1977. In 1982, the government put him under house arrest for six months for helping to organize a strike of Arabs in the Golan Heights.

He thought the best thing now would be for the Israelis to withdraw from the occupied territories and for the Palestinians to establish a state. 'It doesn't mean peace,' he said. 'It means the end of occupation and the independence of the Palestinians. The problem of the refugees would remain to be solved, to give the opportunity for refugees to come back if it is possible. I don't think we should make a problem or a tragedy for the Jews here.' Two states would be the beginning of a process, not the conclusion. 'After that, I think the two peoples should begin to think about real peace, not only between Israelis and Palestinians, but between Israel and all the Arab countries. And I think that the Jews have to think about their status in the Middle East for the future. I think they should not be a minority in the Arab world. They have to be part of the process in the Middle East, the process of democracy and modernization of all the Middle East.' He saw a more profound contest between secular and religious culture, in which he and many Israeli Jews would be on one side and the fundamentalists on the other. 'This is the way to fight against fundamentalism in the Middle East – Jewish fundamentalism and Islamic fundamentalism.'

He invited me to a rally in the village of Yirka on Saturday for the launch of a campaign to urge all Druze to refuse to serve in the occupied territories. He said it would be interesting, and he was right. We would meet again at his house in Dalliet al Karmel on Saturday.

I took a Friday night stroll on Ben-Gurion Street in what had been Haifa's German Colony. There was a similar German Colony in Jerusalem, and both had been built by German Templers. These Templers were not the knights who defended the castle at Acre, but German Protestants who came to the Holy Land in 1868 to await the return of the Messiah. They maintained healthy relations with Arabs and Jews, ran productive farms and built beautiful houses out of local limestone. Haifa's German Colony resembled, in its ordered rows of similar houses, a traditional New England village. Interned and deported by the British as German nationals during the Second

World War, the Templers left behind what became Haifa's liveliest street of cafés, restaurants, nightclubs and boutiques.

Both Arabs and Jews owned businesses along Ben-Gurion Street, the wide boulevard at the heart of the German Colony. It was the only place in Israel where I met Israeli waitresses working for Arab proprietors. Young Arabs and Israelis socialized in the same cafés, and there were a few mixed couples. In Israel, seeing Arab boys with Israeli girls was a bit like finding an African American in Mississippi circa 1960 dating the local sheriff's daughter. Surprising and hopeful. I saw why Sami Michael lived in Haifa.

Ben-Gurion Street ran from the waterfront to the foot of Mount Carmel, beneath the ornate folly that the Baha'is had built as their temple. The temple's lights shone on kids cruising in cars of varying vintages up and down Ben-Gurion Street. The pubs and cafés were filling up for the night. Young Israeli Jews and Arabs were well dressed, trendy and normal. The bars inflicted booming Western rock and Arabic music on their customers whether they liked it or not.

A young woman whom I had met once before took me to an Italian restaurant in one of the old German houses on Ben-Gurion Street. It belonged to a Palestinian friend of hers. Its Israeli waitress spoke to the girl in Arabic and Hebrew. There were other couples, but in large groups. We had spaghetti with wine, then more wine. Someone put on a song by the Lebanese diva Feyrouz. It seemed to make the girl maudlin. Tapping the tune lightly on the table, she asked, 'What am I?' Was she Israeli as her passport said? Was she Arab, as her background was? Was she a Palestinian, whatever that meant? When the *intifadah* broke out in September 2000, some Israeli Arabs made a peaceful protest in solidarity. Police shot and killed fourteen of them. Although aware of discrimination before that, she and most other Arab citizens of Israel were shocked that the state would kill them to keep them quiet. It had been a trauma. She came from a village in the Galilee, but she had lived in Haifa with girlfriends since university a few years earlier. She had a boyfriend. He was away. She was exquisite, and the candlelight on her dark eyes should have inspired any man to compose a poem to her. Looking into her eyes, I knew why fathers had hidden such beauty. Byron wrote, in 'The Bride of Abydos', 'Woe to the head whose eye beheld / My child Zuleika's face unveil'd!' We stayed talking until the restaurant closed, and I did not return to the hotel.

In the early morning before her flatmates awoke, she brewed Turkish coffee without sugar as Sami Michael had done. We listened to a BBC radio report. Israeli forces had killed three people in Nablus – an operation to assassinate a man named Mahmoud Abu Mohammed. The Israeli Defence Forces spokes-man said Abu Mohammed was a Hamas commander. Sami Michael would later tell *Ha'aretz*, 'Imagine the feeling if I woke up tomorrow and saw this neighbourhood, which we inhabit, forcibly conquered by Syrians, and they established settlements here, and in order to go to the bus station, I needed permission from the Syrian army. How would I feel? If I fight them, I will be considered a terrorist. Why am I a terrorist? Why do we call Hizballah or Hamasniks terrorists? Why? Because he fights on his own territory? Suddenly, aliens, occupiers, land on him and tell him: Your house is ours. It's his land. He and his forefathers were born here, and the settlers say, "We will never leave." How would you respond to this?'

Before I left the flat, I suggested we meet again. She thought it was not a good idea. One night, fine. Two, no. I persisted, making a fool of myself several nights running. Sometimes, even a traveller falls in love. With cities like Haifa. With women like Zuleika.

That the rest of Israel was not ready to live the Haifa ex-periment would be proven a while later, when Haifa's mayor, Avraham Mitzna, ran for prime minister and lost to Ariel Sharon. The segregationists weren't ready for change. I could almost hear them claiming they were not racists, they just believed in states' rights.

The Druze Hinterland

In the Druze village of Dalliet al Karmel, Salman Natour sat in
his large study. Its three mainly glass walls opened onto village,
wadi and meadow. On the fourth wall, family photographs
competed with a large portrait of the Lebanese Druze leader
who was assassinated by the Syrians in 1977, Kamal Jumblatt.
Natour had recently been to Amman, where he met Jumblatt's
son and heir, Walid. I told him I was, in a way, on my way to
meet Walid Jumblatt for lunch in Lebanon.

Natour was going to take me to a Druze anti-draft jamboree
in the village of Yirka in the Upper Galilee. While we waited
for his friends, we drank coffee and talked about books and all
that they implied in Israel and the Arab world – his dual worlds
doomed to perpetual conflict. His library took up much of the
house, books in Arabic, Hebrew and English everywhere. He
thought the abysmal state of Arabic publishing was sympto-
matic of all that disabled the Arab world. 'No Arab writer
makes money from his books,' Natour said. 'The regimes are
anti-literature, anti-culture.' Was it easier to write in Israel?
'They are five million here,' he said of Israel's Jews, 'and we are
three hundred million. A. B. Yehoshua can sell here in Hebrew
a hundred thousand copies. In all the Arab world, Neguib Mahfouz cannot sell more than twenty thousand.' The works of
Neguib Mahfouz, Egypt's Nobel laureate, had been translated
into Hebrew by Sami Michael and into English by Abba Eban.
Natour blamed the Arab world's unelected rulers for the fact
that more people read Mahfouz in English than in Arabic: 'I
think we have very bad, very reactionary regimes. There is no
democracy. If there is no democracy, there is no culture. The
Arabs have a very rich cultural tradition. There is no reason for
this situation, it's only because of the regimes. If you have these
regimes, they don't do anything for education, for culture, for
freedom, anything for the dignity of the human being. Because
of that, in the Arab world now, people try to find a solution in

Allah. They don't think they will have good in this life, so they search for it in another place. It's a tragedy.'

What lay at the heart of the tragedy? 'I think there are many reasons. One is that five hundred years of imperialism – Ottoman, English and French colonialism – destroyed everything here. I think the West – the Europeans and Americans – are still thinking in colonialist and imperialist terms about the East. Maybe they changed the instruments, but they have the same aims. But we as a nation are responsible for the facts. I believe that in a few years the Arab nation will realize the tragedy they are living and they will stop it. They have to do it. We have a problem with the regimes. They are not strong regimes. They have strong instruments to repress people. They are not strong in their base. If one Arab regime falls, the others will fall afterwards.'

Wasn't the alternative another form of dictatorship, a religious tyranny? 'Islamic fundamentalism is not the alternative, not the solution of the people. The Arab people will try to find a good solution for this situation. I don't know how they will do it. But I believe there is a process for democracy in the Arab world. I follow what Arab philosophers and writers discuss now about democracy and modernization of Arab society, and I am optimistic. Many of them realize that this situation should not continue for a long time. They are thinking and writing in modern ways. They don't speak in slogans. They know what they are doing. They speak clearly to the people. I think that satellite television and all the Arab newspapers published in Europe will help many forces in the Arab world to speak clearly. Our problem is we didn't speak clearly and directly about our problems. Now I hear very direct and clear voices speaking about democracy, freedom and liberty, about the status of the individual. They speak about the individual, the human being, not slogans about society. It's very important.'

He thought that, while Arab writers in Israel were freer to express such ideas, the literary establishment favoured its own – writers who were Ashkenazi Jews. Sami Michael had said the same. 'In Israel, there is an institute that takes government money to help translate their books. Writers like A. B. Yehoshua and Amos Oz, as soon as their books are in Hebrew, they are available in translation.' There was nothing similar for Arab writers in Hebrew or Arabic, and their works rarely reached the international market. He particularly regretted that his book on Beisan's Sephardim had not been translated into Hebrew or English.

Who were his favourite Israeli writers? 'Sami Michael from Iraq,' he answered immediately. Both had worked on *Al Ittihad*, and both published translations – Natour turning Hebrew into Arabic, Michael the reverse. 'I also like David Grossman. I like very much Yitzak La'or. I don't like Amos Oz.' Why not? 'I don't like him, because he's writing with a colonialist mind, the same way that Peres and the colonialist politicians think. They came here to build civilization because the Arab people are primitive. He tries to be sophisticated with his language. I like his language. But when I read his books, I ask myself what he wants to say. It's the same with A. B. Yehoshua. I began to read his latest novel, but I didn't continue.'

He did not blame Israel, as some did, for Arab woes. 'Israel is a problem, but we have also to think of our responsibility,' he said. 'Everybody should do what he can – writer, teacher, anyone. I don't think mystically that some Arab leader will come to save us. If everybody does the best he can, we will see results. This is what all the time I say to my people. Don't wait for the Mahdi. Don't wait for someone from the sky to make the revolution. Everybody can make the revolution.'

While we drove to Yirka, Natour pointed out where Arab villages had been until 1948. 'This was Birweh,' he said. 'Ghassan Kanafani came from here,' he said of a blank spot on the land. Kanafani was a talented Palestinian writer and spokesman of the PFLP. Mossad assassinated him along with his young niece in Beirut in 1972 after the PFLP murdered twenty-six people at Ben-Gurion Airport. 'This is Jdaideh, where Mahmoud Darwish's family was transferred. He lived here as a boy.' Darwish was Palestine's unofficial poet laureate, who had been exiled for many years and then came to the West Bank after the Oslo accords.

When we reached Yirka, a long line of dignified men were waiting outside the Qasr al Jaleel, the Galilee Palace, to receive Salman Natour. Boys handed us flyers for clothes shops as we went in. The modern Galilee Palace was a hall of white oatmeal tiles and low ceilings, where hundreds of people were gathered as if for a wedding. From the walls loomed large colour portraits of old Druze sheikhs in beards and turbans and one of Yitzak Rabin. Coffee and bottled water were set on a trestle table. Someone served bitter cardamom coffee from a brass pot, and there was sweet black coffee in flasks. A sign said, Yes to Equal Rights for the Arab Citizens. More signs, like political wall-paper, in Arabic and Hebrew admonished: Yes to a Just Peace. No to Compulsory Military Service. Yes to Equal Rights for the Arab Population. Cancel Compulsory Service for Druze Youth. Behind a dais hung a banner for the Public Committee General Congress on Cancelling Compulsory Service.

The great Druze gathering seemed to bring together discontented Arabs from all of Galilee, Muslims and Christians among them. I met a young woman named Rawda Makhoul, who said her family were Greek Catholics, 'but I'm not religious at all'. Her father had studied in Beirut before 1948 and had written a book called *Pages We Don't Forget* in the form of letters to each of his six daughters. Most of the daughters, and their mother, seemed to pop up at demonstrations for Palestinian rights all over the country. I would see them a few days later protesting outside the Jaffa Gate in Jerusalem.

When everyone had found a seat on one of the folding chairs, the speeches commenced. The Druze sheikhs in their white turbans and whiter beards sat in front, much as I had seen them in Lebanon. 'All of the famous Druze are here,' Rawda told me. 'I expected more Druze women. I expected such men to be more socially open.' They had come, among other reasons, to honour the young Druze men who had gone to prison rather than serve

414

in the Israeli army. They wanted to end Israel's policy of dividing the Druze from the rest of Palestine's Arabs by employing them as border police, security officers and soldiers.

'This conference with all of you here reflects the unity of our nation, of all Arabs,' Salman Natour told the crowd. 'I want to stress the fact that we are a part of the Arab nation and of the Palestinian Arab nation.' Applause for the Arab nation interrupted him for a minute. 'Our conference is like a scream against unjust compulsion to do military service. We announce that we support all those who refuse military service. We support all those who have gone to prison.' More applause. 'I greet the Jewish people who are here in solidarity and on the basis of conscience reject military service.' More clapping. 'I warn Arab youth who are from other communities against certain powers who are attracting them to military service. I greet the Golani Druze who have come here – the mayors, writers and the others. I want to welcome Taleb As-Saneh from the Negev.' He also thanked others in the audience – Arab and Jewish Knesset members, the Women's Coalition for Peace and the mother of a young Jewish Israeli imprisoned for refusing to serve in the occupied territories.

Dr Shawki al-Khatib, head of the National Committee for Arab Mayors in Israel, said the meeting was for all Arabs, not only the Druze. 'The Druze suffer from two things,' he announced. 'They die, and their blood is not cheap. And they suffer from discrimination as Arabs. There is a racist wave against all non-Jews in Israel. There is official racism.' He mentioned that six of the Knesset's nine Arab members had been attacked by Israeli extremists and their lives were in danger. I asked Rawda if Azmi Bishara, the most prominent Arab Knesset member, had come to the conference. 'No,' she said. 'He wouldn't come now. He will come late.' Bishara was too theatrical to arrive on time with everyone else. Al-Khatib went on, 'The fact that an Arab boy or girl is born to a certain area or sect should not mean he has to serve in the army.' He referred to the killings of four Palestinian children in Gaza. 'When we oppose serving in the army, it is because we oppose the occupation. They insist on making us a part of it.'

An Israeli woman named Diana Do Lev from the New Profile group addressed the conference in Hebrew. In her soft voice, she said she formed New Profile years before to put an end to compulsory military service. Its members were all women, who offered legal assistance and family support. I remembered a slogan of the Vietnam anti-draft movement in America that would undoubtedly have worked here: 'Girls say Yes to guys who say No'. She said, 'We are sharpening our focus to oppose the militarization of society. Nowadays, it is to the point that all prime ministers, university presidents and other high posts must be generals from the army. It has an influence on our life. Our struggle will lead to a more democratic state. We visit the youth in prison. We write protest letters to the security minister and the defence minister. We now intend to broaden our activities to include the Druze community.' The Druze men stood and applauded.

Hayel Abu Jabal, a middle-aged man in a grey jacket, bore greetings from the Syrian Druze community in the occupied Golan Heights. 'It is a long time,' he reminded them, 'since you opposed being part of this army. American support to Israel gave her a free hand and the broad capacity for action against the Palestinian people. It aimed at making you stand against your Palestinian brothers. The Israeli army destroys houses. It occupies land. It is organised terrorism. We in the Golan rejected Israeli citizenship. We burned our Israeli identity cards in a big bonfire in Majdal Shams. Your youth does not want to contaminate their hands with the blood of their Palestinian brothers.'

Speaker followed speaker all afternoon, and the chairman asked each to limit his or her speech to four minutes. They ignored him. One of the first Druze men ever to refuse military service in Israel, Samih al-Qassem, said the Druze were not required for military purposes. 'We know what lies behind it,' he said. 'They don't need us to defend the Hebrew state. David

Ben-Gurion was the first to test compulsory military service on all Arabs. It was an excuse to expel us. I am quoting the documents. Ben-Gurion divided us. He wanted to enrol the Druze, the Catholics, the Bedouin and the Circassians. In 1948, there were fifteen thousand Druze. The goal was political: to divide and rule. We have witnessed objections to military service since 1956, the date of the law. Most Druze were against it. All of you should not oppose as separate groups, but as Arabs. Not as Bedouin, Sunni or Druze. We have a just cause, and we will win. We will celebrate in a free Jerusalem.'

A poet named Nayef Salim declared that his three sons were in prison for refusing military service. He had just written a poem to honour a Druze soldier named Medhat Yusuf, who was killed in Nablus protecting Israeli settlers. 'He died waiting for an ambulance,' Salim said. 'He was shot by Palestinian Authority police, when he was with five other soldiers. The commander called the army to take him to hospital. They took five hours to reach him, and he bled to death.' The implication was clear: a Jewish Israeli soldier would not have been allowed to bleed to death awaiting an ambulance.

Azmi Bishara entered the hall. Wearing a tie and leather jacket, he shook hands with his admirers as he made his way to the front like a boxer on his way to the ring. The other speakers made way for him. He mounted the podium, held its edges in both hands and jumped into his speech. 'I praise the Druze youth who will not serve in the army.' Applause. 'We are all one soul and one body. You cannot divide a soul from its body. We dedicate our children to self-honour. How can we accept that they will deny us this honour?' His was not an especially provocative speech. He had already provoked the Israeli authorities by addressing a Hizballah rally in Lebanon and by visiting Syria, an enemy state. His house in Nazareth had been attacked, while the police watched a Jewish mob set it on fire. At a subsequent inquest, it emerged that some police had taken part. Bishara would shortly be stripped of his parliamentary privileges and be prosecuted for his statements in Lebanon.

He outlined a programme for the Druze to resist military service, beginning with education of all Arabs – Druze and others – who might volunteer to serve in the Israeli security services. 'Those who choose to go should be aware,' he said. 'Our long-term struggle must be for our national identity. It's a long struggle. I don't have a magic wand. Are we with the occupiers or against occupation? Some struggle against it out of conscience, some out of political motives, some for social reasons, others for national reasons. Our national identity was here before Israel's existence. We should unite in this battle.' Bishara was the first speaker to keep to the four-minute limit. I had met him in his Knesset offices a few weeks earlier and noticed something on the wall that should have had Ben-Gurion scrambling out of his Sde Boker tomb to tear it down: a poster of Ben-Gurion's Arab nemesis, Gamal Abdel Nasser.

Issam Makhoul, another Arab Knesset member, was next. He praised the many Jewish Israelis who had gone to prison rather than enforce the occupation. 'Our present duty now is that all Jewish youth should oppose going to the occupied territories,' he said. 'They should reject the policies of the warmongers. A new lie is being planned. A law is proposed in the Knesset to require all Arabs to do alternative service.' Mohammed Baraki, a Hadash Party Knesset member, said, 'In Israeli society, there is a mentality to give fame to the military. When you are a citizen, you should have rights no matter what religion or nationality or sex you are. More than 50 per cent of Jewish youth don't go into the army. We oppose the policy of forcing people into the army. It is against your rights. We have deep roots in this land. We are part of the wind and the air. They are not granting us a favour. I call everybody here, our sons and our brothers, who are sent to the front line in the *intifadah*. They want occupation, but they want the killed and the killers to be Arabs. Throw down your arms. In front of [Defence Minister Shaul] Mofaz. Tell him we don't want to kill and we don't want to be killed in the name of a war party. Tell him we don't want to kill women and children. We are against raising our hands against Arab women.' He raised his hand in defiance, and everyone clapped. The chairman then read greetings from Walid Jumblatt in Lebanon.

While the speeches continued, delegates drifted outside for cigarettes. A Druze man told me a story about one of his cousins, a woman who was living in Palestine before 1948. It illustrated the predicament of the Druze, divided among the post-First World War mini-states of Lebanon, Jordan, Israel and Syria. This woman married a cousin of hers from Syria, and they had a son. When the boy was still a child, they divorced and she went back to her family in what had become Israel. She was not permitted to bring the child. She married again, and she had six children – three boys and three girls. The son who remained in Syria was conscripted into the Syrian army, and his half-brothers went into the Israeli army. They may have fought one another in the Golan Heights during the wars of 1967 and 1973. When Jordan signed the peace treaty with Israel in 1994, the woman went to Amman to meet her fifty-year-old son. On the way, she had a heart attack and died.

On the way back in the car, I asked Salman Natour why so many Druze went into the army. 'If someone does not serve in the army, he cannot work in any government department. There is a paper saying why he will not serve. It goes to the Shabak and other departments. If he tries for any government job, even as a teacher, he cannot have it. He who resists must know that he's lost his job prospects for ever. It's supposed that we have privileges, that we're trusted. But it's not true. There are no Druze pilots. Why not? They don't trust us. Me, as an Arab Druze, why should I do military service? They say I'm equal, but I don't feel equal to a Jew in the Jewish State. I can do my duty to the state in other domains, not in military service.'

Despite the rallies and the speeches, despite the brave refusal of hundreds of young Jewish and Druze men to police the occupation and despite the organizations supporting draft resistance, most Israeli Jews and Druze answered the government call. Once in the occupied territories, almost all obeyed orders to

demolish houses, to assassinate suspects, to shoot at demonstrators and to bring people in to be tortured. Those who said
no were too few to stop anything.

Natour made a detour for late lunch at J'naini at-Tamr – the
Fruit Garden. He and the owner, Saleh Diab, were old friends.
Diab ran what was probably the biggest restaurant in Israel, if
not the whole Middle East. He built it on family land north of
Haifa in 1977. Diab, as dapper in a dark suit and brush moustache as any character in the movie *Casablanca*, said he could
serve four thousand people at once. His ten children, five girls
and five boys, worked there along with 120 staff. A tree
sprouted in the middle of the floor, as if it were the pole holding
up the tent. It wasn't a tent, but a solid roof, cooled by a
fountain. A very Arab restaurant, J'naini at-Tamr attracted hundreds of Arab and Oriental Jewish families. The salads were
fresh and cold, the hummus as good as in Lebanon and the
mixed grill crisp and well spiced.

With pride, Diab gave us a tour of his domain. Firewood was
ablaze in six long braziers, each with chicken or beef or lamb
or minced lamb kafta. 'I decided to open a restaurant in 1971,'
Diab said. 'But I was told I had to have a Jewish partner. I
found one, and we applied for permission to change the use of
the land. We got the permission in 1977.' He said two of his
brothers were restaurateurs in California – one in Sacramento,
the other in Davis. 'The Arabs and the Oriental Jews are at
home with this food,' he said, 'but the Ashkenazim eat the
hummus with a knife and fork.' Diab said his ambition was to
open another J'naini at-Tamr in London, for which he would
need at least two acres. Did I know anywhere big enough?
I did. Hyde Park.

A Military Vocabulary

While there were those, Druze and Jewish, who refused to join an army of occupation, there were others for whom Israel's army was almost a sacred institution. It preached a doctrine of 'purity of arms' and it indoctrinated recruits in service to the nation. It had grown out of self-defence militias in the kibbutzim. As the Haganah, it had protected Jewish colonists from Arab attack. But the idea of a Jewish army was itself novel. Jews had not fielded an army since Roman times. A new country needed a new army, and the reborn language needed a vocabulary for that army. Ancient Hebrew did not have words for tank, missile, hand grenade, automatic rifle and machine gun. After the war that established both the army and the state, the Israeli army published its first *English–Hebrew Dictionary of Military Terms*. Someone had to make up words for howitzer and fighter plane, preferably adapting old words but sometimes using Hebraized English. The dictionary's author was a young officer who had served in the British army under Orde Wingate. Avraham Akavia still lived with his wife, Ruth, above Haifa in Mount Carmel. Colin Smith, my friend in Cyprus, had met him while he and John Bierman were writing their biography of Wingate, *Fire in the Night*. Colin gave me an introduction. Akavia looked like an ex-officer in grey wool trousers and blue cardigan. A bullish-looking man, still forceful in his eighties, he had the conviction of one who had fought for his beliefs. Faithful to his British military training, he drank whisky and water without ice. He gave me the same. He, Ruth and I met in their small sitting room on Mount Carmel to talk about the past.

A framed photograph of a handsome young man stood on a table. When I asked about him, Akavia said it was his son. A tank commander in the Golan Heights in 1973, he died on the first day of the October 1973 Arab–Israeli war. 'I don't blame anyone,' he said. 'He was a soldier.' So was Akavia. He was

proud to have learned his trade from Wingate, the Gentile Zionist who had trained a generation of what would become Israeli
officers. Akavia believed that, if Wingate had not been killed in
Burma in 1944, he would have become the first commander of
the Israeli army.

Born in Poland in 1916, Akavia was nine when his widowed
mother emigrated with five children to Palestine. He was the
last of the children still alive. 'They've left me a poor orphan,'
he joked. Ruth added, 'That's the way of the world.' Avraham
and Ruth had both grown up in Haifa and married young. They
were well suited.

'I joined the Haganah in 1933,' Akavia said. 'The British were
not supposed to know. I was in the company of messengers,
then was promoted to Signals. I rose to deputy commander,
Signals. At the same time, my job was helping to create military
terms in Hebrew. In 1938, I was at Wingate's training camp at
Ein Herod.' Wingate had established his base at Ein Herod
to suppress the Arab revolt by taking the offensive. There
were stories that he shot prisoners, and he taught his Jewish
recruits to operate at night as what could only be called death
squads. He had the unusual habit of addressing his men in the
nude, sometimes brushing his body hairs with a toothbrush.
Akavia assisted him by translating his training lectures into
Hebrew. He would mimeograph the lectures on a Gestetner
machine for distribution to the class. Wingate did not allow
anyone to take notes. He wanted them to listen. Wingate's
lectures on military tactics, Akavia said, had been discovered
recently and were going to be published. Translating Wingate
forced Akavia to come up with new words. 'Wingate talked
about mortars,' he said. 'Hebrew did not have mortars. So we
did not have a word. No problem. I said, "*Mortira*". Now, it's
margema.'

Wingate thought so highly of Akavia that he requested him
for the Ethiopian campaign of 1941 as part of the Special Operations Executive. 'I belonged to a special section of SOE in
Ethiopia,' he said. 'Until then, we never even heard the word

SOE.' He trained Greek and Yugoslav troops to fight the Italians. When Britain liberated Ethiopia, Akavia returned to Jerusalem and Wingate went to Burma and died in a plane crash. In April 1942, Akavia received his commission as second lieutenant. 'I was with the Jewish Brigade for two and a half years. We were sent to Egypt and to Italy.' As he rose up the British ranks, becoming a major, the Haganah promoted him as well. By the end of the war, he was Haifa District Commander.

When Israel declared its independence in 1948, he said, Haifa staged a ceremony to coincide with Ben-Gurion's celebration in Tel Aviv. 'The idea was that the declaration would be read out and everyone would sing the Hatikva.' Hatikva was Israel's national anthem. 'But we couldn't get a connection to Tel Aviv. They had a text of the declaration, so they read it out. Lorna Wingate turned to me and kissed me. She turned to the other side, but it was the chief rabbi. She couldn't kiss him.' He laughed. Ruth said of Lorna, Wingate's widow, 'She was so beautiful. You cannot imagine.'

The first of many Arab–Israeli wars began, and Haifa's Arabs fled. Akavia did not accept the current histories that said the Haganah expelled them. 'Shabtai Levy was the mayor,' Akavia said. 'He was very sorry to see the Arabs go. I didn't think it was such a terrible thing.' Ruth put in, 'He was a mayor of a town of Arabs and Jews. He was a very nice man.' Akavia thought again, 'Now, I think he was right. It meant the Arabs would not stay with us. Not work with us.'

Avraham and Ruth clung to memories, not only of Wingate and the wars, but of Haifa. They had known the Baha'is who built its famous temple, and Ruth had been born in the German Colony. She spoke fondly of the Templers and particularly of one German woman who taught her the piano. They remembered the little village Haifa was before the British port made it a city. 'They had to build a jetty for the Kaiser to bring him by boat without getting water on his trousers,' Akavia said. I knew he was not old enough to have seen the Kaiser in 1898, but he could have convinced me. 'There was a café near the jetty where

I used to go for swimming competitions.' I wished I had seen Haifa then, and I hated to leave it now.

If not for Mr Sykes, M. Picot and Lord Balfour, I would have driven from Haifa north up the highway through Naqoura, Tyre and Sidon to Beirut. The hostile border that they left was open only to soldiers, guerrillas, spies, UN officials and church prelates. I returned to Paris to write the story thus far. I would then resume the journey in Damascus. Once again, a legacy of 1917 diverted me from the path.

TWELVE

Damascus Is Burning

'During the reign of Ahab, Damascus and Israel fought
as allies against Assyria, but from this event onward
they were foes.'

REVEREND GEORGE ADAM SMITH
The Historical Geography of the Holy Land (1894)

The Road Up and the Road Down

UNTIL TURKEY JOINED THE GREAT WAR as a German ally
in November 1914, Johnny Turk was the plucky friend who
maintained order between the Suez Canal and India. Britain had
defended his domains against encroachments by the Russians
in the north and by the Egyptians under Ibrahim Pasha in the
south. The Ottomans' self-destructive entry into the First World
War gave Britain and France the opportunity to seize an empire
they had long coveted. Britain fought two separate offensives
against Turkey's Arab lands, the first in Mesopotamia, the
second in Syria. Although the twin campaigns were similar land
grabs, the differences affected the natives irredeemably. Syria's
population sought independence from the Sublime Porte. Iraq's
did not. Syria wanted to remain united. The place that became
Iraq for the most part preferred to retain separate identities for
Kurds, Sunni Arabs and Shiite Arabs. Britain united Iraq and it
divided Syria.

At the beginning of 1917, Turkey waged war to preserve not
only its empire but its homeland in Anatolia. The Turks held at
Gallipoli in January, preventing an Allied invasion and occupation of their heartland. In the imperial dominions, however, the

425

Turkish defenders were giving ground. Having defeated a British expeditionary force at Kut, south of Baghdad, the previous April, the Turks surrendered Baghdad to Major General Sir Stanley Maude in March 1917. Britain declared Maude a liberator and later erected a statue of him in what would become the grounds of the British Embassy. When Maude extended the fight north to Kurdistan and Mosul, Britain began the organization – indeed, the creation – of modern Iraq. Colonel Sir Percy Cox, Maude's chief political officer who later became British High Commissioner in Iraq, and his assistant, Gertrude Bell, intrigued among the tribes and urban notables to protect British rule and establish a greater Mesopotamia. They called it Iraq and imposed a centralized system on peoples accustomed to the autonomy afforded them by Ottoman weakness. Britain, the unsought emancipator, had come to stay. 'It was evident,' David Fromkin wrote in *A Peace to End All Peace*, 'that London either was not aware of, or had given no thought to, the population mix of the Mesopotamian provinces.'

Gertrude Bell knew the mix of both Syria and Iraq. Daughter of a coal-rich County Durham baronet, she left Britain, aged thirty-one, with an Oxford First in history, to study the tribes of Arabia. She befriended desert sheikhs from Jerusalem to Persia, learned Arabic and returned to Baghdad with the new rulers in 1917. An ardent member of the Women's Anti-Suffrage League of Mrs Humphry Ward, she believed that an Englishwoman, however unqualified to vote for a member of parliament at Westminster, could direct the affairs of Arabs, Kurds, Assyrians, Turcomen and Jews. 'I'm getting to be a dab hand at Arab politics,' she wrote to her stepmother, Florence Bell, from Baghdad.

Baghdad had the world's oldest, and one of the richest, communities of Jews. They descended from the Babylonian captives who elected to remain in the Fertile Crescent rather than return to the wastes of Judaea. The Balfour Declaration of November 1917 that promised the Jews a national home in Palestine specifically guaranteed that 'nothing shall be done which may prejudice the political and religious rights of existing non-Jewish communities in Palestine or the rights and political status enjoyed by Jews in any other country'. That the rights of Palestine's 'non-Jewish communities', over 90 per cent of the population, suffered for the national home is no secret. The 'rights and political status enjoyed by Jews' in Baghdad would also be forfeited with the establishment of the Jewish State in 1948. Iraq's rulers and the Baghdad mob blamed their defeat in Palestine on Iraqi Jews, who were innocent of any intrigue against their Arab compatriots. There followed a pogrom, expulsions and escapes of a community that had been in Baghdad longer than the Arabs. Palestine and Iraq would affect each other's destinies at crucial intervals from the time of the British conquest to the era of Saddam Hussein and Ariel Sharon.

During the summer of 1917, Britain opened its assault on the south-western flank of Ottoman Arab territory in Syria. The first victory came in July with the capture of Aqaba by Lawrence and the Hashemites. Three hard-fought battles to enter Palestine through Gaza took the British to Jerusalem in time to celebrate Christmas. Allenby won a decisive battle at Megiddo, the biblical plain of Armageddon, and pushed the Ottoman and German armies north through the Galilee. By the end of September 1918, the British were at the gates of Damascus.

The Syrian campaign under Allenby, unlike Maude's onslaught on Iraq, relied on local allies for military and political support. A network of Jewish spies run by the Zionist Aaron Aaronsohn and the Arab revolt both contributed to Allied success on the battlefields of Syria. Syrians – who included Arabs, Armenians, Kurds, non-Zionist Oriental Jews and many eastern Christian sects – believed Britain's assurance to Sherif Hussein bin Ali of Mecca that an Allied victory would leave them independent and united. By the time Britain's other promises – to grant Palestine to European Jewish Zionists and to cede what would become Lebanon and mini-Syria to France – became known, it was too late.

At the end of the war, the Mesopotamian tribes waited to see what the Peace Conference in Paris would offer. Miss Bell's understanding of public opinion was astounding. 'On two points they are practically all agreed, they want us to control their affairs and they want Sir Percy as High Commissioner . . .' Lest local voices express themselves outside Baghdad's tea parties, Britain refused permission for the Commission of Inquiry into public opinion in Turkey's former provinces, appointed by President Woodrow Wilson, to enter Iraq. Instead, the King–Crane Commission limited its investigations to Syria, where it found the population overwhelmingly in favour of the two goals Britain had specifically excluded: independence and unity. If compelled to accept a Mandate – a term invented by South Africa's General Jan Smuts at Paris to disguise what would be protectorates or colonies – Syrians asked that the Mandatory be the United States. In the event, Syria was carved into four Mandate territories – mini-Syria and Lebanon under the French, Transjordan and Palestine under the British. Not for the last time the Western powers imposed their will on the Arabs in defiance of their wishes.

In May 1920, Britain assumed the League of Nations Mandate to govern a united Iraq within its new borders. In June, the country rebelled. In a display of unanimity that shocked the British, who had trusted the efficacy of Winston Churchill's 'dividing up the local powers so that if we have some opponents we have also at any rate some friends', all of Iraq's people fought the British. The Shiite religious leaders in their holy redoubts of Najaf and Karbala declared a jihad. The Arab and Kurdish tribes attacked British troops. *The Times* asked how long Britain would impose on Iraq's population 'an elaborate and expensive administration which they never asked for and do not want?' Lawrence wrote in the *Sunday Times*, 'We have killed ten thousand Arabs in this rising this summer. We cannot hope to maintain such an average: it is a poor country, sparsely populated . . .'

Miss Bell wrote to her father at the height of the rebellion that 'we cannot leave the country in the chaos which we have

428

created, no one can master the chaos if we can't'. By September, Miss Bell was in despair: 'We are now in the middle of a full-blown Jihad . . .' She asked a question that in 2003 America did not: 'How can we, who have managed our affairs so badly, claim to teach others to manage theirs better?' Britain banned all meetings in mosques, imposed a 10 p.m. curfew after which violators would be shot and dispatched Indian army troops. More importantly, it sent aircraft.

Managing Iraq's affairs was becoming both difficult and expensive. Churchill, who left the War Ministry to succeed Lord Milner as colonial secretary, had devised the cheaper strategy of deploying bombers and armoured cars without 'eating up troops and money'. The air squadrons in Iraq launched history's first full-scale aerial bombardment of a civilian population, setting a pattern for future warfare. Only technical deficiencies prevented bombardment with poison gas on those Churchill called 'barbarous peoples'. British bombers at Habaniya air base outside Baghdad became the centre of the Royal Air Force's 'air bridge' between the Mediterranean and India – controlling 'on the cheap' natives who had neither aircraft nor air defences. When Britain restored its position in Iraq, it gave the Iraqis a ruler.

The Arabs of Syria had declared Prince Feisal bin Hussein their king in March 1920. The French expelled him from Damascus that July. Churchill, Sir Percy Cox and Miss Bell agreed he would make an ideal ruler for Iraq, both for his ancient lineage from the Prophet and his dependence on British arms. They staged an arrival in Baghdad to make it appear that Iraqis had invited him. Sir Percy wrote in 1927, without irony, of the 'popular tributes' to Feisal and the British-sponsored referendum, from which the Kurds of Suleimaniya 'abstained' – that is, boycotted. The plebiscite, precursor of hundreds since in the Arab world, produced a miraculous 96 per cent majority in favour of crowning Feisal king of Iraq. Meanwhile, Britain had given his brother Abdallah Eastern Palestine and called it the Emirate of Transjordan.

'When the thorny Shiahs rioted, when the Kurdish *aghas* got out of hand, it was usually the hulking [RAF] bombers from Habaniya that restored things to their grumpy normal,' James Morris wrote in 1959, a year after the Iraqi revolution deposed their Hashemite king and expelled the British. In the meantime, Britain had established a native army with British and former Ottoman officers to supplement the RAF in controlling opposition to the new order. The goal was to protect both oil production and imperial communications. The country's 'backbone', as Feisal called his army, succeeded for the most part in both tasks. It was not designed to protect Iraq's borders or to engage in foreign adventures – as it did in Palestine in 1948, its first mission against anyone other than its own people; and its invasion of Iran, with American approval, in 1980. As a mechanism of coercion, the army effectively massacred Kurds in the north in the 1920s, slaughtered Assyrian Christians around Mosul in 1933 and bombed Baghdad itself in 1936 during the first of many putsches. The army turned against the British in 1941, partly as a result of events in Palestine.

Iraqis resented a British order that was displacing Arab peasants in Palestine to make way for Jewish settlers and refugees from Europe. They sympathized with Palestine's Arabs, who followed the Iraqi example by staging a revolt from 1936 to 1939. A few Iraqis went to Palestine as volunteers, the 'foreign fighters' of their time. In 1939, the leader of the Palestinian nationalists, Haj Amin Husseini, fled to Baghdad. There, his anti-British and anti-Jewish propaganda affected both the public and nationalist army officers. These officers assumed power with an anti-British politician, Rashid Ali Gailani, as prime minister in 1941. They sought assistance from Germany to expel the British. The Baghdad mob started the pogrom, the country's first, against the Jewish community that the writer Sami Michael recalled from his childhood. The RAF at Habaniya bombarded Iraq's army, which was never strong enough to challenge its creators. British troops invaded, overthrew Rashid Ali Gailani and hanged four rebellious generals known as the Golden Square.

Iraq remained loyal for the rest of the Second World War. In the Cold War, the United States asked it to join a Middle East anti-communist alliance modelled on NATO to be called the Baghdad Pact. King Feisal II, grandson of the first Feisal, and his Anglophile prime minister, Nuri Said, made Iraq the only Arab country to join the pact in 1954. A year later, Britain felt confident enough of Iraq's steadfast opposition to communism and, more importantly, to the pan-Arabism of Egypt's Gamal Abdel Nasser, to close its last air base on Iraqi soil. As for the continuing membership of a Western alliance, James Morris noted, 'There was wisdom to the policy, and integrity, but there was one great flaw to it. It disregarded the people's wishes.'

In 1958, the people expressed themselves, and the British were not there to stop them. When the army, under Abdel Karim Kassem, began a *coup d'état*, crowds in Baghdad dismembered the royal family and the prime minister. They invaded the British Embassy complex and tore down the statue of the man who had liberated them against their wishes in 1917, General Sir Stanley Maude. Kassem became the first Arab leader to arm and train Palestinian fighters in military units. From then on, the army or the Baath Party ruled Iraq more and more ruthlessly until both were routed by a professional assassin who had never worn a uniform. Saddam Hussein used the party and the army, and a secret police that kept watch on both, to turn Iraq into an abbatoir. In all his policies, his willing accomplices were Britain, the United States and, for a shorter time, the Soviet Union. He also built modern roads, hospitals and schools to make Iraq the most literate and technologically advanced state in the Arab world. He invaded Iran in 1980, and he laid down challenges to Israel.

When Saddam invaded Kuwait in 1990, he offered to withdraw from the territory he occupied if Israel did the same. This 'linkage', as Washington called it when it rejected the equation, forced the US after the liberation of Kuwait to bring a reluctant Israel to the conference table with the Palestine Liberation Organization, Jordan and Syria in Madrid. In a way, the Oslo accords that wreaked havoc on Palestinians in the Israeli-occupied territories were Saddam's doing.

The Iraqis themselves nearly overthrew Saddam in 1991, when President Bush, Sr, called upon them to rise up and then gave Saddam permission to use his aircraft – as the British so often did – against them. Iraq's helicopter gunships, many made in the United States by the Hughes and Bell aircraft companies, turned the tide against the rebels in 1991. When the Kurds saw them overhead, they feared a chemical attack and fled en masse to Iran and Turkey. The Shiites in the south hid in the marshes, which Saddam drained, and in Iran.

For thirteen years the United States enforced economic sanctions against Iraq that left the people weak and the regime strong enough to control them. When the new Bush administration took office in January 2001, zealous neo-conservatives put Iraq at the top of the foreign policy agenda. Saddam Hussein had to go. By late 2002, they were dispatching troops to prepare for war. I went to Iraq for four months. The Anglo-American invasion was a walkover that reminded me of Lebanon in 1982. Following the PLO departure from Beirut, Israel pushed into the western half of the capital without encountering resistance from Lebanon's leftist and Muslim militias. The militias waited. Slowly, they initiated a guerrilla war. They planted car bombs. They sent the first suicide bombers to their deaths. As the price of occupying Lebanon mounted, Israel slowly reduced the size of its Lebanese holdings in stages until, by 2000, it had nothing left. I suspected the Iraqis would pursue the strategy the Lebanese had, but with – as Iraq's history indicated – greater ferocity. And I was right. Two years after the invasion, the Iraqis had killed more than two thousand American soldiers and confined them to their bases and the Baghdad 'Green Zone' from which their Iraqi collaborators pretended to govern the country.

The mob crashed Saddam's statue onto the Baghdad concrete as it had Sir Stanley Maude's thirty-five years before. On the April evening when American troops helped the Iraqis to pull down the tyrant's brass likeness, I was in the desert near Nasirieh on the Euphrates. US Marines, fearful already of Iraqi suicide bombers, had stopped me at a checkpoint. A call came on my satellite telephone. Baghdad, as symbolized by the statue, had just fallen. Over the telephone came the sounds of the crowd, the journalists and the American soldiers in Firdaous Square – jubilant as if the statue were the man himself. The night before, on a camp bed at an abandoned Iraqi base, I had read and jotted down something from a collection of Jorge Luis Borges's essays: 'From a world of individuals we have passed into an even more passionate world of symbols: the clash was not between parties or opponents of the dictator, but rather among parties and opponents of an effigy or a name.' Saddam's was the effigy, and the name the Americans chanted as they imposed themselves on the Iraqis was 'democracy'. It echoed Britain's promise of 'freedom' to their grandfathers. Freedom, once again, had been given – not taken.

American tanks and bombers and blood did not liberate Iraq the way they had France in 1944. Iraqis did not, as predicted in Washington, shower the liberators in rice and rose water. They threw hand grenades. Yet the Americans may have been bringing liberation to Iraq and the rest of the Arab world, but not as the war's architects sketched it. If the Iraqis liberated themselves from American occupation, they would become an example to other Arabs. That was not what the US Defense Department meant by freedom for Arabs, but it would be freedom nonetheless.

At the end of April I left Iraq and resumed my Levantine journey. The interruptions by kidnapping in 1987 and of war in 2002 and 2003 were behind me. There were no more excuses, and there was not far to go. I had already visited Damascus and Beirut for my previous book, *Tribes with Flags*, but I needed to return to the point where the original adventure was interrupted. Only then would I have completed the journey. I might as easily have picked up the journey in Beirut and gone south to Aqaba, but I had chosen to finish the trip in reverse. Beirut was, after all, the centre of the Levantine shore and the place I knew best. Anyway, Heraclitus had written that the road up and the road down were the same. Having been through the Galilee, my next stop was – as Allenby's had been 1918 – Damascus. From there, it was a short drive through the Bekaa Valley and over Mount Lebanon to the coast road where Hizballah gunmen had captured me. Sixteen years late, I would keep my appointment with Walid Jumblatt, the leader of the Druze, for lunch at his ancestral palace in Mukhtara.

Thawing Alaska

When the British and imperial forces assembled to conquer Damascus at the end of September 1918, the city that the Prophet Mohammed had compared to Paradise had 300,000 inhabitants. They were mostly Sunni Muslim Arabs, and the rest were ancient communities of Armenians, Arab Christians, Shiah Muslims of many sects, Jews, Kurds and Druze. On the eve of liberation, Lawrence argued with fellow British officers that the Arabs under Prince Feisal should enter the city first. It would convince the population they had been liberated by their own rather than by foreign Christian Crusaders. A few Arab nationalists inside the city had hoisted the banner of the Arab revolt over the Town Hall. During the night, Lawrence heard explosions and saw fires erupting inside the city. He wrote in *The Seven Pillars of Wisdom*, 'I turned to [Colonel Walter] Stirling and muttered, "Damascus is burning", sick to think of the great town in ashes as the price of freedom.' Damascus was not, as it happened, burning. The Germans were destroying their ammunition stores before their retreat. The great town did not turn to ash. Lawrence's pledge of Arab independence, however, did.

Australian cavalry, in order to cut the enemy's escape route on the road north, rode straight through the city rather than encircle it via the north-west. On the evening of 30 September, while Lawrence was intriguing with Syrian nationalists, General Sir Harry Chauvel's Mounted Corps were welcomed in Damascus by local leaders. The Arabs entered the next morning. Britain, in accord with Sykes–Picot, invited the French to occupy Lebanon and Syria. General Henri Gouraud, the French commander, drove Feisal out of Damascus in 1920. Gouraud marched to the tomb of the pious warrior who had expelled the Crusaders – many French knights among them – from the Holy Land in the twelfth century. There, he announced, '*Nous revoilà, Saladin!*' The struggle for post-Ottoman Syria was under way.

Long before my return after the Iraq war, Damascus had outgrown its city walls. The 300,000 had become nearly two million. The Syrian capital on the banks of the River Barada had survived eighty years of French, Egyptian, military and Baath Party government. The old president who had ruled for thirty years, Hafez Assad, was dead. Many of the officials I had known before had gone into retirement, while others lingered on spouting the old language of Baathist renaissance, Arab unity and socialism to a new generation that wanted mobile telephones, discotheques and satellite television. Amid the squat concrete towers and traffic bridges of new and expanding Damascus, only a few mud-brick houses were, like Palaeolithic mammals, resisting extinction. Massive apartment blocks on the Soviet model and hotels straight from the American Midwest were transforming the Syrian capital into an ersatz Occident. Oriental structures, struggling under the weight of satellite receivers large enough for families to sleep in, survived on sufferance. Most were in a state of near-destruction, a wall down here, doors falling from hinges there, prisoners shaved for execution. The blame belonged to Syria's modern rulers: the French, who cleared acres of labyrinthine quarters for cannon and tanks to control the natives between 1920 and 1946; the few elected and many military regimes that succeeded them; and, finally, the Baath Party–army–intelligence junta that had held power since 1970.

Only within a corner of Damascus, demarcated by the broad stone walls of its old city, were ancient houses being restored and gentrified after generations of neglect. Damascenes tended to avoid the old city's dilapidated bazaars; but, on my return, I found them rediscovering the charm of mud and wood, stone and marble, running fountains and cobbled paths too narrow for cars. A few old city landlords were reviving their empty palaces as hotels, restaurants and outdoor bars where the young smoked water pipes late into the night in jasmine-scented court-yards as their Ottoman ancestors had done. The difference was that now women joined the men.

When Hafez Assad died in September 2000, there emerged a possibility of escape from the deadening, albeit secure, hand with which he had governed their lives. Power in Syria's heredi-tary republic passed to his son, Bashar Assad, as it had in Jordan seven months before from King Hussein to his son Abdallah. In both countries, the dying leader had acted decisively against his own brother to ensure filial succession. Hafez exiled his bellicose brother Rifaat one last time and arrested his supporters just before his death. Similarly, King Hussein of Jordan, in his final weeks, withdrew his brother Hassan's title of Crown Prince and awarded it to his son Abdallah. In both statelets of Greater Syria, the change proceeded without civil war, sectarian violence or military *coup d'état*. In little Syria, there was a fleeting 'Damascus spring' when the then thirty-four-year-old president, Bashar Assad, encouraged citizens to speak out. A country in which owning a fax machine required security clearance sud-denly found itself awash with mobile telephones and internet connections. The first private newspaper since the declaration of martial law in 1963 began publishing, and hundreds of civil society groups met in houses and public auditoria. More than five hundred societies discussed ending the perpetual state of emergency, holding genuine elections and rooting out the finan-cial corruption that enriched senior officials and their offspring. Then, the old president's inner circle advised the son to be wary of rushing towards a Syrian *perestroika* that would jeopardize his father's legacy and lead to chaos. Police arrested scores of activists, including two members of parliament. Thus did glorious spring revert to familiar winter.

Everyone in Syria knew that, following its invasion of Iraq, the United States had turned its periscope on Damascus and Tehran. American secretary of state Colin Powell, after the conquest of Baghdad, named the price of Baathism's survival in Syria: withdraw the Syrian army from Lebanon, end support for the Shiite Muslim Hizballah militia, close Palestinian offices in Damascus and deport Palestinian leaders. He also told President Assad not to allow Palestinian spokesmen in Syria to speak to the press. 'You promote freedom of the press,' said a Syrian who attended a meeting between Powell and young Assad, 'and you don't want them [the Palestinians] to talk.' Years before, it was the president's father who did not let Palestinians talk. The Popular Front for the Liberation of Palestine's then-spokesman, Bassam Abu Sharif, used to receive me secretly at his Damascus flat in the early 1980s and spoke in whispers while letting water run into the sink to conceal our voices from Syrian electronic eavesdroppers. He used to refer to Syria as 'Alaska', just in case.

Alaska, frozen in the political rhetoric of a 1960s Soviet client, was surrounded. Jordan, Israel, Turkey and Iraq played host to American forces and were formidable foes in their own right. Three contested Syria over water rights, while Syria claimed that both Israel and Turkey occupied part of the land allotted to it under the post-First World War French Mandate – Turkey had Alexandretta and Israel had annexed the Golan Heights. When Iraq became an American protectorate in 2003, the United States told Syria to adapt to the new environment, like a rare bird, or die. The Syrian army and intelligence services were playing their own imperial game in Lebanon, but their presence had become vulnerable to subversion – just as American forces in Iraq were to Syria and Iran.

Syria's precarious military position matched its economic weakness. Assad, Sr, master strategist in foreign affairs and local intrigue, presided for thirty years over financial incompetence that successive *dei ex machina* disguised without correcting. Syria had survived on Soviet subsidies, hand-outs from the Arab oil states who would not themselves confront Israel and remittances from workers in Lebanon. When Syria approached bankruptcy in the early 1980s, deliverance came with the discovery of oil near its border with Iraq. Next came the deals with Iraq in the 1990s, under which Saddam Hussein gave Syria 150,000 barrels of free oil every day and allowed Syrian business to sell Iraqis about $1 billion worth of goods. When the US assumed control of the frontiers on the Iraqi side in April 2003, the oil and the trade stopped. Syria's economy was in trouble. 'By 2010,' Nabil Sukkar, an American-educated former World Bank economist in Damascus, told me, 'we will be net importers of oil.' Half the population was younger than twenty, and unemployment was 25 per cent. No one could employ all of the 300,000 young people coming to the job market every year from school, the universities and the army. A Syrian businesswoman, who ran an industrial firm and whose sons had moved to Canada, lamented, 'Children are our only export.'

Syria – surrounded, broke and threatened by America and Israel – had been down before. In 1967, a few days of fighting Israel cost it the Golan Heights, the prestige of its military dictatorship and a large part of its armed forces. Humiliation led to regime change the old-fashioned way – a coup by brother officers against the war's losers. The air force commander, Hafez Assad, emerged victorious among Baath Party militarists in November 1970. Although Assad provided Syrians with a longer period of continuity than any since Ottoman times, he suffered a defeat of his own in Lebanon. In 1982, the Israeli invasion to install a puppet regime in Beirut pushed Assad's forces out of the southern half of the country and demolished his personal fief, the air force. Almost every Syrian jet that went into the sky fell to an Israeli missile or fighter, and for the next year Syria had no air protection at all. Israel occupied half of Lebanon, and the Americans – dragging the British, French and

Italians into the quicksand with them – set up in Beirut as multinational peacekeepers. It was the 'coalition' of its time, and it set out to create a new Lebanon with leaders and policies acceptable to the United States and Israel. In theory, Assad was finished. His health suffered and his brother Rifaat attempted a palace coup. When Hafez recovered, he expelled his brother, bided his time and rebuilt his armed forces. Lebanese guerrilla operations that he and Iran sponsored against the US, France and Israel forced an American evacuation in early 1984. Assad lived to witness a total Israeli retreat from Lebanon in May 2000, a month before his death. He was probably the only Arab leader to earn America's and Israel's respect, because he beat them both. They were now seeking their revenge on his son.

Syria, for the most part, responded to American pressure by succumbing to it. After the 11 September 2001 attacks in the United States, Syria apprehended Al Qaeda suspects and handed them over to American authorities. Syria voted for America's United Nations Security Council Resolution 1441 to pressure Iraq to display its elusive weapons of mass destruction. When the US declared victory in Iraq, Assad ordered Iraqi regime exiles back home and expelled many other Iraqis as well. He closed the offices of the leading Palestinian guerrilla organizations in Syria, the Popular Front for the Liberation of Palestine, the Popular Front-General Command, Hamas and Islamic Jihad, some of whose leaders quietly left the country. He ordered Hizballah to suspend attacks against Israel from south Lebanon, but he did not disarm it.

An American administration whose diplomatic style meant issuing diktats was not interested in a rehearsal of Syria's case: that the Palestinians were waging a legitimate, legal struggle to end military occupation; that the Syrian people, like Arabs elsewhere, believed in Palestinian national rights; that Hizballah was a legal political party in Lebanon with nine elected members of parliament; that Israel possessed far more weapons of mass destruction, including at least 250 nuclear warheads, than Syria had or could afford to acquire; and that the Syrian government, far from aiding Islamic fundamentalists, had waged war against them for twenty years before 11 September 2001.

'What can we do?' asked Butheina Shaaban, a scholar who worked in the Foreign Ministry and would later join the cabinet as minister of expatriate affairs. 'If we say yes, they will ask for something else. They don't understand the issue of dignity here.' To American and Israeli policy makers, the word dignity was never appended to the word Arab. Like the British and French from 1919 to 1945, America would define Arab policies, draw Arab borders, sustain Arab leaders and stage Arab elections. To the strong, the weak had no dignity.

When I went to meet Butheina Shaaban in the Foreign Ministry in Damascus, I walked into the wrong office by mistake. On its wall was an ethereal portrait of the Assad family, arranged like a Trinity for its subjects to worship. A gold light emanated from the father, Hafez, as if it were an ikon in a Syrian Christian church. Seated beside him on a gilded throne was the son, Bashar. The spirit of the older son, Basil, floated above them. Basil had been the designated heir, when Bashar was studying ophthalmology in London. A car accident that killed him near Damascus Airport in 1994 left the younger brother as the father's vicar on earth. Portraits of leaders – the late one, the one who should have been and the one who inherited – were as common in Syria as in all other Arab countries. The father was always watching.

Across the corridor, where I found the right office, young and serious civil servants of a kind I did not usually encounter in Damascus were tapping computer keyboards, sending faxes, answering telephones in three or four languages and passing documents from one desk to another. The men and women were not afraid of their boss, in a country where fear of those higher up functioned as in corporate America. While Butheina Shaaban and I spoke, a young man took notes of our conversation until she told him not to bother. Then he took part in the discussion. Her staff's enthusiasm and helpfulness reminded me of the young Palestinians of the Negotiations Support Unit in Jerusalem. They bore no resemblance to the Syrian civil servants I had known in days gone by. The story went that, if you worked for the government, all you did was turn up at your ministry, leave your jacket on the chair behind your desk, go out to a café and return at the end of the working day to retrieve your jacket. The Ministry of Information was notorious for lazy and uncooperative officials. A friend of mine called them slurpers, because their only job appeared to be slurping tea and coffee. It was safer to answer requests with a 'no' than to risk criticism from above by taking responsibility for the consequences of 'yes'. Thus, censors said no to the publication of books they did not understand, no to visas for journalists they did not know, no to requests for interviews with senior officials and no to anything else a visitor might ask. Butheina Shaaban's protégés were a new type of functionary, who seemed to believe they could reform a corrupt system from within.

Butheina Shaaban had studied English literature at Damascus University and went to Britain to take her MA and Ph.D. at Warwick University. She met her husband there and wrote a thesis on Shelley and the Chartist Movement. Her new book on Arab women novelists was about to be published. 'Arab women were the first to write novels,' she said. 'Zeinab Fawway wrote *Hasn al-Wakid, Good Consequences*, in 1892. It was the first Arabic novel, although Hussein Heikal's book in 1914 is said to be the first.' Syrian officials did not usually discuss novels. She came to the ministry in 1988 as an Arabic–English translator. 'I got involved in the political scene,' she recalled. 'I was part of the peace process in Madrid and Washington. I became an interpreter for the late President Assad.' Assad's old interpreter, a gentle Palestinian Christian from Nazareth named Assad Kamal Elias, had retired. I had often wondered, watching the late president speak through interpreters whose English he occasionally corrected, how well he spoke any language other than Arabic. 'He understood English, French and Russian,' she said. 'But he believed that, as a president, he should speak his national language.'

American diplomats told me that Colin Powell had read Bashar Assad the riot act when the two met just before I arrived in Damascus. That was not how she, official interpreter and sometime presidential spokeswoman, remembered it. 'The secretary said, "We are going to talk and to discuss the issues of the region." He said, "We are giving our perspective and are ready to hear yours." He gave us his perspective, and it's very far from reality. He said the US had no ambitions in Iraq.' Powell delivered America's requests for Syrian action. 'These were not presented as demands. The secretary stressed that. He said we were conducting a dialogue.' And Assad's reaction? 'The president said that all of these demands have nothing to do with the United States. Prior to the visit, Sharon announced publicly the seven or eight points that the US should raise with Syria.' She said Sharon's points and Powell's were the same. What did she make of that? 'This is my own analysis,' she said. Syrian officials did not often offer their own analyses. 'It is my view. There are countries that are looking at this force as vehement and unstoppable – Egypt, Jordan, Kuwait and Qatar. They say, "Let us try and be in their good books." For Syria, with its history and its pan-Arabism, it does not want to be the country that risks the anger of the United States. But, in the meantime, it does not want to compromise its consistent position in line with United Nations resolutions. I wonder if there isn't room for a margin between the principles and this force.'

For Washington, there was no margin. Syria dithered, waiting to see how long the US would sustain casualties in Iraq before turning the whole mess over to the United Nations. Bashar Assad had revealed uncertainties that the father, whose authority was undisputed, would not have countenanced. Divisions between the old guard and the reformers were paralysing the system. Syria's state television had, in common with the rest of the Arab world, broadcast the American invasion of Iraq with greater emphasis on Iraqi dead and wounded than on the valour of America's soldiers. Until 8 April 2003, when the American invasion of Iraq was under way, Syrian newsreaders were comparing Baghdad's heroic resistance to Stalingrad's. Then, when Baghdad was falling, Syrian television stopped showing news altogether. For four days, there was nothing but drama, sport, archaeology, weather and soap operas. Young technicians and journalists at the television station in Damascus's Omayyad Square said that the minister of information, an old guard Baathist and once respected ambassador in London named Adnan Omran, and the station's director simply went home without issuing instructions. The journalists dared not transmit anything for which they might be called to account later. At another crucial juncture – when the United States proposed the UN resolution legalizing its occupation of Iraq – the Syrian ambassador did not come to the Security Council. There were rumours that Syria would vote no, but it did not vote at all. Veteran hardliners, notably Vice President Abdel Halim Khaddam and Foreign Minister Farouq Ash-Sharaa, were demanding that Syria vote against the measure. By the time the young president came down with the yes faction, the votes had been counted in New York. A few days later, Syria quietly cast its vote in favour. The effect was to antagonize the United States by not voting immediately for the resolution, while showing the Syrian public that it could disregard the pan-Arab principles upon which the regime predicated its legitimacy. Something else happened afterwards that would never have taken place under Hafez Assad: a Syrian former minister of information, Mohammed Salman, admitted on Lebanese television that the government's tardy UN vote had been a mistake. In the old days, there were no mistakes.

Arguments between defenders of the old Baathist faith and partisans of Syrian membership in the brave new world of American imperium were stalling decisions at all levels. At the Damascus Conservatory of Music, a beautiful new building in the style of the Ottoman hospices that surrounded it, auditions were under way for the Diwan Orchestra that Daniel Barenboim and Edward Said established to bring Arab and Israeli musicians together each year in Seville. Young Syrian concert musicians were playing for judges from the Berlin State Opera in a vast ballet rehearsal suite. Those who reached Seville would have international exposure and might be taken up by orchestras in Vienna, Paris or London. There was one difficulty: the Syrian government had yet to grant them permission to play with Israelis. Nor had it forbidden them. I watched their audition, but the violinists and pianists did not know if anything would come of their efforts. The conservatory's director, Nabil Al Lao, was himself an accomplished musician who had studied in France for ten years and Italy for two and a half. Would his students go to Seville? 'It's a little delicate,' he said. A few years ago, the bureaucracy would have prevented any cultural, or other, involvement with Israelis. Nor, in those days, would anyone have asked. 'For reasons you know,' Lao said, 'there is no decision from the [culture] ministry to take part. This is for political reasons.' Musicians from Lebanon, Jordan, Egypt, other Arab countries and the Palestinian Authority had been allowed to play alongside Israelis. The orchestra had a respectable pedigree: Edward Said was not only a virtuoso pianist but the leading Palestinian Arab intellectual in America; and Daniel Barenboim had defied the Israeli government to conduct a concert for besieged Palestinians in Ramallah. In the event, several of the Syrian musicians did go to Seville and toured in an Arab–Israeli orchestra without shaking the foundations of the Syrian state.

Artists were leading the demand for change in Syria. Their declarations appeared in the non-Syrian Arab press, but their novels and films questioning the dictatorship were banned. In 1987, the Syrian film director and actor Doureid Lahham had made a popular movie critical of the bureaucracy called *At-Taqrir, The Report*. It told the story of a government official dismissed for his honesty. The sacked bureaucrat spent the rest of the film investigating the corrupt practices that were destroying his society. He found an official who took bribes, a minister who stole government money to pay prostitutes while beggars went hungry and other figures as familiar to the Arab world as Uriah Heep was to Victorian London. The film achieved mass box-office success in every Arab country. Audiences responded to the little, Chaplin-like hero who took on their criminal governors. At the film's end, the hero was trampled to death in a football stadium where he had come to deliver his report to the public. When I met Doureid Lahham in 1987 for *Tribes with Flags*, he was enthusiastic that film could help to stop government abuses. When I met him this time in his new apartment in Damascus, he told me he had stopped making movies. He had just turned sixty-nine. 'Nothing strikes me any more,' he said. 'With maturity, you think what you did is not up to it. Now that I am older, I don't find anything. Events are running so quickly that there is no time to mature any ideas.' Was anyone else in Syria making political films? No, he said. Why not? He lit a Rothman's and answered indirectly, 'A major leader in an Arab country said to me, "You say what you want, and I'll do what I want." '

Syrians seemed to me to sense a weakening of the old order. There had been demonstrations not authorized by the government, unknown under Hafez Assad. More than a hundred Kurds from the illegal Yakiti Party protested in December 2002 at the parliament in Damascus. Police did not stop them, although some of the Kurds were detained a few days later. That was followed by Kurdish riots in the north-east, near the Iraqi border. Syrians, as ever ill-informed by the state media, wondered whether the Kurds were angry over maltreatment or had been instigated by the Americans and their Iraqi Kurdish allies. A friend who lived near the Republican Palace, the president's modest official residence, parked his car on the pavement to drop letters in a mail box. 'I parked as you park in Damascus,' he said. But no one parked like that near the Republican Palace, because it was surrounded by presidential guards in business suits. For the first time, he knew he could get away with ignoring the guards. One of them told him to move the car, but politely. 'He started pleading with me, saying he would get in trouble if he let me stay,' the man said. 'I don't know why I decided to say no. You see? There is both a change in us and a change in them.'

Ninety-nine Syrian intellectuals – writers, teachers, lawyers, engineers, film-makers – published a letter in the London-based Arabic daily *Al Hayat* that declared a kind of war on the government. Called Charter 99, it demanded an end to the 1963 state of emergency, the release of political prisoners and return of political exiles, freedom of the press and the right to hold public meetings. Two months later, the government freed about six hundred political prisoners and closed Damascus's notorious Mezzeh Prison, where political dissidents had been mistreated since the French built it. A month after that, the government issued a licence for *Ad-Dommari, The Lamplighter*, to publish the country's only non-government newspaper. Then, when *Ad-Dommari* exercised its freedom, its licence was withdrawn. Meanwhile, more civil societies were forming, and more declarations were issued. Although the government press ignored the dissidents, the Lebanese newspapers reported their activities and statements. Some of their pamphlets circulated as *samizdat* in the universities and schools.

On 3 June 2003, 287 'Syrian citizens' published an appeal to President Assad in the Lebanese daily *As Safir*. The petition warned that Syria faced two enemies, Israel and the United States, and was too weak to defend itself from either. It made the familiar demands for ending martial law and releasing political prisoners, but it also said, 'Mr President, the authorities have no remedy for our ills. There is a real cure, which is national reform.' Rather than appeal to America to deliver democracy in Syria, they asked Assad for a democracy to make the country strong enough to stand up to the United States. The Iraqi people had done nothing to defend Saddam Hussein, but many fought the Americans when he was gone. The appeal's signatories asked Assad to avoid making Saddam's mistake. 'Mr President,' they said, 'what is happening in Iraq and in Palestine is just the beginning of what America calls the new era. The characteristic of this era is the use of force by America and Israel. We should stop them from achieving their goals by repairing our society and making our country strong. The way to do this is to have a free people. The masses have been ignored and excluded from public life. You should let them come back and use their power to protect the country.'

One of the signatories was Sadek Al-Azm, a professor of philosophy who had recently retired from Damascus University. I had known him at the American University of Beirut in the early 1970s, when a religious fundamentalist Christian in the philosophy department sought to have him dismissed for atheism. He was from the Damascene Arab–Turkish aristocracy and had been a Marxist. Tall and thoughtful, he was a man of cardigans and comfortable chairs. His sitting room was cluttered with books and papers. Sadek had joined several civil society groups that included both Marxists and Islamic fundamentalists. What did the American war in Iraq mean for Syria? 'In meetings, we asked ourselves, suppose this happened here. Who would go out and fight for the regime? No one said, "I would." The strength of civil society is to tell the regime to be legitimate. There is a difference between defending the regime and defending the country.' He said the Syrian dissidents who wrote the petition in *Al Hayat* had studied Turkish democracy. 'When [Prime Minister Eyup] Erdogan said, "I have to submit to parliament", the Americans could not tell him to go to hell. What Arab leader could say that without the Americans laughing him off the stage?' The Turkish government had agreed that American forces could invade northern Iraq through Turkey, but the parliament refused to allow it. Syria's parliament had no similar independence. Syrian democrats were not awaiting democracy as a care package from the American armed forces so much as seeking a way to seize it themselves as a weapon with which to confront the American empire. In Lawrence of Arabia's words to the Emir Feisal, before he became king of either Syria or Iraq, 'Freedom is taken – not given.'

The regime of Bashar Assad had been reduced to a tactic his father would not have employed: explaining itself to its population. Vice President Khaddam justified government repression to an audience at Damascus University: 'We will not allow Syria to become another Algeria or Yugoslavia.' One of Syria's intelligence chiefs, Majid Suleiman, published an article in *As Safir*, possibly the first Syrian security boss ever to open a debate in print. Suleiman, like the Assad family, came from the Alawi minority whom the French first put into the armed forces and who subsequently took power. He was said to be close to Bashar. In 'Syria and the American Threats', Suleiman wrote that Syria would acquiesce in any arrangement the Palestinians reached with Israel on Palestine. Until then, Syrian policy, stated by Khaddam twenty years before, had been rejection of any arrangement that compromised Palestinian rights even if the Palestinians themselves accepted it. Suleiman admitted that Syria had lost strategic depth when America occupied Iraq. But he insisted that the US needed the Syrian presence in Lebanon. Only the Syrian army could maintain surveillance of Hizballah, the Palestinians and the Sunni fundamentalists. Without Syria, he wrote, the south of Lebanon could be the scene of mass violence that might bring another Israeli invasion. His argument presented Syria as a guardian, rather than opponent, of American interests in Lebanon. That was also how Hafez Assad portrayed Syria to Henry Kissinger and James Baker. In April 2005, however, pressure from the US, the UN and the Lebanese themselves forced the Syrian army out of Lebanon. As for Syria itself, he wrote that the Syrian opposition was loyal. The pre-war Iraqi opposition, in contrast, had been American agents. Surprisingly, Suleiman praised Riad Turk, a communist leader who had been imprisoned by the regime for twenty years, for his fidelity to the country. Turk, nonetheless, was awaiting trial for his criticisms of the government. 'This was the first time ever,' Sadek Al-Azm said, 'that they deigned to discuss problems openly without resorting to the language of bombast and attacking their foes with the old slogans. It was well written, and the points were clear.'

Did the United States really want democracy for Syria and

the rest of the Arab world? Since 1949, when the CIA staged the first of the Arab world's many military coups in Syria, America had helped to suppress democratic movements throughout the Middle East. While writing *Tribes with Flags*, I had interviewed a former cabinet minister and founder of the Syrian Baath Party, Dr Hafiz Jemalli. He had long since left the party and gone into silent opposition. In his eighties when we had met fifteen years earlier, he said, 'If we are democratic, we will be unified.' The unity he meant was of all Syria that the British and French turned into the statelets of little Syria, Lebanon, Jordan and Israel/Palestine. 'If we are unified, we will be a danger to Israel.' Richard Perle, Paul Wolfowitz, Donald Rumsfeld and the rest of the coterie who gave America its Iraq war were not changing regimes to see them become dangers to Israel. American rule in the Middle East faced conflicts: letting the Arabs choose their policies versus America's opposition to their choice when it challenged America or Israel; between representative governments that aligned oil policies to popular will versus American desire to control the oil supply; between independent governments versus the implantation of American military bases in countries that did not want them. Did the neo-conservatives who had counselled Benyamin Netanyahu and were next advising George Bush really want Arab democracy? In Iraq, their test case of the new Arab order, the United States ruled through force and asked Iraqis to legitimize it. Was this a model to attract other countries?

A Syrian journalist friend of mine said the Iraqis' collapse to the swift American invasion disgusted him. He had served as a conscript during the October 1973 war with Israel. 'We will never let the Americans come into Syria like that,' he said. 'We might lose, but we would fight.' His son, who was old enough to be drafted into the army, was playing on a computer. He turned around and shrugged. The shrug said, 'Why bother?'

One night at the Café Havana, Damascus's venerable political meeting house, I had coffee with an old Palestinian scholar. He alternated between pessimism and hope. He had been born in

Nazareth under the British and been banished by the Israelis. To him, Americans were like their British predecessors. He said, 'They cannot rule with force. Ideas are stronger.' The Syrians were behaving no better in Lebanon, he believed. 'Syria should get out of Lebanon and open its borders.' Finally, he was certain the Arab states would never help the Palestinians. He said, 'Israel and the Arab states have the same birth certificate.' To him, they were all illegitimate offspring of Sykes-Picot – step-children of the Great War that drove out the last rulers of a land united and at peace.

I came across a poem about Damascus by one of the Arab world's leading poets, Adonis. Born Ali Ahmad Said in northern Syria in 1930, he studied philosophy at Damascus University until 1956 and joined the Syrian Socialist National Party. The party's goal was the reunification of Greater Syria, the undoing of the Anglo-French enterprise of 1918. After the Damascus regime imprisoned him, he moved to Lebanon. In 'Homeland', he wrote,

> To the faces that harden behind a mask of gloom
> I bow, and to streets where I left behind my tears,
> To a father who died, green as a cloud
> With a sail on his face, I bow,
> And to a child that is sold
> In order to pray and be a bootblack
> (In our land we all pray and are bootblacks.)
> To a stone I inscribed with my hunger
> Saying it was lightning and rain, drops rolling under my
>   eyelids,
> And to a house whose dust I carried with me in my loss
> I bow – all these are my homeland, not Damascus.

Back to the Beginning

In August 1987, the Syrian army had taken me against my
wishes to Damascus so the foreign minister could claim credit
for my escape from Hizballah. My freedom became a footnote
in diplomatic history, when Damascus and Washington – each
as mendacious as the other – took advantage of Syria's 'help'
to reinstate the American ambassador in Syria. He had been
withdrawn when Syrian intelligence was caught trying to blow
up an Israeli airliner from London to Lod. For the next few
years, I flew to Damascus often to cover the releases of other
American and British captives. The last Westerner to come out
alive was the one who had endured the longest, Terry Anderson
of the Associated Press. His release in December 1991 ended
six and a half years of hell for him and concluded the great
game between the United States and Iran that was the hostage
era in Lebanon. From then on, Beirut was safe again for
foreigners.

I waited until 1997, the tenth anniversary of my abduction,
to visit Beirut. Although I had lived there for six years and knew
it well, I needed three days to overcome my fear of kidnapping.
At first, I would walk warily and drive away from every old
Mercedes that looked like the one that had picked me up. Nothing happened. No one threatened. The fear vanished. I was back
on the horse. Friends entertained me, and I explored a city under
reconstruction. The bickering among Lebanon's tribes had
reverted to what it had been before the war – political man-
oeuvring, economic competition and back-biting gossip. Coming back again to complete the Levantine ramble I had begun
in 1987, I saw a city whose downtown had been reborn – albeit
as a soulless imitation of the vibrant and grubby entrepot it was
before the war. Beirut was peaceful, even boring.

Walid Jumblatt, who had inherited his leadership of Lebanon's Druze minority from his father, lived in the Ottoman
palace his ancestors had built two centuries before in the hills

of the Shouf, south of Beirut. I was late for lunch – sixteen years late, not that years had importance. Showing me an old mural of the 1860 war between Maronite Christians and the Druze, he talked about the Turks as if they had only – like the Israelis – just departed. His ancestor Said Bey Jumblatt had beaten the Maronites and massacred many of them, as Walid himself did more than a century later. And, like Said, he lived with the Maronites again. He had invited them back to their houses in the Shouf, a gesture everyone in the Levant apart from the Israelis made to vanquished enemies when wars ended. His interests were less political and military than they had been during the war. He wanted to know the name of my girlfriend in Paris.

My friend Jamil Mroue, who published the English-language *Daily Star* and whose journalist father had been assassinated for criticizing Nasser, tried to persuade me that Beirut was as interesting as it had been before the war. Like a Chamber of Commerce booster, he praised the night life, the skiing and the beaches. But Jamil, like most other Lebanese, was more thoughtful than that. He let his guard down, reminiscing about the golden era before war began in 1975. In those days, political theories and ideas animated our conversations and lent urgency to our lives. Arguments kept us up all night in cafés and bars. Beirut was at the centre of a contest for control of, not merely the oil, but the soul of the Arab world. He lamented the outcome of all the suffering since, saying, 'We have become a bit of a backwater, haven't we?'

Beirut had abandoned kidnapping, urban warfare and suicide bombing. All that had moved to Iraq. Just as the American invasion of Iraq had been more thorough than its half-hearted intervention in Lebanon, the Iraqi reaction was more ferocious. In Baghdad, hostages were not only taken – they were grabbed in their dozens and beheaded. The Lebanese had not kidnapped women, but the Iraqis abducted them and murdered them. In Lebanon, there had been no more than fifty suicide bombings in eighteen years of Israeli occupation. The Iraqis staged them every day. In Lebanon, almost three hundred American soldiers had been killed when the American public demanded their withdrawal. More than two thousand died in Iraq without affecting the determination of the brains trust in Washington. Claiming the imperial inheritance from Britain and France in the Middle East, America had moved its base of operations to Baghdad. Someone told them it would be more secure than Lebanon. Someone got it wrong.

T. E. Lawrence studied Arabic just north of Beirut in the Christian seaside village of Jebail, known in ancient times as Byblos. His teacher was a Quaker named Farida al Akle, an intelligent and perceptive woman who lived to a great age and remembered Lawrence fondly. But, she told Edward Said fifty years later, he never mastered the language. For three months in 1910 and 1911, he laboured in vain towards fluency before embarking on archaeological excavations that deepened his understanding of people whose political future he would help to determine. Had they known what his legacy would become, they might have killed him – as some Kurdish robbers had tried to do in 1909, on his first sojourn through the Levant researching his Oxford thesis on Crusader castles. Lawrence came back to Syria in 1917, conquering Aqaba and persuading the Arabs to fight for their freedom alongside Allies who would ultimately betray them. In Lawrence's time, the natives lacked armed might to protect their independence. Also missing were nationhood and unity, because poor communications and Istanbul's imperial weakness had kept the non-Turks of the Ottoman Empire divided into tribes, regions and sects.

Occasionally, the *indigenes* rebelled – against France, against Britain, against settlers, against America – and usually they were contained. Nationalists were hanged, tortured or exiled during the Mandate years, and popular heroes like Gamal Abdel Nasser were cut down to size by military force. Much of that changed in Lebanon, among the people who lived in the country's rural south and in the suburban slums of Beirut. They drove out the Americans in 1984, and they made the invincible Israeli army leave Lebanon in the spring of 2000. Their weapons were sabotage, ambush, kidnapping, suicide bombing and the refusal to compromise over occupation – all tactics that would be taken up by the Iraqis who from April 2003 did not want the American armed forces to rule them.

In my lifetime, the simple lesson of Lebanon had been ignored. Stir up the population, and it reacts. When their ancestors rebelled in the 1920s and 1930s in Damascus, Nazareth, Baghdad and Mosul, the empires had kept them down with overwhelming force. In Lebanon, the people lost their fear. Perhaps too many had died in their civil war for superior foreign armies to present so terrible a challenge. The Americans and Israelis were not prepared to invest the energy to remain in a country of little significance to either of them. Empires measure profit against loss, and the losses in Lebanon outweighed the profit. The natives did not have to defeat them in major battles; they had only to make the occupation too expensive to maintain.

My kidnapping was but a small incident in the battle by the country's poorest and most backward sect, the Shiite Muslims, to keep the Western world at bay. Shiite peasants and their clergy showed themselves, by some fascinating transformation based on religious education in Iran and Iraq and money making by exiles in West Africa, to be the most sophisticated of Lebanon's many communities – as well as the most determined to redress the balance that had weighed against them from Turkish times.

I went back to Checkpoint Charlie, which is what the Syrians told me they called the military post they had set up at the spot along the coast road in Beirut's southern suburbs where Hizballah took me on 17 June 1987. The checkpoint itself had gone, and life in the tawdry Shiite ghetto was pleasant and normal. An old friend, Qassem Dergham, drove me there. It was not far from the neighbourhood where he raised his children in the midst of a civil war and foreign invasions. He was one of the two men who had answered my urgent telephone calls from

454

the Summerland Hotel on that breezy August night, when I escaped from the bare flat that was my captive's cell. A Shiite who had raised his children in Beirut's suburban concrete maze, he limped a little from an Israeli bullet that had nearly killed him a few years before. His injury forced him to give up golf at which he, a scratch-handicapper, had been a national champion. He still went back to south Lebanon, despite the occasional Israeli bombardment, as a cameraman to take pictures for Western media outlets that for the most part did not broadcast them. His faith that all would be well in Lebanon contrasted with my hard-won pessimism. He had told me the Israelis would leave one day, and they did. He insisted the Syrians would also go, and I visited him again in 2005 when they were withdrawing. More than anything else, he desired to see Lebanon become a country that his children would not have to leave in order to lead normal lives. In that, he shared an unlikely vision with the rest of the Lebanese, as well as the Iraqis, Syrians, Jordanians, Palestinians and Israelis.

SELECT BIBLIOGRAPHY

Fouzi Al-Asmar, *To Be an Arab in Israel*, Frances Pinter Ltd., 1975

Menachem Begin, *The Revolt*, W. H. Allen, 1951

David Ben-Gurion, *Israel: A Personal History*, Sabra Books, 1972

Franz Fanon, *The Wretched of the Earth*, MacGibbon & Kee, 1965

David Fromkin, *A Peace to End All Peace*, André Deutsch, 1989

Nancy Elizabeth Gallagher, *Approaches to the History of the Middle East*, Ithaca Press, 1994

Sir John Bagot Glubb, *Britain and the Arabs: A Study of Fifty Years 1908–1950*, Hodder & Stoughton, 1959

Amira Hass, *Drinking the Sea at Gaza*, Hamish Hamilton, 1999

Flavius Josephus, *The Jewish War*, Penguin Classics, 1980

Walid Khalidy, *From Haven to Conquest*, Institute of Palestine Studies, 1971

Jon Kimche, *Seven Fallen Pillars*, Secker & Warburg, 1953

T. E. Lawrence, *The Seven Pillars of Wisdom* (complete 1922 text), Castle Hill Press, 1997

Udi Levy, *The Lost Civilisation of Petra*, Floris Books, 1999

Basil Liddell Hart, *Colonel Lawrence: The Man Behind the Legend*, Dodd, Mead & Co., 1934

Richard Locke and Anthony Stewart, *Bantustan Gaza*, Zed Press, 1985

Benny Morris, *The Birth of the Palestinian Refugee Problem, 1947–1948*, Cambridge University Press, 1988

James Morris, *The Hashemite Kings*, Faber, 1959

Fr Jerome Murphy-O'Connor, *The Holy Land*, Oxford University Press, 1984

Richard O'Neil, *Suicide Squads: The Men and Machines of World War II Special Operations*, Salamander Books, 1999

Ilan Pappe, *A Modern History of Palestine*, Cambridge University Press, 2003

Tom Segev, *One Palestine, Complete*, Little, Brown, 1999

—— *1949: The First Israelis*, Free Press, 1986

Ariel Sharon, *Warrior: An Autobiography*, Simon & Schuster, 2001

Vincent Sheehan, *Personal History*, New York, 1935

Rev. George Adam Smith, *The Historical Geography of the Holy Land*, Hodder & Stoughton, 1894

Mark Twain, *Innocents Abroad*, Chatto & Windus, 1928

INDEX

INDEX

INDEX